RACE MIXING

RENEE C. ROMANO

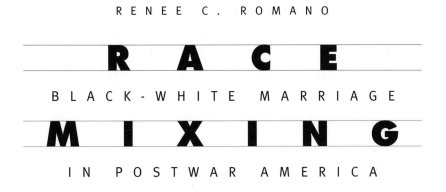

RACE

BLACK-WHITE MARRIAGE

MIXING

IN POSTWAR AMERICA

HARVARD UNIVERSITY PRESS

Cambridge, Massachusetts

London, England

2003

Library of Congress Cataloging-in-Publication Data
Romano, Renee Christine.
Race mixing : Black-white marriage in postwar America / Renee C. Romano.
p.   cm.
Includes bibliographical references and index.
ISBN 0-674-01033-7
1. Interracial marriage—United States.   2. United States—Race relations.   I. Title.
HQ1031 .R65   2003
306.84'6—dc21   2002032929

FOR OWEN AND SABINE

CONTENTS

ACKNOWLEDGMENTS

In the nearly ten years I have spent working on this project, I have bene-
fited tremendously from the assistance and advice of countless people
and institutions. This book would never have been possible without the
unflagging support of two extraordinary women. Estelle Freedman first
encouraged my interest in the topic of interracial marriage, and her insight, knowledge, and good sense shaped earlier drafts and the book that
has resulted. Estelle is, as all who have worked with her know, the con-
summate mentor, and she generously continued to advise me on the
manuscript long after I left the lovely grounds of Stanford University.
Joyce Seltzer, my editor at Harvard, was equally influential in shaping the
manuscript as she pushed me to sharpen my thinking and my writing.
Her tenacious and meticulous editing has made this a far better book,
and I am thankful that I was able to work with her on this project.

Other people from the Stanford History Department also assisted me
greatly. George Fredrickson's keen mind and his ability to ask the big
questions shaped this book more than he knows. David Kennedy and
Richard Roberts provided valuable suggestions for developing and revis-
ing the manuscript. I am also deeply indebted to a wonderful set of Stanford peers who have read this text more times than they probably care to
remember. Karen Dunn-Haley, Ariela Gross, Leslie Harris, Wendy
Lynch, Wendy Wall, and Alice Yang-Murray offered advice and encouragement with good humor and great insight. Our semiannual reading
group meetings on various beaches in California provided me with both
emotional and intellectual support.

I am also grateful to my colleagues in the History Department and the

African American Studies program at Wesleyan for their interest in this project. Claire Potter and Patricia Hill have been both mentors and friends, reading drafts of the manuscript and providing valuable advice about how to balance writing and other obligations. Ann duCille has been exceptionally helpful, and I am fortunate that she returned to Wesleyan when she did. For their suggestions and support, I also wish to recognize my colleagues Liza McAlister, Natalie Brender, Rick Elphick, Ollie Holmes, Maureen Mahon, Gayle Pemberton, Ronald Schatz, and Jennifer Tucker. I would also like to acknowledge my students, especially all those who have taken my course "Race and Sexuality in American History," for their questions and their thoughtful engagement with many of the ideas raised in this book.

The many wonderful scholars I met at the Stanford Humanities Center, the Five College Institute for Women's Studies, and the Wesleyan Center for the Humanities helped sharpen my thinking and taught me a great deal about doing interdisciplinary work. I am grateful for the support I received at each of these centers. A special thanks goes to Peggy Pascoe for her many useful comments on the project, and to Randall Kennedy for his thought-provoking conversation and for his exceptional willingness to share sources.

I am deeply indebted to all those who helped my research, especially the wonderful individuals and couples who generously shared their experiences with me. Yvonne and Chuck Cannon, Shira-Davida Goldberg-Rathell, Gabe Grosz, Grace and Robert McAllester, Chuck McDew, Amy Rollison, Constancia Romilly, and Steve White provided interviews that proved extremely helpful. Others who answered a written questionnaire also provided valuable assistance. I relied on the knowledge and goodwill of many research librarians. Special thanks to the staffs of the Stanford University Library, Wesleyan University Library, the Mount Holyoke College Library, the Schlesinger Library, the Murray Research Center at Radcliffe, the Wisconsin State Historical Society, the Schomburg Center for Research in Black Culture, the Library of Congress, the Beineke Rare Book and Manuscript Library at Yale, the New York Public Library, and the Howard University Library. Thanks also to David Lobenstine and Elizabeth Gilbert at Harvard University Press for all of their work in the final stages of the book.

My biggest debt of gratitude is to my family. My parents, Joseph and Marcia Romano, started me on the path of this book when they insisted we move from our all-white suburb to a racially integrated one when I was twelve. They had no idea, I'm sure, how much that move would shape my outlook and my life. Whatever I have accomplished, it is due to their support and encouragement. My husband, Sean Decatur, is the best partner I could ever hope to have. This book would not have been possible without his intellectual and emotional companionship. As important, his moral support has proved invaluable (as has his willingness to shoulder the burden of childcare during critical stages of the writing of the book). My children, Sabine and Owen, have helped me keep my sense of perspective and my sense of humor throughout the writing process. This book is dedicated to them.

RACE MIXING

E X P L A I N I N G

A   T A B O O

This book had its genesis in an offhand remark by one of my college professors in a 1988 class on racial prejudice and political intolerance. There had been a significant shift in whites' self-reported racial attitudes since the 1960s, he explained, with white Americans claiming to be increasingly willing to live in integrated neighborhoods, to send their children to integrated schools, to work with blacks, and even to entertain blacks in their homes. Yet the vast majority of whites still claimed to disapprove of marriages between blacks and whites. Whatever else had changed, whites apparently remained opposed to integration in the most intimate sphere of family and marriage.

As a white woman involved with a black man at the time (we married in 1991), I was intrigued by this seeming disparity in whites' attitudes. Why were marriages between whites and blacks more difficult for whites to accept than less intimate relationships? What did the continued disapproval of interracial marriage demonstrate about the nature and significance of the racial changes that had taken place in the United States since World War II? Did blacks share whites' misgivings about interracial relationships? As I set out on my own interracial marriage, I also wanted to know how these attitudes had affected blacks and whites who married across the color line.

In researching this book, I realized that my professor's comment was, in fact, misleading. Although whites do express more reservations about interracial dating and marriage than about other forms of integration, their attitudes toward interracial marriage have changed enormously in the years since World War II. The earliest national poll (taken in 1958) found that 96 percent of whites disapproved of marriages between blacks and whites. The most recent polls document a staggering increase in white approval for interracial relationships; in 1997, 61 percent of whites claimed to approve of black-white marriages. Among blacks, too, approval for black-white marriages has increased. When blacks were first polled on the subject in 1972, 58 percent responded favorably. By 1997, 77 percent approved.[1]

This shift in attitudes has been matched by dramatic changes in the legal, political, and cultural arenas. In 1940 marriages between blacks and whites were illegal in thirty-one of the forty-eight states. Many of these laws nullified and voided interracial marriages, regardless of where they were contracted; others made interracial marriage a felony that could be punished with fines and jail terms. As late as 1967, sixteen states still made it illegal for blacks and whites to marry.[2] When the Supreme Court declared all state laws prohibiting interracial marriage to be unconstitutional in 1967, it legalized a relationship that had been criminalized in some form or another in America since the seventeenth century.

Changes have also been significant in the political arena. Since the 1860s interracial relationships have been a constant issue in national politics. Segregation laws were justified by the need to protect white women from "bestial" black men; whites discredited attempts by blacks to achieve civil, political, and legal rights as a desire for "social equality," a coded term for interracial marriage. Since the late 1960s, however, the issue of interracial sex and marriage has fallen out of the national political arena, and openly criticizing interracial relationships is now unacceptable in mainstream politics.

These changes are reflected in popular culture as well. Depictions of interracial love were once quite rare and were almost uniformly negative. Today, interracial couples can be found on movie screens, television, and in the print media. Although not all contemporary portrayals of interracial love are positive, there is a much greater variety in the way in which relationships across the color line are represented. Interracial couples, moreover, have created their own media outlets and Web sites to present a positive message about interracial love and marriage.

In short, there has been an erosion of the taboo against interracial marriage in the last sixty years. In 1940, all types of interracial unions were exceptionally rare. But by 2000, America was becoming increasingly multiracial, with intermarriage rates at an all-time high.[3] In 1960, when the United States Census Bureau first tracked the number of interracial couples, it found only 157,000 marriages (or .4 percent of the total) which involved a white, black, Native American, or Asian American wed to a spouse of a different race. By 2000, there were over one million such marriages, representing nearly 2 percent of the total.[4]

Although the increase in the rate of marriages between blacks and whites has not been as dramatic, there has been a steep rise in the number of black-white couples since the 1940s as well. In 1960 there were approximately 51,000 black-white married couples in the entire United States. That number climbed to approximately 363,000 by 2000. The growth in raw numbers has been matched by an increase in the rate of black-white marriages relative to the total number of married couples in the United States. In 1960 black-white marriages constituted only .126 percent of all marriages; in 2000 black-white couples accounted for .6 percent of all marriages. By another measure, only 1.7 percent of married blacks had a white spouse in 1960, but 4.3 percent had a white spouse in 2000.[5] The actual number of marriages between blacks and whites might still be small, but this increase is striking.

These changes are all the more remarkable when viewed against the backdrop of the long history of the regulation and prohibition of black-white relationships in America. The taboo on intimate personal relationships between blacks and whites served a crucial function in creating the American racial order. Arguably, without such a taboo, the very categories we now think of as "black" and "white" would not have existed in the same way. European settlers to colonial North America could have chosen to mix with the Africans imported into the colonies; widespread racial mixing might have led to erasure of racial differences entirely or to the creation of a "mestizo" class between Europeans and Africans. Instead "white" and "black" racial identity emerged and solidified because regulations and customs stigmatized racial mixing.[6] This binary was further reinforced by the emergence of the so-called one-drop rule that labeled a person with any black ancestry as black. In the United States, there would be no middle ground between black and white.

The taboo on interracial marriage also helped to give meaning to the categories of "black" and "white" by structuring a racial hierarchy that privileged whites over blacks. Regulating interracial relationships was particularly important in establishing the early slave system. Colonies like Virginia took steps to discourage interracial relationships in order to ensure that slave status would correspond with race. Regulations punished whites who married blacks, and reversed traditional English common law by decreeing that a child's legal status would follow from its mother rather than its father. This reversal meant that a child born to a black female slave would be considered a slave, no matter who the father. White men could thus have sex with female slaves without fear that the resulting children would undermine established racial divisions or inheritance patterns. But since status followed from one's mother, biracial children born to white women would be free. Colonial regulations thus aimed at preventing all marriages between free whites and blacks and at discouraging interracial sex between white women and black men. White women who had biracial children could be punished by being indentured into servitude; their children were frequently bound out as servants until adulthood.[7] These early laws shaped American society and were a crucial part of the emerging racial power structure.

Indeed, the regulation of marriage is one of the key defining functions of modern states. Although marriage is often thought of as a private affair between two individuals, the right to marry is a civil right, not a natural one.[8] Marriage organizes community life by establishing rules about the transmission of property and status. Laws prohibiting interracial marriage kept property and economic assets out of the hands of people of color by preventing common-law spouses or mixed-race children from inheriting the estate of a white relative.[9] Common-law spouses in interracial marriages were usually denied their partners' insurance and social security benefits, while biracial children of an unmarried interracial couple could make no claims to be the "legitimate" heirs of the white parent. Preventing blacks and whites from creating socially sanctioned family units protected the wealth, status, and reputation of whites who were involved in interracial relationships and of their white extended families.[10]

Marriages across the race line raised the specter of intimate, private exchanges between individuals that could represent a serious threat to a racial order where relationships were to be governed by an etiquette of white superiority. As a result, marriages between blacks and whites challenged the racial status quo in a way that the mere fact of interracial sex did not. Most interracial sexual relationships involved white men and black women; these relationships were often a manifestation of white male privilege. Sexual relationships between blacks and whites could produce children, but these children would not be considered the legitimate heirs of their white kin. Sexual relationships could be long-standing, but the nonwhite partner would have none of the legal protections accorded to legitimate spouses. States accordingly expended much more effort to prevent interracial marriages than interracial sex per se. In 1940 thirty-one states had laws prohibiting interracial marriage, yet only six states barred interracial fornication.[11] State or colonial legislatures, moreover, had a far greater ability to prevent interracial marriages (which required state sanction) than they did to prevent sexual relationships across the color line.

Prohibiting interracial marriages while condoning interracial sex between white men and black women reinforced gender as well as racial hierarchies. White men were protected from any legal responsibility for their mixed-race children, while white women were given the burden of upholding white "racial purity." Preventing relationships between black men and white women became the responsibility not only of the state but more immediately of white men, who in their role as fathers, brothers, and husbands were expected to control the behavior of women in their family.

The taboo against interracial marriage continued to shore up racial and gender hierarchies long after the end of slavery. Indeed, from the end of slavery through the 1960s, nearly every challenge to the racial status quo was accompanied by a panic over the possibility of "racial mixing." The Civil War generated fear of interracial sexual relationships in a world without slavery. During the presidential campaign of 1864, Democrats made the issue of sex between white women and black men a na-

tional political scandal, coining a new term—"miscegenation"—to tar
the Republicans as a party favoring racial mixing. When southern white
Democrats sought to wrest control of their states away from black Republicans and northern radicals after the Civil War, they did so in part by
demonizing interracial sex and marriage. Black men, many of whom for
the first time held some position of power in the southern political system, were charged with wanting to marry and degrade the purest flowers
of white womanhood. The 1880s and 1890s witnessed not only an intensified concern that black men freed from the bonds of slavery would
rape white women, but that political and legal equality between blacks
and whites would lead to social relationships between the races that
would permit marriage. To prevent such marriages, blacks would have to
be denied political rights, like the right to vote, and civil rights, like the
right to sit on juries.[12]

Concern about interracial sex and marriage was not just a southern
phenomenon. Although the racial hierarchy may have looked different in
states that were not as dependent upon slavery, it nonetheless structured
political and social life outside of the South. In the North and West, as in
the South, interracial relationships were attacked as a symbol of social
disorder. Marriages between black and whites were forbidden, sometimes by law and always by custom. In regions where slavery did not
make the racial hierarchy starkly apparent, preventing mixing between
blacks and whites was a crucial way to maintain "whiteness" as a space of
privilege and "purity." Poor whites who interacted with blacks were thus
described by reformers as degraded and immoral. In the 1910s and
1920s, clubs that allowed interracial mixing became key sites for vice investigations of prostitution and illicit sexuality. In the wake of the Great
Migration of southern blacks to northern cities in the 1910s, northern
whites sought to protect themselves, their jobs, and their social positions
by drawing more rigid lines between themselves and blacks. Fears of intermarriage were used to justify denying blacks jobs and keeping them
out of white residential neighborhoods.[13]

Stoking the fires of racism in both the North and the South was the
popular scientific theory that children of mixed racial heritage were
morally and physically inferior to "pure" blacks, and particularly prone to
diseases such as tuberculosis. Some whites claimed that mixed-race chil-

dren were themselves sterile, much like mules, and they described racial mixing as disastrous for blacks who had to live with these inferior "mulattoes" in their midst. According to one nineteenth-century social scientist, miscegenation was responsible for the increasing black mortality rate, as well as blacks' "consequent inferior social efficiency and diminishing power as a force in American national life."[14]

The importance of preventing marriages between blacks and whites is reflected in the range and extent of antimiscegenation laws in the colonies and later the United States. All but nine of the fifty states had laws barring interracial marriage at one point or another in their history. The Supreme Court, moreover, upheld state regulation of interracial relationships in the crucial 1883 case of *Pace v. Alabama. Pace* held that laws punishing interracial fornication more harshly than fornication between members of the same race did not violate the equal protection clause of the Fourteenth Amendment because they punished the black and white perpetrators equally. With *Pace,* the federal government signaled its support for antimiscegenation laws, a precedent that would hold for more than eighty years. Between 1909 and 1921, when the migration of blacks out of the South nationalized the race problem, twenty-one laws to prohibit interracial relationships were introduced into the U.S. Congress, even though Congress had long taken the position that states, not the federal government, should have the responsibility for regulating marriage. Laws such as the Mann Act, which made it illegal for a man to transport a woman across state lines for "immoral purposes," were used to punish black men who became involved with white women in states where marrying across race lines was legal.[15]

With its potential for providing insight into the construction and operation of race and gender hierarchies, the history of sex and marriage across the color line has become an increasingly popular subject for study. Most historical studies focus either on the regulation of interracial relationships in the nineteenth-century South or on the laws that prohibited interracial marriage and the court trials in which these laws were given meaning. Most sociological studies, in contrast, focus on the experiences of interracial couples themselves, usually documented through intense interviews with a small number of couples.[16] Neither a regional study nor an in-depth case study of a small group of interracial couples, this book explores the political, cultural, and social history of black-white interracial marriage nationwide since the 1940s.

Race in the United States, of course, is not just a black and white affair. Nevertheless, the black-white divide is the most tenacious of all American color lines, and in many ways the regulation of black-white relationships and the taboo against them are unique. Relationships between blacks and whites were the first to be prohibited during the colonial era, and no matter what other groups were forbidden to marry by antimiscegenation laws, all of the laws that existed in one time or another forbade relationships between blacks and whites. The one-drop rule, moreover, implied that mixing with blacks would forever corrupt "white racial purity." Although statutory definitions of blackness in state law rarely relied on the rule, the belief that "black blood" contaminated and overpowered "white blood" served as an ideological barrier to marrying across the color line and made relationships between blacks and whites more controversial than those between whites and members of other races.[17] The "blood" of other racial groups was not so contaminating. Government or religious officials sometimes encouraged whites to marry Native Americans or Latinos in order to speed their assimilation into white society. Intermarriage between blacks and whites, however, was rarely imagined in this way.[18]

The story of the erosion of the taboo against black-white marriage is thus particularly significant, promising to shed light not only onto the changing nature of gender relations and the institution of marriage in postwar America but also onto the state of contemporary American race relations. This story, for one thing, provides a new explanation for the relative success of the civil rights movement of the 1950s and 1960s. While scholars have pointed to a variety of international, demographic, and economic factors to explain the achievements of the civil rights movement, there has been little written about the importance of contesting the heated rhetoric about racial mixing that characterized so much of the southern opposition to integration. There was little chance for activists to dismantle Jim Crow until they could successfully challenge the segregationist claim that integration would automatically end in racial amalgamation. *Race Mixing* traces the hesitant and often painful journey taken by white liberals and black civil rights advocates as they moved to destigmatize interracial love.

Focusing on interracial marriage also offers another angle for exploring the importance of the racial changes that have taken place since World War II. Some argue that the civil rights movement was a revolution that fundamentally transformed America, and that race has become less significant as a factor determining an individual's status and potential for social mobility in modern America. Others insist that the changes since the 1940s have been more symbolic than substantive, that racial inequalities continue to persist despite new civil rights laws, and that race remains a key dividing line in American society.[19] Does the growing acceptance of interracial marriage among whites and a rising number of black-white couples signal that whites have finally fully accepted blacks and that racism and racial inequalities are declining? This book argues that the erosion of the taboo against black-white marriages cannot be read as a simple sign that America has overcome its racist past. There are many reasons why the taboo against interracial marriage has diminished, not all of them having to do with race. Moreover, recent history suggests that structural racial inequalities can persist despite changes in whites' attitudes about blacks.[20]

Nevertheless the erosion of the taboo against interracial relationships is crucial to understanding the workings of race in modern America. Because intimate relationships across the color line strike at the very core of racial identity, the attitudes of both blacks and whites toward intermarriage shed light on what race actually means to individuals and how they perceive their own racial identity. At the heart of this book are the stories of individuals who have been most affected by the taboo on interracial marriage—the blacks and whites who have married since the 1940s and their families. These are the people directly affected by the color line— the structural barriers and cultural beliefs that have separated blacks from whites—and their struggles illustrate the shifting nature of that line since 1940.

The lives of interracial couples also make clear the tenuous nature of the boundary between what is traditionally considered "public" and what is traditionally considered "private." Although the narrative shifts between a focus on traditional politics (often called the "public sphere") and the lives of couples and families (commonly called the "private sphere"), the history of intermarriage demonstrates how the very barriers of public/private are themselves socially constructed and change over time. Interracial marriage has long been considered a public issue, generating political debates and legislative action, and choosing to cross the race line in marriage has been widely interpreted by both blacks and whites as an act fraught with political meaning. Since World War II, interracial marriages have alternately been described as deviant acts of social and economic radicals, the true fulfillment of a quest for racial brotherhood, the ultimate solution to the race problem, and as a betrayal of one's race and one's community.

Yet individuals involved in interracial relationships have tried, with varying degrees of success, to carve out a zone of privacy for themselves. The stories of individuals who have married across the color line, culled from legal documents, memoirs, studies, and interviews, illuminate why people made the choices they did and how their lives and those of their children have been affected by the changing political and social contexts since 1940. These accounts also demonstrate that the erosion of the taboo against intermarriage has had a dramatic impact on the lives of interracial couples. Although marriages across the color line remain rare, they have much to teach us about the meanings of race and the ways in which individuals have sought to craft their own lives within and outside the circumscribed racial boundaries in the United States.

A Note on Terms

Deciding how to write about "race" is always a difficult problem for scholars of American race relations. Although "race" is a social construction, not a biological reality, using terms like "black," "white," and "interracial" runs the risk of making racial categories appear more stable and concrete than they really are. Nevertheless, these terms have social meanings that help construct people's understanding of the world and shape their reality. The social realities of race exist and will not be deconstructed simply by changing our language. This study thus employs the terms "black" to refer to people of African ancestry in the United States (I use "black" rather than "African American" because not all blacks consider themselves African Americans). "White" refers to those people defined by law and custom as "white," a group that has shifted over time. I employ the terms "interracial" and "biracial" because these are the terms people use in their own lives and because there is no easy way to avoid this language. "Intermarriage" and "interracial marriage" will be used interchangeably to refer specifically to black–white interracial marriages unless otherwise noted. The narrative covers only couples where both partners knew they were involved in an interracial relationship. Thus marriages between a black person who was passing for white and a white who did not know about his or her partner's heritage are not included.

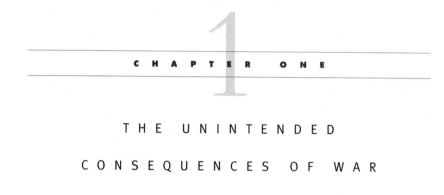

THE   UNINTENDED

CONSEQUENCES   OF   WAR

In 1947, twenty-year-old Hazel Byrne arrived in Chicago after a long flight from her hometown of Manchester, England. Tired from her travels, Byrne eagerly climbed into a waiting taxi to be taken to her final destination. But when she gave the driver the address he balked, certain that she, a nice white woman, must be mistaken about wanting to travel to a black neighborhood. But Byrne knew there was no mistake. After five years of waiting, she was finally going to marry Buford Simpkins, a black American she had met when he was stationed in her hometown during World War II. Although she had to pay the driver an extra fee to get him to take her to the apartment where her fiancé was waiting, the price was small after the long wait they had endured.[1]

Nothing symbolized the enormous impact of World War II on all aspects of American life more than marriages such as that of Byrne and Simpkins. The war had disrupted the everyday lives of Americans, both black and white, in ways that opened new spaces for interracial mingling, at least for the duration of the crisis. The massive military mobilization for the war sent black men overseas, where they met white women outside the confining strictures of segregation. Wartime labor demands pulled millions of American women from their homes to the factories and hundreds of thousands of blacks from the rural South to urban industrial centers in the North and West. Young Americans of all races

moved out of their hometowns, now free to experiment with new identities beyond the close supervision of their parents and familiar communities. Customary racial boundaries seemed to be breaking down under
the weight of the war crisis, testified to by the small but significant number of couples who crossed racial barriers to marry during the war years.

These disruptions of the racial hierarchy did not go uncontested.
Many whites across the country fought to maintain racial boundaries despite wartime chaos and displacement. Torn between the conflicting im-
peratives of boosting the morale of black Americans and maintaining the
support of white Americans, the wartime government preached tolerance while frequently practicing racial discrimination and segregation.

Yet even as the war unleashed massive efforts to reassert white dominance, it also set forces in motion that would set the stage for a more direct reckoning with the taboo on interracial sex. The contradictions between America's own racial practices and its condemnation of Nazism
put a fresh spotlight on American racism and helped to radicalize blacks,
discredit traditional ideas about race, and raise questions about whether
the nation could ever fully assimilate its black population. Before the war,
most whites considered the "Negro problem" a southern one and took
black inferiority for granted. By the end of the war, the status of blacks
had become a national issue and assumptions of racial inferiority were
being seriously questioned. These intellectual and political developments
stimulated public discussions of whites' fears of interracial sex and marriage. During and immediately after the war, black and white liberal
thinkers confronted the belief that whites' revulsion toward interracial
sex doomed any fundamental change in the racial status quo, while popular plays and movies tentatively explored the possibilities of interracial
love. Wartime developments began the process of separating concerns
about "miscegenation" from discussions of racial equality, ultimately lay-
ing the groundwork for a more effective black struggle for political
inclusion.

World War II certainly had the potential to foster a dramatic increase in
the number of black–white marriages on the home front. Before the war,
many Americans had never left the region in which they were born. Al-

though radio had recently become a national mass media, in a large country still lacking the unifying effects of television or an interstate highway system, many Americans grew up in isolated regional subcultures.[2] This was perhaps most true for blacks, 77 percent of whom lived in the South in 1940, primarily in rural areas.

The massive military mobilization that ultimately brought sixteen million young Americans into service had far-reaching implications for American race relations. With the building of wartime defense industries and the increasing mechanization of southern agriculture, the war undermined the traditional southern economic system that relied on a cheap agricultural labor force and helped integrate the South into the rest of the nation's economy.[3] A. Philip Randolph's threatened March on Washington in 1941 forced President Roosevelt to agree to enforce a policy of nondiscrimination in federally funded defense industries. Though weakly implemented, the order did enable blacks to enter some industries that had previously excluded them. They joined the millions of white women who were also drawn into the workforce by the war.

The war stimulated a frenzy of movement. As jobs opened up in defense industries outside the South, offering attractive alternatives to sharecropping, black Americans migrated north and west in record numbers. Over five hundred thousand blacks left the South between 1942 and 1945; two and a half million departed between 1940 and 1960. Millions of white Americans also migrated to find good jobs in wartime industries or to follow loved ones to military bases.[4] As blacks and whites poured into cities in the North and West, whites who had never spoken with a black person before, and blacks who had had primarily subordinate relationships with whites, found themselves working at the same factories and, in some instances, living near each other in city neighborhoods. In Marin City, California, for example, a housing project for war workers quietly followed a policy of nondiscrimination, assigning housing without regard to race. By the end of the war, blacks and whites lived as neighbors in all sections of the project. In Chicago, residential segregation broke down under the weight of the massive migration of blacks to the city, pushing more people into racially mixed neighborhoods.[5]

Those moving to new cities or getting new jobs, moreover, found themselves freer from parental and community supervision, and inevitably they experienced greater sexual freedom. As one young white woman remembered, wartime Chicago provided extraordinary opportunities for sexual experimentation. "Chicago was just humming, no matter where I went," she recalled. "The bars were jammed, and unless you were an absolute dog you could pick up anyone you wanted to. . . . There were servicemen of all varieties roaming the streets all the time. There was never, never a shortage of young healthy bucks." Freed from traditional constraints, both heterosexual and homosexual relationships flourished during the war.[6]

Although most of these relationships were not interracial, the war opened social spaces for some interracial contact. In 1940 the vast majority of blacks lived in states that prohibited interracial marriage by law. As millions of blacks left the South, they had more opportunities to socialize with whites whom they met in their neighborhoods or at work, and their chances of intermarrying increased. The Adams, an interracial couple who married in 1947, would never have met if not for the war. The young white wife, the daughter of Italian immigrants, was fifteen when the war began. She grew up in a sheltered home, forbidden to play with black children and not permitted to date at all. After she graduated from high school, the booming war economy enabled her to get a job at a factory. After repeated clashes with her parents over her dating habits, she moved into her own apartment. Working at the factory alongside her was a black man four years older than she. He had been born in North Carolina, but had migrated north in search of better work. The two began dating in 1945. Two years later they were married, thanks to the wartime circumstances that allowed a southern-born black man to move to a less racially restrictive environment and enabled a young white woman to act on her own without her family's supervision or approval.[7]

The new social conditions fostered by the war, however, generated enormous racial tensions on the home front. Black migrants moved to overcrowded cities where services and institutions were strained to capacity. In the North and West, competition for resources between black migrants and white workers led to race riots that resembled small-scale wars.[8] Throughout the war, white workers sought to contain blacks in existing ghettos and vehemently opposed any encroachment into white neighborhoods. When the federal government built a housing project for black war workers in a predominantly white Detroit neighborhood, white rioters prevented blacks from moving in for nearly two months. Black tenants were able to occupy the Sojourner Truth homes only under the protection of the armed state militia. In Chicago, violence erupted during the war whenever blacks were housed in federal housing projects with whites. The federal government quickly learned that it was easier to follow "local customs" and permit segregation in defense workers' housing in order to maintain the peace.[9]

While white war workers sought to contain the racial disruptions of the war by insisting on maintaining residential segregation, white southerners worried about the impact of the war on black men drafted into the military. Blacks in the army learned how to fight and use arms. In training camps and military units, southern blacks met northern blacks, who were more assertive. Rubbing elbows with these outsiders and learning to fight could only serve to make northern blacks "uppity," many white southerners feared.[10] Service in the military also provided opportunities to learn skills that might allow black soldiers to escape agricultural labor or menial jobs. Most seriously, whites feared that black soldiers who traveled throughout the United States and overseas would be less willing to accept the old segregated order when they returned home.

Eager to uphold domestic morale, the federal government did whatever it could to reassure white Americans that the military mobilization would not upset traditional patterns of black subordination. Despite pressure from blacks to desegregate the military, the U.S. government maintained rigidly segregated armed forces throughout much of the war. Black soldiers were trained in segregated camps; the vast majority served under white officers. The Marine Corps and Army Air Corps refused to even accept blacks at the beginning of the war. Blacks could serve in the navy only as mess men and in the army only in segregated units used primarily for hard labor. As much as possible, the army kept black troops from being used in combat, partly due to doubts about their abilities, but also to preclude claims for equal citizenship based on their willingness to fight. News of those few blacks who managed to get into combat was kept out of white newspapers to help allay whites' fears. When the Office of War Information, the wartime federal propaganda agency, produced a pamphlet entitled *Negroes and the War,* which made the innocuous argument that blacks should support the war effort because life under Hitler would be like a return to slavery, southern congressmen vehemently objected to the pamphlet's photographs, which they thought sent a message of racial equality.[11] The controversy over *Negroes and the War* led Congress to slash the budget for the Office of War Information.

Boundaries that had been established to prevent intimate social relationships between the races seemed to be crumbling, and the level of racial tension rose accordingly. The war crisis, whites feared, allowed blacks to pursue not only greater economic and political opportunities but also equal social, and even sexual, relationships with whites. Integrated defense industries gave rise to accusations that white female war workers were prostitutes who serviced the black workers. In racially tense urban areas like Beaumont, Texas, false accusations of black men raping white women sparked white riots. National radio programs that directly addressed the issue of racial discrimination against blacks generated a massive response by white listeners, who wrote to criticize the programs for encouraging interracial marriage. These listeners heard criticisms of the existing racial status quo as support of, and advocacy for, interracial sex.[12]

The same connections between disruption of the status quo and the possibility of interracial relationships surfaced in rumors that spread throughout the South during the war. The tale of an apocryphal black South Carolinian who supposedly told a departing white soldier, "When you come back from the Army, I'll be your brother-in-law," embodied southern whites' fears that the war was undermining racial boundaries that kept black men and white women apart.[13] Even national leaders suggested that the war might provide an opportunity for blacks to try to overturn the traditional prohibitions on race mixing. Mississippi senator Theodore Bilbo questioned whether American boys were fighting "so that we may become a mongrelized people," while Secretary of War Henry Stimson privately accused "certain radical leaders of the colored race" of using the war crisis to push for interracial marriage. "What these foolish leaders of the colored race are seeking is at bottom social equality," he warned, with "social equality" serving as the familiar shorthand for sexual relationships with whites.[14]

The military's efforts to regulate the personal lives of black soldiers serving overseas makes clear how seriously the federal government took these fears. Military authorities sought to regulate the sexual activity of its armed forces by providing free condoms, preventive treatment of venereal diseases, and even in some cases military-regulated brothels.[15] However, the five hundred thousand black men who served overseas during the war in countries from Australia to Ireland were viewed as a special problem. If these black soldiers became involved with foreign white women, the authorities believed, it could lead to tensions among American troops abroad and raise concerns at home. The army wanted to ensure that black troops serving abroad remained segregated, both from white American soldiers and, as much as possible, from the civilian population of the countries where they were stationed. Yet these goals were difficult to achieve. During World War I, military directives forbade black soldiers in France from speaking with white women or visiting public places where they could socialize with them, and black men who did so were punished, but controlling the social lives of black soldiers during World War II would prove more difficult. Not only did more blacks serve overseas for a longer period of time, but officials found it nearly impossible to segregate black troops completely in European countries.[16]

And while no racial utopia, Europe offered a more accepting environment for interracial relationships. A 1943 British poll, for example, found that only one in seven British disapproved of interracial marriages.[17] White European women might pursue a relationship with a black soldier for any number of reasons—from love to sex and novelty to access to money and resources. And there was no legal ground for the federal armed services to prohibit relationships between black soldiers and white foreign women if those between white soldiers and white women overseas were permitted.

The eagerness of American military authorities to prevent interracial dating overseas created worries for America's European allies, especially for the British, who anticipated that the bulk of black American troops would be stationed in England. British foreign secretary Anthony Eden expressed the fear that if British women fraternized too freely with black Americans, white Americans would object, leading to tensions between the British and white American soldiers. His Conservative Party colleague Maurice Petherick worried more that news of interracial relationships in Britain might demoralize British soldiers serving abroad. He urged the United States to send black troops somewhere more "suitable," like Egypt; other British officials suggested that black troops should be confined to British port areas where the population was already familiar with blacks and might be less likely to mix with them.[18]

Military necessity, however, dictated that black troops be sent wherever they were needed, and by the eve of the Normandy invasion, there were more than 130,000 black Americans stationed in Britain.[19] British military authorities took steps to discourage Brits from fraternizing too freely with black troops. In a 1942 directive, British major general Arthur Dowler instructed that "white women should not associate with colored men." British officers were told to inform their troops that the British should avoid "intimate relations" with black troops and that relationships between white women and black men would "lead to controversy and ill-feeling" between Britain and the United States.[20] Such directives, however, did little to affect the actions of British civilians. The British government had few formal mechanisms to prevent its civilians from dating black Americans. Military authorities could plant rumors about the incidence of venereal disease among blacks, and British women who socialized with blacks were sometimes arrested for breaking curfew or for trespassing on government property, but such prosecution was limited and sporadic.[21]

The U.S. military was unable to prevent all interracial relationships involving black American soldiers and foreign women. Establishing racially segregated camps did little to prevent socializing between black soldiers and white civilian women. In Britain, for example, black and white troops were housed in separate camps that often included their own recreational facilities. To prevent the chances of black and white troops meeting each other off base, Dwight Eisenhower, commander of the American forces, instituted rotating pass privileges and alternate-day policies. Black and white units would have access to canteens, pubs, or Red Cross facilities on alternating days, thus giving each free rein on its assigned days. In some cases, certain towns where black soldiers were located were labeled off-limits to white soldiers and vice versa. These forms of segregation served to prevent black and white American troops from meeting overseas, but they did not necessarily keep black men away from white women.

Many white American soldiers noted with disbelief and disgust the relatively open interracial socializing between black men and white foreign women allowed by such policies. As one white American soldier remarked, the alternate-day policy worked all right "until the white soldiers happened to ask their English girlfriends who they went out with on colored nights." A white first lieutenant stationed in Britain had not only seen black men dancing with white girls, "but we have actually seen them standing in doorways *kissing the girls goodnight.*"[22] The indignation often led to violence as white soldiers attacked blacks out with white women. Some white soldiers feared the long-term implications of the easy interracial socializing taking place in Europe. One Georgia soldier wrote home during the war that he had seen "nice looking" white girls in Europe "going with a coon." What would happen when Georgia got those blacks who thought they were "hot stuff" back again?[23] As this soldier and others like him feared, black men who dated white women while overseas might be more willing to cross racial lines in American society once they returned home.

In order to defuse the situation, American military officials seriously considered importing black American women to socialize with the black men. Shortly after the first black troops arrived in Britain, the War Department requested that black women serving in the Women's Army Corps (or WAC) be sent overseas to "provide companionship for thousands of Negro troops." The implications that WACs were to act as sexual mates to the troops outraged both black leaders at home and WAC director Oveta Culp Hobby, and the War Department eventually canceled its requisition. Black WACs would not arrive in Europe until early 1945, when they acted as a postal service unit, first in Birmingham and then in Rouen and Paris. While the black soldiers stationed near the WAC 6888 unit trucked the WACs in for dances and gave them a warm reception, the approximately one thousand black women who served overseas could not serve as companions for the more than one hundred thousand black troops. Although some black WACs married black servicemen they met overseas, others started dating white European men,

Unable to prevent dating between black American soldiers stationed abroad and white European and Australian women during World War II, the federal government tried to prevent photographs that depicted interracial socializing from being published in the United States. This photo, of the winners of a dance contest at an Italian Red Cross Club, was censored by the army. (National Archives, Still Pictures Branch, photo no. 319-CE-65-SC237349.)

thereby giving authorities a broader spectrum of interracial socializing to cope with.[24]

Eventually realizing that they could neither completely segregate black troops from foreign whites nor effectively prevent all interracial dating, U.S. military officials did the next best thing: to ensure that the interracial dating taking place overseas would not create an uproar at home, they censored stories in the American press. After *Life* magazine ran a picture of black soldiers dancing with white British women in 1943, the War Department's Bureau of Public Relations began to suppress photographs that depicted black servicemen socializing with white women in a way that carried "boyfriend-girlfriend" implications. Photos of black men with white women, Commander Dwight Eisenhower noted, might "unduly inflame racial prejudice in the United States" if they were published. Black troops complained so vehemently about this censorship that they eventually won the right to send home pictures that showed them with white women, but only after such photos had first been stamped "For personal use only—not for publication."[25]

Besides keeping stories about interracial dating out of the American media, the military also moved to prevent relationships between black troops and white civilians from becoming too serious. Tolerating interracial dating did not mean that black soldiers would be allowed to marry their European or Australian girlfriends. Military authorities initially discouraged all overseas marriages, on the grounds that such marriages would distract soldiers from their military duty and lead to complications with soldiers' insurance, allotments, and dependents. However, the military liberalized its policy as complaints from white soldiers denied the right to marry multiplied.[26] No soldier, though, could marry without the permission of his commanding officer. Local commanders reminded soldiers who wanted to marry that they would not be able to live off base, would still be eligible for combat, and would be separated from their wives for long periods of time. Commanders could deny permission to marry if they felt the marriage was ill conceived or hasty, might hinder military performance, or would "discredit" the military. Even if the commanding officer allowed the marriage, there was a mandatory two-month waiting period to ensure that the couple took their vows seriously.[27]

Despite these obstacles, local commanders permitted more marriages as soldiers claimed that the restrictive regulations violated their civil rights. The mandatory waiting period was often waived if the woman involved was pregnant. In Italy and England, white enlisted men who acknowledged paternity and wanted to marry their pregnant girlfriends were granted furloughs for the purpose of marriage.[28] Yet in the case of black American soldiers, the path to marriage was far more arduous. Since there was no federal law prohibiting intermarriage, it was politically difficult for the U.S. military to maintain a blanket policy forbidding black troops to marry white women. Indeed, when pressed, the secretaries of war and of the navy denied that black soldiers were treated any differently than white soldiers who wanted to marry overseas.[29] Yet the headquarters commander in each theater of operations set policies, and many black GIs found that they were prohibited from marrying white women despite official rhetoric.

Documents gathered by the National Association for the Advancement of Colored People (NAACP) illustrate how the air force's policy prohibiting interracial marriage worked to prevent such unions even when local commanding officers were willing to assent to them. In one case an anonymous black soldier was denied permission to marry his pregnant British girlfriend, even though her parents had consented to the marriage and the soldier's superior officer, a captain, had approved the request. Normally, once permission of the commanding officer was secured, a couple was free to marry. But in this case a higher-ranked officer, a colonel at Air Force Headquarters, overturned the permission to marry on the grounds that "such action is against public policy, and on previous occasions has been unfavorably considered by higher authorities."[30] When the frustrated soldier tried to appeal the decision to the commanding general of the European Theater of Operations, another officer at the U.S. Air Force Headquarters refused to forward his appeal, since, as he wrote, "The policy of this headquarters regarding mixed marriages has not been changed. Such marriages are considered to be against the best interests of the parties concerned and of the service."[31]

Although other branches of the service were not as blunt in their official policy directives, black soldiers in the army also found it difficult to secure consent to marry white civilians. Commanding officers routinely denied black soldiers authorization to marry their European girlfriends, pregnant or not, leading the NAACP to accuse the American government of acting as "a partner to bastardy."[32] Black soldiers who requested permission to marry could be sent to another unit or even to the front. According to one black reporter, black soldiers soon learned that if they wanted to be transferred, they simply needed to tell their commanding officer they were in love with a local white woman. After 1950 black soldiers serving in occupied countries in Europe discovered that asking for permission to marry might mean a quick transfer to the front in Korea.[33]

Those black GIs who were dating white women were sometimes confined to camp and assigned extra duties. A black corporal stationed in

Bristol complained in a 1943 letter, "The MPs lock us up for anything and especially if they see us talking with any English women." Black soldiers received disapproving lectures from commanding officers and chaplains. Military authorities often justified their opposition on the grounds that interracial marriage was illegal in a soldier's home state. Yet as one black soldier complained, such an "alibi" for prohibiting intermarriages was unfair: "A man does not have to live where he once lived especially if he wants to be happy and see her [his white fiancée] happy."[34] Soldiers who could not get permission to marry were often forced to abandon their fiancées and children in Europe if they were shipped away or sent back home.

The European women who sought to marry blacks also faced obstacles. American officials, who had their own preconceptions about interracial marriage, took it upon themselves to educate potential war brides about the fate of white women who married black men. Invoking stereotypes about the violence and emotionalism of blacks, one white GI told a European woman that Negro women would kill her if she married a black man, while an officer informed a German woman that she couldn't marry a black man because she would get in "trouble" with colored people and white people would hate her.[35] Although the wartime fiancées of former American servicemen were supposed to receive preference for immigration visas, brides and fiancées of black men were routinely denied visas to travel to the United States. Employees of the U.S. Immigration Department told women involved with black men that they could be refused visas since they might be arrested in the United States as a result of their interracial marriage and they would then become burdensome public charges. If not allowed to emigrate as war brides, women would have to apply for entrance to the United States under the traditional quota basis, which might mean a wait of ten years or more.[36]

Even after they reached the United States, some war brides were pressured to return to their homelands. The Italian wife of Paul Richards, a black veteran from Missouri, found herself in a government hospital in Chicago after contracting typhoid during her trip to the United States. After learning that her GI husband was black, nurses at the hospital tried to convince her to go back to Italy. When that plan apparently failed, the hospital tried to charge the husband for costs supposed to be paid by the Red Cross and tried to label the wife a typhoid carrier.[37] In a worst-case scenario, an English woman came to the United States to marry her black fiancé only to find that she could not marry him in his native state of Virginia. She was arrested for miscegenation after she was found living with him, and was eventually deported back to England.[38]

The road to marriage for Hazel Byrne, the white woman from Manchester, England, and Buford Simpkins, the black soldier from Chicago, illustrates the many barriers erected against interracial marriage. Byrne met Simpkins in 1942 in her hometown of Manchester when she was just fifteen. She had never met a black person before, and was surprised to learn that he spoke English and was "civilized." Although she had been warned not to speak to the colored soldiers, she began a friendship with Simpkins that eventually progressed to dating. When a company of white American soldiers arrived in the area, however, a fight over an interracial couple broke out at a dance and the black troops were sent away. Buford Simpkins managed to come and visit Byrne when he could, but with white American troops in the area, the climate for interracial couples had soured. Friends turned away from Byrne, and at one point she was beaten by a white southern soldier who tried to make her deny that she loved a black man. In 1944 Simpkins asked his commanding officer for permission to marry Byrne. In response, he was transferred to a camp further away from Manchester. Eventually the couple decided they would have to wait until after the war to marry. But when Byrne went to get a visa to come to the States, she found that immigration officials too wanted to prevent her marriage to a black American. She had to wait eighteen months after Buford Simpkins went home even to be interviewed for an American visa. At the American embassy in London, four American women bemoaned the fact that Simpkins was dark-skinned, but then displaced their own objections onto blacks by warning Byrne that "emotional colored girls" might kill her for taking one of their men. One of the women tried to make her understand what it meant to be part of an interracial couple in the United States, telling her in exasperation, "But my dear, you'll have to live with them all your life!"[39] The fact that a white woman might choose to live among blacks seemed beyond the comprehension of American officials. Byrne would not receive her visa to travel to the United States until 1947, three years after Simpkins had sought permission to marry her.

Black servicemen, of course, felt this discrimination keenly. Soldiers complained that there was no legal basis for denying them the right to marry their white girlfriends. As the young air force soldier who was told that his intermarriage violated "public policy" demanded to know, what right did the military have to prohibit him from marrying a white woman when his own home state allowed interracial marriage?[40] By late in the war, the NAACP began to write black soldiers who had been denied permission to marry to ask if they thought the denial was racially motivated.[41] These denials, the NAACP insisted, violated black soldiers' civil rights and were a crude reminder of the military's belief in black inferiority.

Despite all of these roadblocks, some black soldiers did succeed in marrying the white women they met abroad, contributing to the over three hundred thousand marriages involving American soldiers and European women between 1944 and 1950.[42] The U.S. State Department tried to collect figures on the number of interracial marriages from European diplomatic and consular offices in 1945, but it was unable to do so. The British, for example, responded only with statistics about the number of "brown babies" (babies of black soldiers and European women) born during the war, even though most of the parents of these babies never attempted to marry. Anecdotal evidence suggests that several thousand black men married white European and Australian women, while a limited number based in the Pacific married Japanese women. The national office of the NAACP helped a number of black soldiers figure out where they could live with their white brides. The mother of one black soldier, for example, asked the NAACP where interracial couples could legally live in the United States in order to expedite her son's marriage to a French woman. In other cases, the organization helped black soldiers who planned to stay in the military get reassigned to bases in states where interracial marriage was legal.[43]

There are no national statistics on interracial marriage rates before 1960, so it is impossible to determine exactly how many interracial couples there were in the 1940s, but local studies suggest that the number of black-white couples in the United States, which had been decreasing since the turn of the century, began to increase in the 1940s.[44] In large urban areas, clerks noted a rise in the number of interracial couples seeking licenses in the years immediately after the war. The clerk at the marriage license bureau in Chicago was amazed that two hundred interracial couples came in for licenses in 1949; in earlier years, he could recall only a handful of such couples getting married.[45] The war contributed to this small but significant increase in the number of black-white couples nationwide. A 1953 study of interracial couples in Philadelphia found that twenty-one of the ninety-one black-white couples involved foreign-born whites, most of them European war brides. A Washington, D.C., club for interracial couples, founded in 1946, chose as its name "Club Internationale," since so many of the white wives were foreign war brides.[46]

The interracial marriages that took place during the war led to more open relationships between some blacks and whites, but the deeply rooted patterns of American racial discrimination survived the war. Most of the fluidity in social relations was rapidly reversed after the end of the fighting. Black veterans returning to the South were quickly reminded of the color line through threats and violence. Southern politicians berated the performance of blacks in combat and accused black soldiers of raping white women in Allied-occupied areas. Police beat black men in uniform. One black GI from Hattiesburg, Mississippi, recalled that his father brought his civilian clothes to the train station so he would not have to risk wearing his uniform home. And, this soldier recalled, if a black man had a white woman's picture in his pocket, "they'd kill him."[47] The war seemed to have intensified racial tensions by having temporarily afforded mobility and opportunity to blacks.

Most of the economic, like the social, gains of the war were short-lived as well. Blacks, who during the war had for the first time been able to get decent jobs in factories, were the first to be fired. Although some retained positions as skilled laborers, many more were forced to give up their jobs to returning white servicemen. Those who remained ended up in lower-paid, race-segregated jobs. Although residential segregation in some areas had briefly broken down during the massive migrations of

the war years, American living patterns became more, not less, segregated
in the years after the war. Within a decade these mixed neighborhoods
had become predominantly black as ghettos spread and whites moved
outside of the central city to the suburbs. The federal government encouraged these developments by segregating federal housing projects and
by subsidizing the flight of whites to all-white suburbs through guaran-
teed mortgage programs.[48]

Yet even though many of the racial gains of the war were reversed, the
war generated intellectual and ideological changes that would have a
crucial influence on ways of thinking and speaking about interracial
marriage in postwar America. The wartime crisis led to a new sense of
urgency about America's racial problems and contributed to the emergence of a new racial consciousness that questioned the tacit acceptance
of black biological inferiority. By the late 1940s, wartime political, ideological, and scientific shifts began to move the topic of interracial relationships into the national political arena and raised serious new challenges to state miscegenation laws.

World War II had stimulated a fundamental reshaping of ideas about
American national identity. In order to mobilize for a two-front war
against powerful external enemies who made no secret of their contempt
for American democracy or the diverse ethnic and racial makeup of the
nation, the U.S. government had insisted that American pluralism was
the nation's strength, not its weakness. Wartime propaganda and popular
films stressed repeatedly that Americans had to set aside their class, ethnic, and even racial differences to fight the common enemy of fascism.[49]

Yet at the same time, the "arsenal for democracy" was building weapons made in defense plants that discriminated against black workers. The
army fighting fascism was segregated, even labeling blood for injured
troops by race. As Americans fought Hitler and his ideas of a "master
race" abroad, at home black troops were denied service in restaurants
willing to serve German POWs. Such contradictions turned a spotlight
on American racism and led to more pointed criticisms of America's
own structures of racial superiority.

Black Americans understood that the war provided a unique opportunity to force the nation to deal with the fact of racial oppression on the
home front. From the Pittsburgh *Courier's* "Double V" campaign, which

stressed the need to fight both racism at home and Nazism abroad, to A. Philip Randolph's threat to lead thousands of blacks to Washington, D.C., to protest discriminatory hiring in defense industries, activists highlighted the discriminatory treatment of blacks in America. Sensing the possibilities unleashed by the war, the black rank and file in both the North and the South hastened to fight for their rights, joining civil rights organizations in unprecedented numbers, openly defying racial customs, and agitating for the right to vote.[50]

At the same time, the war further eroded the intellectual legitimacy of traditional racism and its assumption of the biological inferiority of blacks. In the first half of the twentieth century, some academics had begun to argue that differences between the races arose from environment rather than from biology. By the end of World War II, as the horrific genocide of European Jews became fully known, biological notions of innate racial inferiority were even further discredited. Scientific racism, as one believer lamented in 1944, "was no longer intellectually respectable."[51] White Americans did not necessarily abandon the belief that there was some biological basis to racial difference, but more began to question how important that difference was, if it went any deeper than skin color, and whether it should be a factor in law or public policy.[52]

The insistent demand by blacks that America deal forthrightly with its race problem and the further discrediting of scientific racism had a profound effect on whites who considered themselves politically liberal. In the 1930s, many white liberals considered issues of race and ethnicity secondary to issues of class and the problem of the unequal distribution of the wealth in the United States. A small group of northern philanthropists and southern whites criticized racial discrimination, but even they focused primarily on improving the regional economy of the South as a way to improve the status of blacks.[53] However, the wartime rhetoric of democracy and antifascism led northern liberals to become increasingly concerned with racial issues and contributed to an emerging liberal consensus that racial discrimination was America's most serious problem.

By the end of the war, the redefinition of the liberal agenda, growing militancy among blacks, and the need for the federal government to distance itself from southern racial practices as it positioned itself as the world champion of freedom and democracy placed the issue of racial discrimination on the national political agenda for the first time since Reconstruction. The new sense of urgency and openness about "the race problem" in the United States, especially in the South, contributed to an increasingly frank discussion of interracial sex and marriage. The Jim Crow racial system, still staunchly defended in the 1940s by most white southerners, had linked segregation to the maintenance of racial purity, implying that only rigid separation of the races could protect white women from "bestial" black men. As Senator Theodore Bilbo wrote in his 1947 political harangue against integration, *Take Your Choice*, "If we sit with Negroes at our tables, if we attend social functions with them as social equals, if we disregard segregation in all other relations, is it then possible that we maintain it fixedly in the marriage of the South's Saxon sons and daughters? . . . The answer must be 'No.'"[54] Even southern whites who thought the existing racial system was unjust argued that some level of separation was necessary to prevent intimate interracial relationships. The Mississippi writer David Cohn believed that blacks should be given justice in the courts, protection of their property, a fair distribution of tax money, and equal wages, but he insisted that the "Negro question" was fundamentally insoluble because it was, ultimately, a sexual question. White southerners would never forgo the segregation that kept blacks and whites separate for fear that any breach in the walls of "social segregation" would lead to racial mixture.[55] The need to prevent "miscegenation," in short, precluded granting full equality to blacks.

An array of books, films, and plays that appeared during and immediately after the war set out to challenge this standard narrative. These works, ranging from Gunnar Myrdal's scholarly masterpiece *An American Dilemma* to *Pinky*, one of the most popular films of 1949, sharply criticized southern racial customs and suggested that the United States must act to ameliorate its long-standing racial problems. Representative of new liberal thinking on race, these works reflected a growing sense among some whites that racial oppression not only was unfair to individual blacks, but was also un-American. Insisting that the "miscegenation taboo" was the linchpin of the entire system of segregation, these scholarly writings and cultural productions implied that no fundamental change in the racial status quo was possible until the issue of race mixing could be somehow separated out from discussions of racial equality. At the same time that black GIs overseas were framing the denial of permission to marry as a violation of their civil rights, these books and dramas were searching for ways to envision a fight for civil rights that would not raise concerns about interracial marriage.

The most influential of the works that tackled the taboo on interracial sex and marriage was *An American Dilemma,* written by the Swedish sociologist Gunnar Myrdal in 1944. For Myrdal, southern whites' opposition to racial amalgamation presented a fatal barrier to America's ability to live up to its democratic creed. Traveling throughout the South, he boldly questioned whites about their feelings toward interracial sex. At southern dinner parties, he often asked his host, "Why don't you want your daughter to marry a Negro?" The leader of an Atlanta organization to preserve white womanhood was horrified when Myrdal asked her whether she ever fantasized about sleeping with a black man.[56] His investigations convinced Myrdal that the taboo on miscegenation was merely a political ploy used by whites to defend black subordination. As he noted repeatedly, whites were largely indifferent "toward real but illicit miscegenation" between white men and black women. Whites defended the caste system, Myrdal concluded, not because of some "presumably biological" miscegenation taboo, but because it gave them economic and political advantages over blacks.[57] If whites were truly concerned about preventing "miscegenation," Myrdal charged, they would seek to improve the status of blacks, since he believed illicit sex would decrease as black fortunes improved while interracial marriages would remain rare.

Myrdal's forthright attack on the miscegenation taboo was echoed in Margaret Halsey's 1946 work, *Color Blind.* Halsey, a white woman, had worked as a captain at a serviceman's canteen during the war. Wartime USO and servicemen's canteens raised general social concerns during the war, as they brought together young, unmarried women with servicemen on leave from their duties.[58] Halsey's canteen served both white and black soldiers, and Halsey demanded that her white hostesses dance with both black and white men. "The canteen considered that a Negro serviceman who was good enough to die for a white girl was good enough to dance with her," she insisted.[59] This policy, however, aroused so much consternation, especially among white southern soldiers, that Halsey felt compelled to write a book that refuted the charges that her white hostesses married blacks or had "coal-black babies" just because they danced with blacks. After all, she wrote, "courtesy is not copulation."[60] Significantly, Halsey questioned the sincerity of whites' anxieties about interracial relationships. Prejudice, she argued, was based not on sexual concerns but on economic ones; the best way for whites to keep blacks as a cheap labor force was to treat them as though they were subhuman. If whites were truly concerned about interracial sex, then segregation was the wrong solution, she charged. The barriers of segregation only served to make blacks more exotic and sexually attractive to whites. Only breaking down racial barriers would diminish their sexual significance for whites, Halsey asserted.

The same willingness to criticize the customary defense of segregation was evident in the 1944 anthology *What the Negro Wants*. In 1943 William Terry Couch, director of the University of North Carolina Press, asked fourteen black leaders to write essays on the titular topic for a volume intended for a white audience. Couch wanted to represent a wide spectrum of black thought; the fourteen essayists ranged from labor leaders to conservative southern educators. Yet despite their diverse political backgrounds, the fourteen essays were remarkably similar. Caught up in the racial militancy unleashed by the war, these black leaders and educators boldly attacked American racism; all of the writers called for an end to segregation and for full inclusion of blacks into America's civil, political, and economic life. Eight of the fourteen essays also directly addressed whites' fears of interracial sex. Opposition to intermarriage, the poet Sterling Brown charged, was a "black herring," used by whites as "the hub of the argument" opposing change in blacks' status. Essayists emphasized that desegregation would have either no impact on intermarriage or would even make it less common. Frederick Patterson, president of Tuskegee University, pointed out that there were very few mixed marriages even in those states that were "comparatively free from the meaner forms of segregation." Virginia Union College president Gordon Hancock, meanwhile, insisted that the social and economic advancement of blacks would result in *fewer* intermarriages. "There is an inverse ratio between race mixture and Negro advancement," Hancock charged. "[T]his alone should relieve the morbid fears that too generally characterize interracial policies." The poet Langston Hughes noted that granting "simple" civil rights did not have to bring with it the complexities of interracial marriage.[61]

The liberal belief that the miscegenation taboo served political rather than biological ends, and that segregation itself fostered racial mixing because it encouraged white male exploitation of black women, did not go down smoothly. W. T. Couch was so appalled by the essays submitted for his anthology that he tried to break his agreement to publish them.[62] Under threat of a lawsuit, he consoled himself by opening the book with a special "Publisher's Introduction" that attacked the essayists for leading America down the dangerous path of racial amalgamation. Whites had the right to separate "cultural from biological integration," Couch insisted, and only segregation would ensure that separation. This hostile reaction was in evidence as well when the black author Richard Wright remarked on a national radio show in 1945 that he had seen throngs of mulattoes in Mississippi despite that state's "airtight intermarriage laws." Outraged whites from around the nation sent letters attacking him and the implication that white men were responsible for racial mixing.[63]

The argument that integration would make interracial sex and marriage less, not more, common was one response to this popular hostility. Writers like Myrdal, Halsey, and the essayists in *What the Negro Wants* asserted that integration could take place without the full assimilation of blacks, as represented by racial amalgamation. Ironically, these efforts to downplay and defuse the issue of "miscegenation" led to increasingly candid discussions of interracial sex and whites' fears of it. Indeed, a survey of popular films, plays, and movies from the mid- to late 1940s suggests a growing public fascination with the meanings and possibilities of cross-racial relationships. Works such as Lillian Smith's 1944 novel *Strange Fruit; Deep Are the Roots,* a Broadway play that opened in 1945; and *Pinky,* the 1949 Twentieth-Century Fox film, dramatized tales of southern racial discrimination through the stories of black-white couples. Like the well-known 1949 Rodgers and Hammerstein musical *South Pacific,* which made an argument for racial tolerance in part by depicting a romantic, if somewhat racist, love story between a white GI and an exotic Polynesian woman, these works used interracial couples metaphorically to stand in for larger messages about the human costs of racism.[64] These representations were certainly not intended to promote interracial love, but they implied that meaningful cross-racial relationships were possible. Their commercial success suggests that millions of Americans were willing to tolerate their relatively sympathetic portrayals of interracial couples.

Lillian Smith, the author of *Strange Fruit,* began attacking segregation in the late 1930s in the pages of *South Today,* the magazine she founded and coedited. She was openly critical of so-called white southern liberals in the 1940s who refused to condemn segregation and who sought to contain the black militancy unleashed by the war.[65] Unlike most southern racial liberals, who focused on the effects of segregation on blacks, Smith was as concerned with how the system of segregation corrupted and stunted whites.

Strange Fruit used the story of a southern interracial couple to underscore Smith's belief that neither whites nor blacks could live up to their full potential under a system of segregation. The novel told the story of an ill-fated love affair between a white man and a black woman after World War I. Tracy Dean, the young southerner who falls in love with a colored girl, is a weak and passive character, economically unproductive and physically handicapped. His lover, Nonnie Anderson, is a beautiful, light-skinned Spelman College graduate, who comes back to her hometown in Georgia to be near Tracy rather than seeking to use her education to better herself. Although Tracy and Nonnie love each other, a full relationship between them is impossible because of racial taboos. Only when he is away fighting in France can Tracy really think about Nonnie as a woman he could love. Within days of his return, Tracy is reminded that white men aren't supposed to "love and respect a colored girl." Nonnie quickly changes back from "the woman he loved" to "a colored girl named Nonnie."[66] Unable to bring himself either to leave the South with Nonnie or to break off his relationship with her, Tracy is murdered by Nonnie's brother for getting her pregnant.

Although Tracy and Nonnie have a loving, fulfilling relationship, Tracy's inability to admit his love for a black woman ultimately destroys him. The book, which Smith called a racial fable about the "White South and Negro South and their relationship to each other," presents no solutions to the vexing problem of segregation and its effect on individuals, both black and white.[67] Yet while the book ends unhappily, its portrayal of a loving bond between a white man and black woman was radical. Their relationship symbolized both the possibility of real connections between the races as well as the destructive forces that prevented such connections from taking place.

The 1949 film *Pinky,* one of several postwar "message movies," also exposed American racism. Directed by Elia Kazan, a leading progressive in the performing arts world, *Pinky* told the story of Pinky Johnson, a light-skinned Mississippi black woman who goes north to train as a nurse and, while there, passes as a white woman and becomes engaged to a white doctor.[68] Just days before her wedding, Pinky's cover is nearly blown when her black coworkers discover her black ancestry. In fear and shame, Pinky breaks her engagement and returns home to her grandmother in the South. The film highlights the ways whites' reactions toward Pinky change when they learn who she actually is. She is harassed by police, arrested without cause, nearly raped by white men, and snubbed by clerks in a store. Just as she is about to head back north, Pinky agrees to serve as a nurse to Miss Em, the elderly white owner of the "big house," who seeks to convince Pinky to stay in the South and work for the improvement of her people. When Pinky's white boyfriend comes south to renew his offer of marriage, Pinky decides instead to stay in the South to open a clinic for local blacks.

Pinky was notable for its portrayal of Jim Crow as unfair and misguided, although in other ways the film romanticized southern race relations and catered to whites' racial prejudices. In *Quality,* the 1945 novel by Cid Ricketts Sumner on which *Pinky* is based, a white mob burns Miss Em's house rather than let Pinky inherit it; in the movie, whites are more willing to allow blacks to succeed. And the role of Pinky in the film is played by a white actress rather than a light-skinned black actress; using a white actress allowed the film to present romantic scenes between the two leads without violating production codes that banned films from depicting "miscegenation," and it probably made the love scenes between Pinky and her white boyfriend more palatable for white audiences.[69]

Publicity for *Pinky* focused on the taboo of interracial relationships and suggested that the key dilemma of the movie was whether Pinky's white lover would discover her black heritage. The poster for the movie featured a large picture of actress Jeanne Crain under the text, "does he know . . . does he know . . . DOES HE KNOW?"[70] Yet what set *Pinky* apart as a film was that Pinky's fiancé, Tom, renews his offer of marriage even after he learns about her racial heritage, has seen the small shack she lives in down South, and has met her grandmother, a dark-skinned washerwoman. The real moral issue of the film is whether Pinky will choose to remain in the South with her people or whether she will choose the man she loves and a life among whites. *Pinky, Life* magazine noted in a cover article, "is one of the rare pictures which presents a central character with a genuine moral choice."[71] The magazine's largely white readership was thus expected to identify with a black character, and to sympathize with her dilemma about whether to marry her white lover.

Deep Are the Roots, a play by Arnaud d'Usseau and James Gow which premiered at Broadway's Fulton Theater in September 1945, dramatized the more threatening relationship between a black man and a white woman. Opening just weeks after the end of World War II, *Deep Are the Roots* charted the return of Brett, a black veteran, to the South after fighting abroad. Before Brett left to go to Europe, he was what white southerners would have described as a "good nigger." He knew his place and he deferred to whites, allowing his white mentor, Alice Langdon, the daughter of a former Georgia senator, to make his decisions for him. He returned to the South, however, a changed man. Instead of accepting Alice's arrangement for him to study for a Ph.D. in Chicago, Brett decides to stay in the South and become the principal of a black school. The turning point in the play occurs when Brett and his childhood playmate, the senator's younger daughter, Nevvie, fall in love. When Alice discovers Brett and Nevvie's love for each other, all her talk of liberalism evaporates. Incensed at the thought of her little sister with a black man, Alice frames Brett for stealing a watch, which results in his being arrested and beaten. When her northern white fiancé suggests that Brett and Nevvie's relationship is none of their business, she exclaims, "Of course it's my business. It's every white person's business. How do you think we live down here . . . When a thing like this happens, we stamp it out."[72]

At the play's end, however, Alice recognizes her own paternalistic attitude toward blacks and offers her support of Brett and Nevvie's marriage. The play thus suggests that southern whites could learn to accept blacks as their equals and perhaps even as their mates. Although d'Usseau and Gow viewed the plot about interracial marriage as secondary to their focus on the unfairness of southern segregation, their message was truly radical.[73] By providing a sympathetic representation of a black man and white woman who loved each other, they implied that hostile opposition to interracial marriage was misguided and unjust.

Ultimately none of these works forced its audience to accept an interracial marriage, since Tracy and Nonnie's relationship ends in tragedy and both Pinky and Brett refuse to marry their white lovers. Nor did these works imply that relationships across the color line could end racial discrimination. As Brett tells Nevvie in *Deep Are the Roots,* they both wanted the world to be different, "but marriage is not the way."[74] Although cross-racial love was as real and deep as other types of love, they suggested, it rarely led to a happy ending. Indeed, these works are best characterized as versions of a white liberal vision of black progress without interracial marriage. Like the academic works, these fictional representations ultimately sent the message that racial progress could occur without interracial relationships taking place.

Despite their failings, *Pinky, Deep Are the Roots,* and *Strange Fruit* used stories of interracial love as a metaphor for the possibilities of racial equality. They provided more positive portrayals of interracial love than had ever previously existed, and their representations resonated with the American public, achieving widespread commercial and critical success. *Pinky* was the second-highest-grossing film of 1949, earning nearly four million dollars. The *New York Times* chose it as one of the year's ten best films, and all of the film's major actresses received Oscar nominations.[75] *Deep Are the Roots* opened to excellent reviews and ran for over a year. *Strange Fruit* quickly became a best seller, selling 140,000 copies in only two months. More than three million copies of the novel were sold by the mid-1960s. The book was so popular that Smith was commissioned to turn it into a play, which opened on Broadway in 1945 and ran for two months.[76]

White audiences may perhaps have been drawn to these stories because interracial love was so taboo and forbidden, but none of these works sought to sensationalize interracial relationships. Instead they wanted to use stories of sympathetic interracial couples to promote a political critique of the racial status quo. Lillian Smith in fact feared that the public's attention to the love story in *Strange Fruit* undercut the book's political message. *Strange Fruit* was too radical for some in its depiction of interracial sex. The book was banned in Boston a month after its release for its "obscene language," and was briefly barred from the mail by the U.S. Post Office.[77] Even though the uproar over the book's graphic language and content contributed to its commercial success, Smith lamented that *Strange Fruit* had become a "sexy, cheap, sensational story about a white man and a colored girl," and worried that the book would not reach its ideal audience (southern whites) because of the publicity. "I think in our ads we ought to stop the passionate love story business," she wrote her publisher shortly after the book's release, asking that the ads instead highlight the book's more important controversy, "its criticism of a whole way of life that has crippled both white and Negro personalities."[78] Yet the fact that Americans were interested in these stories, in part because of their depictions of interracial love, suggests that the longtime taboo on positive portrayals of black-white relationships was eroding. Supporters of the status quo certainly feared as much. As a Georgia newspaper complained, the love story in *Strange Fruit* made "courtship between Negroes and whites appear attractive."[79]

Postwar scholars and artists engaged in increasingly candid discussions of interracial sex and marriage in an attempt to promote their larger civil rights agenda by suggesting that racial progress would not lead to an increase in racial mixing. But as developments in the legal arena showed, the shifting liberal consensus on race raised new challenges to the traditional legal barriers to interracial marriages. A majority of the states in the nation had laws prohibiting or punishing interracial marriage at the close of World War II. Since the era of Reconstruction, when the Supreme Court had ruled that miscegenation laws did not violate the Fourteenth Amendment, no case involving these laws had reached the Supreme Court, and no state court had invalidated its state's bans on intermarriage. In 1944 the U.S. Tenth Circuit Court upheld Oklahoma's antimiscegenation statute and argued that it in no way violated the Fourteenth Amendment.[80] Yet as scientific claims of biological race lost credibility in the 1940s and as race relations became a public issue, new challenges to anti-intermarriage laws emerged in the courthouse.

When the California Supreme Court agreed to hear a 1948 case, *Perez v. Sharp*, there was little hint that it would depart from established precedent. Even though California's law was more lenient than those in most of the southern states—it did not nullify the marriages of interracial couples married legally in other states, and it carried no criminal penalties—interracial relationships had been regulated in some form ever since California first became a state. In 1850, relationships between whites and blacks or "mulattoes" were outlawed; thirty years later, the legislature added "Mongolians" to the list of those whom whites could not marry, and in 1933, after a state court ruled that the marriage of a white woman and a Filipino man was valid under the existing state law, the legislature quickly moved to add the "Malay" race to the list of those who could not marry whites.[81]

Andrea Perez and Sylvester Davis thus challenged a state law that had been strengthened only fifteen years earlier. Andrea Perez was a Latina; Sylvester Davis was black. That made their marriage illegal in California, since Latinos were considered white for the purposes of the state's antimiscegenation law. Their case was brought before the court by the Catholic Interracial Council of Los Angeles, a group that had been looking for a test case to argue that antimiscegenation laws violated the First Amendment guarantees of freedom of religion. Perez and Davis, who were both Catholics, charged that California's ban on interracial marriage was an infringement of their religious rights since it denied them the right to receive the Sacrament of Matrimony. Since their church did not forbid their marriage, they argued, neither could the state. This was an interesting but weak legal argument.[82] Courts had long held that religious freedom of belief did not give one absolute freedom to act on those beliefs. The state could prohibit polygamy or ritual sacrifice even if they were practices encouraged by one's religion. And indeed, the California justices ruled that the law could prohibit interracial marriage even if such marriages were condoned under Catholic doctrine.

But the court did not simply leave the case there; it went on to examine the constitutionality of California's law more generally. California's law, the court argued, would be constitutional if it used reasonable means to prevent a social evil; if, however, the means used were unreasonable or if miscegenation could not be proved to be a social evil, then it "unconstitutionally restricts not only religious liberty but the liberty to marry as well."[83] Two questions were crucial to the court: did the California law use reasonable means to prevent race mixing, and was race mixing a social evil? The majority opinion maintained that if the California law was designed to prevent race mixing, it did not actually accomplish those ends in a reasonable manner. Since the law applied only to people who married in the state, an interracial couple could marry outside the state and move to California and legally "race-mix" within the borders. The statute seemed primarily to apply, as one justice wrote, either to people who were ignorant of the state laws or to those who could not "afford the train fare to a state where the attempted marriage would be valid."[84] The law was too vague, the court insisted, since it nowhere defined what was meant by "mulatto." And it did not actually prevent race mixing, since it placed no prohibitions on marriages between nonwhites and did not prohibit marriages between whites and Latinos or Asian Indians.

But it was on the question of whether amalgamation was a "social evil" that these justices demonstrated the influence of the intellectual forces unleashed by World War II. According to the court majority, miscegenation had not been proved to harm the larger social good. When the state tried to defend the law on the grounds that nonwhites were physically inferior to whites, the majority opinion held that differences between the races were due to environmental factors, not nature. They found "no scientific proof that one race is superior to another." When the state argued that interracial marriage should be prohibited because mixed-race offspring were biologically inferior, the court countered by citing "modern experts" who found no inferiority among mixed-race people. If the goal of the law was to prevent the birth of inferior offspring, it should not use race as the primary tool of categorization, the justices argued. Why not prohibit two sick people from intermarrying? Or two stupid people? The legislature, the court commented, "has not made an intelligence test a prerequisite to marriage."[85] No longer would the court allow race to be used as the unquestioned marker of inferiority.

This landmark decision represented a clear break from earlier judicial assumptions and reasoning. Still, the California court did not expect its ruling to have an impact outside of the state or in other areas of racial law. A state court decision could not overturn the precedents established by

the Supreme Court. And the justices in California did not think this ruling had any bearing on the status of other segregation laws. They, like the
liberal writers, saw the issue of intermarriage as distinct from a broader
civil rights agenda. Antimiscegenation laws were not analogous to other
Jim Crow laws, the court argued, since it was impossible to tell someone
to find a "separate but equal" marriage partner.[86] Other states chose to
ignore *Perez*, viewing it more as an aberration in the long history of
antimiscegenation law than as a trend-setting case. Even in California,
the state senate defied its Supreme Court by voting to keep the invalidated antimiscegenation law on the books. As one state senator reasoned,
the legislature should not remove the barriers to intermarriage, because
"another State Supreme Court may hold the statute completely constitutional."[87]

Despite the consensus about the limited scope of the *Perez* ruling,
the same intellectual and political developments that impelled that decision worried defenders of miscegenation laws in other states. In 1948,
the same year as the *Perez* ruling, Davis Knight, a Mississippi man who
claimed to be legally white and had fought in the army as a white man,
was charged with violating Mississippi's antimiscegenation law. Knight
married a white woman without complications in 1946, but two years
later a distant relative charged that Knight's great-grandmother, Rachel,
was black. If true, Knight would be one-eighth black himself, which
would place him in violation of the Mississippi law that forbade
marriages between whites and those with one-eighth or more "Negro
blood." Although Knight's racial ancestry was nearly impossible to determine, as local townspeople could not decide whether Rachel Knight was
all black or part black, part Native American, Knight was convicted and
sentenced to five years in the state penitentiary. For the jury in Ellisville,
Mississippi, having any black ancestry, whether one-eighth or less, was
enough to convict Knight of miscegenation.[88]

Yet this old-style Mississippi justice was threatened by the new national attention cast on race issues. When Davis Knight appealed his case
to the Mississippi Supreme Court in 1949, even the state attorney general, Greek Rice, agreed that the court should overturn Knight's conviction and throw out the case. Although he, like the local jury, found
Knight's situation "undesirable" and "obnoxious to the sentiments of the

white race," he feared a subsequent appeal to the U.S. Supreme Court was certain to overturn the verdict, given the lack of proof that Knight had "one-eighth or more Negro blood." It would be "dangerous," he argued in front of the Mississippi Supreme Court, for this case to be appealed to the federal court: "In view of the great agitation in many parts of the United States to break down racial segregation in schools, public conveyances and other public institutions, there would be danger if this judgment is affirmed on the testimony in the record of it upsetting our policy of race segregation and forbidding the intermarriage of the white and Negro races within the degrees of the [Mississippi] Constitution."[89] Rice feared that given the present challenges to the racial status quo, the U.S. Supreme Court might be moved to overturn not only this particular verdict but Mississippi's law altogether. The Mississippi Supreme Court agreed, and in November 1949 Knight's conviction was reversed and remanded on the grounds that there was not enough proof that he had one-eighth Negro blood.[90] It would be years before Mississippi's antimiscegenation law was invalidated, but already its defenders saw that outside forces threatened the state's ability to have complete autonomy over its racial customs.

Two years after World War II ended, Theodore Bilbo revealed his anxiety about the ultimate impact of the war on American race relations. He would, he suggested, prefer the death of American civilization by atomic bomb to its slow destruction "in the maelstrom of miscegenation, interbreeding, intermarriage, and mongrelization."[91] As Bilbo saw it, just as World War II had given birth to new weapons that had the potential to destroy humankind, it had unleashed forces that would make his nightmare of racial amalgamation more likely. In reality, the impact of the war was less immediate and more contradictory than Bilbo feared; the disruptions that fostered interracial mixing were short-lived and quickly contained as the military crisis passed. Less easy to reverse, however, were the wartime intellectual and political shifts that reduced the ability of whites to maintain the racial status quo by demonizing interracial sex. The nationalization of the race problem, the critique of the idea of biological racial inferiority, and the wartime celebration of American pluralism changed the environment for discussions of interracial sex and representations of cross-racial love. Although popular books and films did not quite embrace interracial love as a positive good or even urge whites to tolerate it, they did mark a first step toward greater public sympathy and acceptance for black-white relationships. In the wake of the war, the stage was set for a fundamental reckoning with the status accorded the miscegenation taboo in national political discourse.

Despite these tentative steps toward recognition of interracial marriage, black-white couples remained a rarity in the 1940s. Structural barriers such as educational, occupational, and residential segregation ensured that few blacks and whites would be able to meet and socialize as equals. As the next two chapters make clear, hostility to these marriages among whites and fear of them among blacks contributed to the paucity of interracial couples. In many cases, the most serious, and often most effective, opposition to interracial marriage was expressed by the families and friends of those who considered crossing the color line. Whites, many of whom had been able to improve their class and social status during the war, worried that socializing with blacks in any intimate way could adversely affect a whole family's social standing and, even more seriously, might raise questions about their own racial identity, while blacks sought to come to terms with their own ambivalence about interracial relationships as they fought against racial restrictions of all kinds.

CHAPTER TWO

THE DANGERS OF

"RACE MIXING"

America in the late 1940s seemed on the verge of a revolution in race relations. In 1946, President Harry Truman appointed a presidential commission on civil rights to study the race problem. Its 1947 report, "To Secure These Rights," called for an end to segregation, an antilynching law, abolition of the poll tax, and the denial of federal funds to institutions that practiced racial discrimination. In 1948, Truman won reelection despite a mutiny by southern Dixiecrats who bolted the Democratic Party. That same year, Truman desegregated the American armed forces by executive order.[1] The growing federal support for the cause of civil rights reflected not only the impact of World War II but also a more influential black voting bloc and a growing concern for America's image abroad as a result of the emerging cold war with the Soviet Union. It did not, however, reflect a groundswell of protest or clamor for change among most white Americans.

From the late 1940s through the 1950s, racism remained firmly entrenched in American society. The existing racial culture took white privilege for granted. As veterans returned home after World War II, blacks were pushed out of jobs. The fact that black professionals had difficulty finding suitable work and that blacks received less pay for the same work as whites raised few eyebrows in white society in the 1950s. When white Americans moved to the suburbs in record numbers in the

1950s, blacks were excluded not only from new whites-only suburban developments but also from government programs that essentially subsidized the mass migration of whites out of central cities. The new medium of television practiced similar exclusions, showcasing very few minority characters and largely ignoring black America except in news footage. As Henry Louis Gates described life in segregated West Virginia in the 1950s, "seeing somebody colored on TV was an event."[2]

Whites' assumption of this racial order as natural was most clearly reflected in their nearly unanimous opposition to interracial marriage. According to a 1958 Gallup Poll, only 1 percent of southern whites and 5 percent of whites outside the South approved of marriages between blacks and whites. The consensus against interracial marriage cut across class, educational, and regional lines.[3] Even in states where interracial marriage was legal, hostility to the practice was deeply entrenched in the culture and motivated individual whites, schools, and even some courts and medical professionals to discourage it. Almost all whites in the 1940s and 1950s disapproved of black-white marriages, and most saw the possibility of an actual intermarriage involving their family or friends as a crisis that they should mobilize to prevent.

The arguments whites mounted against interracial marriage in the immediate postwar period were similar to those articulated in earlier periods. The bulk of white Americans, one scholar notes, "were just as horrified at the thought of interracial marriage in 1950 as they had been in 1900 or 1850."[4] In the 1940s and 1950s southern whites, as they had in earlier decades, expressed great concern about white racial purity and the mingling of black and white "blood," especially when such "mingling" involved white women and black men. Some insisted too that interracial marriages were sinful because they violated God's creation of separate races. Other whites focused on the ways in which marrying interracially would diminish the status of the white partner and his or her family, and most agreed that black-white marriages could not survive in America's racial environment and that mixed-race children would be stigmatized.

Yet while the underlying rationales for opposing interracial relationships were not new, the mobilization against interracial marriages in the fifteen years after World War II demonstrates what was at stake for white families in maintaining the racial system and makes clear the continued salience of a white racial identity in the years after the war. Preventing interracial marriage served as a way to maintain racial boundaries in a country where having a white racial identity ensured some level of privilege and status. Family honor, a sense of racial superiority, and a distinctive racial identity were all threatened by an interracial marriage in the family. Concerns about the negative consequences of interracial marriage were further exacerbated by the tides of change in the domestic culture of the 1950s. The focus on the importance of traditional nuclear families and of the role of women as wives and mothers, the popularization of psychological experts, and the consolidation of "Caucasian" racial identity to include European ethnics who had not been considered truly white before the mid-twentieth century all served to heighten anxiety about interracial marriage in the postwar years. These varied concerns explain the extreme reactions to the possibility of an interracial marriage within whites' kin networks.

In 1908 James Weldon Johnson wrote a much-quoted analysis of American racism. At the heart of the American race problem, Johnson argued, "the sex factor is deeply rooted. . . . It may be innate; I do not know. But I do know it is strong and bitter."[5] The "sex factor," or white people's seeming revulsion at the idea of interracial sex and desire to maintain white racial purity, has long been viewed as the key reason whites disapprove of interracial relationships. While these supposedly biological concerns cannot be ignored, they must be qualified. Although whites, especially white women, often disapproved of sex between white men and black women, casual or exploitative interracial sex between white men and black women was not prohibited as long as it involved no serious emotional attachment. As in *Strange Fruit,* it was emotional relationships rather than sexual relationships between white men and black women that were threatening; white men were not stigmatized or degraded by intercourse with black women.

The idea of sex between black men and white women, however, repulsed most whites and served as an important dimension of the opposition to interracial marriage involving white women and black men. White women, unlike white men, were stigmatized by engaging in interracial sex. They were tainted by the very act of sexual intercourse with a black man, which implied receiving his semen. The use of the metaphor of "blood" to signify race emerged during the slave period and was further codified in miscegenation law and in late-nineteenth-century theories of eugenics. This metaphor held that racial identity was carried in the blood. "White blood" and "black blood" were not only categorically different, but "black blood" always trumped or dominated "white blood." Having a "single drop" of black blood made a person black. Whiteness was easily corruptible and blackness was all-consuming. This metaphor, as Eva Saks notes, transformed race into an "intrinsic, natural and changeless entity: blood essentialized race."[6]

The language of blood suggested that interracial sex involving white women and black men was far more dangerous than sex between white men and black women. Only men, the assumption went, had the capacity to transfer their blood (through their semen); men were the active spreaders of blood and women the passive receptors. Thus white men could have sex with black women without degrading themselves. White women, however, were tainted through intercourse with a black man, contaminated by his blood/semen. White men could stray and produce half-black children without compromising the "integrity" of the race; the black race might be made more white, but the white race would remain pure and untainted by "black blood." If white women had biracial children, however, it would make the white race less pure; in short, the survival of the white race depended upon its women, who were designated as the guardians of white racial purity.

Although the metaphor of racial blood conflicted with a postwar critique of the biological basis of race, such ideas still resonated with many whites in the 1940s and 1950s. In his 1944 study of American race relations, Gunnar Myrdal found that whites did not consider the illicit race mixing that went on between white men and black women to be amalgamation, since any offspring would be considered black and would live with their mother. Sex between white women and black men, however, was viewed "as an attempt to pour Negro blood into the white race."[7] The language of blood was most often used by white southerners to explain their opposition to interracial marriage. Senator Bilbo employed it at length in *Take Your Choice:*

We deplore the conditions which have poured a broad stream of white blood into black veins, but we deny that any appreciable amount of black blood has entered white veins. As disgraceful as the sins of some white men may have been, they have not in any way impaired the purity of the Southern Caucasian blood. Southern white women have preserved the integrity of their race, and there is no one who can today point the finger of suspicion in any manner whatsoever at the blood which flows in the veins of white sons and daughters of the South.[8]

Bilbo's construction of racial purity excused white men for any sexual indiscretions while suggesting that white women should be carefully monitored since their actions could be so dangerous. White women had it in their power to end the white genetic line. For white southerners, a southern white minister explained, "the presence of the seed of the Black man in the womb of the white woman was the most dreadful thing that could be imagined."[9]

Children born to white women and black men represented the trumping of blackness over whiteness. Biracial children were considered black because of the one-drop rule and likely because of their physical characteristics. The white parent's racial heritage would thus be erased or effaced by the black parent's input. This was the foundational fiction of the American racial dichotomy—blackness polluted and overpowered whiteness, reflected most starkly in the claim that the children of white women and black men would be "coal black." Betty Jeffries, the white wife of the black jazz singer Herb Jeffries, recalled that her family became hysterical when she told them she was pregnant. "Their last words, when I left for good, were 'What if you have a coal-black baby?'"[10] Even when not visible, the black heritage would mark the end of a white kin network.

The sexualized stereotypes of black men as lustful, uninhibited, and virile, moreover, raised questions about the virtue and propriety of any white woman who slept with or married them. White women out with black men were often mistaken for prostitutes by both blacks and whites. Although marriage usually legitimated women's sexuality, especially in the 1950s when marriage experts told the nation that a good marriage required a healthy sexual relationship between husband and wife, interracial marriages continued to carry the connotations of illicit, transgressive sex.[11]

Sexual relationships between white women and black men also challenged the authority and supremacy of white men, politically and sexually, in a way that no relationship between a white man and a black woman could. Although marriages between white men and black women were forbidden by law and custom, white men were far more concerned about controlling and directing white women's sexual relationships. It is no coincidence that the classic question that long served to end all arguments on civil rights was "Would You Want Your Daughter to Marry One?" This query nearly always focused on daughters rather than on children more generally, demonstrating the particular concern about the consequences of white women's actions. Women who married blacks not only challenged the racial order but also rejected the authority of their fathers and brothers. Many men saw these relationships as a challenge to their manhood and sexuality, a fight between a black man and white man for the control of the white man's woman, and they were adamant about preventing relationships that might shame or even "unman" them.

Men sometimes responded to this blow to white masculine authority with murderous hostility. A white father from Norfolk, Virginia, found a 1951 *Life* magazine story about the interracial marriage of a black jazz musician and a white woman so distasteful that he wrote in to express his disgust. "If my daughter ever entertains such an idea [as intermarrying]," he wrote, "I will personally kill her and then myself, thus saving the state the expense of a hanging. This plan of action has the entire approval of my wife and whole family."[12] *Life* did not publish any responses to this horrific threat, which perhaps reflected the not isolated view among white men that a dead daughter was preferable to an "ethnically impure" one. In death, at least, remained some honor.[13]

Gender and family relations in the immediate postwar period intensified fears of white women's liberated sexuality and reinforced the precarious patriarchal authority of fathers over their daughters. The rush to domesticity and eager embrace of traditional gender roles in the 1950s marked an intense concern with sexual order. The insecurities and anxieties unleashed by the cold war and the beginnings of an atomic age were reflected in a fear of sexual chaos and the destructive potential of unrestrained female sexuality. The media and the state held up the post-war nuclear family as a defense against the threatening world, idealizing a traditional middle-class family as the foundation of a strong nation. Marriage and motherhood were celebrated as the path toward true womanhood; men were expected to play the role of benevolent patriarchs supporting and leading the family. Nonconformity in general, and especially among women, became suspect as independent and assertive women were charged with emasculating men and threatening the nation's well-being. While the early marriage age, high birth rate, and low divorce rate of the 1950s were themselves radical departures from previous demographic patterns, those who deviated from them were subject to a type of "McCarthyism of marriage and family."[14] There was no place for interracial couples in this celebration of domestic conformity.

These concerns about racial purity were also reflected in opposition to interracial marriage framed in terms of Christian religious beliefs. A common argument against interracial marriage, especially in the South, was that God had created distinct races and intended for them to remain separate. Interracial marriages violated God's plan for man. A Virginia judge ruled in 1959 that "Almighty God created the races white, black, yellow, malay and red. . . . The fact that he separated the races shows that he did not intend" for them to intermarry. In a 1962 Gallup poll, one-third of white southerners felt that the Bible supported the belief that "God just did not mean for the races to mix."[15] Marrying interracially was a sin in violation of biblical teachings. In the words of one southern mother, her white son had committed a "mortal, black sin" when he moved north to marry his black girlfriend.[16]

The view that intermarriage violated Christian teachings was not shared by all whites. Indeed, less than 10 percent of whites outside the South believed that God did not intend for the races to mix. Most northern religious groups and national religious organizations did not accept a simple equation of intermarriage with sin. Not that religion, which might have been one of the few tolerant spaces in American society, provided much intellectual or social support for intermarriage. Despite the involvement of the Catholic church in the 1948 *Perez* case in California, most organized religious groups either ignored the issue of intermarriage or insisted that such marriages should be discouraged because they were likely to fail. Religious spokesmen did not openly endorse the practice of intermarriage in the 1940s and 1950s, although a few writers did argue that Christians should accept interracial marriage because of their belief in human brotherhood.[17]

Most whites' opposition to intermarriage was driven less by their religious beliefs or even their concern about racial "purity" than by a conviction that associating with black people as social equals would have serious consequences. Working with blacks, living near blacks, or—worst yet—marrying them damaged the social standing of those who were not black. Throughout America's history, other marginalized groups have distanced themselves from blacks in order to gain security and status in American society. Some Native American tribes explicitly made clear their distance from blacks in order to show that they were racially superior and deserved greater rights from the state. Asian and East Indian immigrants argued they should be legally recognized as white, asserting a superiority over people of African descent.[18] For these other racial minorities, maintaining some social distance from blacks was crucial to securing a higher place for themselves in America's racial hierarchy. Richard Rodriguez thus recalled that while his Latino parents rented a house to blacks in Los Angeles in the 1950s, he was not allowed to date black girls. "Back in the fifties, if you dated a black girl, your parents would probably move out of the area," he remembers. "If you were even seen walking with a black girl, [and you were] Mexican, your old man would probably take a switch . . . to you."[19] Forced to share their neighborhoods with blacks, Latinos forbade interracial dating as a way to shore up their own status.

In the postwar period, groups like Slavs, Eastern Europeans, and Jews, who were also considered racially inferior to English or German settlers when they first arrived in the United States, were essentially "remade" as Caucasians as European immigration slowed and as blacks migrated in greater numbers from the South to the North and West. The ability of these groups to be defined as white depended on the racial exclusion of others.[20] Asserting their whiteness as a badge of rank and status, white ethnics who had only recently consolidated an identity as Caucasian fought to distance themselves from blacks in part to prevent marriages that would cause them shame and damage their social position.[21] Indeed, fragmentary evidence of a declining rate of intermarriage between blacks and white immigrants in the postwar period suggests that white ethnics' bid for whiteness may have involved more stringent prohibitions on interracial marriages.[22]

Most seriously, these white ethnics made clear their opposition to sharing their neighborhoods with blacks, fearing both the economic and the social consequences of doing so. In the years after World War II, those with financial resources moved to suburbs that excluded blacks, like the new developments built by Arthur Levitt. Levitt refused to sell to black customers, a policy that he claimed was based not on racial prejudice but on economic reality. Ninety-five percent of his white customers, Levitt charged, would not buy a house in a neighborhood with even one black family. In urban working-class neighborhoods, whites fought racial succession. The value of their homes, their respectability, their status, and their white identity depended on keeping blacks out of the neighborhood, through violence if necessary.[23] Those resisting residential integration feared that living near blacks would lead to interracial marriages. As one Baltimore woman charged, if blacks and whites lived in the same neighborhood, "the children of the two races [would] grow up together and intermarry." The black playwright Lorraine Hansberry poked fun at these fears in her 1959 play, *A Raisin in the Sun*. When whites mobilize to prevent a black family from moving into their neighborhood, one black character asks: "What they think we going to do—eat 'em?" No, replies another, "marry 'em."[24] Marrying interracially was always cast as the greatest threat to whites' status and identity.

Whiteness was always created and defined *against* blackness. In America's racial binary, "white" racial identity had no meaning without its fictive opposite of blackness. This racial identity, moreover, provided economic advantages to whites, who had access to better jobs, housing, and government programs. Whiteness in America carried psychological value, as whites could claim a higher status than others on the basis of their race. Indeed, a white racial identity was perceived to be so valuable that, well into the 1950s, white people who felt they were wrongfully accused of being black could sue for libel because the allegation was seen as likely to cause social injury.[25]

Whereas associating with blacks might lower the social status of whites in contemporaries' eyes, intimate relationships such as marriage could lead to questions about a white person's own racial identity. In other words, it not only was perceived as degrading to associate with blacks, but could also be defining. Racial identity was not determined simply by ancestry, appearance, or any biological notion of "blood"; it was also embedded in social relations in the community. Because whiteness was defined as not being black, being with black people could lead to a reevaluation of white identity. In the largely segregated social world of the 1940s and 1950s, where one lived, whom one lived with, and the color of one's children could reflect on one's race.[26]

Whites who associated openly and freely with blacks called their own status and racial identity into question, since it was assumed that only blacks would marry other blacks. In James Baldwin's 1968 novel *Tell Me How Long the Train's Been Gone,* a young black boy whose light-skinned mother could pass for white tries to understand the racial distinctions between black and white. His older brother explains it to him in this way: "Our mama is a colored woman. You can tell she's a colored woman because she's married to a colored *man,* and she's got two colored *children.* Now, you know ain't no white lady going to do a thing like that."[27] As Baldwin shrewdly noted, being "white" only gained meaning in contrast to not being associated with blacks. A 1960 study of black-white couples in New York City found that several of the white partners had been mistaken for light-skinned blacks because of association with their spouses. "Assumptive racial classification, based upon association, is probably more manifest than is generally known," the author concluded.[28]

Interracial marriages terrified families in part because this line between black and white was so slippery. If having a black spouse could lead to a loss of status, prestige, and perhaps even a racial identity as white for the white partner, there could be similar consequences for having a black son-in-law or black grandchildren. A child's interracial marriage could implicate the entire family in a racial transgression. One sociologist explained in the 1940s that the "profound emotional resistance to racial caste intermarriage" was largely comprehensible given the way that marriage affected an "elaborate network of social relations."[29] A white child's marriage to a black person could upset familial order and threaten a family's community reputation. Families thus had a direct self-interest in preventing a marriage that could shame them in their community.

A final pillar of whites' opposition to interracial marriage in the 1940s and 1950s was the common belief that most, if not all, interracial marriages were unstable and unhealthy. Becoming involved in an interracial relationship might be a sign of some kind of psychological sickness. Postwar America saw the advent of the expert in popular culture, and "expert" opinions about interracial marriage helped shape whites' attitudes. In the 1950s, psychiatric explanations for social behavior were in vogue. Independent women were told that they suffered from a Freudian version of penis envy; unwed mothers were characterized as neurotic or psychopathic. Americans increasingly turned to individual therapy in the mid-1950s, listening carefully to experts who told them how to have a healthy marriage, how to raise their children, and how to be happy.[30]

These experts, moreover, expressed increasing interest in the subject of racial intermarriage. Studies of intermarriage seemed to provide a "precise, quantitative measurement" of vital sociological questions about the process of assimilation, the degree of cohesion within various ethnic and racial groups, and the extent of social distance between groups.[31] Intermarriage also provided an excellent arena for studying deviancy or nonconformity in an age self-consciously concerned with the relationship between the individual and the larger society. At a time of great faith in experts and heightened interest in psychological explanations, sociologists and psychologists weighed in with their own concerns about interracial marriage. At least fifteen sociological studies of black-white couples appeared between 1950 and 1960, while a number of psychologists also studied those who married across the color line.

Rather than arguing against intermarriage on the grounds of black biological inferiority, behavioral and social scientists questioned the mental health of whites who would consider crossing racial lines and suggested that those who intermarried would suffer severe social consequences. Experts from the period generally agreed that marrying across the color line was a neurotic symptom of an underlying psychological disorder, and that those who married interracially were disturbed individuals, exhibitionists who craved public attention. As the Columbia professor of psychiatry Nathan Ackerman argued, marrying interracially "is very often evidence of a sick revolt against society."[32] Being involved interracially became de facto evidence of mental illness. Thus Ackerman contended that any interracial experience was abnormal given the existing state of American society.

Other psychologists turned to Freudian explanations for interracial marriage, accepting, as many postwar analysts did, a modern view that sex "expressed one's deepest sense of self."[33] An interest in interracial sex was read as evidence of sexual deviancy or dysfunction. The psychiatrist George Little, writing in a 1942 issue of *Psychoanalytic Review,* theorized that since blacks served as a "sexual symbol in the white man's life," whites who had difficulty functioning sexually might seek a black mate. An "impotent man seeking a super-heated embrace in the hope of being able to accomplish the sexual act" might well marry a Negro, Little argued, as might a white woman of the "Messalina type" (Messalina was a Roman empress notorious for her sexual profligacy who was executed by her husband, the emperor Claudius).[34] The psychiatrist Robert Seidenberg, meanwhile, believed that interracial sex provided a unique opportunity for whites to gratify their incestuous urges through sex with someone unrecognizable as a father or mother figure.[35] The therapeutic age indulged all manner of individual and group fantasies about those who dared cross the color line.

Several studies blamed interracial marriages on an unhappy childhood or upbringing, tracing nonconformity among adults back to dysfunctionality in the childhood home. This interpretation drew on the paradox of the 1950s: while America celebrated domesticity and family, social critics saw a potential dark side to the isolated nuclear family. Mothers dissatisfied with their life at home might seek to control their children's lives, thus producing weak, effeminate children. Fathers might be emasculated by domineering mothers and as a result provide little direction for their teenaged children. The popular 1955 film *Rebel without a Cause* showcased James Dean as a troubled adolescent, confused and unmoored because of his weak father and overbearing mother. Everything from juvenile delinquency to homosexuality could be traced to insensitive or distant parents.[36] So could a decision to marry interracially. For Eugene Cash, who studied interracial couples in Philadelphia, the personality traits that stood out most among intermarried whites were "resentment, negativism, and rebellion." Most of the intermarried white women resented their mothers and had poor relationships with their parents, he argued. Linton Freeman's 1955 study asserted that a child's decision to marry interracially stemmed from early problems in the parent-child relationship. Young people who married or dated interracially felt alienated from their ethnic group because of a feeling of being rejected by their parents, he argued.[37] In the opinion of these experts, marrying interracially served as a way for disaffected youth to revenge themselves on their ineffective parents.

Another popular theory suggested that whites married blacks for economic gain, which was perhaps the only way that white observers could rationalize black-white marriages. This "exchange theory," outlined by Robert Merton in 1941, hypothesized that marriages involved an exchange of assets. Merton, who claimed that neither "romantic love" nor the American democratic creed were strong enough forces to overcome the barriers to marrying across race lines, argued that whites instead married blacks for crass material reasons. Interracial marriages, he theorized, probably took place between upper-class black men and lower-class white women, with the white partner exchanging her higher "caste" status for the black partner's higher class status. There would likely be few marriages between black women and white men, Merton argued, since white men had no economic incentive to marry black women.[38] Merton's theory was widely influential, motivating a number of case studies of the class and educational disparities between partners in interracial marriages. Although nearly all of these studies found that interracial marriages tended to be class homogamous (meaning both partners were of the same class background), Merton's theory remained popular among scholars. One 1960 study hypothesized that white women who intermarried "tended to be of lower class and of immigrant stock, whereas the male Negro partners tend to be of upper- and middle-class status."[39]

Studies of interracial couples not only argued that whites married blacks either for neurotic or for crass economic reasons, but also contended that such couples would have a very difficult time surviving in

America's hostile racial climate. Although interracial couples certainly faced extra obstacles, experts tended to exaggerate their problems, suggesting that virulent societal opposition doomed most interracial marriages and that those couples who survived would be consigned to a life on the margins of American society, rejected by both blacks and whites. Children of interracial couples had to negotiate this in-between status at their own peril and often suffered permanently for the choice of their parents, experts claimed. Certainly reading marriage and family college textbooks from the era would give cause for alarm. Interracial marriages "present unusually difficult problems, which in some cases are hopelessly insoluble," one decreed, while another called them "inadvisable on social and cultural grounds." All of the existing research, a third warned, "argue[s] against intermarriage."[40] Randall Risdon, writing about interracial couples in Los Angeles in 1954, argued that they lived under a state of siege in American society. Risdon's depiction of the life of interracial couples was bleak: "The accommodation of the interracially married couples to society at large often rests on pseudo, rather than actual accommodation. . . . They appear to live with the feeling that social conflict in some form is always in the offing. These couples are not readily welcomed as friends by most of their contacts in either race." The prognosis for existing and future interracial marriages was grim, according to Risdon. "In interracial marriage, the security and orderly living which most people hope to obtain from marriage are made doubly difficult of obtainment by the nature of society and the cultural heritage which each race brings to it."[41]

These treatises of the 1940s and 1950s provided scientific support for the belief that whites who married blacks were mentally unbalanced and that their marriages and children would suffer as result of their actions. Such pessimistic views on intermarriage came together in a key cultural understanding of the time: that marrying interracially was a form of "sociological suicide," a way for a white person to martyr him or herself.[42] Whites who had low self-esteem could punish and degrade themselves by consigning themselves to a life among blacks. As George Little wrote, a white person might seek to marry interracially because he or she had a "tendency toward self destruction." Interracial marriages, Little claimed, represented the ultimate in self-degradation, a form of "spiritual death" for those with "masochistic tendencies" but not enough daring to actually end their lives. "In those Whites with an urge toward self-destruction and yet without the courage to drink the hemlock, extra racial marriage leaves nothing to be desired," Little contended.[43] Such metaphors of death and suicide were common not only in the academic literature on interracial marriage but also in whites' response to interracial couples. One young white man was repeatedly told by friends and family that it would be social and financial "suicide" for him to marry his "octoroon" girlfriend.[44] This metaphor of intermarriage as social death encapsulated the fears of whites that those who intermarried lacked virtue, shamed themselves and their families, lost social status, and possibly sacrificed property of immeasurable value—their racial identity as a white person.

Concerns about interracial sex, religious tenets, maintaining status, and the social well-being of interracial couples worked together to create an atmosphere of strict societal repression of interracial marriage in the 1950s, despite the transformed postwar environment. White Americans shared a general consensus that interracial marriages were dangerous, socially harmful, and should be prevented whenever possible. This was the atmosphere in which white families operated when they were forced to move from abstract thinking about intermarriage to confront the reality of an interracial marriage involving their own kin.

Any discussion of how white families reacted to an interracial marriage in the 1940s and 1950s focuses by necessity more on the North than on the South. In every southern state in this period, as well as in many in the West, interracial marriage was prohibited by law. These laws prevented couples from marrying or forced them to leave their native states to do so. But despite the laws, there were committed interracial couples in southern states. In fact, when the U.S. Census first tracked interracial marriage in 1960, twenty thousand southern couples described themselves as interracially married. Nearly 60 percent of these couples involved a white man and a black woman, suggesting that it was somewhat easier for white men and black women to forge some kind of life together in the South. In the rest of the country, a little over half of all interracial couples involved black men with white women, but in the

South it was dangerous for black men and white women to show any interest in each other, let alone to live together.[45] These southern couples, however, were not legally married and could make no claims to be.

Finding information about these early southern interracial couples is difficult, since they often had to hide their relationship in order to avoid prosecution. Consider the case of Adeline Young, a black woman who saw herself as the common-law wife of the Italian man she lived with in Mississippi from 1947 until he died in 1963. After her "husband's" death, Young sued for death benefits, but her claim was denied. Mississippi courts ruled that the couple had not had a common-law marriage because they had not publicly presented themselves to the community as married (an action that might have led to their arrest). Their two children, the court ruled, were therefore illegitimate and not entitled to their father's Social Security benefits.[46]

Southern laws prevented most couples from even considering marriage and ensured that they could not have the benefits of a common-law marriage. Southern families, more than those in states where intermarriage was legal, could turn to the criminal system for reinforcement if their child was considering an interracial marriage. When Marry Brown, a white WAF at the Lackland Air Force Base in Texas, married her black boyfriend in Mexico in 1955, her mother wrote the San Antonio police to ask them to do something about the marriage. The district attorney ultimately advised the couple to leave the state of Texas. In the 1948 case involving Davis Knight in Mississippi, Tom Knight also turned to the court system to punish his racially ambiguous nephew, Davis Knight, for marrying a white woman.[47]

A few couples left the South in order to marry, an act that shamed their families. When Burleigh Lester, a Mississippi police sergeant, moved to Chicago so he and his black girlfriend could marry, his mother reacted with disgust. "You must either be crazy or you ain't one of mine," she told Lester, insinuating that whites who intermarried were mentally disturbed. She sent Lester a ten-page registered letter, complaining that he had forever shamed his family (especially his two white children from a previous marriage), and that his actions had embarrassed her. People now pointed her out on the street as the woman whose son married a Negro.[48]

Although community-level studies may well reveal more information about southern couples in the 1940s and 1950s, on the national level there is far more documentation of the response of families in states where interracial marriage was legal. In these states, although families often had the support of the medical establishment and of the courts, they carried far more of the burden of upholding racial boundaries. Of course, few families had to deal with the possibility of an interracial marriage. The 1960 census found a only thirty-one thousand black-white couples in all northern and western states combined. Yet while interracial marriage was rare, it raised immense concern among white families, especially if a daughter announced her intention to marry a black man. Although parents disapproved of the interracial marriages of both sons and daughters, white families regularly resorted to more drastic steps to control their daughters. The special concern about daughters reflected, in part, the greater uneasiness many whites had about interracial sex between white women and black men. But these concerns also stemmed from the patriarchal marital order that assumed that daughters became members of the family they married into, as symbolized by women changing their name. Women, more than men, assumed the status and identity of their spouse, and daughters' actions might thus reflect more directly on the family.[49]

In 1951 a lengthy article by an anonymous author was published in *Harper's* magazine. Entitled "My Daughter Married a Negro," the article recounted the ordeal one white couple had endured when their daughter, Anne, married a black college classmate in 1949. Told by Anne's father, the story described the escalating tensions in a prototypical family faced with the possibility of an interracial marriage.[50] When Anne first told her parents she was serious about her black boyfriend, they were shocked. The photo of him that Anne kept on her bureau during her college vacation "spoiled our Christmas just as completely as the German offensive in the Ardennes had done four years earlier," her father remembered. For the next eight months, the family waged a campaign as organized as that offensive to prevent their daughter from marrying a black man. This offensive began simply with the parents expressing their objections and trying to convince Anne to abandon the relationship. Anne's father wrote to friends and strangers, including a philosopher, teachers, and a social worker, seeking advice about how to prevent the marriage. He introduced his daughter to several available white suitors, wrote letters to her boyfriend making the case for a long engagement, and then pleaded for a postponement when the couple announced their intention to wed.

Anne's father, like many parents, hoped that his child would end her interracial relationship because of his objections. Voicing dismay and horror was the first line of defense. Doris, a young Jewish woman who married Paul, a black man, in the mid-1940s, recalled that when she told her mother she was seeing a black man, "all hell broke loose!" Her mother and father were, "first of all, very angry with me." Doris's mother begged her daughter to stop seeing Paul. When her tears did not work on Doris, she "hit on a different approach: to get to Paul and ask him to stop seeing me. Paul listened to her, and between her pleadings and her tears he finally promised not to see me any more. He said that he couldn't bear to see my mother cry." Doris eventually agreed to stop seeing Paul, although her promise didn't last long. She sneaked out of her home one night and secretly married him. Hettie Cohen also resisted the tears of her parents. When she told her father that she had married the black writer LeRoi Jones in 1958, her father wept and begged her to get a divorce. "You can't do it," he told her. "It'll kill your mother."[51]

Parents and friends frequently turned to "expert" arguments against intermarriage to try to convince their loved ones that marriages across the color line were doomed to fail or would cause great hardship to the white partner. Anne's father, for example, claimed that he did not think interracial marriage was immoral or biologically wrong, but he was certain that a mixed marriage would fail, and he imagined "an alarming list of complications facing a white girl who marries a Negro." When Michelle Ross, a white woman in Atlantic City, decided to marry a black man, a good friend of her father's interrogated her. She recalled that he asked, "Was I doing this to spite my father? Did I expect to have children? Didn't I realize what I'd have to go through all my life, what my children would have to face?" When he finished his litany, he inquired, "Well, have I convinced you?" and seemed surprised that he hadn't. Some parents even accepted the idea that interracial marriage was a form of "sociological suicide." Anne's father, for example, repeatedly employed the metaphors of death and war in describing the impending marriage. The weeks that Anne was home for her summer vacation "passed like a wartime furlough; everything ran against the clock and the calendar." When it was time for Anne to return to college, "it was like seeing her brother off during the war." Another white parent put it more bluntly, telling her daughter's black fiancé in the early 1960s that he would be "signing my daughter's death certificate" if he married her.[52]

The fears of these parents that their children would suffer greatly if they chose to intermarry were often sincere; they reflected the social reality that whites in interracial marriages were likely to face prejudice and discrimination. Nevertheless, even if their fears were valid, the actions of most families in the period demonstrated that they had little interest in challenging the prevailing status quo. Rather than supporting their children and criticizing racism, families accepted as inevitable that interracial couples would be stigmatized and marginalized. In short, they naturalized the negative consequences of intermarrying rather than seeing those consequences as a product of a racist status quo that could be fought and changed.

Instead of working for broader social acceptance for interracial couples, most families exerted their energies in seeking to prevent an interracial marriage, using whatever means they had at their disposal. Some families tried to separate couples, hoping that distance would lead their white children to reconsider their decision to date across the color line. Fran, a white woman who married a black man in the late 1940s, recalled that her mother tried to convince her to go abroad to England to visit some friends after she told her about the relationship. The parents of Dorothy Lebohner, a young white coed at Alfred University, tried to lure her on a Florida vacation so she would forget her black boyfriend. When Ann Marable's parents discovered she was dating a black man, they sent her from New Jersey to California to live with an aunt until she came to her senses.[53]

There is no way to know how many whites were dissuaded from marrying blacks because of familial pressure, but some relationships certainly faltered under the weight of feelings of guilt and betrayal. One young woman broke off her relationship after her father died and her mother became ill. Her family had strenuously objected to her possible marriage and she felt responsible for the turn of events.[54] Archival records left by George Wiley, a black Ph.D. chemist, a leader of the Congress of Racial Equality, and the founder of the National Welfare Rights Organization, provide one of the most detailed accounts of the effects of parental disapproval. While teaching at Berkeley in the late 1950s, Wiley fell in love with Marty Goldsmith, a young white schoolteacher. Her parents, however, strongly disapproved of the relationship, and she eventually broke up with him because of their objections. As she explained to Wiley in a tape recording made after their breakup, her mother had told her that she did not approve of intermarriage, that such a marriage would bring great difficulties, and that she would never be able to accept Wiley or their children. Goldsmith feared that she would have to live two separate lives if she married him, one with him and one with her family, and she decided that while Wiley could move on and find someone else, her mother could not find another daughter. She felt a "greater responsibility to her" than to Wiley, she told him. Although Goldsmith believed that intermarriage was the ultimate answer to America's race problems, since people must "interact socially regardless of race," she was not ready to take the plunge herself. I "won't give up one thing to gain another," she told Wiley.[55] Wiley remained convinced that Goldsmith's parents disapproved only because of their concerns about how their reputation would suffer if people found out their daughter had married a black man, but he could not change Goldsmith's mind. Wiley soon left California for Syracuse, New York. In 1961 he married a white Syracuse graduate student. On their third date, he told her that she had to decide then and there whether she would be willing to marry a Negro or they could no longer see each other. The pain of Goldsmith's decision had affected him deeply.[56]

When parental pressure alone was not successful in breaking up a relationship, families turned to whatever reinforcements they could find. The anonymous father of Anne talked of adding friends and family "to his team" as he desperately tried to postpone his daughter's marriage. Although interracial marriage was not formally illegal in northern states, there were a variety of institutions ready to work on such a team. Some schools and colleges were willing members, prohibiting interracial dating or reporting instances of interracial dating back to parents. At the public high school in Muncie, Indiana, in the 1950s, black boys seen talking with white girls were reprimanded by teachers and guidance counselors. Gregory Williams recalled his teacher's reaction when he was caught talking to a white girl. "You better get it out of your mind that you're ever going to date white girls," the teacher told him. "That kind of thing is just not done in our society. It's not going to be acceptable in my lifetime or yours, and it will never, ever happen here in Muncie."[57] Some integrated northern and midwestern colleges also assumed an "in loco parentis" role, by advising their students against interracial marriages and informing white parents when their children became involved with blacks. At Syracuse University, for example, the administration wrote letters to the parents of white students who dated blacks until student opposition put an end to the practice in 1959. White students at Ohio State University who dated interracially faced reprimands and warnings from student deans, while the black basketball star at Alfred University in upstate New York was advised to quit school by his coach and the dean of men after he began dating the white daughter of the university treasurer. He eventually left Alfred. "I was pressured into leaving school," he told reporters. "I was railroaded out of town, almost." College officials at Alfred worried that parents might hesitate to send their children to a school with a reputation for interracial dating. They took pains to present this affair as a family problem rather than a university one, stressing that this romance should not scare parents from sending their daughters away to integrated colleges because the girl had been living at home when she met and began dating her black boyfriend.[58]

Even some institutions that prided themselves on their lack of racial discrimination went out of their way to discourage interracial dating. In fact, administrators might have felt that a commitment to racial integration necessitated efforts to prevent interracial relationships among students, as a well-publicized 1952 case at Earlham, a Quaker college in Indiana, suggests. In the early 1950s, Earlham was probably one of the most forward-thinking institutions of the day on issues of race. Tom Jones, the school's president, was a self-described racial liberal who had previously been president of Fisk University, a historically black college. Earlham had been founded by abolitionists and had always admitted black students. The college had an official policy of nondiscrimination, boasting that "at no time in its history has it taken the easy road of not admitting students of non-Caucasian races."[59] White and black students lived in the same dorms, ate in the same dining hall, and were equally included in all college activities.

Yet Earlham also had an official policy discouraging interracial dating. In the school catalog, students were warned not to engage in any steady interracial dating "looking toward marriage." Students who dated interracially were counseled by school officials and told not to allow the relationship to become serious. Although Earlham officials claimed that they did not object to interracial marriage per se, they worried that students were not mature enough to seriously consider the full implications of marrying interracially. The college thus sought "to discourage precipitous, youthful interracial marriages because they present extra problems which may be almost insurmountable in the civilization of today," a 1952 college press release stated. "It is our feeling," wrote Earlham's director of public relations, "that usually undergraduate students are not mature enough to evaluate the difficulties surrounding interracial marriage and therefore [we] counsel against dating, and prohibit engagements while they are still students."[60]

In 1952, this policy would be tested by Earlham seniors Grace Cunningham and Robert McAllester. McAllester, a New York native, was white; Cunningham, who was from California, was black. The couple got engaged during spring break of their senior year. Cunningham and McAllester knew about the school's official policy. In fact, Grace Cunningham had been counseled several times about her romantic relationships with whites. But they did not think they would meet serious resistance, given the Quakers' history of racial tolerance. Cunningham's father was a highly ranked black Quaker who had been the first black student to live in the dorms at Earlham. His hallmate was Earlham's future president, Tom Jones. By 1952, he was on Earlham's alumni board. Both McAllester's and Cunningham's parents approved of the marriage, and the couple made clear that they did not intend to marry until after graduation.[61]

Nevertheless, when their engagement was announced in Earlham's newspaper, the school reacted quickly and harshly. Jones and the college board of trustees opposed the engagement. President Jones personally appealed to Grace Cunningham to reconsider. "Movie people" might intermarry, Jones told her, but "good people, upright people didn't do this," a remark suggesting that the college was as concerned about its reputation as Cunningham's.[62] College officials accused the couple of deliberately seeking to defy a college regulation, and when they refused to break off their engagement, the board compelled Robert to leave the campus for the rest of the term and to finish his studies at home.[63] The college's reaction caught many by surprise because of the Quakers' well-known stand against racial discrimination. Students protested McAllester's expulsion and when the story went public, civil rights organizations demanded his immediate reinstatement.[64] Grace was surprised as well. "I had grown up a Quaker. I knew what Quakers stood for," she recalled forty years later. "In this case, they couldn't quite stand for what they stood for." Earlham officials allowed McAllester to return to campus to march in graduation only because of a threatened student boycott. Two days after graduation, McAllester and Cunningham were married in Ithaca, New York. Fifty years later, they are still married and are still somewhat bitter about their experience at Earlham. The couple never returned to Earlham, even when the school dedicated a new black studies center named for Grace's father.[65]

Officials at Earlham apparently felt that if the college was going to admit nonwhite students, there had to be a policy of discouraging serious interracial dating. Whether the policy stemmed more from concern about students' well-being or from concern about the school's reputation is impossible to know. Nevertheless, the fact that this school felt it had the right and the duty to prohibit interracial dating even when intermarriage was not illegal and when both sets of parents approved makes clear that its opposition was deeply held. The case demonstrates as well the limitations of religious tolerance for intermarriage in the 1950s.

Although the reaction to interracial dating in high schools and universities was not uniform, these institutions could provide important reinforcements for parents seeking to regulate the dating choices of their children. Similarly, the medical establishment provided another mechanism for parents to intervene. Women who dated black men were sometimes forced to see psychiatrists against their will or were even committed to mental institutions. There are numerous cases of white women being committed to psychiatric hospitals or dragged to multiple psychologists when their parents found out about their interracial relationships.[66] When Helen Gallahar became romantically involved with a black lawyer in Ohio in 1950, her parents hired an attorney to have her judged insane, kidnapped her and held her prisoner, and, after she escaped, hired a detective to find her. They ultimately disinherited her after she married. Doris, the woman whose mother begged and pleaded with her to drop her black boyfriend, was brought to a psychiatrist by her father, because "he was sure there was something really wrong with me." She eloped with Paul secretly, fearful that if she told her parents, they would "put me away in a hospital." The parents of Dorothy Lebohner, the young coed who fell in love with a black man in her college class, followed a similar path. After they discovered her romance, they put her in a state hospital for several days of "observation."[67]

Police and the courts sometimes aided parents in these attempts to coerce their daughters. Judges could order offenders to be committed to a mental hospital or to be placed under the custody of their parents. When the mother of a fifteen-year-old went to probate court and told the judge her daughter was dating a black man, he replied, "Oh my gosh, a nigger." The judge ordered her confined to the state mental hospital for thirty days. Before he would let her leave, she had to promise that she would not associate with blacks. After a ninety-day stay at the mental hospital she relented and promised to break off her interracial relationship, although she married her boyfriend soon after.[68] While the willingness of some judges to get involved in such cases might be unexpected since interracial marriage was not illegal in these states, judges often shared the belief that marrying interracially was a sign of rebellion or psychological sickness. They intervened when these cases involved teenage daughters who might be considered wayward minors, girls who were still young enough to be considered subject to parental authority. Thus the father of Anne wrote in *Harper's* that he considered calling in the police to force Anne to leave her boyfriend, but dropped the idea because Anne was "of age." She was legally an adult, not a minor. But when Dorothy Lebohner slipped away from her parents' watchful eyes after her return from the mental hospital, her father issued a warrant for her arrest as a wayward minor. Caught with her black boyfriend in a New York City

Taken into police custody in 1960 after escaping together to New York City, Dorothy Lebohner and Warren Sutton experienced many of the tactics whites used to
prevent interracial marriages. White parents sometimes committed their children to
mental institutions, while some colleges expelled students who were dating
interracially. *(New York Daily News.)*

movie theater, she was placed under the custody of her parents, subject to
court supervision. After she married her boyfriend, her father tried to
have the marriage annulled.[69]

Other underage girls who married blacks also feared that their parents
would threaten them with annulment or arrest. Doris, the seventeen-
year-old New Yorker who married a black man in the 1940s, stayed in
hiding for a period after her marriage because she feared her parents
would send the police to retrieve her if they knew where she was. In a

notable case from 1965, courts in New York had to consider the question of whether a teenage girl could still be considered a wayward minor after she had married. When white eighteen-year-old Barbara Friedman married Warner Guy, a young black man, in New York City, her parents sought to have her declared mentally unbalanced; they were able to obtain a warrant for her arrest as a wayward minor made out in her maiden name. Barbara's lawyers argued that her marriage made her an "emancipated woman," but as the case went through court, her parents obtained a doctor's order and had their daughter committed to Bellevue for mental tests.[70] The treatment of these young interracially involved women was not unlike that of other girls in the 1950s who refused to conform to sexual norms. Unwed mothers, for example, found the court system stacked against them if they tried to keep custody of their children.[71]

Drastic measures such as resorting to the courts or to mental institutions were rarely, if ever, used on white men. Although many white men who intermarried faced opposition from their families, relatives instead relied on familiar sociological arguments or behind-the-scenes manipulation to try to prevent these marriages. One white husband said his mother "had a fit" and tried to dissuade him from marrying his black girlfriend by stressing the problems his children would have, the discrimination he would face, and the restrictions on his social mobility he would experience. Another white man who married interracially in the fifties explained that his parents were upset, although not "viciously hostile." Instead, "they harped on the question of the children, saying 'Think of them.' Also, they had concern for our social life. They feared that we would be cut off from society."[72] Other sons found that their parents had secretly tried to undermine their engagements. Several men reported that their mothers called up their black girlfriends or their black girlfriends' mothers to tell them bad things about their sons' personal habits. As one white man explained, his mother "derided" him in every way possible to his future mother-in-law. In the most severe cases, relatives sought to prevent men from making a living. Thus when one young white assistant district attorney in Philadelphia became engaged to a black woman, his parents tried to have him dismissed from his job.[73] But few men were dragged to the psychologist or thrown in jail when they expressed their intent to intermarry. Parents were not only more fearful for their daughters than for their sons, but they may have felt a greater right to assert control over their daughters' lives.

Whites who went ahead with an interracial marriage despite parental objections often strained relations with their families permanently. In many cases, the white child was estranged from his or her parents for years after the marriage. In the most extreme cases, parents actually disowned their children, renouncing them as members of the family. Distancing or disowning of intermarried whites was not done solely because of sociological or psychological concerns about the difficulties of interracial marriage; families who truly feared the difficulties of making an interracial marriage work would have supported the couple if they had the well-being of their children as their utmost concern. Disowning was also not a measure designed to prevent an interracial marriage. Parents sometimes tried to stop marriages by threatening to disown a child, but estrangement usually took place after a marriage had occurred, when parents felt there was little they could do to bring their child into line. Rather, families disowned intermarried whites because it was a crucial way to distance themselves from a child's racial transgression. By disowning a child, a family symbolically declared that the child was dead to them and thus could not cause harm to the extended family. This was made abundantly clear when observant Jewish families sat shiva, a traditional mourning period, when children married blacks.[74]

Even parents who maintained a decent relationship with their intermarried son or daughter worried about what others would think about an interracial marriage in the family. The anonymous father of the 1951 *Harper's* article started his story by describing how his daughter's marriage had caused him discomfort in his community. For a while he and his wife divided everyone in their lives between "those who knew, and those we weren't sure about." He worried about when and how he should reveal the fact of his daughter's marriage and hoped that certain business friends would never find out about it. This father did not disown his daughter. Anne came home to visit when her first child was born, and she kept in close contact with her parents via mail. Yet her parents did not attend her wedding, and they gave Anne and her husband no help at all when they struggled with finding an apartment, going to school, and having a baby.[75]

Many families, concerned about how they were perceived in their own communities, disowned their children in part as a rearguard action to maintain their own fragile status or rank in the racial hierarchy. Cutting a relative out of one's life is an emotionally wrenching task, but it was an act that, as the sister of one intermarried white woman explained, was necessary. "When your mother married your father," she told her grown nephew in the 1980s, "it was like we had to close the pages of a book." Otherwise, she argued, people would have used it against them. Robert McAllester, the Earlham student who married in 1952, was renounced by his older brother. McAllester's brother, who was married to a prominent Virginia woman, believed that Bob's marriage would make his own life more difficult. Another white father whose daughter married a black man contemplated having her arrested, presumably for being a wayward minor, but decided the newspapers would spread the story if he did. Instead he disowned his daughter and tried to keep her marriage secret.[76]

The fact that some parents decided to carry on secret relationships with their children suggests that disowning was often undertaken more out of a sense of necessity than of complete conviction. Often one parent would renounce a child completely, while another would seek to maintain some kind of a relationship. This continuing relationship, however, had to be carried on clandestinely, so others in the community would not find out. In one case, a New York white woman who married a black man was completely renounced by her mother and one of her sisters who "bitterly opposed her marriage," but had a relationship, if strained, with her father and other siblings. Her father would not visit the home of his daughter and his black son-in-law, but he did meet his daughter once a year in his office.[77] This kind of partial disowning was relatively common, but this case was atypical in one respect: it was usually the mother rather than the father who was more willing to carry on a secret relationship with an intermarried child. Whether out of a sense of repulsion at the idea of their daughter engaging in interracial sex, anger at the fact that their child rejected their authority, or shame over the fact that their son or daughter had tarnished the family's reputation, fathers proved more willing than mothers to renounce a child. Many intermarried whites reported that their mothers eventually attempted to open up the line of communication, while their fathers refused to ever see them again. Doris, the woman who eloped with her boyfriend Paul over her parents' objections, reported that her father never spoke to her again after she married. Her mother, however, eventually accepted the marriage and remained on speaking terms with her daughter. After Hettie Cohen's 1958 marriage, her father told her never to call home again. Her mother, however, talked to her rabbi, who told her that Hettie was still her child, no matter what she had done. Hettie's mother met her secretly twice a year, even though she felt that Hettie would "suffer and pay every minute" for the life she had chosen.[78]

Female relatives of those who intermarried sometimes engaged in subterfuge to hide these continuing relationships from males in the family. When Ann Marable, a New Jersey Italian American, married a black carpenter in 1949, her male relatives were totally opposed to her marriage, and they refused to speak to her, telling her she was dead to them. Her older brother, a city official, refused to acknowledge her when he saw Ann out with her children. When Ann's father died, she was not informed, and when an older brother passed away, she had to set up a private viewing at the funeral home to avoid upsetting the family. Her sister and mother, however, were willing to communicate if certain "unspoken rules of the game were followed." They could call Ann, but she could never call them. Sometimes the sister might sneak over for a clandestine visit at Ann's house, but only if no one else in the family knew about it. Forty years after Ann married, and well after her black husband had died, her mother finally invited her to visit the family home—but even then she was anxious about Ann's being seen there. When Ann visited her sister, Rose, in the hospital, Rose "just about freaked out" because she feared that the men of her family and her larger social circle would find out. "She wouldn't eat," Ann's daughter remembered. "She was so nervous and afraid that someone would show up, a family member or a friend, and then she'd be in this very uncomfortable situation. It was just a mess."[79]

Ann Marable's relatives would communicate with her only on their terms, and their actions showed that they thought even this minimal communication was dangerous. As Italian immigrants, this family may have felt a heightened need to disassociate themselves from blacks in order to help consolidate their own identity and status as whites. Although the evidence is admittedly slim, it appears that some of the most violent objections to interracial marriage came from ethnic families from working-class or lower-middle-class backgrounds. The parents in the middle-class professional family profiled in *Harper's* grudgingly accepted their daughter back in their lives and ultimately allowed others to find out about her interracial marriage, but Ann Marable's family members were far more reluctant to have any contact with her. The belief that knowledge of an intermarriage could threaten a family's tenuous economic or social position fueled permanent estrangements. Decades after her sister married a black man, a Missouri woman was still unwilling to forgive her or to accept her sister's children as her relatives. "To be frank about it, I've got to live here," she told her nephew. "I'm not embarrassed by the fact that you're black or anything, but I've got to live here. I don't want to jeopardize my life, and being your aunt would leave me in a hell of a shape."[80]

Uneasiness about interracial sex involving black men and white women, concern about status and racial identity, and worries about the social complications facing interracial couples came together most clearly around the issue of children. Psychologists and sociologists assumed that mixed-race children would be shunned by both races, and whites considering intermarriage were nearly always asked the question "What about the children?" While families had valid and often sincere concerns about the fate of biracial children, their queries masked deeper worries about the implications of the birth of mixed-race children as well. Interracial marriages, though devastating to many families, were reversible. The white partner could get divorced, hide the marriage, and reenter white society. Having a biracial child, however, was not so easily reversed, especially for the white mothers of these children.

Ruth, a white woman who was briefly married to a black man, expressed this knowledge when she commented on how relieved she was that her baby daughter looked white: "I shudder to think what might have happened had my baby been born with a dark skin. She would then have been regarded by everyone as a Negro and would have to live under the handicaps that confront all Negroes. Suppose I had left my husband with a dark-skinned child. What would have happened? Would my parents and friends have accepted her? Would they have accepted me? Frankly, I think not."[81] After her marriage ended, Ruth moved back in with her parents and eventually married a white Jewish man. Her daughter married a white man. Ruth felt she was able to reenter the white world only because her daughter had been born light enough to pass as white. Lee Chennault, a white woman who married a black man in the late 1940s, did not have the same option; her own daughter clearly looked black. Although she and her husband later divorced, Chennault recognized that there was "nothing, nothing I can do to 'make up' for having married a Negro. There is no way whatsoever for me to regain a social status that many would call my 'birthright.'"[82] Her daughter's existence compelled her to tell whites that she had been interracially married; she could not undo or ignore her past like Ruth could. Even though her parents eventually accepted her and her daughter back in their lives, she still felt she lived in between the black and white worlds. Her offspring was living testimony of her "sexual transgression."

Families sometimes urged their pregnant daughters to get abortions or to put their biracial children up for adoption, entreaties reflecting their belief that having a biracial child would permanently remove their daughter from the white community in a way that interracial marriage in itself did not. When Scott Minerbrook's mother briefly retreated to her parents' house with her three small children after a fight with her black husband, her father demanded that she put her children up for adoption. Having black children would slow her down, he told her.[83]

This pressure was most successful when the woman was unmarried and had few people to turn to other than her parents. One unmarried young white woman who became pregnant by a black man in the late 1950s was told by her parents to have an abortion or leave their house. Legal abortions were not widely available in the 1950s, even for white women pregnant by black men. Like many other unwed mothers, this woman carried the baby to term and then placed it for adoption; her parents refused to allow her back in the house unless she gave up her baby.[84]

Even married women were sometimes encouraged by their families to get abortions. When Hettie Jones told her father that she was pregnant and that she had married her black boyfriend, he pleaded with her to end both the marriage and the pregnancy. "I'll take you to Mexico!" he told her. "You'll have an abortion and get a divorce!" When Jeanne Campbell, a white woman married to a black man, discovered she was pregnant, a member of her family suggested she have an abortion. When she and her husband separated, her family advised her to give the baby to her husband to raise. When she refused to give up her baby, her family asked that she tell people the baby was adopted since "people will think more of you that way."[85] Adopting a black child could be seen as a sign of racial benevolence; giving birth to one was a sign of immorality or depravity.

The color of the child was very much at issue. Interracial couples recognized that white grandparents were most willing to recognize their biracial grandchildren if they were light-skinned and looked white. Some white spouses even hoped that having a fair-skinned child might help reconcile their parents to the marriage.[86] In one 1949 case, white relatives decided that a light-skinned biracial child could be brought over into the white world even if her interracially married mother could not. The case involved the five-year old daughter of Marguerite Freitus, a white Buffalo woman, and her light-skinned black husband, Emerson Marshall. Freitus's parents objected violently to the relationship, at one point refusing to allow her to leave the family house to keep her from seeing her boyfriend. A year after Freitus and Marshall married, however, their baby daughter Mary began visiting her grandparents. Eventually, Mary's grandparents tricked her mother into signing adoption papers. They refused to allow Mary to go home to her parents, enrolled her in the neighborhood kindergarten, and undertook a legal battle to win full custody of the child. This case, the trial judge remarked, was about "whether the child is to be raised as a white or a colored girl."[87] Although there is no record of the judge's ruling, the grandparents' actions suggested that they believed that the young girl could have her stigmatizing background erased if she were separated from her parents and raised in a white home.

If biracial children light enough to pass for white could be "remade" as white by being separated from their own racially transgressive parents, then white children could potentially be "remade" as something less than white through association with racially transgressive parents. This was the fear that drove a handful of cases in the forties, fifties, and early sixties involving the custody disposition of white children whose mothers married black men. These cases starkly reveal both the gender ideologies about white women who associated with black men and the racial ideologies that drove whites to distance themselves from blacks as a way to maintain status and privilege.

In deciding whether white women who had married black men should forfeit custody of their white children from previous marriages, courts weighed a woman's racial transgressions against the traditional preference for maternal custody. Most courts throughout the postwar era awarded custody of minor children to their mother after a divorce unless there was extensive evidence that the mother was an unfit parent. The standard rule in custody cases—to do what was in the "best interests of the child"—in the 1950s meant that children of "tender years" should be awarded to their mothers.[88] Yet white women who had initially been awarded custody of their children were taken to court by ex-husbands or other relatives after they intermarried. These mothers, relatives claimed, were no longer fit to raise their children, and courts often agreed, changing custody of white children from their mother to some other party.

Courts were able to act against mothers who would normally be awarded custody because of the negative racial and gender implications raised by interracial marriages. White women who intermarried were easily characterized as "unfit mothers" because of prevailing gender ideology that characterized white women who fraternized with black men as immoral, brazen, or irresponsible. They were also unfit, however, because they subjected their children to an environment that might stigmatize them or harm their social standing. In an era that celebrated motherhood, these white women were characterized as failed mothers because they exposed their children to harmful prejudice and possible ostracism. When Bernice Beckman married a black man in 1951, her ex-husband kidnapped their white five-year-old son and secured an ex parte order from a New York judge granting him custody of the boy on the grounds that Beckman had engaged in "immoral conduct" by taking up with a black man. Not only did the sympathetic judge grant the father full custody, but he also denied Bernice all visitation privileges and issued a restraining order designed to prevent her from ever seeing him again.[89] This harsh ruling was necessary, the judge explained, in order to "protect" the young boy. Eight years later, Bernice Beckman Riggins was still fighting to regain the right to see her son.

Sandra Potter had been awarded full custody of her two-year-old daughter, Donna, after her 1961 divorce, a decision her white ex-husband did not contest. But when his ex-wife moved to California a year later to marry Dr. Percy Baugh, a black surgeon she had met while working at a veterans' hospital in Michigan, Donald Potter went to court to demand that Sandra's custody of Donna be revoked and that he be given legal custody of the young girl. Both a county court and eventually the Michigan Supreme Court agreed that the new situation warranted a change in custody.[90] Although Donald presented no evidence that Sandra was an unfit mother, the court worried about what it saw as Sandra's immaturity. Sandra Baugh, the court charged, was "a picture of a young woman who has been in serious rebellion." The fact that she was pregnant when she married her first husband, that she had gone back to work soon after her daughter was born, that she had secretly dated a black man and then married him nine days after her divorce, and that she had moved to California without first securing permission from the court, proved to the judges that she was not fit to be Donna's custodial parent. Instead, the court decided that it was in Donna's best interest for her to be placed under the physical care of her Michigan grandmother, 2,500 miles from her interracially married mother.

Women who married black men and seemingly put their own pleasure ahead of consideration for their children's well-being were characterized by relatives as selfish and thus undeserving of custody. When Poppy Cannon married NAACP executive secretary Walter White in 1949, Cannon's former husband, Charles Claudius Philippe, asked for full custody of their daughter. Philippe asked Cannon to put aside "any personal feelings or selfish considerations" and to give up Claudia "before irreparable damage is done her." He was sure Claudia would be subjected to insults and gossip and begged Cannon not to "thrust this terrible onus upon her."[91] Philippe never formally sued for a change in custody and Cannon's daughter remained with her, but he clearly saw

Cannon's choice to intermarry as a self-centered act that would hurt their daughter.

Families who took these cases to court cited a variety of reasons why mothers should lose custody, but as the white women's lawyers invariably noted, the only real concern of these relatives was race. When Ann Strasser married a black man in 1949, her mother, Mollie Portnoy, sought custody of Ann's five-year-old daughter. She raised several complaints, arguing that Strasser was a Communist, was not raising her child as Jewish, and had neglected her daughter by placing her in full-time day care, but she admitted that what really upset her was the race of her new son-in-law. She instituted custody proceedings only when her other efforts to break up her daughter's interracial marriage failed. She even told her daughter, "I want you to leave him . . . or I shall take your children away from you," a statement that the National Lawyers Guild argued proved that this mother was using custody "as a weapon to compel her daughter to leave the husband she loves." In this case, the grandmother's efforts were unsuccessful. Although the trial court initially switched custody to the grandmother, the Court of Appeals of New York reversed the custody ruling and gave the child back to her mother.[92]

Racial concerns, however, often proved persuasive to the court. The most concrete fear of those seeking to revoke the custody of interracially married white mothers was that white children raised in interracial homes would be stigmatized, socially isolated, and would face taunts and discrimination. As one grandfather told the Connecticut Supreme Court in 1956, he was supporting a bid to take custody of his grandson away from his interracially married daughter because growing up in an interracial home would injure the boy. There was no way white children raised in interracial homes could have a normal upbringing, he claimed, because of the "stigma that certainly is going to be on them from other children."[93] Donald Potter expressed similar concerns about his daughter. If "forced by order of the Court to be brought up in a bi-racial household," her father predicted, she would "be rejected, shunned, and avoided by the children of both races."[94]

In some cases, claims that white children raised in interracial homes would suffer might well have been true, but the belief that intermarried people were socially stigmatized was so ingrained that relatives did not need to prove a pernicious effect of intermarriage on white children. Donald Potter, for example, provided no concrete evidence that his daughter Donna had been stigmatized because of her mother's interracial marriage. In fact, Sandra and Percy Baugh went to great lengths in their testimony before the court to prove that their interracial family had faced no discrimination in their California neighborhood, that they socialized with their neighbors, and that Donna had made friends with the local children. Yet Donna's father insisted that discrimination directed toward her would increase as her world expanded beyond her neighborhood. As his lawyer explained, "the feelings of . . . other people will impinge upon this child, and the marriage her mother made . . . will have a tremendous and serious effect on this little girl." Courts seemed most concerned that white girls who grew up in interracial homes would have difficulties attracting proper white suitors. The judge in the *Potter* case thus argued that Donna might develop problems as she grew older, "particularly during puberty, when she, in school and other activities, becomes aware of the opposite sex."[95] In a similar case, all three daughters of a Cincinnati woman were placed in protective custody after she married a black man, in part because of the fear that no "decent boy" could call on a young woman with a black stepfather.[96]

Rather than criticizing the racism in society that made life difficult for interracial couples, families and courts reflexively held women responsible for the stigmatization and marginalization that they faced as a result of their marriages. In the 1956 case of *Murphy v. Murphy*, the Connecticut Supreme Court cited the disapproval of those seeking a change in custody as reason enough to remove a child from its mother's care. The court ruled that the white mother should lose custody of her young son in part because her decision to marry a black dentist had "alienated the affections" of her own mother; as a result, the child's relationship with his maternal grandmother would suffer if he remained in his mother's care. The court thus blamed this mother for making her family angry rather than criticizing the relatives who disowned her, a decision, the mother's lawyers noted, that punished "efforts at interracial living and democratic harmony" and encouraged "racial discrimination and prejudice in the critical area of family relations."[97]

These decisions reflected the gravity of the harm that courts and relatives believed would come to white children raised in interracial homes—that they would lose their status, and perhaps even their identity, as whites. Thus the U.S. Court for the District of Columbia denied a black stepfather's petition to adopt the illegitimate white son of his wife, even though the courts normally encouraged the adoption of children born out of wedlock. In this case, however, the fact that the boy and his mother were white, and his stepfather was black, created a "difficult social problem," the court ruled. "The boy when he grows up might lose the social status of a white man by reason of the fact that by record his father will be a negro if this adoption is approved . . . I feel the court should not fashion the child's future in this manner."[98] In another case, a white father won custody of his two young daughters after his ex-wife moved in with her black boyfriend. The father told the court that while he was away from home, "my children were very seldom around white people at all. The only time I even see them they was all around black people and they have no confirmation of what white is, really, I don't think."[99] Donald Potter also feared that his daughter's white racial identity would be compromised if she were raised in an interracial home. If allowed to live with her mother, she "will not grow up and mature as a normal white child should but rather will be rejected, shunned and avoided by children of both races and as a result her entire life could, and unavoidably would, be adversely affected," Potter insisted. In response to these fears, Sandra Baugh presented the expert testimony of a child psychiatrist who argued that the real danger to white children lay in growing up in homes where they would be taught racial prejudice. Prejudiced parents, the doctor asserted, would "convey an attitude to the child that he is, by virtue of being white, inherently of great personal worth."[100] Yet this is exactly the message that Donald Potter wanted to make sure his daughter internalized: that she, by virtue of her white skin, was superior to a black person.

The concerns expressed in these cases—that a child would suffer if raised in an interracial home, that he or she would face social ostracism and stigmatization, that white girls with black stepfathers would have difficulties finding white suitors, and most seriously, that children with black stepfathers might lose their sense of what it meant to be white in American society—demonstrate the deeply held beliefs of many whites and reflect the general state of race relations in postwar America. Being white meant growing up at a safe distance from black people, free from any close association with them, untouched by the stigma attached to them. White children in interracial homes not only might lose the privileges of their whiteness if they grew up around black people; even more dangerously, they might not understand what those privileges were or were supposed to be.

Cases like these exposed the depth of whites' opposition to interracial marriage. The vast majority of whites in the 1940s and 1950s could see only danger when they thought about "race mixing." Most believed that interracial sex degraded white women, that interracial marriages were impossible and impolitic in a racist society, and that being associated with black people threatened whites' social standing and racial identity. No doubt in many cases whites' fear that marrying interracially would lead their children to lose status and racial privileges were justified, but their concern did not lead them to criticize societal intolerance of interracial relationships. Whites generally took their racial privilege for granted, yet they well understood the handicaps black people faced in American society. They recognized racism and its workings in postwar America and did not want their children or grandchildren to have to suffer what black Americans faced every day. Only with the rights revolutions of the late 1960s and the 1970s would white Americans' beliefs about interracial marriage begin to change in any significant way.

AMBIVALENT ACCEPTANCE

In 1960 a white gossip magazine dropped what it called a "bombshell" that would shock millions of whites. Telling the "authentic story" of a young interracial couple who had been accepted by the white spouse's parents, but rejected by the black spouse's parents, *Top Secret* "shed light on a startling fact that runs completely counter to widespread popular belief." Blacks of all classes and educational levels were more bitterly opposed to interracial relationships than whites, the article claimed. They were "in total and unalterable favor of continued sexual segregation."[1] Black disapproval would ensure that such marriages would remain rare even if the races became more integrated, *Top Secret* argued.

Gunnar Myrdal came to the exact opposite conclusion in his 1944 work *An American Dilemma*. Blacks felt compelled to disavow any interest in relationships with whites for political reasons, but Myrdal did not believe there was any serious basis for black opposition to interracial marriage. "After weighing all available evidence carefully, it seems frankly incredible that the Negro people in America should feel inclined to develop any particular race pride at all or have any dislike for amalgamation, were it not for the common white opinion of the inferiority of the Negro people and the whites' intense dislike of miscegenation."[2] Any black opposition to interracial marriage was simply a defensive response to whites' hostility to the practice, Myrdal insisted.

Both the suggestions that blacks opposed interracial relationships more than whites and that blacks opposed such relationships only because whites did misread the black community of the 1940s, 1950s, and early 1960s. The truth lies somewhere between these two polar views. Many whites might have liked to believe, as *Top Secret* implied, that blacks were as unalterably opposed to interracial relationships as they were. If that were the case, then there would be no reason to fear an increase in interracial marriages even if barriers between the races fell. Such wishful thinking, however, did not reflect the reality of the black community's views about interracial relationships. For blacks after World War II, the issue of interracial marriage raised a very different set of concerns than it did for whites. Unlike whites, who worried about maintaining their "racial purity," few blacks had any illusions that race was "pure." Many blacks had white ancestors somewhere in the not-too-distant past; a cry to preserve the purity of "black blood" carried little weight. The alleged difficulties of interracial marriage also fazed blacks less than whites, in part because so many blacks faced discrimination and prejudice every day anyway.

No doubt many blacks were ambivalent about interracial marriage, and some were openly hostile to the practice. Some blacks feared intermarriage could serve as a way to avoid or erase the stigma of race. Much like racial passing, it could potentially allow for individual success at the price of group loyalty and advancement. Many in the black middle class perceived interracial relationships as degrading and disreputable, since most took place outside the confines of marriage. Many blacks were also suspicious of the motives of whites who were willing to make themselves vulnerable to racial hatred by marrying blacks.

Blacks, however, were not uniformly or unalterably opposed to interracial marriage, and many proved willing to accept intermarried whites who proved themselves sincere friends of the black community. Although many were ambivalent about interracial marriage in practice, most black Americans in the forties and fifties supported the right to intermarry in principle. At stake in debates about interracial marriage was nothing less than a black person's autonomy, personal freedom, and right to craft his or her own life and make choices free from state control. Few blacks were willing to take a position against interracial relationships and seemingly acquiesce to laws or customs that limited individual choice on the basis of race.

Assessing the attitudes of blacks toward interracial marriage in this period is a difficult project. National polls focused on white respondents only, assuming that only they would feel strongly about racial mixing. Blacks were not polled on their opinions of interracial marriage until the early 1970s. The black press, however, a cornerstone of the national black community, provides a vital source for community responses among working-class and middle-class blacks to interracial marriage. In its pages, blacks appeared evenly divided between those who approved of interracial marriage and those who disapproved of or were indifferent toward it. In their letters to the editor, a vocal segment of the black community expressed distinct hostility to interracial marriage. A Chicago woman wrote in 1947 that "all clear thinking and racially proud Negroes" oppose intermarriage. I "do not wish to eat with Whites, sleep with them, or above all, marry them."[3] Yet many blacks defended interracial marriage too, and for social and political reasons, blacks seemed more willing to accept interracial marriage than their white counterparts.

Just as few whites could imagine themselves with a black partner, few blacks could imagine themselves with a white spouse. Many blacks disliked or feared whites, the dominant majority they viewed as oppressors and persecutors. Living in segregated worlds, few blacks had the opportunity to get to know whites personally, and blacks harbored fearful and anxious stereotypes about white people. Henry Louis Gates recalled in his memoir of growing up in the segregated South of the 1950s that he was both terrified and thrilled to discover the depths of his mother's hatred of white people. Whites, she insisted, were dirty and smelled. She wanted her children to be able to compete in the white world, but she had no desire to actually be around white people. Or as a black doctor from Alabama explained, he disapproved of interracial marriage because "I just don't like white people socially."[4] Blacks wanted rights equal to those of whites, but they did not necessarily want to socialize with whites or have close personal relationships with them. Whites were "the other," and many blacks viewed them as untrustworthy and inhumane.

Indeed, many blacks doubted whether whites could ever overcome their own internalized racism enough to make an interracial marriage work. In a 1958 poll in the *Pittsburgh Courier,* a leading black newspaper, one of the most common explanations given by respondents for opposing intermarriage was that they did not believe whites could actually see blacks as equals. One woman from Ohio replied, "I wouldn't be sure that I would not be regarded as an inferior by some of my husband's relatives and associations, if not by him, and I might be unduly sensitive, thus spoiling our relationship." Another woman stated that she could not marry a white person because he might slip and call her "nigger" in an argument, and that would be the end of their marriage. Many blacks simply did not believe that whites would be able to overcome negative racial stereotypes.[5]

Although many whites seemed to think that blacks' greatest ambition was to marry a white person, the black community put up its own defenses against being involved in an interracial relationship. Especially among the small but influential black middle class, such relations were often frowned upon and seen as wayward or delinquent. The black elite had its own rules and codes of conduct, often termed "the politics of respectability." Angered by a dominant white society that usually failed to recognize any class distinctions in the black community, black elites sought to reflect their social status and consciousness in their behavior, deeds, and racial pride. Forming elite social clubs and benefit societies, they sought to reform the habits and manners of the black masses and to establish a society for themselves with its own status markers.[6] Marrying a white spouse did not serve as a mark of status in this black social world.

Many blacks associated interracial relationships with sexual exploitation and illicit sex. Since very little of the racial mixing that had occurred in the United States since the colonial period had taken place within the institution of marriage, blacks often viewed interracial couples as disreputable or immoral. A white wife, the black sociologists St. Clair Drake and Horace Cayton noted in their 1945 study *Black Metropolis,* never strengthened the social position of her black spouse "vis-à-vis Negroes." One self-described "Loyal American Negro Mother" explained, "All decent colored people disapprove of mixed marriages." Omattée Carrasco, the child of an interracial marriage, was raised by her black paternal grandparents in a middle-class black section of Oakland after her parents divorced. For years, her grandmother nursed anger over her son's interracial marriages. As Carrasco recalled, marrying a white person "was not *tolerated*—not where I grew up, not by my experience of life, not from my family experiences, not from my community, school, nowhere. It was unacceptable."[7]

For the black middle class, dating whites was frowned upon. This was especially true for black women, since white male–black female relationships had traditionally been sexually exploitative. There seemed little chance that an interracial relationship, even in the forties and fifties, would lead to a marriage, since it was assumed that few white men would put their own social status at risk by marrying a black woman. St. Clair Drake and Horace Cayton argued that elite black women had good reason to avoid dating white men: "It would seriously depreciate her value in the Negro marriage market; and, of course, there is almost no chance for her to marry a white man."[8] A black college student who traveled extensively with her military family was strongly influenced by her parents' views on interracial dating. Her parents "objected wholeheartedly to my dating white boys," she explained, because they were Southern born and had only negative images of relationships between white men and black women. She came to believe that interracial relationships were "cheap and generally unhealthy." Whenever a white boy approached her, she made sure to keep her distance.[9]

Fear of community censure even led some black women to hide their interracial relationships. The white boyfriend of a professional black woman complained in 1949 that she refused to marry him because of fear of how other blacks would react. She would socialize with him with their white friends, but in three years of dating, she had refused to introduce him to her black friends. The "prejudice of her own race" doomed him to a life of loneliness, he charged.[10]

For black women who saw little chance that a white man would ever marry them, interracial marriages between black men and white women could be galling. Even though the number of black-white couples in the 1940s and 1950s was very small, and a roughly equal number of these marriages involved black women, some black women opposed interracial marriage because they feared losing black men in a competition with white women.[11] As one young black woman explained to Drake and Cayton, "Why should Negro men marry white women? White men don't want to marry us. They just use us when they can." Drake and Cayton claimed that black women often opposed intermarriage because of its perceived "one-sided nature," that black men married white women but white men did not marry black women. With white antipathy focused on black men with white women, much of the coverage in the black press focused on this combination as well. Such coverage contributed to some black women's perceptions that black men alone crossed the race line in marriage. One letter writer to the black magazine *Ebony* charged in 1951 that the marriage of black men and white women "creates a problem for Negro women. [E]very time we lose a man to a woman of another race, it means one more Negro woman will be husbandless."[12] These women frowned upon interracial marriage because they feared it posed a serious danger to their own marital opportunities.

Other black women charged that black male–white female marriages were unhealthy manifestations of the sexualized racial hierarchies that defined white women as more beautiful than black women. Black men, this small group claimed, were attracted to white women as status symbols, as an ideal of beauty. White women were the "forbidden fruit" that black men craved. Violet Coburn, a black woman from Brooklyn who expressed her anger at the 1949 interracial marriage of a prominent black leader, thought perhaps it was "a good idea that the white men lynch these Negroes men to keep them from there [*sic*] white women. If they didn't poor black women would never get a husband. Soon as Negroes men get in position to support a family they must find a white wife or some one next to same complexion while the poor black devils of womanhood suffer on bread lines with there brats."[13] Black men, Coburn felt, did not value or respect black women, and they would always turn to white women or lighter-skinned women if they had the chance. An anonymous black society woman whose own husband had left her for a white woman echoed these charges in a 1951 *Negro Digest* article. Although she believed that marriage was a personal decision between two adults, she worried about "upper-crust white sisters . . . walking away with our prize providers." The men were flattered, she asserted, and black women had little hope to retaliate because they had little hope of marrying a white man.[14]

Marrying interracially was also perceived by some blacks as evidence of a lack of pride in black identity and a desire to be absorbed into the white world. Violet Coburn argued that blacks who intermarried were ashamed of their race and such feelings prevented blacks from working together to improve themselves. "Black people will never be much help to one another as they don't know who they are and they don't like there [sic] black skin, the whole truth they don't like themselves." Others argued that intermarried blacks did not appreciate their own racial distinctiveness or "natural beauty," a claim that implied that whites and blacks were fundamentally different. Interracial marriage was perceived by critics such as Nannie Burroughs, the president of the Women's Auxiliary of the National Baptist Convention, a black Baptist denomination, as a form of assimilation into the dominant white group and as a denial of black identity. Blacks, she wrote, "should pitch in and make the race worth belonging to instead of escaping into a race that is already made." John Banks of El Paso, Texas, also feared that efforts at economic and political integration would lead to racial disintegration. "Instead of allowing our species to fade away through interracial marriage, why not reclaim our own African heritage?" he wondered. Few others would refer to Africa in their critiques of interracial marriage, but a vocal minority insisted that such marriages heralded a loss of black racial pride.[15]

Blacks who were perceived as trying to distance themselves from the black community particularly feared criticism of their interracial marriages. When the famous black singer and actress Lena Horne decided to marry a white man in 1947, she kept it a secret for over three years, in large part because she feared the reaction of other blacks. The black community and black press were dubious about her because she had been built up by Hollywood as "a glamour girl," that is, looking almost white save for her darker skin, and she already faced charges in the press that she was becoming a "white Negro." To her, it seemed that announcing her marriage "would only confirm their worst suspicions." Eartha Kitt, another glamorous actress and singer, was criticized for her dating habits and her 1960 interracial marriage. In response to one story in the black press about the marriage, a reader insisted that Kitt seemed to have a complex about being a Negro and was trying to disassociate herself from own people. "No Negro has a right to be a 'turncoat,' not so long as the southern situation exists. . . . Your article might have been entitled 'The Assimilation of Eartha Kitt.'"[16] Blacks openly condemned those who married interracially seemingly with the ulterior motive of seeking personal advancement.

Yet the realities of interracial marriage in the forties and fifties did not lend themselves to a well-developed critique that blacks who married whites abandoned the race. Few blacks who married whites could realistically assimilate into the white community; hostility among whites was so widespread that marrying interracially did not gain blacks entrance into, or status in, the white world. White society shunned those whites who intermarried, and they were far more likely to assimilate into the black community. Indeed, only a very few of the hundreds of letters to *Ebony* and *Negro Digest* on the subject in the fifteen years after World War II openly denounced interracial marriage as a form of betrayal of racial identity. Blacks more commonly argued that an interracial marriage would make life more difficult, not easier, for the black partner. As one New York black man noted in 1950, "Marriage to a white leaves one still a negro, a victim of the same old irrational discrimination even by his white-in-laws, and subjected to the same social insults and contempt which he may be trying to avoid. In fact, sometimes, his situation becomes worse."[17] Except in the rare cases, few seemed to believe that marrying whites would enable blacks to leave the community behind or to deny their racial identity.

The belief that opposing interracial relationships was a form of racism also tempered blacks' disapproval. Many cautioned blacks not to accept the kinds of racial thinking that whites did; blacks who opposed interracial marriage were criticized for "racial chauvinism" and "stupidity and obtuseness." According to Carl Rowan, a black journalist who would eventually help break down the color line at the State Department, those who accepted the "warped notion" that it was an insult to the race when other blacks intermarried were "insecure and bigoted."[18] When one *Ebony* letter writer insisted interracial marriages "shamed the race," another responded that what truly shamed the race was knowing blacks practiced

the same forms of racism and discrimination as whites. For these critics, blacks who opposed interracial marriage were implying either that
whites were inferior to blacks or that whites should not be judged on
their individual merits. Blacks, these observers argued, should know better than to develop a blanket negative characterization of whites. George
Schuyler, the iconoclastic columnist for the *Pittsburgh Courier,* who was
himself interracially married, asked repeatedly, "Are Negroes more prejudiced than whites?" in stories about black elite society ostracizing interracially married whites. Schuyler believed that prejudice against
whites would only redound to blacks' detriment. Blacks could not criticize the Ku Klux Klan "while accepting their basic premise" about the
importance of racial purity. As the *Pittsburgh Courier* noted in one of the
articles in its series about interracial marriage, "if Negroes themselves
were guilty of the same racial prejudices as some whites, the black man's
dedicated fight for justice would be defeated."[19] In an era when blacks
were seeking equality and racial integration, any public support for racial
separatism, even in marriage, was suspect.

Some blacks went further to insist that there was no connection
between marrying interracially and black racial identity. Indeed, many
blacks seemed willing to question whether the very idea of race had
much meaning. The argument that marrying interracially represented a
lack of racial pride or a betrayal of the group did not resonate at all with
those who wanted to downplay the idea of racial difference. For this
group, talking about "interracial marriages" made no sense; marriages
called "interracial" were just examples of one human marrying another.
It is not "kosher to think in terms of interracial marriages," one *Negro
Digest* reader insisted in 1950, since "among the civilized minority there
is but one race, the human race." An NAACP field secretary in Los Angeles expressed a similar idea when asked whether interracial marriages
hurt race relations. "We of the NAACP believe there is but one race, the
human race. Those who believe some marriages are interracial and others not, do not believe in equal human rights." A black Washington, D.C.,
woman hoped that "race" would eventually be viewed in the same way
as ethnicity. "A Negro marrying a white should cause no more comment
than a Frenchman marrying a German, or a Norwegian marrying an
Englishman," she insisted.[20] She stressed the similarities, rather than the

differences, between blacks and whites. For the many blacks who insisted in their letters to the black press that "love is a greater power than the color of one's complexion," interracial marriages were proof of the shallowness of racial difference.[21]

Some African Americans even viewed interracial marriage as a positive step toward ending racial discrimination and solving America's race problems, a view that was very uncommon among whites. A New York man "believed strongly" in interracial marriage because it would eventually erase racial differences. "When this happens, men of all races will exchange ideas, customs, dance, play, worship, and love together. Prejudice will be destroyed." According to another black man, racial mixing would knock out prejudice and "kill Jim Crow."[22]

A group of new national black magazines made this case most energetically in the postwar period, presenting interracial marriages as a step toward full equality that should be celebrated, not criticized. *Ebony, Jet,* and *Negro Digest* were all founded by John H. Johnson, a black self-made millionaire. Johnson started *Negro Digest* in 1942 with a five-hundred-dollar loan, and three years later he launched *Ebony,* a glossy monthly magazine aimed at blacks. *Jet,* founded in 1951, was a pocket-sized weekly news magazine.[23] The emergence of these magazines, whose circulation would quickly surpass that of any of the leading black newspapers, reflected the growth of a national black community in the post–World War II era, as blacks migrated across the country, their economic clout grew, and their expectations rose.[24] Johnson believed that through hard work and perseverance, blacks could win the respect of whites and succeed in white society. As he once told *Fortune* magazine, "I don't want to destroy the system—I want to get into it."[25] The best way to achieve such acceptance was by highlighting respectable black subjects, often from the middle class, who were much like their white middle-class counterparts. *Ebony* in particular focused on blacks who had succeeded in the white world; many of its stories reflected the aspirations of a black middle class that Johnson presented as deserving of white Americans' acceptance and respect. The magazine emphasized black success stories, mirroring, Johnson explained, "the happier side of Negro life."[26]

The Johnson publications exhibited a fascination with interracial marriage that bordered on the obsessive. *Negro Digest* featured testimonials by famous interracial couples who wrote about their lives together under headlines like "Does Interracial Marriage Succeed?"[27] (The answer was always yes.) *Ebony* featured major articles on interracial marriage, with topics ranging from "Famous Blacks Married to Whites" to the fate of black servicemen's white war brides. *Jet,* the most tabloidlike publication of the three, contained short pieces in nearly every issue about interracial couples. In all three magazines, interracial relationships were presented as proof that blacks and whites weren't so very different, and that whites could love, respect, and admire blacks. Such articles refuted segregationists' claims that the color line was a permanent barrier that could not be crossed and that whites could never accept blacks as their social equals.

The magazines' frequent coverage of lavish wedding ceremonies suggested that interracial love that once had to be hidden could now be celebrated openly among family and friends. Thus *Jet* trumpeted the 1952 wedding of black Beatrice Williams to white Raymond Stough, which it called "probably the biggest interracial marriage in Chicago's history." Not only did one thousand guests pack the Good Shepherd Congregational Church to witness the ceremony, but the groom's entire family came to the wedding and gave the couple their blessing. A 1951 church wedding of an interracial couple who marched down the aisle "with hundreds of their friends in attendance" demonstrated the change in atmosphere from when interracial romances were "hush-hush secret affairs." A photo of the white bride feeding her new husband a piece of the wedding cake showed her "effervescent happiness."[28]

Ebony and *Jet* also provided extensive coverage of the small group of elite blacks who married whites in the 1940s and 1950s. Well-known singers such as Lena Horne, Pearl Bailey, Anne Brown, Mattiwilda Dobbs, Eartha Kitt, and Billy Daniels, musicians William Grant Still and Leroy Smith, actresses Dorothy Dandridge and Hilda Simms, and political activists Frank Curle Montero, Walter White, Leslie Perry, and Julian Steele were all featured with their white spouses.[29] By highlighting interracial marriages among the black and white elite, the magazines portrayed interracial love as respectable and even commonplace among the most talented and brightest members of both races. Ann Mather, who married Urban League Fund director Frank Curle Montero, was a steel heiress, a Smith graduate from a family that could trace its lineage back to the Pilgrims. Mary Bradley Dawes, the white wife of settlement house director Julian Steele, was a Boston socialite and "a direct descendant of William Dawes, who rode with Paul Revere on his historical ride." NAACP executive secretary Walter White's bride Poppy Cannon did not have a "blueblood background," *Ebony* noted, but she still "rates high in the Park Avenue set."[30]

Johnson's magazines paid particular attention to whites who expressed a desire to marry blacks. In the late 1940s, *Ebony* and *Jet* received hundreds of letters from German women in search of black men who would marry them and bring them to America. Even though *Ebony* editors recognized that many of these women were "motivated by the ulterior motive of wanting to come to the States," they published a selection of the letters on the grounds that many of the writers sincerely sought love and recognized the worth of black men. To *Ebony,* the letters demonstrated "the wonderful public relations job which Negro GIs did in Germany," while *Jet* pointed out that nearly all the letters praised black men as "kind husbands and desirable lovers." *Negro Digest's* 1948 article, "I Want to Marry A Negro," written by a white woman who did not reveal her name, pointed out the "many virtues of the Negro male." Black men were virile, more beautiful than whites, and had a "great nascent nobility." Oskar Heim's 1954 piece, "Why I Want a Negro Wife," made a similar case for the superiority of black women to white women, describing black women as warm, vital, and possessing a natural grace.[31] Although laden with clichés, such pieces showcased whites who preferred black mates.

Ebony and *Jet* particularly emphasized relationships between white men and black women. These articles demonstrated that white men were willing to marry blacks, not just carry on sexual affairs with them, and they could be used to show disapproving black women that black men were not the only ones who married whites. Black women had long had white lovers; for white men to marry their black paramours signaled a new level of equality. As *Jet* emphasized in one article, a "trend" of white men marrying black women indicated "that the traditional views against race-mixing are a thing of the past." Another stressed that modern black female–white male relationships were categorically different from those that took place during slavery. Unlike those of slave days, these romances were "on a high plane of respect and devotion, untouched either by scandal or notoriety."[32] For *Jet,* such articles served to disprove the "propaganda" that mixed marriages involved only white women, while the *Chicago Defender* hoped that publicity about black women married to white men might lessen the opposition of "embittered Negro women" to intermarriage.

Interracial marriages here provided "proof" that blacks were human beings who could be loved by whites. The coverage of interracial marriage highlighted the similarities between blacks and whites, and implied that evidence of successful assimilation into the white world would speed the fight for full equality. Although the outspoken advocacy of interracial marriage in *Ebony* did not reflect the feelings of the majority of blacks, many accepted the magazine's basic premise that social relationships between blacks and whites would ultimately help race relations. A 1958 poll found that 66 percent of southern blacks and 87 percent of northern blacks believed that social meetings between blacks and whites would help overcome racial discrimination and prejudice. In contrast, only 49 percent of northern whites and 10 percent of southern whites believed social contact between the races would improve race relations.[33] Not many blacks would go as far as *Ebony,* but many agreed that better interpersonal relationships between blacks and whites was a step in the right direction.

Whatever their personal opinions about interracial marriage, blacks found themselves embroiled in the very complicated politics surrounding the issue. On the one hand, white opponents of racial equality invoked fears of "racial amalgamation" and "miscegenation" in order to defend segregation and black subordination. For blacks to openly advocate or celebrate interracial marriage invited the wrath of whites, potentially making it more difficult to achieve basic civil rights reform. Thus *Ebony* readers often criticized the magazine's articles on interracial marriage, not because they disapproved of interracial relationships per se, but because they thought such open discussion of the practice could have negative political ramifications. A black soldier serving overseas complained that stories about interracial marriages were "immensely embarrassing," especially when a white soldier happened to look at the magazine. "I'm not one of those people who say Negroes should marry Negroes, etc., but why play it up?"[34] When *Ebony* magazine ran a two-page spread on interracial relationships in postwar Europe, readers chastised the magazine. Pictures of black-white couples would only "uphold the timeworn contention of the bigoted enemies of our race who reiterate that all the Negro means by social equality is association with white women," responded one reader. The story, another argued, gave "plenty of pictorial ammunition and from a Negro source" that black men wanted to marry white women. A reader from Kansas was concerned that *Ebony*'s coverage of interracial marriage would intensify demands for segregation. As he saw it, it was not "good race relations" for a magazine like *Ebony* to feature interracial marriages "at this or at any other time in the conceivable future."[35]

Yet on the other hand, in an era where black leaders and black newspapers were united in their attack on segregation in all its forms, it was difficult for blacks to accept limitations on the right to marry across racial lines. Black Americans certainly could not agree with whites that intermarriage was wrong because blacks were biologically inferior. For blacks to oppose intermarriage seemed a major concession to white supremacists. White supremacists must rejoice, wrote one reader, "to hear an outstanding Negro say, 'Yes, we are different. Keep us in our place—our separate place.'" As black Harlem congressman Adam Clayton Powell noted, any coherent attack on segregation had to include condemning antimiscegenation laws, which were a form of segregation that clearly codified white beliefs in black inferiority: "You can't have a position on one hand against segregation and on the other against interracial marriage."[36] At a time when "miscegenation" was still illegal in many states and when whites defended segregation as necessary to prevent racial mixing, many blacks who supported the cause of integration felt compelled to condemn barriers on interracial marriage.

By the late 1940s most prominent blacks had developed a public position on interracial marriage that reconciled their need to support the right to intermarry with their interest in refuting charges that they advocated intermarriage: they defended the right of individuals to marry whomever they chose, but insisted that such marriages should be considered a personal matter that affected only those individuals involved. With this position, black leaders sought to divorce the issue of interracial marriage from the larger civil rights agenda. Black spokespeople denied any interest in intermarriage while at the same time being careful not to condone antimiscegenation laws, which they viewed as just one more manifestation of the system of legal segregation. Thurgood Marshall, the chief legal counsel of the NAACP, thus argued that blacks did not want to marry whites, but "there must be no law saying they can't do it if they happen to choose to marry someone of another race." When, in 1957, *Ebony* asked a host of prominent blacks whether interracial marriage hindered the cause of integration, nearly all the respondents insisted that marriage should be viewed as a personal matter rather than as a political issue. Intermarriage was a "personal relations" question, the labor leader A. Philip Randolph insisted, while Carl Rowan argued that the right to pick a marital partner was "not a racial right, but an individual right."[37]

Moreover, whatever their own ambivalence about interracial relationships, blacks closed ranks when whites condemned such unions. Black opinion was never more united than when interracial marriage was attacked by whites. Blacks thus harshly criticized Dr. Norman Vincent Peale, a prominent white Protestant spokesman, when he advised a young black woman to give up her white boyfriend in his advice column. Dozens of blacks chastised him, arguing that marriage was a personal matter and urging the couple to marry if they were in love. Peale was criticized for his "un-Christian" attitudes and for bowing to societal prejudices. "Love has no racial barrier," wrote a black salesman. "No one has the right to dictate who one must spend the rest of his life with because of color, regional or national origin. This should be solely the decision of those involved." As one *Courier* reporter found, blacks felt Peale stepped beyond his bounds in giving advice on such a profoundly personal matter. Intermarriage might not be easy, but neither law nor prejudice should forbid people from deciding to marry if they so chose.[38] The former baseball star and black columnist Jackie Robinson took the same position in response to the popular 1960 media story about the attempts by Dorothy Lebohner's family to thwart her college interracial romance. In the *New York Post,* Robinson defended the right of the two young people to make decisions for themselves. "Marriage between any two parties is a greatly personal thing which by and large is nobody else's business," Robinson insisted. No one, not even parents, had a moral right to interfere with a couple who wished to marry.[39]

In rare cases, the position that marriage was a personal matter brought blacks into conflict with white liberal supporters of interracial marriage. George Wiley, a successful black chemist and later welfare rights activist, became embroiled in an argument about intermarriage with his white ex-girlfriend, Carol Stout, in 1960. Writing about a young interracial couple who wanted to marry, Stout argued that the marriage was ill advised because the couple seemed immature and unstable. "This is the kind of marriage which I feel could set integration back a long way," she maintained. Intermarriages should only take place between mature people who could not be labeled deviant and who would not be likely to divorce, since a failed interracial marriage would be "grist for the anti-integrationists' mills." Wiley, however, disagreed, because he felt that the decision should be left up to the couple. The real issue, he claimed, was "the good and well-being of the individuals concerned, much more than societal considerations."[40] Wiley did not believe that interracial couples should have to carry the weight of integration's potential success on their backs.

The political complexities of interracial marriage in the black community were brought into stark relief in the late 1940s, when one of the foremost black political leaders of the day married across race lines. In 1949 Walter White, the executive secretary of the NAACP, divorced his black wife of twenty years and married Poppy Cannon, a white woman. The NAACP, founded in 1909 with the goal of ending segregation and pursuing full racial equality, had mounted legal challenges to Jim Crow laws, championed victims of racial discrimination, and worked to promote interracial cooperation. White opponents had long accused the group of seeking to promote "racial amalgamation." The governor of Georgia, for example, claimed that the NAACP's ultimate goal was the "complete intermingling of the races . . . even in marriage."[41] When White married Cannon, it seemed to confirm opponents' charges that the NAACP sought to promote race mixing and that the crusade for civil rights was just a front for black men seeking relationships with white women. In this light, White's marriage could do serious damage to the NAACP's image.

Walter White was a prominent public figure and his marriage ignited controversy in the black community. A very light-skinned African American, White became an associate secretary of the NAACP in 1918, building his reputation by conducting undercover investigations of lynchings while passing as a white man. In 1929 he became executive secretary of the organization, leading it through the crises of the Great Depression and World War II. His public visibility ensured that his decision to marry a white woman was a major news item in the black community. In black newspapers, within the leadership circles of the NAACP, and on the streets of black neighborhoods, blacks debated whether White could continue in his job despite his interracial marriage.

Although White publicly defended the right to intermarry, Cannon wondered "whether the course he believed right for others could be applied to himself, since he had been for so many years an acknowledged leader, and in many ways a symbol of the Negroes' fight for freedom." White recognized that once the relationship became public, his leadership might become a liability to the NAACP and to the black community more generally.[42] He also feared that his prominence as head of the NAACP would lead bigots to target Cannon and her family. As he wrote to Cannon, "I would gladly give up every bit of the publicity or reputation I've gathered if I could and thereby take away from the enemies I've made the weapons they could use against you and the children."[43] When the couple finally decided to marry, White tendered his resignation to the NAACP board of directors on the grounds of ill health (he had recently suffered several heart attacks). Although the board refused to accept his resignation, it granted him a year's leave of absence. White began his leave in June 1949; a month later, he and Cannon were secretly married. Three days later, they left for a round-the-world trip and were outside the United States when news of the marriage broke.[44]

White's critics, including his own family, argued that his marriage would cost him the support of rank-and-file blacks. To White's sister Helen, the romance was "tragic news" that would lead to his personal downfall. His sister Madeleine warned that marrying Cannon would disgrace White in the eyes of the black community. "The little people in the alleys and slums" worship you, she argued, in part because he, a very light skinned black, had married someone who was of darker complexion. "You were one of them. You personified the doctrine of race."[45] White's most outspoken critic, J. Robert Smith of the *Los Angeles Sentinel,* argued that White had deserted the black community and sacrificed his racial pride by marrying Cannon, a writer, editor and advertising executive who was not known for her commitment to the cause of racial equality. Other journalists agreed that black opposition to interracial marriage would compromise White's effectiveness as a race leader. As the *Oklahoma Black Dispatch* editorialized, White could no longer be useful because "thousands of blacks . . . actually feel it is a crime for black people to marry out of their race."[46]

Major black newspapers, members of the NAACP board, and White's own family were also concerned that White's marriage would provoke a white backlash against the NAACP. White's sister Madeleine thus advised him to resign from his position well before his divorce and then to wait for a few years before marrying Cannon. C. C. Spaulding, the powerful president of the North Carolina Mutual Insurance Company and a member of the NAACP board of directors, charged that with his marriage, White had "snatched at the rug of economic, social and political advancement upon which the feet of Negroes rest."[47] Many leading black newspapers echoed this sentiment, arguing that White had given "firewood to the white man's theory that the Negro's greatest ambition is marriage within the white race." The *Norfolk Journal and Guide* worried that White's actions would undermine blacks' claims that they meant something more by "equality" than the right to marry whites:

The detractors of the association have made much of the charge that its anti-segregation program is in reality a disguise of the Negro's yearnings to marry whites. This is a fallacy, of course, which is vigorously denied by friends of the organization, but the denial is subjected to a deflating slap when it is recalled that the association[']s most vocal official hopped across the race line in matrimony.[48]

It was incumbent upon black leaders to placate the fears of whites, to reassure them that the NAACP was, in fact, not interested in "race mixing."

The reaction to Walter White's marriage echoed an accommodationist compromise first proposed by Booker T. Washington. In 1895 Washington, the most important black leader of his day, told whites gathered in Atlanta that black equality did not have to lead to more intimate social relations between blacks and whites. In an era when black men were stereotyped as beasts who would ravish white women without provocation, denying any interest in social relationships with whites was a matter of life and death for blacks. Black men could be lynched for looking at a white woman too directly, let alone for socializing with her. Washington told whites that blacks would not seek social equality as long as whites treated them fairly in the realms of economics and politics: "In all things that are purely social we can be as separate as the fingers, yet one as the hand in all things essential to mutual progress."[49] Washington sought to appease whites' fears of racial mixing in order to continue his fight for fairer treatment in other areas. Those who attacked Walter White similarly hoped to alleviate concerns that the fight for integration was really a front for intimate relations between the races.

Yet despite the apparent similarity, those who attacked Walter White's marriage made clear that they were not opposed to interracial marriage per se; rather, they criticized this particular marriage because of White's public position. Interracial marriage was all right for everyday folks, but not for blacks in symbolic leadership positions. Madeleine White argued that "when you became the leader and spokesman for 10,000,000 Negroes you sacrificed any private life you might have had." The stipulations and qualifications black newspapers and other black leaders made in their criticism illustrate the power of the postwar public imperative to support the right to intermarry. Even as they attacked White, writers insisted that marriage was a "purely personal proposition," that White had acted within his rights by marrying, and that everyone should have the freedom to choose his or her spouse freely (except, presumably, civil rights leaders). White should resign not because interracial marriage was wrong, but because his marriage would prove a liability in the fight for equality.[50]

The NAACP board of directors, who ultimately had to decide whether White could keep his position, eventually decided that punishing White for his marriage would subvert NAACP principles. Board member Palmer Weber argued that "the whole existence, the fighting existence of the Association is premised on the inalienable rights of every American." William Hastie, a federal judge and another member of the board, insisted that the NAACP must adhere to its basic principles, no matter what blacks or whites thought. Giving in to those who disapproved of intermarriage would be like bowing to blacks who favored segregated institutions, Hastie charged.[51] Ultimately Weber and Hastie's view carried the day, and the board voted to reappoint White as executive secretary.[52] Upholding the right of the individual to marry across racial lines ultimately outweighed the need to accommodate to whites' fears.

Walter White remained the leader of the NAACP until his death in 1955. Although the early 1950s was a difficult time for the NAACP, as the organization suffered through the repressive domestic atmosphere of McCarthyism, White remained an outspoken public spokesman, and the NAACP did not seem to lose the support of blacks as a result of his marriage.

Many blacks were simply unwilling to take the public position that marriage across race lines was wrong. They insisted, as one wrote in 1958, that "a person, regardless of color, should marry whom they please. They have to live their own lives."[53] This "live and let live" attitude went beyond mere rhetoric among blacks. The reactions of blacks who had to deal with interracial marriages firsthand provide the best evidence of their willingness to accept them. Black families proved far more tolerant of interracial relationships than white families. While nearly all whites reacted with dismay at the possibility of an interracial marriage in their own families, blacks claimed in polls that they could consider the prospect calmly. When the black newspaper the *Pittsburgh Courier* asked its readers in 1958 how they would feel if one of their children wanted to marry a white, only 30 percent of those polled said they would object either mildly or vigorously; nearly 70 percent said they would not object at all. Even those who expressed personal disapproval commented that they would not try to rule their children's lives. One black housewife from Virginia wrote, "While I don't believe in it [intermarriage], I don't feel that I should dominate my child's life."[54] A 1964 study of more than seven hundred black families in Chicago found that half of the families were neutral toward interracial marriage, half opposed it, but over 80 percent said they would permit their child to marry a white if a romance had already developed without their knowledge.[55]

LeRoi Jones thought his parents took his 1958 interracial marriage in stride because of their attitude about the right of individuals to craft their destiny free of racial controls. "Such is the disposition and tenor of the oppressed they are so in love with democracy!" he later cynically explained.[56] Jones would come to see his family's acceptance as evidence of their own racial oppression, but his family was not alone in accepting a white spouse with open arms. Ruth Shilsky McBride, a white Jewish woman who was completely disowned by her own family when she became romantically involved with a black man, recalled the different reception she received from her black fiancé's family. The first time she met them, they were shocked, but once they got to know her, "They took me in with open hearts and made me one of their own; the only thing was it sometimes took a minute for them to get over the shock of seeing a black and white together." One elderly aunt who had never been close to a white person before took a while to warm up to her, but it was this aunt who helped McBride most when her husband died. McBride became part of her husband's extended black family, and she turned to them whenever she needed help. Jean Northrup, who had also been disowned by her family when she married a black man in the 1940s, found the contrast when she visited her husband's family "astonishing. Aunts and uncles were called in and they had a family celebration."[57]

Although some black families accepted their child's white spouse without question, families more commonly disapproved when they first learned about an interracial romance. Some feared for their child's safety. When Paul, a seventeen-year-old black man from Massachusetts, told his family that he wanted to marry Doris, a young white woman, his relatives "almost exploded." Although they liked Doris, they knew that her parents would oppose. the marriage, and as Paul recalled, they were "worried about what Doris' folks might do to me if they got the police on my neck." His mother tried to break up the romance by giving him a one-way train ticket to Washington, D.C., to stay with his older brother. Another black man's mother became livid when she found out about his interracial relationship. She feared it put her son at risk of great physical harm, and blamed his white girlfriend, who she thought might get him killed.[58] As these concerned relatives realized, the pervasiveness of racism in the broader society made it likely that interracial couples would face taunts and perhaps worse in public spaces.

Some families saw an interracial marriage as a personal insult and even a threat to their own reputation. The mother of one black woman who intermarried made clear to her daughter that she saw marrying a white man as an "insult to the Negro race," and she told her white son-in-law that there were a lot of black men her daughter could have married. Although she eventually moved in with her daughter and son-in-law, her relationship with her son-in-law was strained.[59] Katherine Minerbrook, a member of Chicago's black elite, felt so insulted by her son's interracial marriage that she took pains to embarrass his white wife whenever possible. She referred to the marriage as "a long-term affair" and never fully accepted her daughter-in-law. Another black mother who lived in a small southern town feared the social disapproval of acquaintances who might accuse her son of "deserting the race" and the hostility of local whites if they ever discovered what her son had done. Blacks who lived in the South knew that their son or daughter would not be able to bring their spouse home with them. In these circumstances, parents might resent an interracial marriage because it would limit their ability to see their own children. As one black husband explained, his mother accepted his marriage, but would be "scared to death" if he tried to bring his wife to visit her in the South. He had visited her alone, but the couple had never gone south together.[60]

Yet even among the most disapproving relatives, blacks exhibited far less willingness than whites to cut their family ties completely. Initial disapproval quickly became grudging tolerance for the sake of maintaining kin networks. Disapproving relatives often continued to see the couple and remained a part of their lives. Few blacks who intermarried were ever totally cut off by their families. One black man who married a white woman in the 1950s recalled that neither his sister nor his mother was happy about his marriage, but both had resigned themselves to the marriage and accepted his wife, even if they were not "enthusiastic supporters."[61]

Arthur Lambkin, a Massachusetts black man who married in the late 1930s, discovered that some of his sisters resented that he had married a white girl. One was particularly bitter, but he and his wife regularly visited her as if they weren't aware of her feelings, and eventually she came to accept them. And the mother who sent her son, Paul, away when she discovered he was in love with a white woman became sympathetic once Paul showed his determination to marry his white fiancée. After he snuck back home to Boston from Washington, D.C., his mother facilitated the wedding, even going to city hall to give her permission for the marriage since Paul was underage. The couple married in the home of Paul's sister.[62] In this case, the seriousness of the commitment convinced the black partner's family to support the marriage.

Black families proved more tolerant than white families for less personal reasons as well. Disapproving black parents had fewer options for controlling their children. Black parents did not appeal to state institutions, like the courts or police, to prevent an interracial marriage; they were more likely to fear such institutions than to see them as allies in an effort to establish parental authority. Blacks might also see the potential for economic and social mobility through such marriages. The embattled status of blacks in a white-dominated society constrained black opportunities, and perhaps some blacks saw such marriages as openings to a wider world. Most important, the extended family was a crucial survival system for blacks coping with racial persecution, and few blacks seemed willing to sacrifice their kin networks over disapproval of a child's choice of spouse.[63] Indeed, even families who bitterly disapproved of an interracial marriage rarely disowned the offending black relative.

The common pattern among whites was disapproval followed by distancing; among blacks, disapproval tended to diminish once the wedding had taken place. Black families objected when they still had a chance to stop the relationship, but once the couple married, many families made an effort to give them a chance. When Chuck Cannon, a black man who had migrated to San Francisco from Fort Worth, Texas, married a white San Francisco woman in 1952, his mother temporarily disinherited him. Angry both that he married someone she had never met and that his new wife was white, Cannon's mother wrote him out of her will. For Cannon's mother, whose own mother had been a concubine of a white slave driver, her son's interracial marriage must have come as a shock. Some of her own family looked nearly white, testament to the sexual exploitation black women had suffered at the hands of white men. Her anger was short-lived, however. She decided to come visit the young couple in California, and determined that she liked her new daughter-in-law. After she returned home, she changed her will back and sent the couple a wedding present. Similarly, a 1964 study of nine black-white couples in Indiana found that some black parents disapproved of their child's romance, but "in no case did a Negro parent remain hostile to the white member of intermarriage after its consummation."[64]

Families who decided to "give the white partner a chance" may well have recognized how much whites sacrificed when they married blacks. It must have reassured some parents that a white partner chose their son or daughter even though it meant probable hardship. For them, the marriage signified the commitment and seriousness of the white spouse. Black mothers may also have wanted to bring their white daughter-in-laws into their kin network to teach them how to care for their sons. Ann Marable, the white woman who was disowned by her New Jersey family for years after her 1947 marriage to a black man, found a surrogate mother in her black mother-in-law. She was accepted, Marable's daughter later remembered, "as my father's wife, and also as this young woman who didn't know very much about cooking, especially about cooking for a black man. So they showed her a lot."[65]

Lois Jones, a white California woman who married her black husband in 1946, was not initially accepted by her husband's family. No one in his family liked her, and his mother treated her with "much disdain." Nothing changed until the day when her husband asked her to cook some of his favorite dishes. She had no idea how to prepare collard greens and black-eyed peas, so she asked her mother-in-law to teach her. She cooked the meal under her mother-in-law's supervision. "I used her pots and pans and listened. Afterward, I left her kitchen spotless. I had won her respect. After she tasted the meal I had cooked . . . I had won her friendship!" Efforts like these demonstrated that a white person was serious about becoming part of a black community. Lois Jones reported that her husband's family eventually came around and "treated me like one of their own." For her, the lesson was clear. White women who married black men must "stand by their Black men and be a part of their culture . . . They must embrace the Black community." A study of fifty black-white Philadelphia couples found this same pattern. Black families moved from tolerance of an interracial marriage to more sincere acceptance only after the white partner demonstrated some sense of connection and appreciation for the black family.[66]

In contrast, whites who seemed to distance themselves from blacks were viewed with suspicion. Katherine Minerbrook was disappointed when her daughter-in-law said she was going to let her children choose for themselves what race they would be. Minerbrook believed that the young woman should have recognized that her children would be black and needed to be prepared for the racism they were sure to encounter. Convinced that her daughter-in-law had not fully accepted the implications of marrying a black man and entering the black community, she told her, "LaVerne, you're such a *white* white girl."[67] Some of the opposition of black female relatives, who were more outspoken in their disapproval than black fathers and brothers, may well have stemmed from a sense that children raised by white women would not be as fully schooled in black culture as those raised by black women.

Yet those whites who were willing to take their place among blacks and confront the challenges they would face as part of an interracial couple were often treated as worthy additions to the black community. At a time when few whites were willing to ally themselves with blacks, intermarried whites who proved themselves true to their partner and proud of their decision to become part of the black community were generally accepted. Whites who were willing "to keep proving one's identification with the group" often found welcome acceptance in the black communities where they took refuge. In the early 1960s Arthur Lambkin, a black man who had been married to a white woman for twenty-four years, discussed how he and his wife had been received socially. He did not care if the white community accepted him; he was only concerned that the black community accept his wife. "If the white woman, married to a Negro, accepts the fact that she is really a part of the Negro group, as my wife did, then all suspicions and uncertainties are overcome," he explained. Josephine Schuyler, the white wife of the black journalist George Schuyler and a longtime resident of Harlem, felt much the same way. Members of the black community, she had found, though often critical of interracial marriages, became friendly when they learned that an interracial couple was sincere and decent. "If a white person conducts himself in a dignified, friendly way in Harlem, as elsewhere, he will be met in a like manner," she explained.[68] Hazel Byrne Simpkins, the English war bride who married a black man in 1947, claimed that she had many good black friends, and that her black neighbors treated her just like anyone else and were willing "to accept me into their race." Other white wives living in black neighborhoods in the 1940s and 1950s described their relationships with their black neighbors as friendly as well. When Michelle Ross wrote about her experience as half of an interracial couple for *Ebony* magazine, fifty of her black neighbors wrote to express their love and support for her and her black husband. "They are doing more to make people understand than all the shouting about equal rights will ever do." Michelle Ross was a "wonderful woman" whom they loved and respected. After Ruth McBride's husband died, leaving her with seven young children, she discovered the depth of the black community's support. Friends and neighbors stuffed her mailbox with checks and cash. People sent food, clothes, and anything else they had. McBride was so touched she vowed to remain part of the black community forever. "That's how black folks thought back then," she later told her son. "That's why I never veered from the black side."[69]

Whatever their personal feelings, political considerations made it difficult for blacks to formulate a coherent critique of interracial marriage in the twenty years after World War II. Having had limits imposed upon them for so long, blacks were keenly aware of the importance of upholding the ideal of the right of individuals to act free of racial constraints. By the late 1960s, blacks would move toward a position that the right to intermarry should be limited for the sake of maintaining a strong black community, and black women would become far more vocal in their attacks on black men who married white women. But in the 1940s and 1950s, interracial marriage did not raise the same level of concern about the dangers of racial assimilation or of black men deserting black women. The tolerance of the black community and the intolerance of the white would have a profound effect on those blacks and whites who married during this period, influencing how and where they lived, the challenges they faced, and how they defined themselves racially.

NOT JUST COMMIES

AND BEATNIKS

Society, a soon-to-be interracially married white woman wrote in 1953, "has not found a way to dominate the human heart."[1] In the 1940s and 1950s, whites were openly hostile to interracial marriage while blacks were only ambivalently tolerant of the practice. Yet the 1960 U.S. Census documented fifty-one thousand black-white couples in the United States, many of whom had married during the prior two decades. These couples had to face discrimination, persecution, and sometimes even violence, their marriages constantly challenged as illegitimate and abnormal. What brought them together and how they built lives for themselves tell us a great deal about the workings of the color line in postwar America.

Structurally, racial segregation was endemic in American society and intensified as whites moved to suburbs and black migrants crowded into central cities in the war years and after. Blacks and whites commonly lived in different neighborhoods, attended separate churches, and joined segregated social organizations. Black students, in the South and elsewhere, attended predominantly black schools. Few blacks attended majority-white colleges, and most professional workplaces remained all white. Although many blacks and whites mixed on the streets and in random daily encounters, such brief meetings did not encourage cross-racial friendship or intimacy. The single most important factor preventing blacks and whites from marrying in the 1940s and 1950s was the de jure and de facto segregation that made it unlikely that an individual would meet someone of another race in a situation that fostered the development of a personal relationship.

Ideological barriers that stressed the difficulties of bridging the social and cultural distance between the races further reinforced the structural hurdles that kept blacks and whites apart. Those who intermarried defied societal taboos and challenged prevailing racial and gender norms. Not surprisingly, the spaces most open to racial mixing in postwar America were on the margins of respectable society, places that brought together individuals who were adventurous and sometimes critical of America's racial norms. The Beat subculture in Greenwich Village, jazz clubs, dance halls, and leftist political events were all important meeting sites for interracial couples. But not everyone who married interracially in the forties and fifties was a "bohemian," a political radical, or a member of the "sporting world."[2] Sustained opportunities for cross-racial intimacy, though rare, did occur in some workplaces and schools, and many interracial couples in postwar America came from typical working- or middle-class backgrounds.

Whatever their background, couples had to have a strong relationship if they hoped to withstand the external forces that worked against their marriages. Hostility and ostracism drove some interracial couples to divorce. Many others, however, found ways to cope with rejection, persecution, and job and housing discrimination. Couples forged friendships with like-minded individuals and sometimes created their own support networks. Most minimized the role that race played in their relationships in an effort to present themselves as legitimate and respectable. Yet even as they downplayed the importance of race, it constantly impinged on their lives, determining where they could live, how they identified themselves to the world, and how they raised their children. Most black–white couples, especially those involving white women and black men, had little choice but to build their lives within the black community. No matter what they may have wanted for themselves, couples were forced to consider themselves as black families and to raise their children as black. The color line, most couples of the forties and fifties found, was relatively inflexible and unyielding. Perhaps society could not dominate the human heart, but it severely limited the ability of interracial couples to craft lives on their own terms.

––––––––––––

When E. Franklin Frazier, the well-known black sociologist, made an outline for a planned (though never completed) book on interracial marriage, one of the first questions he intended to address was how interracial couples met. Most meetings between blacks and whites, Frazier noted, did not happen on terms where marriage would be considered a possibility. How was it that in the 1940s and 1950s blacks and whites might "come to know each other so that marriage ensues as a consequence?" he asked. Lee Chennault, a white woman who married a black man in the late 1940s, found people were very curious about how she met her husband. "Usually when people want to know how you met your husband, they are being romantic," Chennault wrote in 1960. "But with me, they are really asking how I got from such a lily-white background into a situation where I could meet and marry a Negro."[3]

Indeed, there were not many places in postwar America that enabled blacks and whites to meet in situations conducive to marriage. School, while generally a site where young couples meet and begin dating, did not afford many opportunities for black-white couples. Not only were public schools racially segregated, with nearly 60 percent of black students outside the South attending schools that were 80 to 100 percent black, but it was difficult for young people to embark on an interracial relationship while living at home if their families disapproved.[4] Public schools with racially diverse student bodies, moreover, often formally forbade or informally discouraged interracial dating.

The greater freedom accorded to university-level students made interracial socializing more of a possibility at colleges, although segregation in higher education ensured that few marriages would develop on campus either. As late as 1960, there were only 141,000 blacks enrolled in college nationwide, and the majority of these students went to historically black colleges where there was little chance they would get to know whites.[5] Still, some couples did meet at college in the forties and fifties. Paul Robeson, Jr., the son of the great black singer, met his future wife when they were both freshmen at Cornell University in 1946, while Jean Thomas, a black woman studying at Columbia University in the 1940s, met her white husband, George, in a college class. Cheryl Wolfe, a light-skinned black woman born in the late 1920s to middle-class parents, attended Dunbar, a prestigious segregated high school in Washington, D.C. She went to college at Wellesley and then attended Yale University Law School, where she was one of the only black students in 1949. She soon fell in love with a white fellow student. "We did not know what we were going to do with this relationship," Wolfe recalled years later. "I mean, we felt this was the right thing for both of us, but we knew the world wasn't going to think it was so perfect." One of their professors suggested they move to the Virgin Islands when they married. Instead, they both moved to Boston after graduation; they were married a year later.[6]

Other couples met in public venues such as grocery stores or restaurants. Jimmy Ross, a black Atlantic City man, met his wife, Michelle, when he happened to stop into her fried-chicken shop one day. He came back every night and they would talk long after the shop closed. After two weeks, Michelle got the courage to ask Jimmy over to her house, and they began dating more formally. White eighteen-year-old Hazel Ballard met her husband Bill while working as a cashier at a café near the university he attended; she eventually went with him to Washington, D.C., when he was offered a job there. Yet such random meetings were not likely to develop into relationships unless the individuals involved had a chance to meet each other repeatedly. It could be dangerous for a black man to ask a white woman he had just met out on a date, while white men who did the same thing were likely to be rejected by black women for being too forward. A woman, black or white, who might want to pursue a partner of another race would violate both gender and racial norms if she expressed interest before the man did. Couples had to have the opportunity to evaluate each other's attitudes and sincerity before taking the risk of suggesting a more personal relationship. Jimmy Ross and Bill Ballard went back to the restaurants where they met their wives repeatedly before the relationships became romantic. Similarly, another interracial couple met while the white wife was working as a nurse at a hospital where her black future husband was recuperating after an auto accident, a situation that gave the couple an opportunity to get to know each other before they began dating.[7]

It was more common for interracial couples in this period to meet at work than at school or in commercial establishments. Some workplaces brought blacks and whites together in positions of relative equality. Doris and John Wilson met while working for the same wealthy family, Doris as a housekeeper and John as a chauffeur, while Phil and Dorothy Garrett met while working in a Kansas City hotel. He was a janitor and she was a waitress.[8] Other couples met as more professional and clerical jobs opened up for blacks in the years after the war. Although the number of blacks holding such "white-collar" jobs would begin to climb dramatically only in the mid-1960s, even in the 1950s, more blacks were going to college, earning professional degrees, and finding at least some opportunities open to them as more states passed fair employment laws. A surprising number of interracial marriages in the 1950s evolved along the lines typical of same-race marriages, with a woman working as a secretary or assistant marrying her boss or a coworker. One young black woman in Philadelphia met her white lawyer husband while working as his secretary; another who worked as a secretary in a real estate office met her husband there. Joan Connors met her black husband, Mike, while working as a secretary at a plant where he was a research chemist, while white Dorothy Murphy got to know her future husband, Wendell Urling, when she worked as a receptionist in his dental office. Murphy was married to a white man when she began working for Urling in 1952, but the work environment encouraged a relationship, since as the Connecticut Supreme Court noted in a case concerning the custody of her white son, "she saw him and was with him every working day that the office of Dr. Urling was open."[9]

The industry that most commonly brought blacks and whites together in the forties and fifties was entertainment. Successful black actors, singers, or dancers commonly worked closely with whites, and white entertainers often respected their successful black counterparts. Although some blacks criticized celebrities who married whites as sellouts and status seekers, others recognized that the frequency of intermarriage among famous blacks was in part due to the fact that they had more contact

with whites than the "average Negro."[10] Both black and white commentators theorized that black and white musicians were more likely to
intermarry because music provided a kind of "common ground" that
could transcend racial lines and foster relationships. When Pearl Bailey,
the black jazz singer, married white jazz drummer Louis Bellson in 1952,
New York Post columnist Max Lerner saw their union "as enclosed in
music." Music, Lerner argued, was "an international language that laughs
at barriers of race, nation or religion," a language that could cut across
"diverse birth and breeding and background." Lena Horne, who was attacked by blacks for her 1947 marriage to the white composer and ar-
ranger Lennie Hayton, thought that a common background in music
helped her overcome her reluctance to become involved with him.
"Music was and perhaps still is the area of my life where the question of
color comes second and the question of whether you play well or not
is the one you have to answer as a test of admission into society," Horne
wrote in her 1965 memoir.[11] Similar artistic interests helped black
and white entertainers like these get beyond the racial stereotypes of
the time.

Meeting places such as school and workplaces neither encouraged interracial relationships nor had the goal of questioning racial boundaries.
But some spaces in rigidly segregated postwar America allowed or even
fostered cross-racial interactions. In urban areas, individuals who considered themselves bohemian or artistic might socialize across the color line
at parties. At certain dance halls and jazz bars, black bands played for
white patrons and sometimes black and white patrons even shared the
dance floor. Left-leaning political and religious organizations brought
some blacks and whites together to fight poverty or racial discrimination.
Many interracial couples in the forties and fifties met in such spaces.

Lee Chennault met her black husband at a party after she started
hanging out with artists who, as she recalled, talked a lot about the race
problem. This was a social circle where interracial gatherings were seen
as chic and fashionable. The "arty" or "bohemian" atmosphere attracted
black and white intellectuals who wanted to test social and sexual
boundaries. LaVerne and Alan Minerbrook met in Chicago at a party of
"an interracial set who all knew each other." Other couples, such as Walter and Jean Northrup, met at dances or nightclubs. Jean, a white woman

in Gary, Indiana, became drawn into the black community by working at a community center in a black neighborhood. She began socializing with blacks, meeting her future husband at a dance in 1939 and marrying him in the mid-1940s.[12] Whites who were attracted to blacks or black culture could also head to jazz clubs where black musicians played. Black jazz musicians Billy Taylor, Herb Jeffries, and Oscar Pettiford all married white women. Herb Jeffries met his wife in a Los Angeles jazz club; Billy Daniels met white socialite Martha Braun at Club Zanzibar in New York City. One black female drummer met her white husband at the nightclub where she performed.[13]

Those whites drawn toward black society or those simply rejecting the perceived cultural conformity of the 1950s were also creating their own subculture. The Beat scene, most fully developed in New York City and San Francisco, attracted young Americans disillusioned by the complacency of their generation. Antimaterialistic, critical of sexual mores, and eager to experiment with drugs and alternative lifestyles, Beat writers, artists, and hangers-on forged their own small communities on the basis of the ideals of individual liberty and personal freedom. White Beats were drawn toward black culture because they believed that blacks were less inhibited than whites. For them, as Norman Mailer's famous 1957 essay "The White Negro" argued, blackness represented the ultimate in existential awareness; only blacks truly lived in the moment and were free enough to experience the height of sexual freedom. Jazz was like an orgasm, and white hipsters wanted a piece of it. For the women of the Beat crowd, an attraction to black men and culture could be a form of rebellion against the strict gender-role expectations of the 1950s. "Darkness, whether in the form of rock n' roll or boyfriends or fantasies," noted the white writer Wini Breines, "offered girls danger and models that broke with 'the nuclear family, white house, and picket fence.'"[14]

The Beat scene fostered an atmosphere where blacks and whites could come together to experiment with new social relations. Hettie Cohen, a Jewish girl from suburban New York, met LeRoi Jones (later Amiri Baraka), the son of a middle-class black couple from New Jersey, in the heady atmosphere of 1957 Greenwich Village while both were working for *The Record Changer,* a small music magazine. They went together to jazz clubs, roamed the streets of New York City, and hung out with

Beat poets and writers. Cohen wanted to become "something," she re-called. "I never had 'normal' fifties plans—they seemed preposterous," she wrote in her 1990 memoir. When one of her friends predicted that she would end up a housewife in the suburbs, she wondered, "What un-foreseen catastrophe would send me up the river to decorate a home in Westchester?" Becoming involved with a black man ensured that Cohen would not end up in suburban Westchester. For Jones, dating a white woman seemed like a natural extension of his new life as an artist in Greenwich Village, hanging out with beats who flouted societal con-ventions. Before moving to the Village, Jones contends, he had never thought much about white women, but "the idea that you could go with a white woman seemed like one of the 'down' aspects of the whole Bo-hemian scene." Dating white women seemed to Jones like "part of the adventure of my new life in the Village. . . . Some kind of classic Bohe-mian accouterment."[15]

Marriage, in contrast, was not considered a bohemian act. Although the Beat world produced some interracial relationships (Cohen remem-bers a "half-dozen" steady interracial couples in Greenwich Village in 1957), there were fewer interracial marriages. Jones and Cohen married only after Cohen became pregnant for a second time in 1958 (she had an abortion with the first pregnancy). Other Beat interracial couples who married included the black poet Bob Kaufmann and his white wife Elaine, and black artist Bob Thomson, who married the white clothing designer Carol Plenda. As LeRoi Jones later wrote in his autobiography, "The black-white thing wasn't no normal US shit; it was out." But "marriage was some normal US shit. . . . Hey, it was a kind of middle-class thing to do."[16] For the Beats, the same impulses that led them to re-ject traditional racial boundaries also led them to question "middle-class" conventions like marriage, although some marriages did emerge.

These interracial social and cultural spaces had their counterparts in religious or political organizations that brought like-minded blacks and whites together to work for the cause of racial equality or social justice. Organizations with the goal of improving race relations or fostering hu-man brotherhood provided a safe atmosphere in which couples could get to know each other. Vincent Parks, a white man, met his black wife, Julia, in the early 1950s while volunteering at the Friendship House, a

Chicago organization working for interracial justice, while Nancy and Charles Jones, an older couple who were each widowed, met at an interracial social sponsored by a group of churches. A young couple who attended university together got to know each other when they participated in a political discussion group. As the white husband recalled, the atmosphere in the group was "conducive to such relationships as ours." Mainstream civil rights organizations did not actively encourage cross-racial relationships, in part because opponents portrayed civil rights groups as licentious supporters of race mixing, but marriages could develop in these groups as well. James Farmer, the first director of the Congress of Racial Equality, met his white wife, a member of a CORE chapter in Illinois, at a 1943 CORE fundraiser in Chicago.[17]

Political groups further to the left proved even more friendly to interracial couples. The American Communist Party had begun to focus on racial discrimination in the late 1920s, looking to expand the party's following among black Americans and hoping to exploit racial divisions in the United States to foster political instability. By the 1930s, the party had begun to attack segregation and the legal persecution of blacks in the South. In the midst of the Great Depression, the American Communist Party sought to work with civil rights organizations and labor unions as part of its effort to forge a "popular front" of leftist groups against fascism. The party undertook important civil rights initiatives, from defending the Scottsboro boys (a group of nine young black men unfairly charged with raping two white women) to leading rent strikes and boycotts of discriminatory stores in Harlem. It also actively recruited black members and encouraged blacks to assume leadership positions. Although by the early 1940s the party was eager to move more into the mainstream since the Soviet Union desperately needed America's help during World War II, it maintained far more radical positions on race and racism than other political groups.[18]

Communists viewed racism as a tool used by capitalists to divide the working class and urged all workers, regardless of color, to fight together for the common revolution. Blacks and whites had to share a common social and cultural life if they were to going to share the same political struggle. The party thus urged "the greatest degree of fraternization, the closest association of the white with the Negro comrades in social life inside and outside of the Party." The party was, in the words of one proud member, "a working model of racial integration."[19] In order to foster such socializing, the party sponsored interracial dances and parties for its members. White Communists who seemed hesitant about inter-acting with blacks were reprimanded as racial "chauvinists." Between 1949 and 1953, the party undertook a heated campaign against "white chauvinism," denouncing and expelling members who were accused of being racist. The campaign quickly became obsessive, with even very trivial suggestions of racism (like serving watermelon at an interracial gathering) attracting censure, but it demonstrated the party's commit-ment to eradicating all forms of racial discrimination.[20] Members who objected to interracial relationships were rebuked; in Harlem in the 1930s, white men were even given dancing lessons so they would feel more comfortable asking black women to dance at parties. Blacks who voiced concerns about interracial marriages between party members were chastised for giving voice to "nationalistic deviations." It was con-sidered a political duty to foster interracial social relations.[21]

The Communist Party brought together strong-willed, radical people who wanted to integrate their political beliefs into their personal lives. Not surprisingly, even though the party was small (with fewer than twenty thousand members in 1955 and only three thousand by 1959), it produced a significant number of black-white marriages in the forties and fifties.[22] Susan Moscou's parents were drawn together by their shared political beliefs. They met in a Flint, Michigan, automobile factory. Her white father was a union organizer; her black mother worked on the as-sembly line, drawn toward progressive politics because "she desired an interracial life." The family moved to New York after her father was fired and blacklisted for his party activities in the mid-1950s. Chuck and Yvonne Cannon were another interracial couple who met through the party. Chuck had moved to San Francisco from Fort Worth, Texas, in 1944, when he was just seventeen. He found a job working as a welder, and he soon became involved in radical politics, joining the Young Communist League (YCL), a youth organization for the Communist Party. Yvonne had grown up in a well-to-do suburb of New York City, but even as a child she remembered being interested in people who were less privileged. With her mother, she challenged her Long Island Girl

Scout troop to accept black girls in the early 1940s. After her parents divorced, she and her mother moved to Los Angeles, where her mother joined the Communist Party. Yvonne met intellectuals, artists, and writers who shared her mother's radical political beliefs. She moved to San Francisco when she won a scholarship to an art school, but was soon expelled for her political activities, which included taking classes at a Communist-run labor school and doing organizing work for the YCL. When Chuck and Yvonne met, introduced by a mutual friend on the street in 1949, they were both active in the Communist youth movement. They were married in the home of friends who were also party members and found support and acceptance among their radical friends, most of whom were white.[23]

Given its small numbers, which dwindled dramatically during the anti-Communist repression of the McCarthy era, the Communist Party fostered only a fraction of interracial marriages in the postwar period. Nevertheless, the party's history suggests the kinds of social relationships that could develop across racial lines in a supportive environment. Indeed, only one organization during the postwar period would go further than the Communists in supporting interracial relationships. Bahá'í, a religion of Middle Eastern origins, was introduced to the United States in 1893. Bahá'ís believe that the unity of mankind is a prerequisite to achieving peace on earth; religious differences, ethnic differences, and racial prejudice must all be overcome. One of the few groups that made a case for the positive benefits of cross-racial love in the forties and fifties, the Bahá'í faith instructed followers to "close your eyes to racial difference and welcome all with the light of oneness." This call to obliterate racial prejudice proved challenging for the predominantly white American Bahá'í community. But Bahá'í spiritual leader Abdu'l Baha urged Americans to overcome their racism and even to unite in the most literal sense through intermarrying. He instructed Washington, D.C., followers to "gather together these two races, black and white, into one assembly and put such love into their hearts that they shall not only unite but intermarry," and he personally encouraged the first intermarriage among Bahá'ís, which took place in 1912.[24] Although the group had very few American practitioners (perhaps seven thousand in the early 1950s), it encouraged its members to intermarry. "If you plant a garden, you wouldn't want to grow flowers of all one color," one intermarried Bahá'í member explained. "We are God's flowers in His garden, so there is no reason why His flowers can't live together and intermingle harmoniously to produce a colorful beautiful garden." Of the seventy-five black Bahá'ís in Chicago in 1952, at least six were married to whites.[25]

Interracial relationships, no matter how they began, took place in a highly politicized context. Determining why any couple chooses to marry is difficult, but especially so in the case of interracial marriage since so many have assumed it to be neurotic or unhealthy. There was little societal, cultural, or ideological support for the idea of love across the color line in the forties and fifties, and those couples who chose to marry across the color line did so for a wide variety of reasons. Although many couples sincerely loved each other, some individuals were impelled by racial stereotypes, a desire to escape from a negative home environment, or by the hope of material gain. But many same-race marriages were motivated by similar concerns, and in most respects, interracial couples were similar to their same-race counterparts.

Some whites exoticized blacks, as did a white woman who wrote an anonymous *Negro Digest* article in 1948 explaining that she wanted to marry a black man because she found black men physically and spiritually attractive, with "sun-bronzed skin and generously molded eyes and lips," and a great "nascent nobility." She could imagine nothing more fulfilling than mingling her blood with that of a "Nubian son of the sun" to create a beautiful mixture. Lois Jones, a California woman who began dating black men in 1939 and married one in 1946, became interested in blacks while attending business college. She had not grown up around blacks and she became intrigued by them, purposely seeking them out by making friends with black women. When she realized that some black men were interested in her, she was "undaunted." Although she was familiar with the negative stereotypes about black men, "I wanted to experience for myself," she recalled. She pursued her first black boyfriend, and soon was dating blacks exclusively. An attraction to blackness motivated some white men as well, like Oskar Heim; he claimed he hoped to marry a black woman because they had dignity, natural grace, warmth, and a vitality that white women lacked.[26]

An interracial marriage could serve as a form of rebellion or a means of escape. For some young white women, getting involved with a black man offered a way to get out of an abusive home. Rachel Shilsky, later Ruth McBride, the daughter of Orthodox Jewish immigrants living in Virginia, suffered at home from a father who sexually abused her and forced her to work long hours in the family store. She became involved with a black boy who frequented the store when she was fourteen or fifteen. Shilsky was drawn to him because he was kind and treated her well. Although their relationship ended, Shilsky eventually moved to New York, where she married a black man in the 1940s. Ruth, another young white woman, was eighteen years old when she married her black boyfriend. Raised by a mother who pressured her to become a stage performer and a father who sexually abused her, Ruth was eager to leave home. She also saw herself as a crusader for equality, having grown up believing that all people were equal in the heady atmosphere of 1930s leftist politics. Although her parents opposed the marriage and her friends advised against it, Ruth thought that by marrying interracially she could "prove that I believed that all people are equal and that I was not a hypocrite; and . . . get away from both my father and my mother." The marriage lasted only two years, but it helped Ruth establish a new relationship with her parents.[27]

Racial considerations or stereotypes could impel interracial relationships among blacks as well. Don Terry's parents never married, although they had two children together. Terry believed his black father pursued white women in part because he wanted to have light-skinned children to make up for the fact that his own mother thought he was "too dark," and in part because he wanted to assert his manhood by dating white women. John Blake also felt his father was "really into white women" because he always wanted to do whatever was forbidden to black men. For some black men, a relationship with a white woman was a way to challenge their subordinate status in American society. White men, meanwhile, could represent a form of stability and protection for black women. Melba Patillo, one of the nine students who desegregated Little

Rock's Central High School in 1957, ended up marrying a white student she met at San Francisco State University. He reminded her of the white guard who had protected her during her year at Central High, and she married him, in part, for the "safety that my black uncles and father could not provide me in the South."[28]

Given the higher status accorded to whites in American society, blacks could also view having a white spouse as a status symbol or a form of accomplishment. Some black partners thought marrying white provided a chance for upward mobility or assimilation. Several adult biracial children believed that their black fathers married white women in an effort to achieve fuller acceptance into American society. The journalist Scott Minerbrook describes his black father as a middle-class social climber, always seeking to achieve more. His 1949 marriage to a white woman was both an idealistic act and an ambitious one. Although the couple remained together, on and off, for nearly twenty years, the marriage became increasingly abusive as Minerbrook's father took his anger over racism and the limits he encountered in his life out on his wife. Neisha Wright believed her black father married a white woman in the early 1960s because he wanted to assimilate into white mainstream culture by "being bigger than his race." "My father was raised by his father to believe that assimilating into the white culture was the only way to make it. Obviously, my father and his brother both married white women; that's got to tell you something about the way they were raised."[29]

Other blacks consciously wanted to pass into the white world and saw marriage to a white person as an important part of that project. Tony Williams grew up in Muncie, Indiana. His mother, an uneducated black woman, had become pregnant while working for a wealthy white man. Tony, who never met his white father, was light-skinned and ambitious. He briefly attended Howard University, but eventually dropped out and married a white woman he had met in Muncie. The couple moved to Virginia, opened a tavern, and lived as a white family for years. When the marriage and the business fell apart, however, Tony Williams had to return to Muncie with his two older children, who learned only then that they were "colored." Although things didn't work out for Tony Williams, he encouraged his son, Gregory, to follow the same path, repeatedly telling him that he should pass as white and marry a white woman: "You might have to live in the ghetto, but you'd don't have to subsist on its food. Life is going to be easier for you if you have a white wife."[30] The only way for a black man to get ahead, such instructions suggested, was to escape the stigma of the black race entirely.

Few blacks involved in interracial marriages admitted to wanting to escape their race, but having a sense of distance from their own racial community clearly predisposed both blacks and whites to consider inter-marrying. Some blacks who married whites in these years described themselves as independent thinkers or loners who were unconcerned about other people's opinions. Grace McAllester had few qualms about her decision to marry a white man. As she explained years after her marriage, "I'm not a great lover of people, so it was not that overriding a threat to me, because I never have cared that much whether people like me or not." Arthur Lambkin, a black man who met his white wife at a meeting of the Socialist Party, also attributed his willingness to inter-marry to his self-sufficiency and independence. "I am the kind of person who doesn't require very many contacts with the outside world—Negro or white," Lambkin told an interviewer in the early 1960s. "I really don't need people around me all the time, nor do I concern myself overly much about what other people think of me or my ways." For some blacks, this tendency toward self-sufficiency led them to question what they saw as a rather constraining black culture and community. Chuck Cannon, who met his white wife through the Young Communist League, described himself as a loner who felt that black culture limited black people. His decision to marry a white woman was due in part to his unwillingness to be constrained.[31]

Just as blacks who questioned their community ties might be more likely to intermarry, individuals with a less stable position as "white" were more predisposed to marry blacks. By the 1940s, American Jews were the group perhaps least consolidated into a larger sense of "white" identity. Although there are no national statistics on the Jewish-black in-termarriage rate, Jewish Americans made up a disproportionate number of the whites involved in interracial marriages, considering that there were fewer than five million Jews (about 3.5 percent of the total popula-tion) in America in the late 1940s. In a 1960 study of twenty-four inter-racial couples in New York City, twelve of the white partners were Jewish, as were 16.7 percent of the white spouses in a study of Washington, D.C. In the mid-1960s the sociologist Werner Cahnman estimated that 70 to 80 percent of the white spouses of black men in the New York metropolitan area were Jewish. Although these figures are skewed since they focused on New York City, a city with a large Jewish population, many of the stories of interracial couples from this period involve a Jewish spouse.[32]

Several factors help explain the high numbers of black-Jewish couples. Jews were more likely than non-Jewish whites to be engaged in radical politics in the forties and fifties and thus more likely to meet blacks in an open and supportive environment. Fully one-third of the members of the American Communist and Socialist parties were Jews. In part because of their experiences with oppression and persecution, some Jews were sympathetic to other oppressed minorities. Penny Rhodes believed that her Jewish upbringing prepared her for an interracial marriage, even though her neighborhood was very segregated and she met almost no non-Jewish children growing up. Judaism itself, she believed, predisposed her to marry an "outsider." Jews, she felt, "understand persecution and can generalize past their own experience to another group's experiences."[33]

Some Jews in the United States, furthermore, did not see themselves as part of the "white" community. Before World War II, Jews were commonly perceived as belonging to a distinct race. The war helped speed the process by which Jews became viewed as "Caucasians," but for many Jews, an ambivalence about their own racial identity remained.[34] Hettie Cohen, the young Jewish woman who married LeRoi Jones, wrote about her life in the 1950s, "Black/white was still a slippery division to me." As an "outsider Jew," she thought about identifying herself as white by aspiring "to the liberal intellectual, potentially conservative Western tradition. But I was never drawn to that history, and with so little specific to call my own I felt free to choose."[35] Uncertainty about their own racial position made some Jews more willing to consider relationships with blacks.

Yet seeking "deviant" or unique motives for marrying interracially can obscure the similarities between interracial and same-race couples and imply that same-race marriages are undertaken for "better" reasons.

The 1940s and 1950s were marked by a celebration of marriage and a rush toward the altar. In 1940, 31 percent of the American population were single. By 1960, only 21 percent were.[36] Many of these young couples married for reasons other than love. White women in the 1950s rushed into same-race marriages in part because of peer and parental pressure, fear of spinsterhood, a desire to establish their own home, or an eagerness for sexual intimacy. A woman who married her husband three months after she met him recalled, "I didn't feel I was in love. I thought, everybody else is doing this and I need to get my life on some sort of course." The equation of marriage with adulthood, especially for women, led many fifties women to embrace marriage, even with men they did not love. As one young wife explained, "I had a tremendous drive to get married, to get out of my house. I didn't fall madly in love." Another claimed that she "would have done anything to get out of the house."[37] Many women looked for men who could provide them with security and stability, while some chose spouses they believed could provide them with glamour and excitement. Men often looked for stable women who would be capable homemakers or dutiful corporate wives.

Marriages across race lines could provide similar benefits: an opportunity to escape from the home, the chance to begin a new adult life, glamour and excitement, perhaps, some thought, even the opportunity for social climbing—but such motivations were not incompatible with feelings of love or genuine affection. Lois Jones, who admitted to being particularly attracted to black men, was married to her black husband for seventeen years, until his death. Jones had little patience for whites who implied that her reasons for marrying a black man were neurotic or wrong. "I chose him because I *wanted* him. I *loved* him," she told one white critic. Ruth McBride, who made her way to Harlem after surviving childhood sexual abuse, was also aware of how white outsiders might view her relationships. "Folks will run with that, won't they?" she remarked when she told her son about her experience with incest. "They'll say, 'Oh, she felt low, so she went on and married a nigger.' Well, I don't care. Your father changed my life."[38]

In many respects, interracial couples in the forties and fifties were not unlike their same-race counterparts. Most individuals who intermarried, like most who married within their race, wed others from similar class and educational backgrounds. Interracial couples married less across economic or educational lines than within their particular socioeconomic brackets, and couples often shared similar occupational levels as well.[39] Although most interracial couples lived in the Northeast, interracial couples could be found in every region in the United States, including the South, and while most often in urban areas, in rural areas or in small towns as well.[40]

Where interracial couples differed from their same-race counterparts was in their age at the time of marriage. In the 1950s, the median age for marriage was 22.6 years for men and 20.3 years for women, but those who married interracially were significantly older than their same-race counterparts. In California, the median age for white men who married black women between 1948 and 1951 was 39, as compared with 26 for those who married other whites. Forty percent of the black women who married white men in California were over 35, although only 17 percent of black women who married black men were.[41] One reason partners were older was because, for many, these were second marriages. During a decade when the divorce rate hovered around 10 percent, the number of previously married people involved in interracial marriages was exceptionally high. Case studies of couples from Philadelphia, Washington, D.C., New York City, and Indiana found that anywhere from 25 to 50 percent of those entering into interracial marriages had been married before. This data is supported by the 1960 U.S. Census, which found that 35 percent of individuals who married interracially during the 1950s had been married before, as compared with only 19 percent of whites who married within their race.[42]

Individuals who were slightly older, divorced, or widowed were often better equipped to handle familial or societal opposition to their marriages. They had established some distance from their families, both emotionally and often geographically, marrying, as one study noted, at an "age that parental influence had little or no effect." Many already lived on their own and were economically independent. This was particularly important for white women, who often found it difficult to carry on an interracial courtship while still living with their parents. Those who were divorced, moreover, had already violated one social taboo by ending a previous marriage and may have been less hesitant to challenge another.

Few people who were married interracially had been married to a partner of a different race before, but having had an unhappy same-race marriage may have made them more likely to take a chance on an interracial
relationship. One white woman married to a black man insisted in 1950
that she knew true love had nothing to do with skin color, "because I
have had a white husband and got deceived." For blacks, having already
been married to someone of their own race may have made it easier to
answer criticisms that might arise when they married outside their race.
An interracially married black woman pointed to her previous marriage
to a black man as evidence that she had nothing against her own race, no
matter what anyone said.[43]

Interracial couples, no matter how they met or why they married, however, could not escape familial and societal disapproval. Most interracial couples were viewed as deviants, as people who had crossed racial
boundaries and who threatened customary hierarchies. As such, they
were forced to pay a price for their transgressions—whether losing their
jobs, being denied housing, being persecuted by police, or being stared at
or even attacked on the street. The risks and costs any given couple in-
curred, however, were influenced by variables of gender and class. Couples with fewer economic resources were more vulnerable to discrimination in employment and housing, and many of these couples would
retreat into the black community for support. Black husbands and white
wives faced a more hostile environment than white husbands and black
wives, although neither type of couple escaped opprobrium. Couples
who belonged to progressive political or religious organizations had a
preexisting support system in their friends and comrades, and thus reported less social isolation. Yet whatever a couple's political convic-
tions, class background, or gender composition, racial boundaries defined their lives.

Couples invariably encountered not only curiosity but also verbal,
and sometimes physical, abuse when they went out together in public.
Michelle Ross found that people on the streets of Atlantic City stared at
her and her black husband, Jimmy, "with their mouths wide open." Even
in the relatively progressive Greenwich Village of the late 1950s, Hettie

Cohen and LeRoi Jones encountered stares and worse when they went out on the street together. "Hatred," Cohen remembered, lurked "phantomlike in every face except the most familiar, and [could] at any time become overt." Subjected to jeers and catcalls when they went out, Cohen had to learn to control her impulse to fight back. If she said anything, her black husband might be in danger. "People stop and stare and we sail on—what else should we do, fall on our knees and ask their permission? Sometimes I still want to toss my head or stick out my tongue or shriek, 'We are not illegal,' but I have learned and I am learning every day."[44] Hostility could escalate to physical violence, as black Alan Minerbrook and his white girlfriend LaVerne Smith discovered when they were attacked by a gang of white men outside a Chicago movie theater in 1948, the year before they married. Other black male-white female couples reported similar attacks by gangs of angry white men.[45]

Some of the open hostility directed at interracial couples stemmed from the common belief that a woman with a man of another race must be a prostitute. Hazel Byrne Simpkins, the English war bride who married a black American in 1947, quickly learned that both blacks and whites assumed she was a prostitute when they saw her out with her husband. People on the street "freeze up and look us up and down as if we were very cheap," Simpkins recalled. "Not many of them say anything, but their expressions are enough." Black men she met while out with her husband acted like she was "for sale." Another white woman complained that she was "rushed" by black men whenever she was out with her black husband.[46]

Similarly, white men and black women were assumed to be engaged in casual or commercial sexual relationships rather than married. White husbands out with their black wives were sometimes attacked by blacks as interlopers who were sexually exploiting black women. One interracial couple in New York City was repeatedly harassed by blacks who thought they weren't married. Out on the street in 1950, the black wife was hit in the face by a black man who thought she was a prostitute or was involved in a cheap sexual affair. Informed that the couple was married, the assailant reacted in disbelief. This same couple was stopped by a group of young black men who threatened the white husband for being out with a black woman. He avoided a beating by convincing the group that they were married. "Leave him alone," he remembered the ring-leader saying, "he's a regular." For these young black men, at least, it was more acceptable for a white man to marry a black woman than to carry on a sexual relationship with her.[47]

In fact, it is likely that a significant majority of cross-racial relation-ships in the United States in the postwar period were extramarital and illicit. Many blacks and whites who would never consider marrying interracially engaged in some form of illicit interracial sex. Before his conversion to the Nation of Islam, Malcolm Little (later Malcolm X) worked for a madam to arrange meetings for white men who wanted a black woman. For some black men who left the South, having sex with a white woman was a rite of passage, tangible proof that they were in a new place and free to have sex with whomever they wished.[48] It was thus not uncommon for either white or black men to assume that a woman involved in an interracial relationship was sexually available.

City police forces, who were usually overwhelmingly white, also commonly assumed that interracial couples were together for illegal commercial transactions. A Chicago couple, seen by police leaving a the-ater together, were arrested and held for fourteen hours on suspicion that they were a prostitute and pimp. No charges were ever brought against them, and the couple successfully sued for false arrest. In one particularly egregious case, a black woman who went to the police to get help after a white gang beat up her white husband was herself arrested on the grounds that she must be a prostitute. Loretta and Joe Johnson, who mar-ried in 1946, were stopped so frequently by police in San Francisco that they began carrying their marriage license with them wherever they went just in case they needed to prove that they were married.[49]

Police abuse of their public authority sometimes continued long after they determined an interracial couple was married. Elaine and Carl Neil found themselves the victims of a New York City police sting to round up prostitutes in the early 1950s. After they moved into a white neigh-borhood, the police tapped their phone line and then arrested Elaine, who was white, on prostitution charges. Although the case against Elaine was dropped due to a complete lack of evidence, the police quickly fab-ricated other charges, including vagrancy and narcotics possession. Elaine Neil discovered that she was seen by the New York police as a rescue mission; they were going to save her from her interracial marriage, even if they had to accuse her of being a prostitute to do so. After one arrest, the assistant district attorney demanded that Elaine confess that Carl was her pimp, called her a "whore," questioned whether she was really married to "that black bastard," and told her that he was going to "get every nigger that's with a white woman." The police, he explained, were simply trying to rescue Elaine from the life she had chosen. "Take my advice," he told her. "When this whole thing's over, leave Harlem and go back to your family. Carl's going where you can't see him for a long, long time. We're just trying to be helpful and afford you a new start in life." Eventually the Neils threatened to sue the state for false arrest, harassment, and illegal wiretapping, which compelled the police to drop all charges against them.[50]

These egregious forms of persecution were reinforced by other types of discrimination that made daily life difficult for interracial couples. Some who intermarried discovered that their marriages made it harder for them to earn a living. Working-class white women who were married to black men seemed particularly vulnerable to employment discrimination. Many white women feared they would lose their jobs if their marriages were public knowledge, and some of them did.[51] One white woman who had married a black man in Washington, D.C., lost her job after a coworker saw her husband drop her off at work; her employer told her that it was company policy to dismiss anyone who was interracially married. After she found another job, she made sure to keep her marriage a secret out of fear that she would be fired or paid less if it were discovered. A Los Angeles woman was fired after her boss saw her with her black husband at a baseball game. Michelle Ross had a similar experience. She lost several jobs when her bosses discovered that she was part of an interracial couple, information they deduced from her address in a black neighborhood.[52]

Problems at work, however, did not affect all intermarried individuals. Only 14 percent of the forty-six black-white couples who participated in a 1960s Seattle Urban League survey, for example, believed that their marriage had handicapped their attempts to get or keep jobs.[53] In the workplace, individuals in interracial relationships could present themselves as single or could try to hide the fact that their marriage was interracial. There are few instances, moreover, of black women, or of men—white or black—losing jobs because of their interracial marriages, although some encountered disapproval at work. Melvin Jackson's supervisor made it clear that he did not like the fact that Jackson was married to a white woman, but he did not fire the black accountant. White women probably faced greater problems at work because they were less likely than men to be self-employed and were less likely to be employed as professionals, where their skills might grant them some level of protection from discrimination. Women may have had a harder time keeping their personal lives out of the workplace, as coworkers and bosses felt free to ask women workers about their marital status. White women's economic vulnerability might also have reflected white men's particular disgust about their relationships with black men, since most white women worked under white male bosses.

Gender patterns also had some influence on couples' success in finding housing. Black male–white female couples had somewhat less freedom in where to live than white men married to black women. But few interracial couples of the forties and fifties escaped housing discrimination completely. Couples could not easily hide the fact of their interracial marriage when apartment or house hunting, and whites often feared that if an interracial couple moved into a predominantly white neighborhood, property and rental values would fall. Interracial couples, like black couples who sought to move into white neighborhoods, faced resistance and harassment, and their presence sometimes triggered "white flight" out of the neighborhood.[54]

Recognizing the existence of housing discrimination, the white spouse frequently took charge of finding a place to live, hoping his or her white skin would make it easier to secure an apartment. Henry, a white husband in a Boston couple, always went to rent houses and apartments by himself, hoping to sign a lease before the landlord discovered his mixed-race family. When Chuck and Yvonne Cannon went apartment hunting in 1950s San Francisco together, doors were slammed in their faces. Yvonne continued the search on her own, hoping that landlords would not find out that her husband was black. All of these couples discovered, however, that the privileges of the white partner would not necessarily gain or keep them housing. Robert McAllester found many suitable apartments, but they became unavailable once he mentioned his wife's race. "Each time I located a place that was offered to me, I would say casually, 'Of course, you won't mind that my wife is a Negro.' A typical reply was, 'Well, I wouldn't mind, but I'm afraid some of the other tenants would.'" The couple looked for months before Grace was able to rent a small apartment in an all-black apartment complex in a racially mixed neighborhood. The Boston man, Henry, took an apartment, but he and his wife were later evicted for "racial reasons." Chuck and Yvonne Cannon eventually found an apartment, but when the manager discovered that Chuck was black, he raised their rent from $37.50 to $75 a month. They thought about suing, but decided to move instead.[55]

Some interracial couples believed landlords were reluctant to rent to them because they could not accept that interracial couples were really married. Many whites found it hard to believe that another white would marry a black person and willingly enter a relationship certain to bring hardship and downward mobility. Their disbelief also aroused suspicions as to motives or personal character. Doris, a white woman married to a black man in the forties, complained that landlords saw interracial marriage as a "sign of decadence or something."[56] When Elaine and Carl Neil rented an apartment in a predominantly white neighborhood in New York City in the mid-1950s, they were harassed by other residents, even though the building already had some Asian families. Elaine had assumed this seemingly integrated building would tolerate her and her husband. Yet the other tenants were not happy to find a black-white couple in their midst. Soon after the Neils moved in, their neighbors slashed their tires and began sending them hate mail. The landlord accused them of having loud disruptive parties and tried to force them out of the building. The harassment was so emotionally draining that the couple decided to move back to Harlem.[57]

As a result, probably the majority of interracial couples were forced to live in, or on the edges of, black neighborhoods. As a 1955 *Ebony* article pointed out, whites who married blacks frequently found themselves "for the first time denied the right to live in a white neighborhood." The result was that some white partners in interracial couples lived almost exclusively among blacks. The white wife of a black policeman was the only white resident in their apartment building in 1948. Ruth McBride, who was married to black men for most of her adult life, raised her large family in black neighborhoods in New York City. She went to a black church founded by her first husband and socialized with black friends and with his extended family. Sallyann Hobson, a biracial child who grew up in Orange, New Jersey, in the fifties and sixties, remembers living in a black neighborhood where her mother "was the only white woman for blocks." Like McBride, Hobson's mother had been cut off from her own family and community, but was welcomed into her black husband's extended family networks.[58]

White male–black female couples were, in some instances, able to break these boundaries and live quietly in white neighborhoods. The race of the "head" of the family helped determine the acceptability of couples among whites. White men could, to some extent, seek a place for their interracial families outside of black communities. As one study of twenty-two New York couples in the late 1950s found, dwelling areas tended to be "patrilocal." The seven families headed by white men lived in predominantly white neighborhoods, while twelve of the fifteen families headed by black men lived in black or racially mixed neighborhoods. Henry, a white Boston man, and his black wife lived largely among whites. They felt they had encountered few problems because they hadn't tried to become active members of the community and hadn't forced themselves on anyone.[59] Intermarried white men, it seemed, were able to retain more of their status and privileges than intermarried white women.

But gender privilege did not always shield intermarried white men from white hostility. One white husband found that his neighbors went to great lengths to get him and his black wife to leave their white neighborhood. The neighbors refused to talk to the couple, they threw rocks at their windows, and even put sand in the gas tank of their car. White men with black women sometimes felt compelled to live in all-black neighborhoods. Bernette Ford recalls that her Long Island interracial family was "really circumscribed by what society dictated." Perhaps her white father and black mother would have preferred to live in a white neighborhood, but in the 1950s, they couldn't, "at least not comfortably and not without worrying all the time."[60]

As a result of public hostility and job and housing discrimination, many whites, especially white women married to black men, believed that they had little choice but to embrace the black community. As Michelle Ross learned after her 1951 marriage, if she insisted on defying "the stupid dictatorship of the color line," she would be ostracized, able to operate in the white world only if she hid the fact of her marriage. White spouses, especially white wives, often assumed the status of their black partners, becoming "Negroes socially."[61] Many couples reported that their social life changed dramatically after their marriage. Older friendships were discontinued and were "replaced by new contacts, mostly in the Negro community."[62] Some whites were open, even defiant, about their choice to live among blacks. A white Chicago woman who married a black man she'd met as a child on a farm in Alabama declared in 1950, "I have no white friends and don't care." Ruth McBride, the white woman who twice married interracially, explained her decision to build her life among blacks: "I stayed on the black side because that was the only place I could stay. The few problems I had with black folks were nothing compared to the grief white folks dished out."[63]

Contrary to the traditional understanding of interracial marriage as an avenue for assimilation for the minority partner, in many black-white marriages in the forties and fifties, it was the white partner who assimilated into the black community. A black photographer married to a white woman summed up the common pattern in 1955, asserting, "When a colored man marries a white woman, she comes to him. He doesn't go to her."[64] Indeed, stories of violent and abusive interracial marriages frequently involved black men who had hoped to use their marriage as a way to improve their own status in American society but discovered that marrying a white woman did not help them enter white society or achieve greater prestige.[65] In postwar America, the white majority was unwilling to accept blacks as equal citizens, and intermarriage did not help many blacks cross over the deeply rooted racial divide.

Whites who were involved in progressive political or religious communities were best able to resist this "reverse assimilation." Those couples who had met through artistic or political circles often found that their life changed very little after their marriage. Although their immediate families might disapprove, they had already surrounded themselves with supportive friends who shared their political or cultural beliefs.

Such couples were more likely to live in mixed neighborhoods than in the black community and to socialize with white friends. Yvonne and Chuck Cannon felt themselves "insulated and protected" by their like-minded circle of friends, fellow radicals who accepted them and their decision to marry. Most of their friends continued to be progressive whites, and the couple eventually settled in a house on an integrated block in a primarily white neighborhood. Grace and Robert McAllester, the Quakers who met at Earlham College, had a similar experience. They socialized with other young Quaker couples, most of whom were white and who accepted them as members of the Quaker community. Susan Moscou, whose parents were followers of the Communist Party, grew up in a progressive community surrounded by other interracial families. "In my world, all the moms were Black and all the dads were Jewish," she remembers. Her family lived in the "most integrated neighborhood possible" for the 1940s. Their community went beyond their neighborhood to encompass "a rich, culturally diverse society of progressive politics and interracial families." It took her a long time to realize how sheltered her upbringing actually was. In a study of fifty black-white couples in 1950 Philadelphia, the transition to being intermarried was found to be easiest for those couples "who had associations with radical or Bohemian groups before marriage." In their cases, "the marriage brought about no perceptible effect on their social position."[66]

Yet even for couples in progressive communities, the challenge of finding a racial identity and community could be acute, especially once they had children. In the forties and fifties, raising children as biracial was not a realistic option. In a highly racially stratified America, any children who looked black were labeled black. Interracial couples before the 1970s tended to accept that their children, perceived as black, needed to be raised like other black children. As Brunetta Wolfman, a black woman who married a Jewish man, explained, there were simply no other options available for children who looked black. Henry and Violet, the white man and black woman who met in a university political group, felt that there was no question about how to raise their children, since color was something visible. The children are "definitely Negro. We know it and they know it," Henry explained. It was imperative to raise their children as black, Violet added. "They are that not only in the eyes of the world but in their own eyes as well." Other parents raised their children as black out of a sense of necessity or of pride. Jeanne Campbell, a white woman raising her mixed-race daughter on her own, thought it crucial to teach her child that she was black. Her daughter needed a sense of identification with the Negro race, Campbell explained, because she would be far happier if she loved instead of hated "the race with which she is identified by the people with whom she comes in contact." Bernette Ford, the daughter of a black woman and white man who married in 1949, was taught by her proud black mother that she was black. "My mother felt strongly, and my father probably went along with the idea that because she was black, we were black," Ford remembered. The family always lived in black neighborhoods and "we just knew we were black people."[67]

Courts further reinforced this racial identification when interracial couples divorced. The Supreme Court of Washington decided in 1950 that the children of Marylynn Ward and James Ward should be placed in the custody of their black paternal grandmother. Although the court did not doubt that Marylynn, the children's white mother, loved her daughters, it ruled that "both children are colored" and would have a "much better opportunity to take their rightful place in society if they are brought up among their own people." The Cook County Circuit Court in Illinois similarly ruled in 1956 that two biracial children who had the "basic racial characteristics of the Negro race" should be placed in the custody of their black father rather than of their white mother, although this decision was later overturned by the Illinois Appellate Court.[68]

Some couples with light-skinned children considered the possibility that their children might eventually want to "pass" as white. Michelle and Jimmy Ross joked about whether their daughter, Cookie, would be able to pass when she grew older, while another couple decided when their first-born was still a baby that they would be willing to stay in the background if he wanted to pass once he grew up.[69] This attention to passing highlights the inability of couples to conceptualize an identity for their children outside the boundaries of prevailing racial constructions.

Some parents fought the pressure they felt to define their children as black or to encourage them to pass for white, but they had few alternative solutions. Few could easily conceptualize an identity that combined or transcended racial categories. The black father of a little blond child complained that others were pressing him to put his son into one racial group or another rather than leaving him in an ambiguous zone. "Why must David be 'Negro' or 'White,'" he demanded to know. "Why can't he simply be David Evans, Jr.: blond, tall for his age, full of questions, fond of cheese?" On the one hand, this father did not want to lie and teach his son that he was white. On the other hand, he did not want his son to be limited by having an identity as black. He wanted his son to be accepted as an "individual and not on the basis of his race." Yet even this man who insisted on his son's individuality quickly slipped back into traditional racial categories, making clear that his son was black and referring to him as a "blonde Negro." Similarly Lee Chennault, a white woman who was raising her biracial daughter on her own, wanted her daughter to choose to be a "Negro-Caucasian," but at the same time she titled an article about her experiences "How I Face the World With My Negro Child" and focused on what she was teaching her daughter about being "a Negro."[70]

Couples who sought an alternative identity for their children had to invent their own language or assert the insignificance of racial categorization in a world where racial categories ran very deep. Bill and Jeanne Lowe, an interracial couple in California, tried to teach their children to be proud of both sides of their heritage by teaching them that they were "children of the universe." Other parents stressed that people should be viewed as individuals rather than as members of races. As one white mother explained in 1961, she was teaching her daughter to "grow up as a person, thus eliminating the need to choose to be anything." Teaching children that they belonged to no race or that racial identity was unimportant, however, was unrealistic and impractical in preparing children for the outside world. Chuck and Yvonne Cannon raised their children to embrace their complex racial background by stressing the common humanity of all people and tried to teach their children to be humane, kind, and egalitarian. Chuck Cannon now expresses some regrets about their choice, feeling that his children had a "hell of a time" figuring out who they were and often felt inferior to children with two white parents. Biracial children who were brought up in the black community as black, he believed, probably grew up more emotionally secure. Many parents seemed to share the sense that while it was nice to teach young children that every individual was unique and good, mixed-race children eventually needed to be taught "the values of defensive racial solidarity and of race pride" so they could survive outside the safe confines of the family.[71] Racial definitions could perhaps be minimized within the family, but couples knew that racial categories retained great power in the outside world.

These outside pressures and racial boundaries had a negative impact on many interracial marriages. Interracial couples who married in the forties and fifties were more likely to divorce than same-race couples. For first marriages that took place during the 1950s, 90 percent of white couples and 78 percent of black couples were still married in 1970. But only 63 percent of black male–white female and 47 percent of white male–black female couples were.[72] The strain of societal hostility and family disapproval tore many of these couples apart. Edmond Whitfield, who met his white wife while he was a student at Yale University preparing for a career in medicine, could not withstand the social pressure directed at interracial couples. He suffered a nervous breakdown and was committed to a California mental institution in 1949. A black navy officer living in New Jersey was convinced that two years of threatening phone calls had finally led his white wife to leave him, taking their three children with her. Couples attracted to interracial marriage for very different reasons could also have a hard time making a marriage work. Neisha Wright theorized that her parents' early 1960s marriage failed because her mother and father had conflicting motivations: her black father hoped the marriage would make it easier for him to enter into mainstream white culture, while her white mother was interested in cultural rebellion. "My mother became a hippie and my father was trying desperately to assimilate," she recalled. With all of these pressures, it could seem that interracial marriage was doomed to fail, as sociological experts of the time predicted. Rose Warder, who grew up in an interracial family in San Francisco in the early 1950s, remembered that most of the biracial families she knew were divorced. "It's hard for me to say exactly what percentage but I know as a kid, of my contemporaries who were biracial, my family was the only family that was intact." From the perspective of a child, this instability must have been terrifying.[73]

Cognizant of these pressures, many couples thought long and hard before deciding to marry. Sylvia and Marshall Goodwin, educators who married in 1933, believed they had given more thought to their marriage than had many others. "We've paid more attention to solving personal problems than most couples," Sylvia told an interviewer in the 1960s. "In a way, it was more important to us to make sure our marriage succeeded." And as she recalled, isolation from family and community had meant that they had early on learned to turn to and depend on each other. New York couples interviewed in the late fifties generally agreed that outside pressure and skepticism about their marriage had strengthened, rather than weakened, their marital bond. Interracial couples, one black husband remarked, "have no one else to lean on but themselves," while another felt that the lack of support from their immediate families led him and his wife to focus on developing their own family.[74]

Because of the societal opposition they faced, interracial couples in the 1940s and 1950s had a unique vantage point. Living on the color line, they were frequently reminded of the importance of race in American society. Yet their interpersonal relationships helped them see the ways in which racial identity and definitions were superficial, and the threat of violence and ostracism led couples to stress their similarity to same-race couples, rather than their differences from them. Thus when couples spoke publicly about their relationships, most stressed how ordinary and "normal" they were. The effort to present themselves as ordinary served a variety of needs for couples. It probably helped them psychologically by allowing them to downplay the very unordinary treatment they received at the hands of society at large. They also sought to shield their relationships from the extra burdens that others who saw them as crusaders or deviants tried to impose on them. Most important, presenting themselves as legitimate or respectable could perhaps reduce the societal discrimination they faced and diminish the negative stereotypes many whites and blacks held about them.[75]

Couples' claims that they were "ordinary" and just like everyone else came through most clearly in their defense of marriages as acts of love, rather than manifestations of neurotic tendencies or political crusades. Interracial couples presented themselves as living proof that "love conquered all." The vast majority of couples went to great pains to insist that

their marriages were ultimately motivated by, and based on, love. Intermarried white women thus angrily denied that they turned to black men
because of uncontrollable sexual desires. As one white woman married
to a black man complained in 1950, "People always feel a Caucasian
marries a Negro because he's wealthy or sexy. It's always got to be something different. They never figure people are just plain people." Another
complained that people thought she married her black husband "because I am oversexed and only a Negro can satisfy me."[76] Other couples
insisted that they did not marry to further any political project. One
black woman married to a white man insisted in 1952, "Ours is a marriage, period. It is not a sociological experiment." Another young couple
resented that others assumed they were "crusaders" just because they
were interracially married. "We married because we loved each other,
not because we were trying to further any cause," they explained in
1960.[77]

Given the societal opposition they faced and the danger they could
encounter in the outside world, seeking to challenge negative stereotypes
about interracial relationships was an important coping strategy. Couples
emphasized the strength and normalcy of their marriages in their efforts
to change the public discourse about interracial relationships. When Ebony ran a story entitled "The Case against Mixed Marriage," one Los Angeles couple called the article a "gross libel," and insisted that interracial
couples had no major social problems any different from those of any
other couple. "We are nothing spectacular nor side show freaks. We are
just ordinary people, leading an ordinary life, asking no favors and need-
ing none." Another interracially married white woman had a different
reaction to Ebony's regular coverage of interracial marriage, believing that
the magazine's stories would help people understand interracial marriage
more. Such publicity would help people realize that marriages like hers
were "good, sound marriages."[78]

Couples' quest for respectability was reflected in their public behavior
as well. A white Los Angeles woman who married a black man in the
early 1940s argued that interracial couples had to "dress, live, and act
better than others. If we wear bluejeans and they see us walking down
they street, they say, 'Look at that trash.'" In a society where racism was
pervasive, whites tended to project all the negative images held about

blacks as a group onto any mixed couples who entered their white world. Michelle Ross thus felt that if she was not well dressed, people would criticize her black husband more than they would a white man. Another couple explained that they always tried to present themselves in a dignified manner, "because people seem to expect the opposite." The black husband always wore trousers to the corner store instead of jeans; his white wife wore skirts, not slacks, when they went out together. Another couple, a white husband with a black wife, always tried to dress "very well" when they went out "so as to eliminate one source of criticism." One intermarried black woman explained to a reporter that she always kept her house very clean to contradict the stereotype that blacks were naturally sloppy. She also went out of her way to ensure that her biracial children appeared respectable in public. "Our children," she explained, "will have to be neater and more polite than their white playmates. If they aren't, people will say, 'You see, that's what comes of John's marrying a Negro.'"[79]

Couples often avoided public displays of affection, not only because it was dangerous for them to openly express their affection but also because they did not want to give people the wrong idea about their relationship. One black woman married to a white man explained that she disliked when he put his arm around her in public because of the "loose woman connotation." She did not want people to think that they were simply having an affair. Some couples even decided to have children in part to demonstrate the legality of their relationship and their commitment to each other. Children could give a stamp of legitimacy to a relationship that the world viewed as abnormal, deviant, or only sexually motivated. When Elaine and Carl Neil were harassed by their neighbors and arrested by the police as a prostitute and her pimp, they reacted not by ending their marriage but by deciding to have a child. Although Elaine had previously worried about bringing a mixed-race child into the world, after the episode with the police she became convinced that "the natural result of any marriage, the complete consummation of the union, is the flesh and blood proof." Having a baby would prove that theirs was no fly-by-night sexual relationship, but rather one that was permanent, stable, and procreative.[80]

Postwar couples also made clear their concern for normalcy and respectability when they formed their own social organizations. Interracial couples formed a number of clubs in major U.S. metropolitan areas after World War II. Club Internationale, a name chosen to reflect the high number of foreign war brides among its fourteen couple members, was founded by an interracially married black man in Washington, D.C., in 1947. The Club of Tomorrow, formed in Detroit in 1948, consisted of ten black male–white female couples. In Los Angeles, twenty-three mixed couples banded together to form Club Miscegenation soon after the legal ban on interracial marriage in California was overturned in 1948. Primarily social organizations where interracial couples could socialize and share advice, these clubs focused on helping interracial couples demonstrate their respectability. The philosophy of the Club of Tomorrow, as expressed by one of its members, was to show people that "we're not trash, that we're just as capable as anyone else. We intend to start businesses together, buy property. We want to make things easier for the children of mixed couples." Club Miscegenation held its meetings in a Catholic church and had an anti-Communist oath in its constitution, presumably in response to the common assumption that those who married interracially had to be Communists or non-Christians, while the founding members of Club Internationale emphasized that contrary to the connotation of the group's name, "no political implications whatever are intended."[81]

The desire to claim respectability and to present themselves as "normal" may also have helped couples who were trying to hold their marriages together in the face of external hostility. Many couples were aware of the stereotypes about interracial marriage and did not want to fulfill them. Couples spoke of the maturity needed to make an interracial marriage work and warned those who were not completely committed not to try it. As Paul, a black man who married a white woman in the 1940s argued, individuals who married interracially had to be "better than an average person" because "average people don't work hard enough at something to make it succeed where it might otherwise fail." He did not feel that an "ordinary guy" should marry interracially. Some couples even worried about the negative consequences of interracial marriages between immature blacks and whites. "Marriage is for adults, not children," one white man argued. "It is not something to be tested or tried for the thrill or expected excitement." Couples had to enter an interracial marriage with an appropriate and realistic attitude. "A humanitarian attitude—such as the 'look, haven't I done a wonderful thing' feeling—is dangerous because it implies that you're doing your partner a favor," a white woman in a fifteen-year interracial marriage explained. A couple needed "basic training" before undertaking the challenge of a mixed marriage, this woman argued.[82]

These couples in the postwar era challenged their social marginalization by insisting that they were normal, no different from anyone else. Despite the fact that they had transgressed popularly condoned social boundaries, most couples claimed that they were not transgressors. They stressed their similarity to other married couples and positioned themselves within the respectable confines of family, love, and domesticity. By high-lighting the ways in which their marriages were like any other, interracial couples made a radical statement about race in postwar America, challenging the widely accepted belief that race defined people and that the gulf separating blacks and whites was too vast to cross.

Yet whatever their rhetoric, their lives demonstrated the power and inflexibility of the color line in postwar America. Whites who transgressed the color line were largely forced out of white communities and lost the protections against employment and housing discrimination that a white racial identity usually allowed. Although gender privilege allowed white men married to black women some limited immunity from the harshest discrimination, the vast majority of interracial couples were forced to craft their lives among blacks. The unyielding color line limited where they could live, how open they could be about their relationship, and even how they could raise their children.

And even as interracial couples struggled to demonstrate that race mattered little in their private lives, political events of the 1950s showed the power of those who defended the importance of racial distinctions. The 1954 Supreme Court decision in *Brown v. Board of Education,* which threatened segregation laws in the South, pitted those who insisted that preventing interracial marriage was an important public policy objective against a growing number of racial liberals who argued that the issue of interracial marriage should be seen as a private, not political act. *Brown* and its aftermath would make clear how much preserving "racial purity" mattered to many whites.

CULTURE   WARS   AND

SCHOOLHOUSE   DOORS

In 1952 the social psychologist Otto Klineberg appeared on ABC's political events show, *Horizons,* to discuss "The Future of American Race
Relations." A professor at Columbia University, Klineberg had demonstrated that black children's scores on IQ tests improved when they
moved from southern states to New York City. An important member of
a group of scholars who were building the case that living in a segregated
society hurt black children, he would work with the NAACP in its legal
challenge to segregated public education.[1]

Asked on *Horizons* to assess the state of American race relations,
Klineberg was optimistic. As he saw it, World War II had awakened
America's conscience, science and social science had shown that whites
were not innately superior to blacks, outstanding black figures like Jackie
Robinson had changed the attitudes of many whites, and the cold war
made practicing democracy vital to American national security. All of
these signs suggested that America was making steady progress in its
march toward greater racial equality. Indeed, Klineberg's remarks themselves provide some evidence of change. When asked the inevitable
question about the possibility of marriages between blacks and whites,
Klineberg told his 1952 audience that interracial relationships should
be of little public concern. Long regulated or prohibited as a way to uphold the "public good," interracial marriages, Klineberg argued, should

instead be considered personal affairs. Not only would such marriages remain rare in the foreseeable future, but "marriage is a pretty personal matter and ought to be left to personal decision. I would leave it to the individuals themselves of whatever race to decide."[2]

Although the vast majority of whites across the country disapproved of interracial marriage, as revealed in national polls, southern laws, custom outside the South, and the consignment of interracial couples to a life among blacks, the seeds of change that would eventually culminate in increased white tolerance for interracial marriage were planted in the 1950s. The decade's seeming cultural conformity masked the nation's increasing heterogeneity, revealed most dramatically in a youth culture where black and white cultural forms freely mixed. Young whites listened to black artists and went to see films depicting taboo interracial love, such as the 1957 drama *Island in the Sun,* foreshadowing a liberalization of representations of interracial relationships in popular culture. More immediately, racial liberals and southern segregationists engaged in a heated conflict about the role interracial relationships should play in political discussions of the "race problem." While segregationists insisted that any change in the racial status quo would lead to more interracial relationships, influential white liberals in the 1950s, like Klineberg, began to argue that fear of "miscegenation" should not stand in the way of black equality.

Nothing brought this home more clearly than the reaction of southern political leaders to the threat of school desegregation raised by the 1954 Supreme Court decision in *Brown v. Board of Education.* Southern political leaders, and many ordinary white southerners, claimed that the *Brown* decision would lead to an explosion of interracial sex. Although the claim that "miscegenation" would be the inevitable result of racial integration had been part of white southern politics since Emancipation, this reaction was exacerbated in the 1950s by white southerners' fears that they were losing the ability to socialize their own children, because of both potential federal meddling in southern schools and the cultural "miscegenation" of emerging youth culture. White southerners felt besieged by the federal courts, by academics who argued for an environmental understanding of racial difference, and by the music and movies their children were embracing. Fighting to stave off political, legal, and cultural change, they articulated an opposition to integration that would bring the issue of interracial sex and marriage to the forefront of public discussions of race. As a result, proponents of integration increasingly came to understand that they would have to challenge the primacy of sexuality in the political discourse of American racial politics if the nation was ever to move forward in its quest for meaningful racial equality.

If World War II led to the nationalization of the race problem as the country began to discuss segregation and the racial issues that had long concerned the South, the 1950s gave notice that traditional southern practices would not easily withstand the scrutiny of national attention. Intellectuals and northern political elites largely accepted the idea of liberal environmentalism in the wake of World War II, thus denying the existence of significant biological differences between the races. Coupled with a concern about how state-sanctioned racism affected United States foreign policy aspirations during the cold war, these beliefs gave rise to a new paradigm of "color blindness." The color-blind ideology suggested that race should not limit an individual's life opportunities, especially as determined by the state. Government, in short, had no right to treat people differently because of their race, which is exactly what the web of Jim Crow laws in the South did. By the 1950s, these ideas had found important supporters in the federal courts, as the ruling in *Brown v. Board of Education* made clear.

When the Supreme Court announced its ruling in the *Brown* case in 1954, it crowned an intense legal struggle against Jim Crow segregation and marked the beginning of the end of federal acquiescence in state-sanctioned racial discrimination. Decades of hard work by the NAACP had highlighted the impossibility of achieving true equality in segregated schools. America's claim to leadership of the "free world" in an ideological battle with the Soviet Union made dealing with the race problem perhaps more important than ever before. The federal government felt impelled to show the world that the United States could practice what it preached about democracy and equality, and the Truman administration pushed the Supreme Court to rule that segregation in public education was unconstitutional.[3] On May 17, 1954, the Supreme Court embraced the understandings of race that had become popular among academics and racial liberals in the postwar period. Speaking for a unanimous court, Chief Justice Earl Warren declared that "in the field of public education the doctrine of 'separate but equal' has no place. Separate educational facilities are inherently unequal."[4] Segregation in schools, the court held, injured and stigmatized black children and denied them the ability to live up to their true potential. In one stroke, the Supreme Court deprived segregation of its moral and political legitimacy and gave legal support to the ideology of color blindness by stressing the ideal that race should not limit an individual's ability to succeed in American society.

The *Brown* decision exploded throughout the South. Although many southern communities prepared to voluntarily submit to the court ruling immediately after the decision, southern moderation quickly disappeared as those committed to maintaining the status quo organized and mobilized people's passions and fears. Politicians campaigned for office by stressing their unswerving commitment to uphold segregation and their willingness to challenge the authority of the federal courts and the federal government in order to preserve the southern "way of life."[5] *Brown* came to represent change imposed from the outside, insensitive to southern culture and traditions. Initial caution about the need to follow the rule of law soon gave way to an organized battle to maintain segregation, one mounted in part on the grounds of states' rights, as southerners charged that the federal government violated state sovereignty by interfering in the province of education. But the battle was also undertaken on a more emotional terrain, as an editorial in the *Daily News* of Jackson, Mississippi, from the day after the decision makes clear, "White and Negro children in the same schools will lead to miscegenation. Miscegenation leads to mixed marriages and mixed marriages lead to mongrelization of the human race."[6]

Since the emergence of the black rapist myth in the nineteenth-century South, sexuality had played a crucial role in southern racial politics. As Gunnar Myrdal argued in *An American Dilemma,* sex was the principle "around which the whole structure of segregation of the Negroes" was organized. "No excuse for other forms of social segregation and discrimination is so potent as the one that sociable relations on an equal basis between members of the two races may possibly lead to intermarriage."[7]

The social order of segregation was described as necessary to preserve a particular sexual order in which blacks and whites did not mix or marry. Inevitably, any attack on that social order led to fears of sexual chaos that would threaten the survival of the white race. While Myrdal described southern fears of interracial sex as a rationalization for defending segregation, the response to the *Brown* decision suggests that many whites saw a very real possibility of racial mixing if schools were desegregated.

The *Jackson Daily News* editorial demonstrated the rhetorical battle that southern leaders would pitch to defend segregation. In public forums from speeches to newspaper editorials, southern political elites played on whites' fears of interracial relationships to attack the decision, arguing that desegregation of the schools would inevitably lead to "amalgamation" of the races. Mississippi senator James Eastland, a key architect of the massive resistance movement, told Congress ten days after the *Brown* decision that America's greatness depended upon "racial purity and maintenance of Anglo-Saxon institutions." In Louisiana, state senator William Rainach argued that the ultimate goal of those supporting integration was "extinction of both the white and black races into a shade of brown," while Mississippi congressman Edwin White expressed his view in the *New York Times* that the true reason the South resisted integration was because southerners sought to "preserve the racial integrity of its people."[8]

Just a few weeks after the *Brown* decision, Mississippi judge Tom Brady published *Black Monday,* a handbook for segregationists. It would take an army of "one hundred million men" to compel school desegregation, Brady warned integrationists. "You shall not mongrelize our children and grandchildren! . . . Whenever and wherever the white man has drunk the cup of black hemlock, whenever and wherever his blood has been infused with the blood of the negro, the white man, his intellect and his culture have died." *Black Monday* became a bestseller in the South. In 1956 the Mississippi House chose *Black Monday* as one of the books it required the State Library Commission to buy for public libraries. Seven years later, Brady was appointed to the Mississippi Supreme Court, a hero to many southerners who believed themselves to be victimized by northern liberals and black activists.[9]

The many organizations that led the fight against the *Brown* decision also used the rhetoric of mixed blood and the decline of the white race in order to prop up the besieged segregation laws. Hundreds of thousands of southern whites, from the elite to the working poor, joined organizations like the Citizens' Councils, the Ku Klux Klan, and the National States' Rights Party, which used demonstrations, pamphlets, and newspapers to wage an ideological and rhetorical war against integration on the basis of defending white racial purity.[10] Thus a 1957 full-page newspaper ad, paid for by the Montgomery Citizens' Council, noted, "There are only two sides in the Southern fight. [T]hose who want to maintain the Southern way of life and those who want to mix the races."[11]

These organizations and their leaders argued that the attack on segregated schools was a conspiracy led by those who wanted to mix the races and undermine whites' racial integrity. They characterized the NAACP as an outsider group bent on "mongrelizing" the South. Alabama state senator Walter Givhan luridly described the NAACP's goal in 1955 as opening "the bedroom doors of our white women to the Negro man." The American Nationalists, a hate group based in California, distributed postcards in the South with suggestive pictures of black men with white women, claiming that these represented "the ultimate goal toward which the National Association for the Advancement of Colored People and every other professional race-mixing organization is striving."[12] Segregationist publications were quick to remind their readers that NAACP executive secretary Walter White had married a white woman, and they pointed to stories about interracial couples in *Ebony* and *Jet* to demonstrate that "what the negroes really want is complete and unequivocal integration and equality, not only with reference to opportunity, but with regard to sex and inter-marriage."[13]

Segregationist groups saw in integration not only a conspiracy by black elites who, as one newspaper charged, were all mulattoes who wanted everyone to look like them, but a much more dastardly plot by America's sworn enemies, the Communists, to undermine the country's strength and vitality. Leander Perez, the district attorney and political boss of Louisiana's Plaquemines Parish who spearheaded resistance to integration in Louisiana, attacked *Brown* as a Communist plot to mix the races. As he saw it, the Communists sought to use the Supreme Court

THE WHITE SENTINEL

THE TRUTH THAT SHOULD BE PRINTED

OFFICIAL ORGAN OF THE NATIONAL CITIZENS PROTECTIVE ASSOCIATION

JOHN W. HAMILTON, Editor   HELEN M. WOLF, Associate Editor

P. O. BOX 156 ST. LOUIS 3, MO.

Subscription $2.00 per year

Vol. IV No. 7   *Racial Integrity - Not Amalgamation*   July, 1954

COMMUNISM'S SECRET WEAPON - THE MONGRELIZATION OF THE WHITE RACE

NEGROES ATTEMPT TO INVADE MEMPHIS STATE COLLEGE

Encouraged by the Supreme Court, a gang of blacks accompanied by an NAACP lawyer, sought to force their way into Memphis State College. When denied admittance, they threatened legal action. As they left the premises, onlookers heard one negro remark, "We'll take this place over soon."

THEY WENT TO SCHOOL TOGETHER AND THEN MARRIED

The disgusting picture is of William Vargus and his negress bride examining their wedding gifts shortly after their marriage in Medford, Mass. They "fell in love" while at Tufts College. The wedding was performed by Dean Eugene Ashton (Universalist) of Tuft's School of Religion and was attended by a large number of negroes and a few curious Whites.

LET ELEANOR GO TO SCHOOL WITH THEM

Eleanor's kids never went to school with negroes. They went to private schools. Yet, she is leading the fight for race-mixed schools. Last month she was escorted to Haile Selassie's shindig at the Waldorf Astoria by negro Adam Powell who is leading an anti-Catholic campaign in Harlem. It's all right with Eleanor to hate Catholics if you love negroes.

RACE-MIXING IN LOS ANGELES In a demonstration of contempt for the White Race L. A. City College crowned a black buck as "King" and gave him a White girl for his "Queen." Shown above are "Queen" Barbara Lee Cooke and her negro "King" being crowned by Dr. Howard S. McDonald of City College and Kim Novak, would-be actress. This is what race-mixing in school leads to.

The White Sentinel, like other segregationist publications, claimed that racial integration was a secret Communist plot to undermine American racial purity and strength. The newspaper used photos and stories printed in *Ebony* magazine to make its case about the dangers of "race-mixing" in schools. (General Research Division, The New York Public Library, Astor, Lenox and Tilden Foundations.)

to destroy the public school system and ultimately white civilization. "What would lead to the more certain destruction of our country than a mongrelized race?" Perez asked. "How much resistance do you think would be offered to the Communists by a mongrelized race?" *The White Sentinel,* a white supremacist newspaper published out of St. Louis, called the mongrelization of the white race "communism's secret weapon," while Robert Shelton, the Imperial Wizard of the Ku Klux Klan in the 1950s, declared that "amalgamation is ultimately the goal of the Communist element . . . because it would destroy the morals of the people."[14]

In labeling *Brown* a Communist plot to weaken America through racial amalgamation, segregationists directly challenged the prevailing view that winning the cold war demanded that the United States take steps to live up to its rhetoric of freedom and democracy, instead insisting that desegregation would ultimately hurt the United States. Georgia senator Herman Talmadge argued that the lessons of history proved that "nations composed of a mongrel race lose their strength and become weak, lazy and indifferent. They become easy preys to outside nations." Federal efforts to undermine southern tradition through court orders would lead America down the path of authoritarianism and totalitarianism. To Robert Patterson, the executive secretary of the Association of the Citizens' Councils of America, integration represented "regimentation, totalitarianism, communism and destruction," while segregation meant "Americanism, state sovereignty, and the survival of the white race."[15] Only states' control over their own schools—state sovereignty—could ensure that white southerners were not forced to interact with blacks in ways that could lead to race mixing.

In the tense years following *Brown,* those who opposed school desegregation made the most of any evidence they could find that the end result of integration was intermarriage. *The White Sentinel,* for example, reprinted an *Ebony* story on interracial marriages at colleges, noting that the story demonstrated "that where there is integration the inevitable result will be mongrelization."[16] When anyone working against segregation admitted that there might be a connection between integration and intermarriage, segregationist politicians seized on the remarks as proof that the ultimate goal of *Brown* was to desegregate the bedroom. An offhand remark by Albert Kennedy, the legal counsel of the South Carolina branch of the NAACP, that intermarriage would be the "natural consequence" once the two races were integrated, provided fodder to segregationists for years, cited in speeches by Georgia attorney general Eugene Cook, repeated at Citizens' Councils rallies, and quoted in the segregationist press.[17]

When the court-ordered integration of a southern school actually led to an intermarriage, segregationists advertised it with a combination of glee and dismay. Such was the case when, in 1963, Charlayne Hunter, one of the first two black students to desegregate the University of Georgia, married Walter Stovall, a white student she met there. Here was a concrete example of the relationship between integration and amalgamation: a black student, admitted to a formerly all-white institution by a federal court order, who "inevitably" ended up with a white spouse. Secretly married in the spring of their senior year, Hunter and Stovall were, in their own words, "every segregationist's nightmare," choosing to live together as husband and wife rather than as concubine and master.[18] When, having left the state, they publicly revealed their marriage the September after their graduation, white southerners expressed disapproval tinged with a sense of disbelief as they tried to understand what could have led Stovall, the son of a prosperous Georgia chicken-feed manufacturer, to turn his back on his heritage. His parents called it "the end of the world," and their neighbors dropped by to offer their condolences. Townspeople wondered what had changed Stovall, who had won his high school's Citizenship Award, had been president of a popular youth club, and had made the all-state football team. According to one neighbor, Walter was "a right good boy when he was here, but after high school he went a little haywire." State officials were just as upset. Officials at the university reported that they were "greatly surprised and shocked" and reassured the public that the couple would have been dismissed from school if their marriage had been public. Georgia's attorney general explained that Hunter and Stovall were not married under Georgia law and would be prosecuted under the state's antimiscegenation statute if they returned. The governor described the marriage as "a shame and a disgrace."[19] Hunter and Stovall's marriage provided concrete evidence of the dangers of integration as segregationists saw it. As an article in *The Citizen* pointed out, this case suggested that "a propensity to mix may be greater than we have hitherto imagined."[20]

Although southern political leaders and the organizations formed expressly to fight integration articulated these concerns most vehemently, their fears were shared by other southern whites, from intellectuals to the general public. South Carolinian Herbert Ravenal Sass, a prolific nonfiction writer, explained that nearly all white southerners believed that the integration of the schools "would open the gates to miscegenation and widespread racial amalgamation" in a 1956 *Atlantic Monthly* article. Church groups echoed these concerns. The Missionary Baptist Association of Texas, which included some three hundred churches, argued that desegregation would "inevitably lead into a hybrid monstrosity that would defy the word and will of God," while members of a Baptist church in Sumter, South Carolina, declared their love for the Negro but their opposition "to amalgamation of the races, to which integration inevitably leads."[21]

The breadth of this "anti-amalgamation" discourse was made clear whenever integration of a school became a realistic possibility. When nine black students attempted to enter Central High School in Little Rock, Arkansas, in 1957, a member of the mob standing outside the school explained that Little Rock whites wouldn't "stand for our schools being integrated. If we let 'em in, next thing they'll be marrying our daughters." Much the same thing was said to Melba Patillo, one of the Little Rock Nine, by an older woman inside the school on that first day. "Nigger bitch," the older woman yelled as she spit in Melba's face, "Why don't you go home? . . . Next thing, you'll want to marry one of our children." Patillo recalled her surprise at the remark. At fifteen, she wasn't even allowed to date yet, and she couldn't imagine why anyone would think she would ever want to marry one of those nasty white people at the high school.[22]

When a foreign reporter arranged a meeting between segregationist students and some of the Little Rock Nine several weeks later, the concern about intermarriage surfaced again. Asked why the white students at Central objected to the presence of the nine black students, a white student leader replied it was because of fear of race mixing, that blacks and whites might marry each other. Ernest Green, one of the black students, protested that "school's not a marriage bureau," adding that he was there for an education, not to find a spouse. Nevertheless, the fear that even this token level of integration would somehow end in intermarriage remained.[23]

The fact that all southern states had laws prohibiting interracial marriage, and that both black and white supporters of integration seemed willing to allow those laws to continue unchallenged, did little to halt the uproar over *Brown*. Just weeks after the decision was handed down, Walter White told *U.S. News and World Report* that the NAACP had no interest in formally challenging antimiscegenation laws.[24] White liberals, meanwhile, attacked a controversial article in *Dissent* by Hannah Arendt about the desegregation crisis in Little Rock. Arendt, a refugee scholar from Nazi Germany, had doubts about the wisdom of forced school integration, which she believed placed the burden of change on children. She argued instead that antimiscegenation laws should be attacked first, since the right to marry was a basic human right "compared to which 'the right to attend an integrated school, the right to sit where one pleases on a bus, the right to go into any hotel or recreation area or place of amusement, regardless of one's skin or color or race' are minor indeed." *Dissent* prefaced the article with a disclaimer and accompanied it with two critical commentaries, one of which suggested that it was well within the power of states to prohibit interracial relationships. This defense of antimiscegenation laws was motivated by political pragmatism. David Spitz argued in his critique of Arendt's piece that southerners would come to accept school desegregation only if they were convinced that integration would not hasten intermarriages. There was, he felt, "no surer way to prevent acceptance of the principle of equal educational opportunity for the Negro in the South than to push the issue of miscegenation into the forefront at this time."[25]

Arendt's position, while certainly principled and probably legally sound, was not politically viable. At a time when southern states were defying both the Supreme Court ruling in *Brown* and the federal government's authority over them, a ruling invalidating antimiscegenation laws would have intensified southern resistance. The Supreme Court seemed to sense this, and the Justices were careful through their actions to reassure southern states that antimiscegenation laws would remain safe for some time to come.

The Supreme Court had been very concerned about how southerners would react to *Brown*. Chief Justice Earl Warren insisted that the decision be unanimous in order to present a united front. The Court also sought to soften opposition to the decision by ruling that desegregation could be gradual rather than immediate. Southern resistance to *Brown,* the justices recognized, could set off a crisis like the one that preceded the Civil War, when certain states declared themselves not subject to federal law. As Tom Clark, one of the two southern Justices on the Court, noted, "We don't have money at the Court for an army and we can't take ads in the newspapers. We have to convince the nation by the force of our opinions."[26] A difficult task already, convincing the South to follow federal law would have been even harder had the Court showed any interest in antimiscegenation laws. Instead, the Court went out of its way to avoid ruling on the constitutionality of antimiscegenation statutes in the years immediately after *Brown,* refusing to review both a 1954 Alabama case and a 1955 Virginia case that challenged their legitimacy.[27] Philip Elman, a former clerk to Supreme Court Justice Felix Frankfurter and the lawyer in the U.S. solicitor general's office who wrote the federal government brief in the *Brown* case, later claimed that "the last thing in the world the Justices wanted to deal with at that time was the question of interracial marriage." They wanted to "duck it. And if the Supreme Court wants to duck, nothing can stop it from ducking." As one Justice at the time supposedly remarked, "One bombshell at a time is enough."[28]

This seeming willingness to ignore laws prohibiting interracial marriage, at least temporarily, reassured few white southerners, who saw *Brown* as a direct attack on their ability to socialize their children as they chose. Of all the forms of segregation that the Supreme Court could have invalidated in the 1950s, probably the most threatening to southerners was that of public education. Segregated public schools socialized white and black children to a racially segregated social order. Black children, whose schools were dilapidated and underfunded, understood that they were considered inferior and less worthy of education than whites; white students, meanwhile, learned that whites deserved a superior education because of their race and that they must keep a proper social distance from blacks. One supporter of segregation explained in 1960, "There is a definite and deliberate relationship between a given culture and educational patterns aimed at perpetuating that culture."[29] If southern culture was based on racial segregation, then it was the job of the schools to reproduce that culture on a smaller scale.

Schools were social institutions, the site of many students' social lives. Not surprisingly, parents worried that white children who attended desegregated schools would also be forced to interact with blacks outside the classroom. This was a key concern of white parents in Little Rock, Arkansas, when plans were being made to desegregate the high school there in 1955. If the schools were desegregated, where would race mixing stop, parents asked the superintendent. Would black children be allowed to attend school dances "or would discrimination be permitted here?" Would black children go on the out-of-town school field trips? Would black and white students share the same bathrooms? What about drama classes? Would romantic parts be assigned without reference to race, "or would discrimination be permitted in this situation?"[30] The superintendent of the school system, Vergil Blossom, assured concerned parents that any social functions that involved race mixing would not be held. Social affairs, he admitted, would need to be drastically curtailed or even eliminated in integrated schools, but, he reasoned, "Many present schools would be better off with less emphasis on social affairs and more emphasis on education."[31]

These parents' questions acknowledged that schools were more than academic institutions. They were the place where children spent the greatest part of each weekday. High schools, as much as they might be instruments of socialization, were also age-segregated institutions that provided adolescents a forum for the development and transmission of a peer culture and a space where they could act independently of their parents' control. Integrated schools, one letter in the *Greensboro Daily News* complained in 1954, would bring black and white children together "discussing the real life needs of children and the problems of high school youth, such as the problem of developing and maintaining acceptable boy-girl relationships, including dating, dancing, playing and entertaining on a general scale." Social activities were an inherent part of the "modern school routine," and students at integrated schools would inevitably have to socialize together. *The White Sentinel* also emphasized how normal school activities would inevitably lead to "race mixing" in integrated schools. The October 1954 issue ran a picture of the homecoming king and queen at Central High in St. Paul, Minnesota. The queen was a sixteen-year-old white student; the king was a black student. "This picture is a sample of what the 'integrationists' plan for your daughter whether you like it or not," the *Sentinel* warned. "Mixed schools lead to mixed sex." The Savannah-Chatham County Board of Education filed a court case to reverse *Brown* on the grounds that free social contact between the races would "create special social problems that immature school children are not equipped to handle in the prevailing social climate such as interracial social intercourse, interracial dating, interracial dancing, etc." If such activities were cut back in order to prevent interracial socializing, the suit contended, all of the children would be denied the opportunity to mature socially in a healthy way.[32]

Supporters of desegregation were quick to point out that such arguments implied that white boys and girls in the South would find blacks so attractive they would be unable to resist them. After all, no one could force someone else to marry them, so any marriages that occurred would have to involve a willing white. Only an "overwhelming physical attraction between the races" could account for all of the efforts that went into keeping them apart, a *New York Post* columnist argued in 1956. The black lawyer and writer Pauli Murray claimed that the South's fears implied that the white race was "so lacking in self-restraint it will commit suicide unless the Negroes of the South are continually oppressed and kept in an inferior position," while *Pittsburgh Courier* columnist Joel Rogers found whites' fear of intermarriage laughable; the only plausible psychological explanation for these worries about school integration was that segregationists knew their children would be attracted to blacks, much like they probably were themselves.[33]

Some southerners insisted that their main concern was that black boys, emboldened by desegregation, would attack unwilling white girls. Drawing on stereotypical assumptions about black men's supposedly uncontrollable sexual appetites, Judge Tom Brady claimed in *Black Monday* that integration would lead arrogant black men to "perform an obscene act, or make an obscene remark, or a vile overture or assault upon some white girl." Leander Perez argued in New Orleans that the black man "is not too far removed from the jungle in his morals, and . . . he wants that white woman." School desegregation would lead to a rash of brutal "Congo style" rapes, Perez contended.[34]

With the southern system of segregation under attack, the slightest provocation by a black male was met with brutal repression, as in the tragic lynching of fourteen-year-old Emmett Till for allegedly whistling at a white woman in Mississippi. In Monroe Country, North Carolina, in 1958, two young black boys, aged eight and ten, were sent to a state reformatory after kissing a seven-year-old white girl on the cheek. Charged with assaulting a white female, the two boys were held incommunicado in a county jail cell for six days while the police went out of their way to frighten them. The judge who sentenced the boys thought he was being merciful; before the reformatory was built, "Negro boys like these might have had to go in the chain gang," he explained. The Committee to Combat Racial Injustice, a group formed in New York City to help secure the release of the boys, saw the overreaction to this juvenile case as "part of the pattern of vindictiveness against the Negroes of Monroe because of their stand on desegregation issues and their defiance of the Klan."[35] White southerners felt their way of life was under attack and their deepest fears and anxieties surfaced. They were certain that black men would become "uppity" with white women as a result of desegregation.

Yet southern parents were ultimately more concerned that white students in integrated schools would be taught that the races were equal, and thus would not understand the importance of racial distinctions. This "miseducation," as segregationists described it, would counter the inherent instinct of "race preference" and would undermine whites' instinctual propensity not to marry across the color line. Children in integrated schools "would be indoctrinated with that alien theory from the first grade up, that there is really only one race and that is the human race; that each child or adult is as good as any other child or adult," one Greensboro man predicted. The NAACP targeted southern schools precisely because it knew the students' young minds were vulnerable, Herbert Ravenal Sass insisted in 1956. The "nearly universal instinct" of race preference, he argued, was not active in the very young, and "could be prevented from developing at all." White southerners educated in mixed schools would not find the idea of interracial marriage repugnant, Sass claimed. "A very few years of thoroughly integrated schools would produce large numbers of indoctrinated young Southerners free from all 'prejudice' against mixed marriage."[36]

It was not merely physical proximity that would stifle whites' natural race instinct, but also the ideas that southerners argued would be taught in racially integrated schools. Segregationists railed against what they perceived as a new ideological climate, one where the ideas of "tolerance" and the "brotherhood of man" were more legitimate than those of "white purity" or "racial preference." The head of the Citizens' Councils of America complained in 1954 that Americans had been subjected since the 1930s "to a relentless propaganda campaign of press, screen, radio and pulpit" that told them segregation was "unamerican" and "immoral"; this "equalitarian dogma" could lead nowhere but to more interracial marriages. William Workman, Jr., a southern journalist who sought to defend the anti-integration position in his 1960 book *The Case for the South,* saw in a handbook on intergroup education by the National Education Association (NEA) evidence of a disturbing focus on tolerance, diversity, and equality. The guide, he argued, attacked "old-fashioned ideas" like "racial purity, natural affinity of like-minded and like-cultured individuals, and parental concern over children's associations." The NEA wanted to mix together all people "to an even textured blend devoid of distinctive color, culture, or flavor." In the wake of *Brown,* textbooks in the South were examined and discontinued if they seemed to preach ideals of human equality. Thus the Morehouse-Parish School Board in Louisiana voted to discontinue use of its ninth-grade science textbook because it declared that all men on earth belonged to the same species, which was defined as a group of living things that have similar physical traits and could "breed freely with each other."[37]

Even children's books seemed intent on undermining children's "natural race preference." The 1958 children's book, *The Rabbit's Wedding,* which depicted the marriage of a white rabbit and black rabbit, was vehemently attacked by segregationists as a liberal attempt to sell race mixing to young children. The author, Garth Williams, denied that the book had any political significance, but the *Montgomery Home News,* a publication of the Montgomery White Citizens' Council, attacked it as integrationist propaganda "obviously aimed at children in the formative years of three to seven." Alabama state senator E. O. Eddins demanded the book be removed from library shelves and burned, while popular *Orlando Sentinel* columnist Henry Balch denounced *The Rabbit's Wedding* as the "most amazing evidence of brainwashing" designed to condition young southern minds to accept the idea of integration. "As soon as you pick up the book, you realize these rabbits are integrated." In Alabama, the book was withdrawn from the open shelves of the Alabama Public Library Service Division and placed on the reserve shelves where public libraries could gain access to it only by special request.[38] Although this reaction might seem "incredible," as *Time* magazine described it, one South Carolina reader insisted it was reasonable. "I know, and you should know," he wrote *Time,* "that this book is readily adaptable to planting in the mind of a child receptiveness to the idea of marriage between white and black human beings."[39]

The uproar over *A Rabbit's Wedding* reflected a fear that young children would be particularly vulnerable to the effects of integration. In some southern locales, school systems integrated the upper grades first, because they feared too much resistance if young white children were forced to attend school with blacks. One Mississippi white man explained that he was in favor of integration on the college level, but not in elementary schools, since if young white children went to school with black children, it would be more difficult to instill in them the value of racial purity. Teenagers, parents hoped, would have already developed such values. Thus when Superintendent Vergil Blossom in Little Rock planned to start desegregation with incoming first-grade students, parental opposition led him to propose desegregation of the high school first.[40]

Segregationist propaganda graphically depicted what the inevitable result of integrated education would be. Young whites, sent to integrated schools and bombarded with cultural forces that seemed to sanction "miscegenation," would turn against their better instincts and become involved with blacks. The ultra-segregationist *White Sentinel* harped on this theme. A picture of a young white girl playing on a beach with a black toddler ran above a caption accusing the girl's parents of teaching their daughter to "integrate" in her "tender, most impressionable years" before she knew the difference between right and wrong. If she eventually came home with a black baby, who would be to blame, the *White Sentinel* asked. "No venomous serpent that lurks in the deepest jungle is as dangerous to this beautiful little girl as the fate which her parents are exposing her to." In another case, the *Sentinel* argued that white girls who flocked around black teenage star Louis Gossett, Jr., in a New York City high school could not be held responsible for their actions. "Their immature minds have been corrupted and perverted by the preachers, teachers, politicians and others who advocate mongrelization."[41] Forced to attend integrated schools and social functions, their heads constantly filled with the propaganda of brotherhood, racial equality, and tolerance, these poor girls knew no better than to compromise "White Womanhood" by socializing with blacks. The American Nationalists distributed postcards during the Little Rock desegregation crisis in 1956 that argued that the real criminals were not the young people who intermarried, but the school teachers and clergy who taught America's youth that racial tolerance was moral and that the races were equal. If you teach your children that segregation and racial pride are wrong, how can they be expected to believe that intermarriage is wrong, one handout asked. "Educate them together . . . let them play together . . . send them to church together . . . and the result is inevitable."[42]

Segregationist organizations presented dramatic parables and cautionary tales about the consequences of school integration. The Atlanta branch of the Ku Klux Klan staged one such morality tale at a 1961 rally. It began with a young white boy in blackface walking across the stage, holding hands with a white girl. The narrator informed the rapt audience that this was only the beginning of the story, telling them, "Oh no, these two will grow up and then here's what you'll be seeing in the schools of this great state." The couple reentered, now in their teens, the boy with his arm around the girl's waist. Soon a minister appeared and the three pantomimed a marriage ceremony. But this was not the end of the story, the narrator warned the audience. "Because if we don't do something, here's the kind of thing you're going to be looking at." Now the girl reappeared with her head bowed, being led roughly across the stage by the young man in blackface. Behind the couple were three children, all in blackface. This progression was seemingly inevitable: young

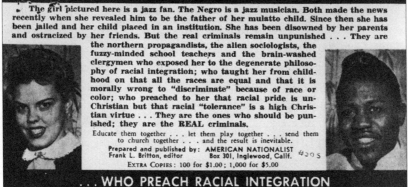

Postcards like this one, distributed in Little Rock, Arkansas, in 1956, claimed that teaching racial equality would lead innocent young whites to lose their "natural instinct" for race preference. (Wisconsin Historical Society, WHi3325.)

naive white children—usually girls—forced to go to school with blacks would end up dating them as teenagers, which would lead to marriage, and finally, to the birth of mixed-race children. A poem that appeared in a 1961 segregationist religious journal graphically portrayed the grief young white women would endure if they chose the wrong path: "When a white girl marries a negro / Her sun of life goes down, And glaring spots of sin appear on her / White wedding gown." The woman in the poem begins to have regrets within days of her marriage, but by then she is pregnant. When she gives birth to a biracial child, she can only look at it with "tear-stained eyes" and hang "her head with shame": "I sold my birthright for a mess / I mixed my white-born blood / With black blood, so I languish here like / One bogged down in mud." Once the child was born, even leaving her black husband could not erase her shame since her "mis-spent life" would follow like "footprints in the snow." The only way out, she concluded, was death.[43]

Such rhetoric reflected both the belief that women held the responsibility for maintaining white racial purity and the sexual stereotypes that girls were naive and easily manipulated. Girls, more than boys, needed the protection of mature adults who would teach them the truth about race mixing and help them stay on the right racial path. In the face of the

betrayal of the public school system, the segregationist press implored
parents to take responsibility for preventing racial mixing, goading them
to become more active in fighting integration. A 1955 article in *The
White Sentinel* blamed interracial relationships not only on "integrationists" who were pushing "negroized" public schools but also on "the parents and all other self-respecting White adults" who were "guilty of
sitting idly by and allowing this to happen. Our sins of omission are coming home to roost." A lengthy description of the steps from integrated
schools to intermarriage in *The Virginian* ended with the admonition, "It
will come to this and it could happen in your own family. . . . What color
will your grandchildren be!"[44]

Such rhetoric also reflected the more sweeping fear that parents were
losing control of their children to an increasingly foreign youth culture and to mass media's ever-expanding reach. The *Brown* decision was
handed down at a time when American adults were growing more and
more concerned about a gap between them and their children, an era
when teenagers established themselves as an independent group with
their own culture, different from that of both children and adults. Ironically, the fight to maintain the "southern way of life" took place at a
time when black culture was assuming greater visibility in American
daily life. Young whites in the segregated South were already listening to
music their parents did not approve of, rock 'n' roll clearly based on black
musical forms that reflected a new cultural mixing, a coming together of
white and black cultures. In 1955, the year after *Brown,* black and white
artists began to have crossover success, finding listeners among both
blacks and whites. Bill Haley's hit *Shake, Rattle and Roll* rose to number
one on the white pop chart and number four on the black rhythm and
blues chart. Chuck Berry had similar success with his song, *Maybellene,*
which went to number one on the rhythm and blues chart and number
five on the pop chart.[45] The panic over school integration stemmed
at least in part from fears that this increasing "cultural miscegenation"
would corrupt white youth. As one White Citizens' Council flyer read,
"Help save the Youth of America—DON'T BUY NEGRO RECORDS." The
"screaming, idiotic words, and savage music" of black records were undermining the morals of young whites.[46]

Although concerns about new music abounded, it was Hollywood that earned the most contempt from segregationists for its attempt to "sell" the idea of interracial love. Segregationist publications pointed to films such as *Love Is a Many Splendored Thing*, which depicted the love affair of a half-Asian, half-European woman and a white American journalist. Through films like these, Hollywood could plant the idea of interracial love in the minds of the young, who would have few means to resist since they were already being taught in "progressive schools" that racial differences didn't matter. Although a single movie might not seem important, "this is all part of a pattern, an organized campaign," a 1955 article in *The Virginian* explained: "Each radio or television program, each movie, each novel or story which encourages interracial love and marriage is just one more well-oiled cog in the smoothly-coordinated machine which works unceasingly toward the inevitable goal; total amalgamation of the races."[47]

From 1934 on, production codes had barred the depiction of romantic relationships between blacks and whites. Film companies belonging to the Motion Picture Producers and Distributors Association agreed not to release any film until it received a certificate of approval from the Production Code Administration. These codes, developed by the Catholic Legion of Decency, forbade the depiction of a wide variety of acts considered immoral, including homosexuality, incest, abortion, drug addiction, suicide, and interracial intimacy. The 1949 film *Pinky*, for example, could show embraces between the light-skinned Pinky and her white fiancé only because the character of Pinky was played by a white actress. But by the 1950s, the codes had begun to crumble. Confronted with a rapidly declining audience stemming from the advent of television (movie attendance was down 50 percent between 1946 and 1960), movie studios sought to liberalize the code to draw in viewers. Shifts in the studio system gave local theaters more choice in deciding which films to show, and the emergence of drive-in theaters led producers to make films targeting the increasingly important adolescent audience.[48]

At the same time, local censorship of motion pictures came under attack in the courts. On the grounds that the film industry was more a business than a medium for the communication of ideas, the Supreme

Court had long upheld the right of localities to censor and prevent the showing of "objectionable" films. In the early 1950s, however, the Court decided that the film industry deserved some First Amendment freedom-of-speech protections, and soon a flurry of rulings limited the power of local censors. This would have an immediate impact on films dealing with controversial subjects such as interracial love. When the local board of censors in Marshall, Texas, denied theater owners permission to show *Pinky* on the grounds that it was "of such character as to be prejudicial to the best interests of the people of [the] City," the Supreme Court overturned the board. If a board of censors could tell the American people what they could see, read, or hear, the Court ruled, "then thought is regimented, authority substituted for liberty, and the great purpose of the First Amendment to keep uncontrolled the freedom of expression defeated."[49] This decision would make it far harder for local communities to prevent the showing of films that promoted ideas they opposed.

By the mid-1950s the production codes had been revised to allow the portrayal of many previously taboo topics, including abortion, drugs, and miscegenation. Soon a wave of movies featuring interracial couples appeared. These were not "race problem" movies like those of the 1940s. Instead they exploited the melodramatic possibilities of interracial love to titillate their audience; they were designed to entertain by walking carefully around the edges of a social taboo. The first post-code movie to feature "miscegenation" was *Island in the Sun,* a 1957 Darryl Zanuck film about politics and love on a Caribbean island. *Island* was daring for its time in that it cast black actors in romantic roles opposite whites in a story that centered on the fate of two interracial couples, but the film still shied away from presenting explicit physical relationships between the black and white actors. One of the couples, a black shopkeeper played by Dorothy Dandridge and a white British aide played by John Justine, had to fight to say the word "love" on screen, and at the end of the movie they leave the island so they can be married off-camera in England. Joan Fontaine battled for a scene in which she and her lover Harry Belafonte drink out of the same coconut, but the filmmakers insisted that the couple not kiss and that they give each other up at the end of the movie.[50]

Despite the film's advances, the actors were not allowed to engage in any physical displays of affection on the screen. The most daring shot of Belafonte and Fontaine, which showed the two embracing, did not make it into the final cut of the picture.

Even so, *Island in the Sun* triggered a flurry of protests from segregationists. The *White Sentinel* lambasted *Island* as "the first open portrayal of mongrelization to be filmed by any American motion picture company." The film represented a victory of organized racial minorities who had long pressured Hollywood to glorify interracial romances, the paper claimed. It encouraged its readers to boycott the film, to pressure their local theater manager not to show it, and to protest in writing to its director. "If Zanuck loses a goodly part of the $3,000,000 being invested in the film, he may not produce any other insults to White womanhood and manhood." A South Carolina state congressman introduced a bill that would impose a $5,000 fine on any theater in the state showing the film. The *White Sentinel* also publicized Harry Belafonte's 1956 divorce from his black wife and remarriage to a white woman soon after finishing filming of *Island*. Belafonte had taken the message of the film seriously, the paper crowed. Hollywood press agents, meanwhile, were looking for other black "matinee idols" to foist on an unsuspecting public: "It is all part of the brainwashing to integrate and mongrelize America."[51]

Despite these segregationist complaints, *Island in the Sun* proved to be a huge box-office success, grossing over three times its cost of $2.5 million. After the commercial success of *Island,* more films featured stories about miscegenation. Several B movies aimed at young adults and particularly at teenagers going to drive-ins sensationalized the story of the "tragic mulatto" woman in a secret interracial relationship. The 1960 film *I Passed for White* focused on a young black woman tormented by the possibility that the birth of her first child might reveal her black ancestry to her white husband. The 1959 *Night of the Quarter Moon* depicted a light-skinned black woman removing her clothes in a courtroom scene in order to prove that her white husband knew that she was "dark" all over and not just tan on her face before their marriage. Films such as these that openly titillated audiences with the possibility of illicit interracial relationships represented a growing cultural liberalization, and they further fueled segregationists' fears that they were losing the ability to properly socialize white children.

Under siege from the federal courts and popular culture, defenders of school segregation sought to discredit *Brown* with the argument that integration would lead to intermarriage. Senator Eastland made this clear in his call to take the fight against integration into the arena of national public opinion. "The law of nature," he said, "is on our side. After all, the average American is not a racial pervert. We must place our case at the bar of public opinion." Once northern whites realized the "inevitable biological effect" of desegregation, they would join the South's opposition to *Brown,* Herbert Ravenal Sass charged. In focusing on the sexual outcome of *Brown,* segregationists sought common ground with whites outside the South, who for the most part shared southerners' concerns about interracial relationships. An American Civil Liberties Union observer even found that some whites in working-class Chicago neighborhoods feared that *Brown* would lead to intermarriages in their own communities.[52]

As prominent a national leader as President Dwight Eisenhower empathized with southern opposition to school desegregation. He told Chief Justice Earl Warren shortly before the decision was handed down, "These [white southerners] are not bad people. All they are concerned about is to see that their sweet little girls are not required to sit in schools alongside some big black bucks."[53] At least one major national magazine was sympathetic to the segregationist position; *U.S. World and News Report* ran articles in which sociologists discussed whether integration would lead to an increase in interracial marriage, as well as exposés of interracial dating at an integrated high school. In a 1958 article, an anonymous white student at an integrated school argued that every white girl at her school had a secret crush on a colored boy. "Integration is a gradual process. At first it is difficult to see anything but that they are Negroes. Later you think of them as just people and then as friends," the student wrote. "As one girl I know put it, from there it is just a hop, skip and jump before you think of them as more than friends."[54] With articles like these, *U.S. News* suggested that segregationists' concerns had some basis.

Young girls were bound to see black boys either as exotic experiments or, worse, as ordinary guys.

Yet many white racial liberals who wanted to see *Brown* fully implemented were not so quick to accept the link between integration and interracial relationships. The vehement attack on *Brown* forced white liberals to confront southern rhetoric about "race mixing" more directly than they had in the past. Indeed the number of articles in white publications about interracial marriage increased dramatically as supporters of *Brown* came to recognize that they could no longer simply ignore southern arguments about the sexual consequences of integration. As Milton Mayer argued in a lengthy piece in the *Progressive,* as long as segregationists turned all discussions of civil rights into attacks on "racial amalgamation," those who supported integration had to be willing to talk candidly about "miscegenation."[55] National religious organizations that supported the *Brown* decision also came to this realization. Within several years of the decision, religious groups that had previously ignored the issue of interracial marriage began to argue that no fundamental social change would be possible until concerns about race mixing were discussed more openly. Lutherans gathered at the Valparaiso University Institute of Human Relations insisted it was time to take "the skeleton out of the closet" to show people "the unfair way in which the question [would you want your daughter to marry one] is usually used as a device to stop the discussion and win the argument." The Presbyterian journal *Social Progress* printed a symposium addressing the question of interracial marriage since concerns about racial amalgamation lurked "in the minds and hearts of many persons sincerely and positively concerned about race relations."[56]

Most white liberals suggested that even if southern fears were sincere, they were misplaced or misguided. Integration, they charged, would not necessarily lead to an increase in interracial relationships. From the moment *Brown* was handed down, northern political and intellectual leaders emphasized that the ruling was about legal, not social, equality. The *New York Times* editorialized the day after the decision, "the court is not talking of that sort of 'equality' which produces interracial marriages. It is not talking of a social system at all. It is talking of a system of human rights which is foreshadowed . . . in the Declaration of Independence."[57]

In her 1955 book *Now Is the Time,* southern liberal Lillian Smith argued
that nothing in *Brown* compelled social interactions or social equality between blacks and whites. While everyone, black and white, had the right
to move freely through a common public life and share its opportunities
(such as public schools), people also had the right "never to be intruded
upon in home or club, or interfered with in our personal relationships."
The government could not force people to socialize with one another,
Smith insisted. "There is nothing in the decision that affects anyone's
home, friends, private clubs or social affairs."[58] Smith emphasized this
point in discussion groups she led about ending segregation. When one
young white participant asked about the increased possibility of intermarriage with integration, Smith stressed every citizen's right to a private
life. "No one has the right to make you have Negroes in your home, or
in your club; or to marry one. No one can make a Negro invite you to
her home, either, or to his club; or compel a Negro to marry you."[59] Arthur Krock, the editor of the *New York Times,* even suggested that southerners segregate their public schools by sex if they were concerned about
the dangers of potential race mixing.[60] Abandoning state-supported segregation, such statements implied, did not have to limit the ability of
southerners to regulate interracial relationships.

Some liberal *Brown* supporters suggested that racial integration would
even decrease the incidence of interracial sexual relationships. Interracial
sex, they suggested, was more common not when the races were equal,
but when one group was held in a subordinate position and was vulnerable to exploitation or so distanced as to appear exotic. Thus the Harvard
social historian Oscar Handlin argued that there was an inverse relationship between blacks' status and racial mixing. Desegregation would actually be a disincentive to intermarriage, because it would improve the
status of blacks, thus increasing their self-respect and decreasing their desire to marry whites. Lillian Smith charged that there would be far fewer
interracial marriages as a result of integration than there had been "irresponsible sexual adventures" as a result of segregation. Black women who
were given real opportunities wouldn't be interested in being any white
man's concubine, she insisted, and white youth would have little incentive to intermarry and face the "burden of social taboos." Carrying
this argument to its logical conclusion, the *Pittsburgh Courier* columnist

George Schuyler charged that politicians who were concerned about preventing "mongrelization" should lead the charge to desegregate the schools, since a strict color bar made interracial relationships seem more risky, dangerous, and attractive.[61]

For further proof that integration could take place without the sexual or marital assimilation of blacks into white society, many pointed to the low rate of intermarriage in the North, even though interracial marriage was not illegal there and no formal system of segregation separating the races existed. The sociologist Robert MacIver of Columbia University told *U.S. News and World Report* that the apprehensions of the South were "exaggerated," noting that "the experience of the North would suggest that sex is not a grave problem."[62] Critics of segregation maintained that blacks had no great desire to marry whites, no matter what white southerners thought. The *New York Journal American,* which published a series of articles on the segregationist movement in 1956, found it "dishonest and shameful" that so many southerners claimed that the step from a white school to white bedrooms was inevitable. Citing several interviews and an argument by Gunnar Myrdal that black Americans were more concerned about political and economic equality than about social equality, the series argued that blacks did not seek to marry whites and would not choose to do so even if they achieved legal and economic equality.[63] Because interracial marriage would remain rare even in an integrated world, arguments about segregation's being necessary to maintain racial purity were misleading, even irrelevant.

A number of influential white liberals went even further than this to argue that interracial relationships should not be considered dangerous or socially harmful even if they did occur. This position was a direct challenge to southerners who insisted that segregation had to be upheld for the larger public good of maintaining racial purity. The segregationist position rested on the conviction that interracial relationships were so injurious to society that they had to be prevented no matter what the cost. As William Workman wrote in *A Case for the South,* even if southerners' fears were subsequently proved groundless, they could not risk a fully integrated society. "The chance is too great a one to take, for if intermarriage on a considerable scale were to result, there could be no effective turning back by the time the mistake were discovered."[64]

After *Brown,* a number of influential white liberals began to question the very premise of the miscegenation taboo by challenging the insistence that interracial relationships were a dangerous threat to the social order. For the emeritus history professor Allan Nevins, who believed intermarriages would become more common with integration, the real threat to the social order was whites' opposition to such relationships. Nevins contended that accepting interracial relationships would be the great moral crisis for whites in the modern era, just as their need to reconcile themselves to the end of slavery had been the great moral crisis of the nineteenth century. A growing willingness by whites to challenge the accepted view that interracial relationships were socially harmful was evident immediately after *Brown. Esquire* ran a tongue-in-cheek article under the headline, "Rankin is Right," asserting that while desegregation would end in "racial mongrelization," all types of race problems would be solved when the United States became a "nation of mongrels." No longer would there be race riots, since there would be no races to riot. Southerners could stop worrying about black men raping white women; there would be no white women to rape. And taxpayers would save money since there wouldn't be any more lawsuits enforcing antimiscegenation laws. Walter Stevens, a speech professor at the University of Washington, granted that intermarriage might result from desegregation, but argued that the national advantages of racial equality far outweighed any danger posed by intermarriage. "I would rather see mixed marriage eventually accepted than to continue to play the game of 'limited brotherhood,' and the Constitution applies to me but not to you,'" he wrote. A white man who had married a black woman in the 1930s, meanwhile, wrote a piece in *Negro Digest* using his own marriage as evidence that the whole controversy over "miscegenation" was "a lot of calculated baloney." He and his wife were nothing scary or dangerous; they were an ordinary couple with ordinary concerns like paying their bills and putting their daughter through college. "Idiots" who frightened themselves "into a lather" about miscegenation needed to grow up, he insisted.[65] Marriage, after all, was a personal matter, not an issue for political concern.

This idea—that interracial marriage was personal rather than a issue for political debate—was the most radical of the reactions to the southern defense of segregation. Although this response was not widespread, at least a few racial liberals, including Otto Klineberg in *Horizons,* carried these arguments to their logical conclusion by insisting that intermarriage should be understood as a personal matter between two individuals rather than a topic for discussion in the realm of formal politics. Even if interracial couples faced a hostile society, some argued, they should have the right to marry and their marriages should concern only them. The controversy over *Brown,* in effect, led some white liberals to move toward a position that blacks had long held. Thus the Lutheran group who met at Valparaiso in 1958 warned of the "life of misery" that might accompany interracial marriage, but they argued that since the Bible taught that all races were part of a single unified mankind, interracial marriage should be a matter of individual choice, left up to the individuals involved. Lillian Smith also insisted that since blacks and whites belonged to the same species and could produce healthy children, interracial marriages should not be feared. If an interracial couple loved each other, were mature, and understood the obstacles they faced, they should be allowed to marry, Smith asserted.[66] Eleanor Roosevelt, who addressed the issue of interracial marriage several times in her syndicated *My Day* column, agreed in 1958 that "marriage is a purely personal matter." Although people of the same color and religion generally tended to prefer each other, some mixed marriages would occur, and in these cases, the individuals themselves had to make decisions about what to do.[67] In effect, these writers advocated according interracial marriages the same protective zone of privacy given to other marriages, which was a crucial first step in removing the issue of intermarriage from whites' public and political debates about civil rights.

The cultural and political shifts of the 1950s were admittedly tentative. The embrace of an ideology of color blindness by northern political elites and the courts did not immediately doom antimiscegenation laws or many other forms of segregation. The popularity of black musical forms did not lead most young whites to start dating across the color line, and even the growing number of titillating films about interracial love still made clear its dangers. Racial liberals moved quite slowly to discredit southern arguments about the inevitability of race mixing in a world without segregation, and few took a strong stand in favor of interracial relationships. Yet in contending that marriages between whites and blacks should be discussed and negotiated between individuals rather than in the formal political sphere, some racial liberals continued the process begun by black civil rights activists of redefining black-white marriages as a private, rather than a political, concern. These changes would come to fruition in the 1960s, when mass activism and a revolution in notions of individual rights would influence the courts, make interracial relationships harder to regulate, and provide intellectual and cultural justifications for interracial love.

THE RIGHTS REVOLUTIONS AND

INTERRACIAL MARRIAGE

Neither of them could have possibly imagined that they would end up together. Although they grew up only twenty-five miles apart, Johnny Ford and Frances Baldwin Rainer lived in separate worlds. Ford's world was the mostly black town of Tuskegee, Alabama. He grew up poor, the son of a low-paid employee at the Tuskegee Veterans Administration Hospital. Ford graduated from the segregated schools in Tuskegee in 1960 and then attended predominantly black Knoxville College in Tennessee on a scholarship. Frances "Tas" Rainer lived on the other side of the proverbial tracks. The daughter of one of the leading white families in Macon County, Tas grew up in the neighboring white town of Union Springs. Her father was a member of the White Citizens' Council before his death in the mid-1950s. The family was personally acquainted with George Wallace, Alabama's staunchly segregationist governor. Tas grew up knowing almost no blacks personally and idolizing George Wallace. In the mid-1960s, she studied at the segregated University of Alabama, where she joined an elite sorority and thought little about the civil rights protests going on around her in the South.[1]

In the 1950s, there was little chance that the paths of a poor black boy from Tuskegee and a well-to-do white girl from Union Springs would cross, except, perhaps, if the black boy ended up working for the white girl's family. But Ford and Rainer came of age in a South that was changing at a time of national upheaval. In 1969 they would meet in Tuskegee as social equals, both seeking to improve the lives of poor blacks in Macon County.

After working for the Boy Scouts and as a political organizer for Robert Kennedy's 1968 presidential campaign, Ford landed a job as the administrator of Tuskegee's Model Cities program, in charge of dispensing federal funds to improve housing, education, and health care for the urban poor. Tas Rainer, meanwhile, found her comfortable acceptance of the status quo challenged after graduation when she took a job as a caseworker with the Welfare Department of Macon County and began working with poor black families. Within a few months, she had rejected most of what she had been taught about race as a child. Rainer and Ford met in 1969 at a conference for Model Cities and welfare officials and began dating secretly in Montgomery, some forty miles away. Six months after they met, on October 28, 1970, Johnny Ford and Tas Rainer were married in Alabama, where they would make their home.

The Fords' story dramatically illustrates the extent of the changes that took place in the United States during the 1960s. They were able to marry in Alabama in 1970, three years after the U.S. Supreme Court declared state antimiscegenation laws unconstitutional. They consciously chose to stay and raise their family in the South, where only ten years before, a black man and white woman who lived together openly risked arrest and even death. Perhaps most surprisingly, Johnny and Tas Ford did not become pariahs or outcasts in their native South. Ford became the first black mayor in Tuskegee's history in 1972, just two years after his marriage, a position he would hold until 1992. His marriage was "no big thing in Tuskegee or in the Deep South," Ford insisted after his election. "This is 1972 and people ought to have a right to do what they feel is constitutionally and morally right. We're just man and wife, that's all."[2]

A black man with a white woman had never been "just man and wife," and in 1972, interracial couples were still a long way from being just like any other married couple. But the Fords' marriage reveals an extraordinary shift from the 1950s, when even the most token school desegregation unleashed a torrent of fears among southern whites about impending "miscegenation," to the 1970s, when an interracial couple could legally marry and live openly in the Black Belt of Alabama. By the end of the 1960s, the long battle of blacks against the Jim Crow system finally culminated in the overturning of the most entrenched of the segregation laws, those that prohibited interracial marriage. In the realm of politics and popular culture, white supporters of civil rights began to come to terms with their own ambivalence about interracial marriage. Young whites increasingly rebelled against the traditional rules and customs that discouraged interracial dating, and a growing number of young blacks and whites would meet and choose to marry as spatial segregation decreased on college campuses and in professional workplaces. Indeed, by the end of the decade whites of all age groups expressed greater tolerance for interracial relationships, even if a majority still disapproved of intermarriage. It seemed as if, in the words of the intermarried black sociologist St. Clair Drake, "the white sides kinda got all right."[3]

If the white side had "kinda got all right," as Drake believed, the transformation had its origins in the black freedom struggle of the 1950s and 1960s. Although commonly referred to as the civil rights movement, the black struggle extended well beyond the narrow realm of civil rights, as southern blacks challenged discriminatory laws, their political disfranchisement, and white supremacy in all its manifestations. In Montgomery in 1956, a united black community proved its economic power in a year-long boycott that ultimately forced the desegregation of the city's buses. Four years later, black college students challenged Jim Crow laws by the simple act of demanding service from segregated establishments. National civil rights leaders such as Martin Luther King, Jr., and James Farmer, and organizations including the Southern Christian Leadership Conference (SCLC) and the Congress of Racial Equality (CORE) skillfully manipulated the media to win national support for their desegregation and voting campaigns, while college students formed the Student Nonviolent Coordinating Committee (SNCC) and worked at the grassroots level to empower local blacks to take control of their own lives and demand change.

In the 1940s and 1950s, blacks struggling to win legal and political equality usually disavowed any interest in interracial marriage. Not only was the issue explosive to whites, but most civil rights activists believed that fighting segregation and disfranchisement was more important than trying to change laws and customs prohibiting personal relationships across the color line. The activists of the 1960s, however, were not content to challenge racism through the courts or to focus solely on political equality. SCLC and SNCC envisioned a world where blacks and whites would relate to each other as brethren and social equals. They talked of love, brotherhood, and creating a "beloved community" where people would respect and value each other without regard to color. In short, they were concerned with not only political and legal equality but also social equality. Movement activists encouraged interracial organizing and refused to accept the traditional southern racial and gender order. CORE and SNCC welcomed white women's participation in southern protests, deciding that the movement should challenge southern assumptions about the sanctity of white womanhood, even if "sending a white woman up was just like sending dynamite."[4] Movement activists would not allow any of their activities to be limited by southern mores. When the Kennedy administration asked civil rights organizations to respect southern taboos by not putting black men and white women together in demonstrations, activists refused to yield on principle.[5] If they were fighting for integration, they would not segregate their own protests.

Marriages across racial lines could even be seen to represent the ultimate expression of the political ideals of the early movement, which stressed human brotherhood and pushed for a transformation in social relationships between blacks and whites. As one white volunteer explained, she and the black activist she married in 1965 were the "living embodiment of 'black and white together,'" the popular SNCC slogan. Although SNCC activists did not encourage interracial relationships as a way to overcome racial hatred, they recognized that such relationships were a symbol of the integrated world they were seeking to create, and were to be expected among young people who were politically active and were not "hung up on racial differences."[6] Civil rights organizations, moreover, provided a meeting space for young blacks and whites committed to the ideal of racial equality. Although the number of whites involved in the movement was not large, both SNCC and CORE had long-term white organizers. Furthermore, at least 650 white northern college students were recruited to come work in Mississippi in 1964.

These volunteers were largely young and single. They faced danger constantly and, as a result, forged strong ties with one another and with southern blacks—ties that could easily lead to romantic relationships.[7]

Yet while interracial love might ultimately be symbolic of the larger goals of the movement, pragmatic concerns made the issue of interracial love and marriage far more complicated for movement activists and ensured that the number of movement interracial marriages would remain relatively small. It could be both dangerous and politically foolish for people involved in the movement to openly engage in interracial dating or marriage. Most civil rights organizing took place in southern states where being part of an interracial couple could be fatal. Although people in SNCC didn't object to interracial dating, the attitude was "don't do it down here, because, c'mon, people are crazy, they'll kill you." Southern police took special pains to harass young people who went out in racially mixed groups of any kind. Even walking across the street in an integrated group was considered a crime in some southern towns during the movement; walking outside as an interracial couple was virtually unthinkable. Dottie Zellner, a white SNCC field secretary, recalled seeing few serious interracial couples. Folks might get together casually in the Freedom Houses civil rights workers shared, but pursuing an "open, stable, committed public relationship in Mississippi, that would be enough to get you killed!"[8]

When large numbers of northern whites volunteered with the movement during the summers of 1964 and 1965, veteran organizers strongly discouraged them from dating interracially. Planners feared that the legacies of sexual racism would undermine healthy relationships between blacks and whites and would impede their ability to work together effectively. Fearful that whites would come south and pick up a "token summer Negro" as a way to prove their liberal credentials or that black men would eagerly seek to experiment with taboo white women, Freedom Summer organizers warned volunteers to shy away from interracial dating. At orientation, white volunteers were told not to sleep with a black person as a way to atone for racial guilt, and white women were warned that some black men might be sexually aggressive toward them. "Don't think it's because you're so beautiful and so ravishing that this man is enamored of you," a black staff member warned them. Black men, he told them, would sleep with any willing white woman as a way to express their manhood by having what white society denied them.[9]

Project directors also feared that interracial dating during the summer would incite white violence. Ivanhoe Donaldson, a Freedom Summer project director, warned his volunteers that interracial dating would provide "local whites with the initiative they need to come in here and kill all of us." Indeed, northern white volunteers' ignorance of southern sexual and racial taboos put other civil rights workers in serious danger. The veteran activist Chuck McDew received a particularly savage beating from his southern jailers after a naive white supporter posed as his wife in order to find out whether McDew had been hurt during his captivity. His previously uneventful prison stay changed suddenly, as the enraged police began to beat him mercilessly, telling the unmarried McDew, "Son of a bitch, that's what you get for marrying a white woman." Danny Lyon, a young white SNCC photographer, bore the brunt of the punishment when a white woman he took to a bar in Albany, Georgia, announced loudly and repeatedly that she was married to a black man in the North. When the two left the bar, they were met by police, who arrested Lyon and told him he might be prosecuted under the Mann Act for bringing an underage girl across state lines for the purposes of prostitution.[10]

Given the explosive situation in the South, potential volunteers who told Freedom Summer interviewers that they might engage in interracial sex were not accepted, while those volunteers already in the South who openly engaged in interracial sexual activity might be told to leave. SNCC staff sent one white woman Freedom Summer volunteer home when she had sex with a black man in his car parked out on the street. White volunteers complained about whites who wanted to come down South and "screw around."[11]

The black men who engaged in such public escapades were not forced to leave the group, although they faced disapproval and censure for their actions. They were warned in no uncertain terms that SNCC would not expend energy to look for them or bail them out if they got in trouble because of their relationships with white women. SNCC staffers responded angrily to one black worker who rode through Mississippi on his motorcycle with a white woman. "People were mad and hated things like that because you use your resources to protect something foolish," one Mississippi SNCC staffer explained.[12]

If veteran activists had feared only that interracial dating would invite the violence of white southerners, they might have been more willing to challenge the ultimate southern taboo. But project directors were equally concerned that open interracial relationships would alienate the conservative, religious rural southern blacks they were trying to organize, a group likely to be shocked by and disapproving of interracial relationships. The prohibition on interracial dating reflected an effort by SNCC to ensure that its workers behaved in ways consistent with southern rural norms of respectability. Ivanhoe Donaldson told his Freedom Summer volunteers that interracial dating was strictly prohibited: "Even if the whites don't find out about them, the local people will, and we won't be able to do anything afterwards to convince them that our primary interest here is political. Our entire effort will be negated if we lose the support and respect of the people." Interracial dating, Donaldson proclaimed, was a form of "bullshit" the movement could not afford. Stokely Carmichael, the project director in Greenwood, Mississippi, listed interracial dating as one of his taboo behaviors, a list that also included public drunkenness, disrespecting local blacks' religious beliefs, and women wearing pants.[13]

Interracial dating could also impede project unity and create tensions between volunteers. As one white male CORE worker explained, although he joked with the black women he worked with in Louisiana, he tried to stay "completely away from sexual relations, because I know how it can screw up a project." If you started dating one girl, "you have the problems of the Negro men, even though they say it in a kidding way, that old, underlying current of distrust and dislike is coming up all the time, the comments about it."[14] Some black women activists, meanwhile, felt betrayed when a black male worker dated a white woman, and some worried that such relationships would undermine movement solidarity both among blacks and between blacks and whites. Fannie Lou Hamer, the black sharecropper turned SNCC activist, scolded white volunteers who dated black men. Resentful of these middle-class white women's sense of freedom, and aware that their actions could harm black men in Ruleville, Hamer declared, "If they can't obey the rules, call their mothers and tell them to send down their sons instead!"[15]

Serious relationships were not immune to criticism either. When Candi Law, a white CORE volunteer, became involved with a black activist in Durham, she was surprised by the hostility she encountered from the Durham CORE people, who began "cold-shouldering" her black boyfriend because of his association with her. Law called on CORE's national director, James Farmer, to show his support of their relationship and to defend the right of volunteers to date interracially. This kind of reaction to an interracial relationship should be "fought and won, not run from," Law insisted, stressing that those working for equality could not expect her to be ashamed for loving a black man. Farmer, who was himself interracially married and thus perhaps more likely to defend such relationships, instead saw the issue as a distracting nuisance. He told Law that she should leave North Carolina and gave her money for a train ticket. Law left, but her boyfriend soon joined her and the couple moved to Michigan, where they were married. The next year, the national office sent the young couple a congratulatory telegram wishing them success in staying active in the movement. Having the movement run smoothly was, in this case, more important than defending the rights of individuals to date interracially.[16]

Interracial relationships did occur among movement activists, but the movement environment was ultimately more conducive to short-term, furtive sexual relationships than to those that might lead to marriage. Sexual relationships between black and white civil rights workers were quite common during the summers of 1964 and 1965 when large numbers of white volunteers came south on a temporary basis. Most of these relationships, however, were brief and experimental. During the Freedom Summers, northern middle-class liberal white volunteers worked with southern blacks, many of whom had never worked with whites before. Movement workers were young, away from the supervision of parents and community, and working under stressful conditions with people who represented the ultimate sexual taboo; interracial relationships were bound to occur.

Some found adventure in flouting southern sexual and racial norms; white women sometimes slept with black men out of a combination of thrill-seeking and guilt, or to prove themselves free from racism and middle-class norms. Mary King, a white woman who worked for SNCC, believed some white women volunteers "fluttered like butterflies from one tryst to another" in an effort to prove their own liberalism. Black men sometimes manipulated this anxiety and guilt to get white women into bed.[17] Alvin Poussaint, a black psychiatrist who studied Freedom Summer volunteers, theorized that black men in the movement saw white women more as symbolic conquests than as individuals. The black men he studied viewed "sexual intimacy with the white girls as a weapon of revenge against white society," Poussaint argued. Although psychologists were often predisposed to view movement interracial relationships as unhealthy and neurotic, as they did interracial dating more generally, the movement environment could indeed foster relationships between individuals who had little in common. Beula, a nineteen-year-old white college student who volunteered with the movement in Mississippi, met and began dating a black Mississippi man who had little education and who ridiculed her interest in music, art, and literature as "boss class fancies." Beula, her psychologist Hugo Biegel argued, belonged to the "great mass of college students whose rebellion against their personal situation or whose protest against social injustice demands sexual communion with the victims as ultimate proof of the sincerity of their beliefs." The relationship did not last long after Beula left the South.[18]

The few interracial relationships that progressed beyond dating to marriage usually involved long-term white civil rights activists, not summer volunteers. Some veteran activists remember perhaps a half-dozen interracial marriages; others put the number slightly higher. Frank Nelson, a young white engineer from New York, met his black wife during a demonstration in Poplarville, Mississippi, in 1962. John Perdew, a white Harvard student, moved to Albany, Georgia, in 1963 to work for SNCC. Arrested in Americus, Georgia, on charges of insurrection (which carried a possible death penalty), Perdew served three months in jail before dropping out of Harvard and joining SNCC's field staff full time. He would marry a black woman he met in the movement. Dinky Romilly, a white daughter of Communist parents from California, came to Atlanta to work in the SNCC office in 1962. She fell in love with James Forman, SNCC's black executive secretary, who eventually left his black wife for her. Although the couple were never legally married, they considered themselves married, raised two children, and stayed together for more than ten years. Other SNCC activists who married interracially include Lawrence Guyot, Chuck McDew, Ruthie Buffington, Tim Jenkins, and Bill Hansen.[19]

Yet as these civil rights veterans well knew, if they chose to marry across racial lines, they would likely have to leave the southern movement behind. Marrying interracially remained a crime in every southern state until 1967; couples who stayed in the South risked arrest or worse. Some, like Bill Hansen, a white man who served as head of SNCC's operations in Arkansas, and Ruthie Buffington, a black student at Arkansas A&M who became a SNCC field secretary, chose to use their marriages as an opportunity to challenge state antimiscegenation laws. The Hansens returned to Arkansas and released notices to the press after they married in Cincinnati in 1962. But their challenge was fruitless; arrested and convicted of miscegenation, they ultimately moved to Germany while their case was still on appeal. Chuck McDew never expected to stay in the southern movement after marrying Fredrica Greene, whom he met while on a SNCC fund-raising trip to Sarah Lawrence College in New York. McDew and his wife were prepared to leave the country rather than make a political issue of their marriage. They thought about moving to England, but eventually settled on Minneapolis, which was conveniently close to Canada.[20]

The black and white activists of the modern freedom struggle sought to create a new world and new ways of relating across racial lines. As Casey Hayden, a long-time white SNCC staffer, explained, "Our struggle was to break down the system, the walls, of segregation. This implied no barriers in our relations with each other." One of the most important aspects of the movement was, in Hayden's words, "real meetings of people across racial barriers, fostering healing and relationships that transcended race."[21] The movement did help break down racial barriers, and it provided some young and idealistic blacks and whites the opportunity to experiment with cross-racial sexual relationships and to experience interracial intimacy. The environment in the South and in the movement itself, however, kept most of these relationships from progressing to marriage.

Although the number of interracial marriages that developed out of the civil rights movement itself was small, the movement had enormous ramifications for interracial couples and for the ability of states to regulate interracial relationships. The movement's most important legacy for interracial couples was its effectiveness in discrediting all types of segregation laws. From the mid-1950s through the 1960s, black protesters challenged the legitimacy of Jim Crow laws in courtrooms and in the streets. Their actions forced federal courts to reevaluate the role that race should play in the legal arena. As courts moved to declare racial segregation in transportation, public accommodations, and federally funded institutions unconstitutional, laws prohibiting interracial sex and marriage came under new scrutiny. Although antimiscegenation laws would be the last segregation laws to fall, in 1967 the U.S. Supreme Court would declare them unconstitutional in the groundbreaking decision of *Loving v. Virginia*.

Some movement activists of the sixties urged a direct confrontation with antimiscegenation laws. Wyatt Tee Walker, an important figure in the Southern Christian Leadership Conference, used the occasion of a Catholic Conference for Interracial Justice to urge churches to take the lead in abolishing state antimiscegenation laws, which, he argued, denied black people their freedom to choose a mate. The retired military man Frank Van Vranken sought the support of CORE for his proposed crusade against antimiscegenation laws. Van Vranken planned to move to New Orleans, rent an apartment, and find a companion of color who would join with him in the fight to eradicate "the barriers of hate and fallacious race designation" that resulted from the laws prohibiting intermarriage. He wanted CORE's help in convincing a suitable woman to join him in his crusade.[22] CORE, not surprisingly, ignored Van Vranken's rather bizarre request, but other civil rights organizations proved open to more legitimate attacks on antimiscegenation laws. When an unmarried interracial couple was arrested in Florida in 1962 for violating the state

law prohibiting interracial cohabitation, the NAACP appealed their conviction all the way to the Supreme Court.

This direct attack on antimiscegenation laws, however, was ultimately
less important in achieving the decriminalization of interracial marriage
than was the indirect effect of the larger battle against all forms of legal
racial segregation. Before 1954 the federal courts had accepted the fiction of "separate but equal" in ruling that segregation laws did not violate the Fourteenth Amendment. With *Brown,* however, the Supreme
Court began to develop a body of legal precedent that would require
strict scrutiny of any laws that relied on racial classifications. If the mere
existence of segregation stigmatized blacks as inferior, as the Supreme
Court ruled in *Brown,* there could be no such thing as "separate but
equal." State laws that made distinctions based on race, then, had to be
subjected to the strictest forms of judicial scrutiny to ensure that the racial classifications in the laws were not "invidious and arbitrary." As
movement activists challenged Jim Crow laws in the streets and in the
courts, the Supreme Court sided with blacks and invalidated laws that
mandated segregation on buses, in parks, and in public accommodations.

Although none of these rulings directly affected state antimiscegenation laws, by the 1960s some state legislatures outside the deep South began to view laws prohibiting intermarriage as part of the larger system of
racial regulation that was being discredited as the federal courts slowly
invalidated all other forms of segregation. Indeed, many states that had
few other segregation laws reconsidered the legitimacy of their antimiscegenation statutes in the years after *Brown.* In 1959, twenty-nine states
still had laws barring interracial marriage. By 1967, only sixteen states
still had antimiscegenation laws on their books, all, except for Oklahoma,
former slave states. States that legalized intermarriage in the years between *Brown* and the 1967 *Loving* decision include Arizona, Idaho, Indiana, Nebraska, Nevada, South Dakota, and Wyoming. Indiana repealed its
antimiscegenation statute in 1965, at the same time that the state passed a
fair housing law.[23]

Antimiscegenation laws also became more vulnerable in some southern border states as entrenched conservative political interests lost control of their states for the first time since Reconstruction. In a series of
reapportionment cases in the early 1960s, the Supreme Court ordered

states to redraw voting districts that were weighted to favor rural areas against cities and suburbs. In border states such as Maryland, fairer representation of urban areas led to the election of some black representatives to the state legislature. In 1966 Verda Welcome, the only black member of the Maryland Senate, sponsored a bill to overturn the state's antimiscegenation law. When the bill was defeated, Welcome reintroduced it. It passed, only to be defeated by the House. But the next year, the same law passed both houses of the legislature. As the *New York Times* noted, less opposition was raised because of a newly reapportioned legislature; an 80 percent turnover in the membership of the Maryland General Assembly passed control from rural legislators to those from the city of Baltimore and the Maryland suburbs of Washington, D.C.[24]

In this climate, racial liberals recognized the new vulnerability of antimiscegenation laws and called for renewed efforts to get rid of them entirely. National church organizations launched a campaign against antimiscegenation laws, passing resolutions urging states to repeal them and calling on the Supreme Court to invalidate them.[25] An upbeat 1964 *Negro Digest* article advised potential couples that if their state did not allow intermarriage, they should seriously consider going through the courts to attempt to have the law changed. "Since so many states dropped their anti-miscegenation laws recently, perhaps your state is just waiting for a case such as yours to test the law" so they could "dispense with it on legal precedent," the author optimistically suggested. Of course, she noted, couples who lived in the Deep South might find the courts "reluctant to do so just yet."[26]

States in the Deep South were not about to abandon their antimiscegenation laws voluntarily; southern state courts repeatedly upheld antimiscegenation statutes in the years after *Brown.* In 1959 the Louisiana Supreme Court insisted that states had the right to prohibit interracial marriages as a means to prevent the birth of mixed-race children, whom the Louisiana court described as social misfits unlikely to be accepted by either community. When Virginia's antimiscegenation law came under the scrutiny of the U.S. Supreme Court in 1967, lawyers for the state argued that each state legislature should have the right to decide for its own people whether intermarriage should be prohibited.[27]

The new legal precedents on race, however, opened the door for the

Supreme Court to reconsider its 1883 ruling in *Pace v. Alabama,* which held that states could prohibit interracial sex as long as both the black and the white members of an interracial couple were punished equally. By 1964, when the Supreme Court was faced with a Florida case that directly raised the issue of the constitutionality of state laws that criminalized interracial sex, the stage was set for a radical departure from federal precedent. The case involved a black Honduran hotel worker and a white Alabama woman who were arrested in Miami for violating a law that forbade men and women of different races from living together. Convicted in a jury trial, each was sentenced to thirty days in prison and a $150 fine. The NAACP, which usually shunned cases involving interracial sex, agreed to lead the appeal—a clear sign that the respectability of antimiscegenation laws was waning.[28]

The Florida Supreme Court held that Florida's law was constitutional since it punished both the black and the white perpetrators equally, but it recognized that the Supreme Court was likely to rule otherwise. Congress had just passed the 1964 Civil Rights Act and the Supreme Court had dismantled nearly every other form of segregation except those that related to sex and marriage. As the Florida court openly recognized, the defendants hoped that "in the light of supposed social and political advances, they may find legal endorsement of their ambitions" in the U.S. Supreme Court. And in *McLaughlin v. Florida,* they did, as the Court used the case to overturn the precedent it had set in 1881 in *Pace.* "In our view," wrote Justice Byron White for the unanimous Court, "*Pace* represents a limited view of the Equal Protection Clause which has not withstood analysis in the subsequent decisions of this court."[29] The Florida law punishing unmarried interracial couples more harshly than unmarried same-race couples was unconstitutional, the court ruled. Although the Supreme Court did not extend its ruling to overturn the state laws prohibiting interracial marriage, the legal reasoning in *McLaughlin* left little doubt that as soon as the Court had a case that directly raised the issue of the constitutionality of the bans on interracial marriage, it would be compelled to declare these bans in violation of the Fourteenth Amendment.

That chance would come with a case that began years before the *McLaughlin* decision. In 1958 Richard Loving, a twenty-four-year-old

Richard and Mildred Loving made history when they challenged Virginia's prohibition of interracial marriage all the way to the Supreme Court. In 1967 the Justices finally declared all bans on interracial marriage unconstitutional. The decision was almost anticlimactic, although it nullified sixteen state antimiscegenation laws and made it possible for interracial couples to marry and live openly in the South. (©Bettmann/CORBIS.)

white bricklayer from Caroline County, Virginia, married his black childhood sweetheart, eighteen-year-old Mildred Jeter, in Washington, D.C. Five weeks later, Caroline County sheriffs walked into the Lovings' bedroom while they were sleeping and charged them with violating Virginia's antimiscegenation law. The county judge sentenced the Lovings to one year in jail unless they left the state and agreed not to return together for the next twenty-five years. The couple moved to Washington, D.C., in order to avoid prison time, but they hated it there, and in 1963 they wrote Attorney General Robert F. Kennedy to see if he could help them. Kennedy forwarded their letter to the ACLU, and shortly thereafter, the Lovings began the process of appeals that would bring their case to the Supreme Court.[30]

By 1967 the outcome of *Loving v. Virginia* was almost preordained. The Supreme Court's ruling in *McLaughlin* left little room for a constitutional defense of antimiscegenation laws. Although Virginia tried to defend its law by questioning the Court's new reading of the Fourteenth Amendment's equal protection clause, in *Loving v. Virginia,* the Supreme Court unanimously concluded that antimiscegenation statutes contained invidious racial discrimination that could not be justified on any grounds. "There can be no doubt that restricting the freedom to marry solely because of racial classifications violates the central meaning of the Equal Protection Clause," the Court ruled.[31] Thirteen years after *Brown,* the Supreme Court finally carried that ruling to its logical conclusion and invalidated antimiscegenation laws.

Although several legal scholars had predicted that such a ruling would seriously hurt the civil rights movement or lead to a severe violent reaction in the South, in fact there was no organized "massive resistance" to the *Loving* ruling as there had been in the case of *Brown.*[32] Not that there was instant compliance. In Delaware, a county clerk had to be forced by a U.S. District Court to provide a marriage license to an interracial couple two weeks after the *Loving* ruling. Three years after *Loving,* the U.S. Department of Justice had to file suit to force Alabama judges to issue marriage licenses to interracial couples. Mississippi and Georgia also had to be enjoined by the federal government to stop enforcing their now unconstitutional antimiscegenation laws. South Carolina, Mississippi, and Alabama refused to remove bans on miscegenation from their state constitutions. Yet the remaining antimiscegenation laws could not be enforced. When the right-wing Southern National Party sought to prevent one of the first legal interracial marriages in Mississippi's history with a state court injunction, a federal court order allowed Roger Mills, a white law clerk for the NAACP Legal Defense Fund, and Berta Linson, a black legal filing clerk, to wed as planned in Jackson in August 1970.[33] By 1967 all justifications for prohibiting marriage between blacks and whites had lost their legal legitimacy. States that had before arrested and exiled blacks and whites who had dared to marry now had to sit by as interracial couples were legally married in public ceremonies.

The decision in *Loving v. Virginia* did not generate a dramatic increase in the number of interracial marriages, but it forever changed the terms of the debate among whites about intermarriage. Before *Loving,* interracial marriage had been considered a matter suitable for public regulation. In *Loving,* the Supreme Court firmly insisted that interracial marriage, like marriages more generally, should be considered a fundamental personal right that, as Justice Earl Warren wrote in his decision in *Loving,* "resides with the individual and cannot be infringed by the State." As the *New York Times* editorialized, "choosing a husband or wife lies in the inviolable area of personal freedom that government may not enter."[34] Although the Court waited to act until the illegality of antimiscegenation laws could not be seriously questioned, its ruling made clear that interracial couples deserved the same privacy and state protection as same-race ones. The decision, moreover, influenced public opinion in important ways. When the Gallup Poll asked whites in 1965 whether they approved of laws forbidding intermarriage, 72 percent of southern whites and 42 percent of nonsouthern whites said yes. By 1970 only 56 percent of southern whites and 30 percent of nonsouthern whites favored such laws.[35]

This shift in public opinion was crucial to changing the actual practice of interracial marriage. The decriminalization of interracial marriage was an important step, but interracial marriage had long been regulated by more than laws. Marriage across the color line was rare even where it had been legal, in large part because of what had been almost universal opposition to interracial marriage by whites. At the beginning of the 1960s, perhaps 5 percent of whites nationwide claimed to favor interracial marriage. The decriminalization of intermarriage would prove relatively insignificant if whites' attitudes about intermarriage remained the same.

The civil rights movement, however, explicitly sought to change whites' attitudes about blacks, to force whites to confront their own internalized racism and to see beyond the color of blacks' skin to, in the words of Martin Luther King, Jr., "the content of our character." Racial discrimination, the movement highlighted again and again, was unfair, immoral, and illegitimate. Although scholars debate the extent of change in whites' racial attitudes that resulted from these efforts, there is no question that by the end of the decade, open expressions of racism had declined and whites more readily claimed to accept blacks as their social equals. One poll, for example, found a dramatic change in white Texans' attitudes about working with blacks, being with blacks in public places, and living near them. In 1963, only 40 percent of white Texans felt comfortable with blacks eating at the same restaurants they did. By 1971, 80 percent said they would not mind blacks sharing their restaurants. National polls found whites more accepting of daily public contact with blacks at work and in schools, and a growing number of white Americans supported the ideal of racial equality and agreed that blacks had been victims of unfair discrimination.[36]

These changing racial attitudes threatened those who wanted to maintain traditional forms of white supremacy. Defenders of the racial status quo feared a loss of white consensus on the basic idea that blacks should have a lower status than whites. Nowhere is this clearer than in the sexual narratives constructed by segregationists about the civil rights movement, narratives that focused far more on the whites who participated in the black struggle than on the blacks they worked alongside. Challenges to white supremacy have always been accompanied by sexual stories, whether during Reconstruction, when panicked rumors spread about black-beast rapists, or during the 1950s, when segregationists envisioned school integration ending in widespread racial amalgamation. The stories of the 1880s and the 1950s were similar: both portrayed sexual disorder as the inevitable result of black equality and both represented whites as innocent victims, either of black rapists or of misguided attempts to indoctrinate them with false claims about human brotherhood. In oral and published stories from the 1960s, however, whites were portrayed as responsible for leading the attack on white supremacy for the sake of cheap sexual thrills. The narratives of the movement focused on the sexual depravity of whites who knowingly and willingly allied themselves with the black cause.

This focus on white participants is particularly revealing of the mindset of those who opposed the civil rights movement. For segregationists, whites' interest in interracial sex seemed the only plausible reason why a white person would come to the aid of the black cause. Whites had a racial identity that afforded them some level of status and security no matter what their class position; blacks had little to offer, except perhaps for their alleged sexual superiority. In the eyes of many segregationists, those whites who chose not to protect the value and integrity of white racial identity could be motivated only by their desire to experience the taboo of interracial sex. White activists, especially women, constantly faced vulgar questions and taunts about their sex lives. White mobs yelled at white women during protests and labeled them sluts and whores. For Sally Belfrage, a white Freedom Summer volunteer in Greenwood, Mississippi, in 1964, handling the litany of obscene phone calls at the movement office was one of the greatest challenges of her summer. Volunteers would spend the day dealing with callers who asked questions like, "You ever been raped by a nigger?" or "How many nigger cocks y'all got to suck 'fore you can go to sleep at night?" When Belfrage and a group of other white women volunteers were arrested after picketing the Greenwood courthouse during a voter registration campaign, their jailer repeatedly accused them of sleeping with blacks, and taunted that they would all end the summer pregnant by black men. The white daughter of the civil rights lawyer William Kunstler faced similar verbal abuse after the car she was driving in with black civil rights workers was pulled over by the sheriff in Oxford, Mississippi. "Which one of them coons is you fuckin'," the sheriff asked before an appreciative white crowd. "Slut, I know you fuckin' them niggers. Why else would you be down heah?" Any white support for the cause, no matter how minor, was interpreted by southern opponents as a desire for interracial sex. A white Atlanta woman who berated a white mob tormenting twenty picketing black students was told, "If you feel that way, why don't you marry one of them?"[37] Any white woman so debased as to defend sit-ins must be degraded enough to want to marry a black, too.

The obsessive, even paranoid, stories of orgiastic interracial sex in the movement revealed a deep psychological fear of the loss of a racial consensus among whites. In focusing on whites who were willing to work against their own presumed racial self-interest, segregationists revealed they found the fissures among whites even more disturbing than militancy among blacks. One white priest from Birmingham recalled, "The Klan hated the whites who were helping the blacks more than the blacks themselves."[38] Such stories also suggested that whites' loss of racial control heralded the loss of white male privilege as well. Brazen and bold white women were willing to risk their own reputation and status for the chance to have sex with a black man; their independence threatened

white men who could not control them and the structures of white supremacy more generally. White men involved in civil rights, meanwhile,
were depicted as either driven purely by their desire for sex, or as weak
and emasculated. Selma sheriff Jim Clark, who penned his own version
of events in Selma, Alabama, during voting rights demonstrations in
1965, painted a picture of sexual degeneracy. Describing the enemies of
the traditional South as Catholics, sexual radicals, and gender deviants,
Clark wrote of white priests who openly slept with black women, of a
beatnik white man who claimed to have been recruited to come march
in Selma by offers of free food and "all the sex he could handle," and of
gay interracial couples kissing and holding hands in public. Southern police made clear to white male civil rights workers that they didn't consider them "real" men, and, in some cases, threatened to castrate them.
White men who worked with blacks as their equals would thus be
feminized, the symbol of their manhood forcibly removed.[39]

These stereotypes about whites who became involved in the movement also served to excuse violence toward white activists. Painting
white activists as avid "race mixers" helped legitimate the right of other
whites to put them in their place or even murder them. When Viola
Liuzzo, a white Detroit mother of five, was shot and killed while driving
marchers back and forth from Selma to Montgomery in 1965, the mur-
derer's lawyer painted Liuzzo as a sexual pervert who did not deserve the
protection due to white women, or even the moniker of "white." White
people who joined the cause of "black supremacy" became "white niggers," he charged, and riled the jury with insinuations of interracial sex:
"Do you know those big black niggers were driven by the woman, sitting in the back seat? Niggers! One white woman and these niggers.
Right there. Riding right through your county." Describing Liuzzo as a
wanton woman eager to give herself to black men, the lawyer justified
her brutal murder and successfully defended his clients. The murder of
the white seminary student Jonathan Daniels was similarly rationalized
with innuendoes about his sexual interactions with black people. Daniels
came to Selma in 1965 as a volunteer and was arrested in Lowndes
County several months later for participating in a protest there. After his
release, Daniels and three other civil rights workers—another white man
and two black women—went to a local store to buy drinks while waiting

for a ride back to Selma. But the storekeeper met the group at his door with a gun, shooting and killing Daniels and seriously injuring the other white man. At the trial, the storekeeper's lawyer focused on all the ways in which Daniels had violated southern custom. He had been known to walk around Selma with his arms around black girls' shoulders, he had corresponded with a black woman while in jail, and most damningly, the county deputy charged that right after Daniels was released from jail, he kissed one of the black women on the mouth. Even though white southern men had been raping and sleeping with black women for years, a kiss on the mouth was beyond the pale, suggesting a level of intimacy and equality that was not permitted in the stratified racial order. Although there was no proof of Daniels's interracial kiss, this sexual story resonated with the jury, who found the shopkeeper innocent of Daniels's murder.[40]

Segregationists used these stories to try to reestablish control of the racial narrative and to shore up a white consensus against black equality. Sexual stories aimed not only to degrade and debase whites who allied themselves with blacks, but also to discredit the black fight for civil rights more generally. The movement was not a legitimate struggle for better treatment for blacks, such stories implied, but an unnatural, disturbing, immoral quest for sexual gratification. When Jim Clark described the marchers in Selma as "filthy, promiscuous degenerates" who inflicted "almost indescribable indecencies" on Selma, he was consciously responding to media accounts that presented marchers as well-meaning individuals involved in a campaign for human dignity.[41] Once segregation itself was under siege, describing activists as sexual degenerates seemed the easiest way for segregationists to take back the moral high ground from protesters and to discredit the motives of the movement. According to Clark's outrageous account of the Selma-to-Montgomery march, mixed couples had sex in public, half the women marching in Selma wore no underpants, and prophylactics littered the ground wherever the marchers went. Clark attested that he had personally seen white girls "rubbing up against Negro men and kissing them in the street," while black men openly fondled white women marchers. This was the "untold story" of the movement that segregationists tried to sell to the larger public, whether through books like Clark's or in the pages of southern newspapers. The taboo on interracial sex had taken on a life, and a psychological currency, of its own, and was now leading "sexual maniacs, dope addicts, mentally deranged communists and a few well-meaning brainwashed people with no understanding of human decency," in the words of one Mississippi man, to act against the interests of white supremacy.[42]

If their stories are any indication, segregationists seemed to assume that, no matter what other fissures might be developing between whites, a strong consensus about the undesirability of interracial relationships remained. But even as opponents of the movement sought to smear it by characterizing it as a hotbed of interracial sex, the movement was influencing some whites to reconsider their opposition to interracial relationships. In the ten years from 1958 to 1968, as whites became more tolerant of all forms of racial integration, approval of interracial marriage among whites quintupled, from 4 percent to 20 percent. These numbers, however, reflected a growing tolerance for interracial marriage in the abstract. When whites were asked how they would feel about an interracial marriage in their own family, disapproval remained extremely high. A 1963 *Newsweek* poll found that while less than a third of white Americans would oppose working with a black person or sitting next to one on a bus, 90 percent would disapprove of their own daughter dating a Negro; among white southerners, disapproval reached a near–unanimous 97 percent. Even those whites who claimed they knew blacks well and were friendly with them disapproved of interracial dating when their own child was involved. Interracial dating and marriage in their own families were where whites seemingly drew the line, no matter what their other racial attitudes. As one Lewistown, Pennsylvania, man told a *Newsweek* interviewer in 1966, "I have nothing against Negroes—as long as it doesn't get too personal like dating and marriage."[43]

Perhaps a consensus could still be found, one that would revolve around that old question, "Would you want your daughter to marry one?" This "final question" of the race problem, as it was described in one 1966 article, was publicly acknowledged by both supporters and opponents as the most powerful weapon in segregationists' ideological arsenal. As *Ebony* magazine noted in 1965, the question was still "Southern racists' most effective squelch for 'broad–minded white liberals' from the

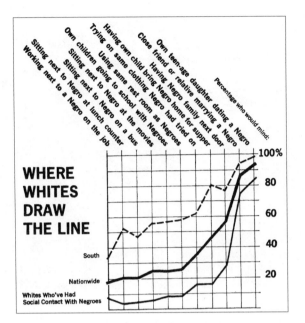

The results of this 1963 poll in *Newsweek* suggest how much more difficult it was for whites to accept a romantic relationship than other types of interracial social contact. (*Newsweek,* October 21, 1963. © 1963 Newsweek, Inc. All rights reserved. Reprinted by permission.)

North." That question, an article in the segregationist magazine *The Citizen* insisted, had been the "most effective single argument against the social intermingling of the races."[44]

The famous question not only played to whites' emotional reactions to interracial sex, but also powerfully personalized the racial issue. Black equality might mean accepting a black person into the family or even having black grandchildren. By focusing particularly on daughters, the question brilliantly reduced the racial problem to one of the proper parental, and particularly fatherly, concern for the well-being of one's little girl. The race question became a battle between men, white and black, for young, innocent white daughters. As *fact* magazine theorized in 1966, the "final question" suggested that it was a personal reflection on a white man's power if his daughter married a black man. "A Negro having rela-

White residents in a Chicago neighborhood, angry at a civil rights march, claim to be protecting "white womanhood" during a 1966 demonstration. Protests such as these suggested that northern and southern whites might rally together against integration because it posed a threat to the "racial purity" of white women. (AP/Wide World Photos.)

tions with a white man's daughter, his own precious virgin, is in effect a storming of the castle, the penultimate act of castration." The segregationist Bob Weems agreed, making even more explicit the connection between interracial sex and white male patriarchal power: "Overpowering *a* white girl is to overpower *the* white man." "Would you want your daughter to marry one?" made the possibility of interracial sex a direct threat to white male manhood and control, implying that all rational white men would oppose interracial relationships in their own families. Thus the humor of a 1965 cartoon in *Negro Digest* which showed a white man on a psychiatrist's couch declaring, "And one morning, Doc, I woke up not giving a damn whether my daughter married one or not."[45]

Before the 1960s, whites who supported racial change either ignored this question or attacked it as misleading by insisting that racial integration would not lead to intermarriage. In the 1960s, however, white liberals began to grapple with the "final question" in a more serious way. In religious forums, mass media articles, and on the movie screen, liberals directly faced the question of whether they could fully accept blacks as their daughters- and sons-in-law. As one southern Christian liberal wrote in a 1964 *Community* article, it was not enough to cite statistics about the rarity of intermarriage or to assert the general principle that every individual should be free to marry whomever he or she chose; those who wanted to deal with the "question" would have to address the "subterranean feelings on which the question is based."[46]

The willingness of racial liberals to engage in a discussion of their personal feelings toward intermarriage also reflected a sense, intensified by the movement, that these "subterranean feelings" were perhaps the most important barrier to fundamental change in the racial system. For years segregationists had insisted that racial discrimination was, at its core, sexual, psychological, and emotional rather than economic or political. In the decade after *Brown,* racial liberals began to agree that the emotional basis to racism was more of a barrier to racial change than they had previously thought. The intense resistance to change in the South, the hatred that the television showed on the faces of white mobs, and the willingness of seemingly decent people to inflict cruelty on nonviolent protesters and even children, led those who supported the fight for black equality to focus on the psychological and emotional dimensions of racism. Whites' aversion to interracial marriage, which symbolized their inability to accept blacks as their equals, became an important part of the racial problem that had to be addressed. One 1970 work even warned that the issue of whites' attitudes toward intermarriage was the only racial question of any importance. Until whites began to liberate themselves from their "keystone fear" of interracial marriages, Joseph Washington argued in *Marriage in Black and White,* there could be no real racial progress. "To the degree we come clean on marriage in black and white, everything else can be worked out, and to the degree we are dishonest about marriage in black and white, nothing else will work."[47]

Writings by white liberals in the 1960s were often confessional in tone, characterized by personal soul-searching in the authors' efforts to be brutally honest about their own attitudes toward blacks and about interracial marriage. Religious figures, grappling with the conflict between

disapproving of intermarriage and preaching human brotherhood, decided that if they followed their religious beliefs, they would have to
accept and support interracial marriages. Most respondents to a 1960
United Presbyterian Church survey decided that they would approve of
a daughter's interracial marriage, as long as the Negro involved was an
upstanding Christian, the couple was committed, and they understood
the obstacles they would face. Any other position, several writers noted,
would violate their Christian beliefs in human brotherhood. Reverend
Eugene Askew, from a Texas Congregational church, explained that if he
didn't want to be a hypocrite, he would have to say, yes, he would want
his daughter to marry a Negro. He could not "now reverse myself when
the basic issues about equality, brotherhood and love are on the verge of
becoming personal in a way they have not yet been."[48]

For Norman Podhoretz, the liberal Jewish editor of the left-wing
magazine *Commentary*, coming to terms with the emotional aspects of
racism meant admitting his own deep-seated antipathy for blacks and his
aversion to interracial relationships. In the 1963 *Commentary* article, "My
Negro Problem—and Ours," Podhoretz explored his own experience
as a poor boy growing up in Brooklyn in the 1930s, where gangs of Jewish boys fought constantly with the black boys in the neighborhood.
Podhoretz feared and hated—but also envied—blacks, who seemed not
to care about authority and seemingly had the courage to rebel against
parents, teachers, and authority figures. These childhood experiences,
Podhoretz admitted, had influenced his own view of blacks, and he could
not imagine whites who had grown up free of such feelings. All American whites, Podhoretz argued, were "sick in their feelings about Negroes." Yet Podhoretz took the psychological dimension of racism not as
an excuse to maintain the status quo, but as evidence that change would
have to start at the level of the individual psyche. For him, the first step in
solving the race problem was dealing with his own feelings, especially the
"disgusting prurience" that stirred in him whenever he saw an interracial
couple. Feelings must be made to yield, Podhoretz insisted. "One's own
soul is not the worst place to begin working a huge social transformation." The place to start, Podhoretz argued, was with the old question,
"Would you like your daughter to marry one?" No, he wouldn't. He
would "rail and rave and rant and tear my hair." But then, he hoped he

would have "the courage to curse myself for raving and ranting, and to give her my blessing." How else could he be the man he had a duty to be? As Podhoretz expressed it, accepting a daughter's interracial marriage was a sign of his manhood, not his lack of it.[49]

The angst white liberals, especially men, felt about their ability to overcome internalized racial feelings and to truly accept blacks as their equals received its most extended discussion in 1967's *Guess Who's Coming to Dinner,* a film that argued that white liberal opposition to intermarriage was misplaced and outdated. In the film, Johanna, the twenty-three-year-old daughter of a well-to-do racially liberal San Francisco couple, brings her black fiancé home to meet her parents for the first time. Joey's mother, Christina, runs her own modern art gallery; her father, Matt, publishes the progressive city newspaper. The black fiancé, John, played by Sidney Poitier, is a highly educated, successful doctor who is about to take a job with the World Health Organization in Geneva. In the film's main plot device, John gives Johanna's parents only one evening to decide if they can accept the marriage without reservations. If they cannot, he tells them, he will call off the wedding, since he doesn't want to alienate Johanna from her family. Most of the film thus focuses on Johanna's parents and whether they will give their blessing to an interracial marriage. By making the black partner an exceptional person, the film made the case that racial prejudice was the only possible reason for Johanna's parents to oppose the union.[50]

The film presents interracial marriage both as a result of white liberal teachings and as a challenge to liberal beliefs. Johanna has no qualms about marrying John, because she has grown up in a racially progressive home and has internalized what her parents taught her. As her mother, played by Katharine Hepburn, explains:

We answered her questions, she listened to our answers. We told her that it was wrong to believe that the white people were somehow essentially superior to the black people, or the brown or red or yellow ones for that matter. People who thought that way were wrong to think that way. Sometimes hateful, usually stupid, but always, always wrong. That's what we said and when we said it, we did not add, but don't ever fall in love with a colored man.

Having been raised in this environment, Johanna assumes that her parents will accept the idea of an interracial marriage as uncritically as she has. She repeatedly reassures John that her liberal parents will not have any objections to the marriage. John, who is far more attuned than Johanna to racial tensions, is dubious. When Johanna's father, played by the archetypal American father figure, Spencer Tracy, demands to know why he needs to make up his mind so quickly about the marriage, John tells him that it was Johanna's idea that things be settled so fast: "Your daughter said . . . there's no problem, she said my dad, my dad is a lifelong fighting liberal who loathes race prejudice and has spent his whole life fighting discrimination and my parents, well, they'll welcome you with open arms—and I said, oh, I sure want to meet them."

Although both of Johanna's parents are shocked when she brings John home, her mother recovers quite quickly when she decides the young couple are truly in love. Matt Drayton, however, considers his wife an impractical romantic, and he insists that the young couple wouldn't have a "dog's chance" of making a successful marriage in the face of a hostile and oppressive world. Citing his patriarchal responsibility to protect his daughter, he refuses to give his blessing to the marriage. The film, however, presents his opposition as the misguided act of a man whose racial liberalism cannot withstand the real test of racial equality. His oldest friend, a Catholic monsignor, attacks Matt as a "broken-down old phony liberal come face to face with his principles."

Significantly, Matt changes his mind only when John's mother accuses him of being an old man who no longer understands what it feels like to be in love or to feel sexual attraction. His manhood thus challenged, Matt makes a dramatic final speech in which he gives his approval. "Anybody can make a case, a hell of a good case, against you being married," he tells John and Johanna:

> But you're two wonderful people who happened to fall in love, and happen to have a pigmentation problem. But I think that now, no matter what kind of case some bastard could make against your getting married, there'd be only one thing worse. And that would be if knowing what you two are, knowing what you two have, and knowing what you feel, you didn't get married.

In the 1960s, white liberals began to critique the long-standing definition of white manhood that centered on the ability to protect white women from the supposed threat of black men. In the 1967 film *Guess Who's Coming to Dinner*, Spencer Tracy plays an archetypal father figure who eventually comes to terms with his daughter's choice of a black fiancé. (©Bettmann/CORBIS.)

By the end of the film, Matt Drayton has overcome his reservations about the marriage, labeled the position he took earlier in the film as that of a "bastard," and implied that it would be cowardly for the couple not to marry.[51] The dramatic tension has been relieved: white liberals can overcome their own emotional reluctance to accept blacks fully and white men can accept an interracial marriage without compromising their manhood.

Guess Who's Coming to Dinner was both commercially and critically successful, breaking box-office records and garnering ten Academy Award nominations. The film resonated with members of an American public who were themselves worried about how the racial and social changes of the sixties might affect their own families. One mother who went to see the film with her teenaged daughter explained, "We've never talked about interracial dating at home—the subject just never came up. But when we left the theater I said, 'Gosh, this poses a whole new question.'"[52] *Guess Who's Coming to Dinner,* however, posed the question of intermarriage in as safe and controlled a way as possible. By giving Matt Drayton the power to prevent the marriage, the film gave the white patriarch ultimate control of the situation. And while John and Johanna's relationship in the film is described as passionate, little of that passion is shown on the screen. Only one real kiss made it into the final cut of the film, and even that kiss is seen only through a taxi rear-view mirror. The audience is assured that the couple has not slept together, because John refused to until they were married. Neither does the film does show their wedding, which would have brought the reality of the marriage home to the viewer more directly. Yet in spite of its limitations, the film represented a very public refutation of the long-accepted white position on interracial marriage. It not only argued that interracial relationships could be healthy, but also suggested that social opprobrium should not prevent couples from marrying and placed whites who opposed interracial relationships in the wrong.

An even more telling shift in white attitudes was the reaction to what was arguably the most famous interracial marriage of the decade, the real counterpart to the fictional drama of John and Johanna. On September 21, 1967, Peggy Rusk, the eighteen-year-old daughter of Secretary of State Dean Rusk, walked down the aisle with twenty-two-year-old Guy Smith in a small private wedding on the campus of Stanford University. Rusk had met Smith, the light-skinned son of a black Washington, D.C., professional family, when she was only fourteen during regular horseback riding outings in Rock Creek Park. The couple dated while Smith earned his degree at Georgetown University, and when Rusk went to Stanford, Smith took a job at the NASA's nearby Arms Research Center to be near her. A member of the ROTC who volunteered for active duty in Vietnam, Smith was in many ways an ideal match for the daughter of Dean Rusk. Appointed secretary of state in 1961 by John F. Kennedy, Rusk was a political insider who became the symbol of the administration's policy in Vietnam. The interracial marriage of the daughter of a high-ranking member of the cabinet (who was a native-born

Georgian, no less) attracted widespread media attention. This wedding, as *Time* magazine noted, was more "social history rather than society-page fare."[53]

Although no civil rights crusader, Dean Rusk practiced racial tolerance in his personal life, and in the glare of national publicity, he showed the nation that even the most divisive racial issues could be dealt with in a dignified way. Rusk and his wife, Virginia, attended the wedding and Rusk walked his daughter down the aisle. After the short ceremony, the beaming bride and groom emerged from the church and obligingly kissed for the cameras before heading to the reception. Their parents also left with smiles on their faces. Dean Rusk told waiting reporters that he was "very pleased" with the wedding and with his new son-in-law. Rusk understood that the wedding might have political ramifications, voicing his concern to Lyndon Johnson that the marriage might compromise his relations with some members of Congress. But he did not offer to resign, despite press reports to the contrary, and he stood by his daughter, both publicly and privately, calling the wedding a "family matter" that would be handled in a family way.[54]

Although Rusk's calm acceptance of his daughter's marriage angered some of his Georgian relatives, who accused him of abdicating his paternal responsibility to prevent an embarrassing interracial union, the media praised Rusk for handling the marriage with dignity and grace. To *Time* magazine, Peggy and Guy's union was "a marriage of enlightenment" that would long be remembered as "a benchmark in the troubled history of race relations in the United States." Most white readers responding to coverage in *Time* and *Newsweek* approved of the marriage. One called Peggy and Guy "prophets for our time"; another felt that their marriage would have a "great effect on all Americans and was another step towards a 'more perfect union.'"[55]

Although the State Department received several hundred hate letters and phone calls about the wedding, this type of outspoken opposition was increasingly out of step with the public mood. To *Time*, those who attacked the marriage were "kooks and bigots" relieving themselves "of excess bile at Rusk's expense." In 1963, only four years earlier, former president Harry Truman told a reporter that interracial marriage violated biblical teachings and that he had personally "edited" the men his daugh-

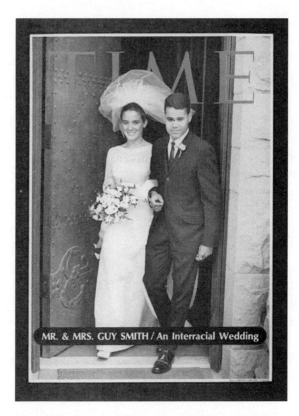

MR. & MRS. GUY SMITH / An Interracial Wedding

The 1967 marriage of Peggy Rusk and Guy Smith attracted widespread media attention and demonstrated
changing attitudes toward interracial marriage among
whites. *Time* and other publications portrayed the couple
sympathetically and presented whites' objections to the
wedding as misguided. (*Time,* September 29, 1967. Reprinted by permission of TimePix.)

ter had dated so she would end up with the right mate. In 1967, although
President Johnson made no comment on Peggy Rusk's marriage, his
support of Dean Rusk was viewed as tacit approval. First Lady Lady Bird
Johnson publicly congratulated the couple, saying she hoped everything
went well for them, "just as we all feel when one of ours gets married."[56]
Peggy Rusk, Lady Bird Johnson suggested, was "one of ours," a young
woman the entire country should wish well. Peggy Rusk was no hippie;

she was studious, sober, and had a "wholesome" appearance, *Time* magazine claimed. "Almost any parent could visualize her as their own young
daughter, plunging into intermarriage."[57] If Spencer Tracy was the symbolic father figure coping with a daughter's intermarriage, Peggy Rusk
became the symbolic national daughter who forced whites to consider
their own personal reaction to intermarriage.

By 1967 interracial marriages no longer generated the same violent
hostility or fear among whites that they once had. An interracial couple
could be seen as a positive sign of the times, and accepting intermarriage
could be a sign of maturity rather than of weakness. Outspoken critics of
interracial marriage were on the defensive. When Dean Rusk was asked
to join the faculty at the University of Georgia Law School a year after
the wedding, the segregationist leader Roy Harris, a member of the university's board of regents and chair of George Wallace's 1968 presidential
campaign in Georgia, tried to have his appointment rejected because of
Peggy's interracial marriage. The regents overrode Harris and appointed
Rusk. That same year, a Texas history teacher was fired after telling a student who asked him about Peggy Rusk's wedding that he did not think
there was anything wrong with interracial marriage. The state Board of
Education and the courts overturned the decision, ruling that he should
not have been dismissed simply because he approved of intermarriage.[58]

The public approval of Peggy Rusk's marriage stemmed in part from a
change in attitudes among whites as more came to accept the idea of racial equality, at least in the abstract, and as blatant expressions of racism
became less politically acceptable. But it was not only attitudes about
race that were changing. Large-scale cultural changes that took root in
the sixties would also have an important influence on whites', especially young whites', ideas about interracial relationships. These younger
Americans had been raised during an era when racial discrimination was
under attack and biological notions of racial supremacy had been largely
discredited, and national polls documented a growing gap between their
attitudes and those of their parents. In a 1968 Gallup poll, 34 percent of
whites in their twenties approved of interracial marriage as compared
with only 13 percent of those over fifty. By 1972, 44 percent of Americans aged 18 to 30 expressed approval of interracial marriage, while only
28 percent of those aged 30 to 49 and 19 percent of those over 50 did.

According to a 1971 Harris poll, 81 percent of Americans thought the
adults they knew would be upset if they saw an interracial couple out
together, but only 33 percent thought the young people they knew
would be.[59]

Young people ridiculed the uneasiness older white liberals felt about
interracial marriage. When Stanley Kramer, the director of *Guess Who's
Coming to Dinner,* showed his film on college campuses around the country, students were openly critical of the movie and its message. They criticized Kramer for making Sidney Poitier ridiculously accomplished and
for downplaying the sexual aspect of the relationship between John and
Johanna. According to Kramer, students around the country bluntly told
him that they had long ago accepted interracial marriage and did not see
it as a problem.[60] Children of racial liberals openly questioned their parents' disapproval of interracial dating. One young white man complained
that he couldn't understand why his parents were happy to see a black
family move in next door, but told him that he couldn't ever marry a
Negro. "I'd been raised to believe Negroes were just like anyone else.
Two and two just never made four." A white schoolteacher was shocked
that her "ultraliberal parents" opposed her engagement to a black man.
When you're brought up in a liberal atmosphere, she complained,
"you're not supposed to succumb to irrationality the way my parents
did." A young white man engaged to a black woman summed up the
mood succinctly in a 1968 letter to *Ebony.* "The college-age generation,"
he insisted, would accept no "sacred cows" from the past, especially the
notion that love should be bounded by color.[61]

The teenagers and young adults of the 1960s were representatives of
the post–World War II baby boom, an explosion in the birth rate that
led to an astounding increase in the number of young Americans. In
1960, sixteen million Americans were eighteen to twenty-four years old.
By 1970 that number had climbed to twenty-five million.[62] Raised in
an affluent America, many of these young people would have the luxury
of attending college or living on their own before settling down to
family, career, and domestic responsibilities. By the end of the decade,
nearly half of all eighteen- to twenty-one-year-olds were enrolled in college. Growing up during the civil rights movement, these young whites
became more aware of the structures of authority in their own lives.

Baby boomers transformed American cultural values as they angrily rejected institutional and parental authority and demanded their freedom as individuals to pursue self-gratification regardless of societal or family opposition.

Spurred by the idealism of the movement, young Americans of the 1960s would challenge accepted societal values and launch what would be a revolution in rights consciousness. Many rejected the morality and perceived conformity of the 1950s. Politically minded students joined in civil rights demonstrations or protested the war in Vietnam. At Berkeley, students in the Free Speech Movement criticized university authorities for ignoring student input and for running the university like a dehumanized machine.

At the same time, this sixties generation came of age in the midst of a sexual revolution that redefined acceptable sexual behavior in modern America. Erotic literature became more available as the Supreme Court liberalized its rulings on pornography. Films and plays dramatized sex more explicitly. Inspired in part by the success of *Playboy,* launched by Hugh Hefner in 1953, advertisers looking to capitalize on the youth market increasingly sold their goods by promising sexual excitement and titillation. Just as *Playboy* preached sex for pleasure and without commitment, Helen Gurley Brown's 1962 *Sex and the Single Girl* told young women that they should enjoy their time before marriage in dating and sexual experimentation. Sexual pleasure, a more candid society would now admit, was an important aspect of personal happiness that should not be denied, even if the couple involved was not married.

These cultural developments could not help but have a profound effect on whites' attitudes about interracial relationships. Dating interracially became a "hip" way to challenge authority and to strike a blow for sexual freedom. The Sexual Freedom League, a group founded in New York City in 1964 to fight all "unreasonable restrictions, legal and societal" on sexual behavior, wanted to see the decriminalization of everything from fellatio to miscegenation. College chapters of the Sexual Freedom League launched attacks on miscegenation laws, while at Berkeley, a student group intent on overcoming sexual restrictions urged its members to "make special efforts to . . . find lovers of different races." Interracial dating on campuses became more common, and observers

noted that it seemed to be tolerated in the protective campus atmosphere. The relaxing of prohibitions on interracial relationships, the authors of a study of an Arizona campus surmised, was a "side effect of the
general youth revolt."[63] *Time* magazine noted in 1968 that interracial
dating took place openly on college campuses, the "strongest enclave"
for interracial socializing in the country. Some parents even approved of
this "youthful experimentation" as long as it didn't progress to marriage.
When one University of Minnesota student told her parents she'd begun
dating a black man, they responded calmly, "Go ahead, but date others
too and don't let it get too serious."[64]

Underlying these cultural developments was a wholesale reconceptualization of the relationship between the individual and the larger
society. A new ethos of individualism stressed not only the importance of
personal gratification but also the primacy of individual rights vis-à-vis
larger societal institutions, from the family to the government.[65] Adopting these new values, young whites asserted that they had the right to
challenge all kinds of constraining social rules, including the taboo on
interracial dating. The song "Society's Child," written in 1966 by then
fifteen-year-old folk singer Janis Ian, highlights the changes in some
young people's attitudes. Telling of a white girl who decides to break
up with her black boyfriend because of the opposition of her mother,
schoolmates, and teachers, the narrator laments that she does not have
the courage to defy those around her. She tells her boyfriend, "One of
these days I'm gonna stop my listening, gonna raise my head up high . . .
but that day will have to wait for a while. Baby, I'm only society's child."[66]
As the young Ian noted, by the mid-1960s a hip, "liberated" person who
was free from societal conventions would be willing to date across the
color line. It was society that was wrong, not the individual who wanted
to date interracially.

With the new focus on individual freedom, interracial marriage could
be redefined as a courageous act of individual nonconformity. Psychologists and sociologists in the sixties increasingly characterized intermarriage as the act of a strong individual able to free him- or herself from
rigid racial thinking. Charles Smith, of New York's Post Graduate Center
for Mental Health, argued that the individuals involved in interracial relationships had good ego structures and were more prepared to accept

change than their parents, while the psychologist Ari Kiev insisted that those who married interracially had to be self-assured in order to act independently of their families and communities. To Paul Adams, a marriage counselor, interracial couples served as a reminder that "all deviance is not madness: some kinds of nonconformity can be wholesome and creative."[67]

According to this new understanding of interracial relationships, those who risked ostracism and persecution were brave and should be applauded, not attacked. When a group of college psychology students were interviewed about interracial relationships in the early 1970s, they agreed that a person who would date interracially would have "to be strong enough not to care about what other people think. A person who depends on what somebody else thinks would probably not be found in an interracial relationship." Not conforming to a group was neither "deviant nor abnormal," students stressed. As a short story in Negro Digest emphasized, it took a "special kind of courage" to marry interracially.[68]

The same social forces that allowed some whites to see intermarriage as a courageous act of nonconformity also affected the ability of families to prevent interracial relationships. In the 1940s, 1950s, and through the early 1960s, the most effective force in preventing interracial marriage was family pressure. Parents regularly used a variety of means to stop a potential interracial marriage. They might forbid their child to see his or her black lover, they might threaten the child economically, and in extreme cases, they might turn to the police and the courts to impose their parental will. Yet in the 1960s, the ability of parents to control and dictate the actions of their children decreased. Family historians point to a "profound shift in cultural values" in the late 1950s and 1960s, from an understanding that happiness was a by-product of hard work and family obligations to a belief that happiness arose from self-gratification and individual fulfillment. Family obligations were reconceived as an impediment to personal growth and satisfaction. Americans in the 1960s increasingly claimed their right to act as individuals, free of familial and societal constraints.[69]

Even as white liberals finally came to grips with the question of intermarriage in their families, cultural changes were taking place that would make the premise of a movie like Guess Who's Coming to Dinner, in which the white father has ultimate say about whom his daughter marries, irrelevant. When segregationists asked, "Would you want your daughter to marry one?" they assumed that a daughter would ask her father's permission. By the late 1960s, it could not be safely assumed that a daughter (or son) would ask permission to intermarry, or that young people would have the same qualms about intermarriage as their parents did. Rabbi Albert Gordon, a staunch critic of both interracial and interreligious marriage, complained in a 1964 book that young people increasingly looked upon romantic love as a "natural right" that their parents had no authority to question or hinder. "The current belief that whatever one does is one's own business, and is only indirectly of concern to society, assures a steady increase in the number of interfaith and interracial marriages," Gordon predicted.[70]

White families who faced the issue of interracial dating lamented this decline of familial authority. When her son married a black woman, one Jewish woman recalled that she and her husband were "devastated" because they were worried about how the marriage would reflect on their status in the community. Her son, however, "was a child of the 1960s," who not only was color-blind but who also refused to worry about what others thought of his marriage. Faced with the choice of cutting her only son out of her and her husband's life or accepting his black wife, this mother chose the latter. Although she said she had come to love her black daughter-in-law, she still thought it would be easier for the family if she were white.[71]

Another woman blamed her "perfect" daughter's interracial marriage on the fact that the black movement was the "in" thing in the 1960s. Her daughter started out "snubbing her nose at society" and ended up falling in love with a black man. She was rebelling at a time when "everybody was jumping on the bandwagon for black people." After their daughter had been dating her boyfriend for more than five years, her parents finally gave their blessing for her marriage. The mother, however, never completely accepted her daughter's black husband and, nearly a decade after the marriage, was still waiting for the relationship to fail. She would never have done anything like this herself, the girl's mother emphasized, and if she had ever dated a black, she was sure that everyone in her hometown would have told her mother about it. "It was everybody's business to tell your mother when you were doing something wrong too. Everybody was sort of another mother."[72] This mother believed that the type of community controls that existed when she was growing up would have served to deter marriages like the one her daughter had chosen.

A widowed white woman who strongly objected to her daughter's interracial marriage refused to talk to her daughter for more than a year and a half after the wedding. Finally, she came to accept the marriage, although she never questioned her own negative stereotypes about blacks, instead coming to see her son-in-law as an exception to the rule. "In front of our parents we [people of her generation] put on different faces," she claimed. "I ha[d] other thoughts and ideas, but if my mother disagreed, I never would have done it." She also felt the social climate of the 1970s had contributed to her daughter's decision to intermarry. Children in the 1970s didn't feel ashamed when they did something their parents disliked, she asserted. "But if I did anything I thought my mother would disapprove of and she found out about it, I was terribly ashamed."[73] Shame, in other words, no longer effectively controlled an individual's actions.

In all three of these cases, the mothers eventually accepted their children's interracial marriages, even when they continued to dislike them. All realized that there was little they could do to prevent their children from marrying blacks. All, furthermore, felt that the environment in the late 1960s and 1970s enabled their children to assert their choices more forcefully, and that there were fewer methods parents could employ to control their sons and daughters. The same cultural changes that led some young whites to question racial distinctions and limitations on their personal freedom made them less willing to accept parental dictates.

Young middle-class whites like these, moreover, were increasingly likely to meet blacks in situations where dating relationships might take place. The success of the civil rights movement enabled more blacks to gain access to mainstream institutions. The end of legal segregation, the emergence of affirmative action programs that helped black Americans gain access to schools, government jobs, and corporate workplaces, and the robust American economy all contributed to the growth of a black middle class. Between 1960 and 1970, the number of blacks employed in middle-class occupations more than doubled, from 13 percent to 27 percent. During the 1960s, as the economy expanded and blacks found unprecedented opportunities to move into white-collar occupations, the middle class grew by 108 percent. It would increase by another 62 percent between 1970 and 1980.[74] The small black middle class of the 1950s often served the black community, working in segregated settings as teachers, doctors, small-business owners, and ministers. By the 1960s, however, members of the black middle class were more likely to interact with whites, working for national corporations or with government agencies, as did Johnny Ford, who became the mayor of Tuskegee. These class gains were matched by increases in educational attainments. More blacks graduated from high school, and an increasing number attended college with whites. Between 1960 and 1970, the number of blacks enrolled in college increased from 141,000 to 437,000. By 1980, 718,000 blacks were enrolled in college, many of whom attended predominantly white universities. In 1964, more than half of all black college students attended historically black colleges. By 1970, over 75 percent of black college students were enrolled in institutions with predominantly white student bodies.[75] The spatial segregation that mitigated against interracial marriage in the twenty-five years after World War II was decreasing.

The 1960s changed whites' responses to intermarriage on many levels. The success of the black freedom struggle contributed to the decriminalization of intermarriage, to a significant change in white people's attitudes about blacks, and to a wide variety of "rights revolutions" in the United States that stressed the importance of individual rights. The greater tolerance for interracial relationships among whites was a sign of the civil rights movement's success in transforming whites' attitudes about blacks and discrediting openly racist discourse in national politics. The changing reactions to intermarriage also stemmed from societal and cultural changes of the 1960s unrelated to race. The celebration of individual rights and the pursuit of sexual and personal gratification led more whites to experiment with interracial dating and weakened the social controls available to prevent intermarriage.

These developments resulted in an increase in the rate of black-white interracial marriage nationwide. The number of black-white couples counted by the U.S. Census increased 25 percent between 1960 and 1970, rising from 51,000 in 1960 to nearly 65,000 by 1970. By 1980, only ten years later, the number of interracial married couples nationwide would climb to 167,000. The 1960s marked the beginnings of a steady and dramatic increase in the rate of interracial marriage. Black-white marriages did not become commonplace, but interracial couples were no longer so unusual.

Yet just as interracial marriages became more accepted among whites, they were becoming more contested in the black community. With the resurgence of the philosophy of black nationalism in the mid-1960s, disapproval of interracial relationships among blacks soared. As blacks became more integrated into white institutions, marrying across the color line would increasingly be seen as an attempt at assimilation and as a sign of racial inauthenticity among blacks. The rising rates of intermarriage, especially those involving black men and white women, also sparked contentious debates between black men and women about gender-role expectations and the duty of individual blacks to the larger racial community. As that wry observer, St. Clair Drake, concluded in 1969, the primary source of the pressure against interracial marriage had changed. "In the last two years the white sides kinda got all right since Sidney Poitier came to dinner in the movie and Senator Rusk's daughter got married out here at Stanford. . . . The white side has eased up but now it is the black side, particularly the black women, who give it to you."[76]

TALKING BLACK AND

SLEEPING WHITE

Offstage, explosions signal the advance of the black rebellion in the middle of a bloody race war. Onstage, the leader of that rebellion returns to the home of his white ex-wife to claim their two young biracial daughters. Thus begins the 1964 drama *The Slave,* written by the interracially married black author LeRoi Jones. In the heated exchange that follows, the black revolutionary Walker Vessels tries to understand what happened to his marriage. Vessels desperately wants his ex-wife, Grace, to understand that he has never betrayed her personally or stopped loving her, despite his strident antiwhite rhetoric. He tells her, "You were my wife . . . I loved you. You mean because I loved you and was married to you . . . had had children by you, I wasn't supposed to say the things I felt." He could condemn the white race and still love a white person. "I was crying out against three hundred years of oppression," Vessels explains, "not against individuals." Yet Vessels never fully reconciles his personal feelings for Grace with his political attack on white oppression. The play ends ambivalently. Grace is killed by an explosion, and Walker leaves without taking the children, who are heard crying offstage.[1]

The Slave is an autobiographical work that illuminates the personal anguish Jones faced when he moved away from his life in the interracial Beat community toward an identity as a black nationalist.[2] Like Walker Vessels, LeRoi Jones was a black poet with two biracial daughters and a white (soon-to-be ex) wife. Jones had married Hettie Cohen in the Beat milieu of the 1950s, at a time when interracial marriages could be viewed as hip and radical. Jones's interracial marriage and his involvement with the primarily white Beat community, however, soon came into conflict with his increasing commitment to the struggle for racial equality. In the early 1960s, he began politically organizing young blacks in Harlem, associating with Malcolm X, and writing dramas that highlighted the vast gulf between the experiences of whites and blacks, even middle-class blacks like himself. By the mid-1960s, Jones was publicly attacking whites, telling one young white woman that whites were "a cancer" who could only help in the racial struggle by dying.[3]

The ambivalence of *The Slave* mirrored Jones' own uncertainty about the relationship between the personal and the political at a time of momentous political and cultural transition for black Americans. In 1964, after twenty years of widespread, though by no means unanimous, belief among blacks in the desirability of integration, the entire ethic of integration was challenged by young black activists who instead began to call for "black power" in a resurgence of the philosophy of black nationalism. Nationalists argued that blacks needed to build their own institutions separate from whites, celebrate their African heritage and personal beauty, and reject whites as allies in the fight against racial oppression. With their emphasis on racial solidarity and self-reliance, nationalist ideas provoked a reevaluation of the meaning of interracial relationships. Black power advocates charged that blacks involved in interracial relationships were "sleeping with the enemy," and they attacked intermarriage as an attempt to assimilate into the white world and to reject black culture (and even, perhaps, black identity). No longer a courageous and symbolic act of racial brotherhood, interracial marriage was redefined by nationalists as the conservative choice of "Uncle Toms" who were selling out the race.

Ironically, at the same time that nationalists attacked interracial marriage, the number of black men dating and marrying white women began to climb. In 1960, there were approximately 25,000 black men married to white women; by 1980, that number had jumped to 122,000. For some black men, becoming involved in an interracial relationship was a way to test a newfound sense of freedom in the wake of the civil rights movement. In other cases, these relationships simply reflected the increasing social integration of blacks and whites. But for a variety of reasons the rate of interracial marriage climbed far faster for black men than for black women in the 1970s. In 1960, roughly equal numbers of black men and black women were married to whites, but by 1970, 64 percent of all black-white marriages involved black men and white women, a number that would reach 73 percent by 1980.[4] These lopsided numbers gave rise to intensified opposition to intermarriage among black women, who feared being left without suitable marital partners. Asked one black woman plaintively in 1974, "The white man is marrying the white woman; the black man is marrying the white woman; who's gonna marry me?"[5]

Both the nationalist reconceptualization of intermarriage and the heightened criticism on the part of black women were in part a reaction to the new political atmosphere after the demise of legal segregation. In the post–civil rights era, as antimiscegenation laws fell, whites became somewhat more tolerant of interracial couples, and more blacks entered white institutions, many blacks expressed the concern that marrying interracially might become a way for blacks, especially those in a growing middle class, to reject their own community and to fully assimilate into the white world. Interracial marriage became more contested among blacks in the late 1960s because it was increasingly seen as an engine for assimilation that would allow successful blacks, especially black men, to leave the community behind as they focused on their own economic and social advancement. Debates about interracial marriage reflected a growing concern about how the black community could continue to produce strong families and inculcate a sense of racial responsibility at a time of expanding individual opportunities.

Black Power, the modern variation of black nationalism that was widely influential for nearly a decade beginning in the mid-1960s, emerged from the civil rights movement of the first part of the decade. Spurred by the pride and confidence that they had developed in the movement, young blacks in the mid-1960s began to express their frustration with the scope and pace of change and to demand their rights more forcefully.

Although the civil rights movement had ended legal segregation in the South, it had done little to help northern blacks or to end economic inequality. Disillusioned with the possibility for fundamental change within the American political system, and radicalized by their experience working with large numbers of white volunteers during the Freedom Summers of 1964 and 1965, civil rights activists in groups like SNCC and CORE began to question whether whites could truly be allies in the struggle for racial justice. In 1966, both organizations rejected the notion of interracial organizing and expelled their white members. Tired of being beaten and killed with impunity in the South, black power advocates turned away from nonviolence and began to call for blacks to defend themselves.[6]

In its simplest form, Black Power was a call for blacks to achieve control of their own lives "politically, economically, and psychically." Advocates of Black Power stressed the need for blacks to build their own communities apart from whites, rather than seeking access to white institutions. Blacks should own the businesses in their communities, run the schools their children attended, and control the police force that patrolled their streets. Some black nationalists saw this separatism as an end in itself; others viewed building group solidarity as a necessary stage before black Americans could enter American society as equals, arguing that blacks would be able to bargain effectively for their rights only if they established an independent political power base. Trying to work with whites had failed, as had the strategy of integration, nationalists contended. Integration, SNCC's Stokely Carmichael insisted, was just a subterfuge for maintaining white supremacy. As he explained in 1967, integration was "despicable" because it reinforced the idea that white was automatically superior and black was by definition inferior. Blacks who integrated into the white world would be forced to give up their racial identity and their culture. "Acceptable" blacks, moreover, would be encouraged to forgo their heritage as a means of maintaining white supremacy over the black masses. Integration, therefore, would result not in equality, but in assimilation and even in cultural annihilation.[7]

With this emphasis on black pride, racial consciousness, and the need for racial unity, interracial marriage became a natural target for black nationalists. Until the mid-1960s, most blacks viewed interracial marriage as a personal choice that had little to do with the larger racial struggle. Black nationalists, however, argued that blacks who married whites cut themselves off from the black community and hindered the fight for black liberation. As nationalists saw it, they were traitors to the race.

Although sociologists had long described intermarriage as an act of social and cultural assimilation on the part of the minority partner, blacks, for the most part, had not viewed marrying interracially as a sign of a lack of racial or black cultural identity before the 1960s. Indeed, blacks who intermarried before the sixties rarely assimilated into the white community. Instead, whites who married blacks were far more likely to assimilate into the black community, moving into black neighborhoods and becoming part of black extended families. Before the 1970s, interracial couples usually raised their children as black, not as white or even as biracial. Intermarrying did not gain black partners access to better jobs or to the resources of the white community; instead, intermarriage cost the white partner status and privileges. In other words, interracial marriage was not an engine for assimilation for blacks in the 1940s and 1950s and thus did not raise the same concerns about a loss of racial identity or community.

Yet in the late 1960s, an increasing number of blacks began to claim that blacks who married whites abandoned their distinctive cultural practices and values to enter the white world. These accusations reflected both the heightened concern in the post–civil rights era with racial authenticity and the new forms of cultural politics that were rapidly becoming the key markers of racial identity. In the years after the end of legal segregation, the cultural arena became an increasingly important site for delineating a distinctive black racial identity. The cultural politics of the Black Power period took many forms. Blacks were encouraged to leave their hair natural rather than straightening it. Across the country, African-inspired fabric and clothes like Kente cloth and dashikis became popular urban outfits. Nationalists created new holidays such as Kwanzaa, which celebrated African values.[8] A wide variety of acts assumed greater political and symbolic weight. Personal acts such as dressing, listening to music, speaking, and dating were politicized as markers of black identity.

Cultural politics, of course, were not new in the sixties; ways of dressing and speaking, for example, have long been understood as potentially political.[9] But in the post–civil rights era, as some blacks were able to gain access to white institutions, these cultural markers of identity became even more important. If a black person grew up in a predominantly white neighborhood, went to a predominantly white school, and ended up working at a predominantly white corporation, how could his or her allegiance to the race be determined? Even those blacks not involved with whites might find themselves in social situations with whites. How, in a postsegregation world, should blacks maintain their distinctive racial identity? And how should the actions of other black people be judged? The politics of racial authenticity that emerged in the late 1960s reflected a struggle by blacks to find new ways to mark their identity. As Charles Hamilton, the coauthor of *Black Power,* wrote in 1969, blackness was no longer just a matter of skin color; it was an ideological issue as well. "Real" blacks supported black neighborhoods, black businesses, black political power, and—according to some definitions—did not marry whites.[10]

For Black Power advocates, the focus on the importance of a positive black racial identity went hand in hand with a condemnation of race mixing. The Nation of Islam, the Black Muslim organization that rejected racial integration, disapproved of interracial marriage as much as any southern white organization. "Why should we chase white women?" Malcolm X asked at a Freedom Rally in Harlem. "Our women are the most beautiful, like a bouquet of flowers. . . . Let the white man keep his women and let us keep ours." In a 1960 radio interview, he explained that the Nation was opposed to integration if it meant "that a black man should run out and marry a white woman or that a white man should run out and get my woman, then I'm against it. We're absolutely against intermarriage!"[11]

To nationalist critics, black-white relationships were unhealthy manifestations of black people's internalization of white standards of beauty. They claimed that blacks were interested in whites because they had been told for so long that whites were superior and more attractive. This was particularly true for black men, who had been conditioned—or brainwashed—to see white women as the pinnacle of beauty and femininity. Eldridge Cleaver, the minister of information for the Black Panther Party, saw black men's desire for white women as another aspect of their oppression. Because black men and women had been indoctrinated with white standards of beauty, interracial relationships signaled a devaluation of the black race and of black women. Loving a white woman was a "revolutionary sickness," a sign of one's desire to be white.[12]

In this highly charged political context, proponents of assimilation came under attack. *Ebony* magazine, which unabashedly celebrated those blacks who succeeded in the white world and portrayed interracial marriage as a positive sign of whites' ability to accept blacks as their social equals, was sharply criticized by its readers in the late 1960s. The new militancy among younger blacks first became an issue in late 1964, when the magazine ran a cover story on black artist Sammy Davis, Jr., and his Swedish-born wife, Mai Britt. The story was no different from dozens of other stories *Ebony* had run about interracially married black celebrities in the previous twenty years, but the responses it elicited from readers contrasted sharply with previous reactions to similar features. The story, one New York reader complained, was "morally offensive and an affront to the Negro race." Black people weren't proud of this marriage; by featuring the couple, *Ebony* revealed itself to be "as shallow and sick as Sammy obviously is." Other readers pleaded with *Ebony* not to put any more pictures of "white devils" on its cover and criticized the magazine for holding up Davis as an example for other black men. "He is one of the kind that is not fighting for civil rights for his own race, but is fighting for a way to get to a white woman that is the frightening part about the fight for civil rights," Arsola Thompson of Toledo, Ohio, declared.[13] Throughout the late 1960s and 1970s, *Ebony* readers openly and vehemently challenged the magazine's favorable portrayal of interracial couples. *Ebony,* one reader argued in 1966, was an "Uncle Tom magazine," full of stories about successful black men with their white wives, while another responded to a story about actress Leslie Uggams's marriage to a white Australian with a plea to stop printing articles on "these treacherous deceivers." Articles about interracially married blacks only encouraged blacks to lose identification with their people.[14]

On newly integrated college campuses, blacks students faced intense peer pressure to maintain a distinct black racial identity, even to segregate themselves from whites. As one black woman lawyer who attended college in the late 1960s explained, "you just did not associate with white students if you had any leanings towards being black. It was just not done." A black freshman at New York University in 1968 described her resident fellow as "totally black power." Blacks were not even supposed to speak to white people, let alone date them; at one point, a line was painted down the middle of the dormitory hall, one side for blacks and the other for whites. Courtland Milloy, who in 1968 became one of the first fifty blacks to integrate the campus of Louisiana State University, initially hoped that he would be able to socialize with whites. Yet he found intense pressure at LSU not to mix with whites, especially from black women, who castigated the black men who dated white women on the campus, and from campus nationalists, who stressed that blacks needed to take pride in their identity. Milloy recalls that "it was decided that we had not come to LSU to integrate. We had come to start our own black organizations."[15]

The rapid shift in the political landscape stunned blacks who had been proud supporters of integration or who did not view interracial dating as politically harmful. One thirty-three-year-old black woman who had grown up in a small southern black farming community, had taught in Harlem, and had supported the civil rights movement, even wrote to *Ebony* to ask if being proud of famous intermarried blacks and liking the film *Guess Who's Coming to Dinner* made her "anti-black or Uncle Tom." No, replied Regina Jones of New Jersey, a subsequent correspondent, she was not a "Tom," but was an "unhip black woman who must get herself together." Not knowing the current state of black politics was not "anti-black," but not trying to overcome her ignorance was "indeed a 'cullud' attitude."[16] Tony, a black medical student who had been involved with the Black Panthers, tried to come to terms with the disapproval and shock of his friends when he moved in with a white woman. As his friends saw it, he failed to understand the connections between the personal act of interracial dating and his political commitment to black people. "A lot of them felt that interracial couples are just politically devastating," his then girlfriend, Judy, remembered. Yet while Tony could understand blacks' resentment of interracial dating intellectually, he couldn't relate to it himself. "Emotionally he was in love with me and to be blocked out because I have white skin, to Tony was absolutely incredible." The couple eventually broke up, though not because of racial differences.[17]

Not surprisingly, blacks who had white partners faced bitter attacks in the 1960s and 1970s. How the black members in the relationship reacted to these new criticisms depended on their level of commitment to their white partner, whether they were dating or married, and whether they were drawn to the ideas of black nationalism. The new political climate led both black men and black women who had been interracially involved to reassess their relationships, and even to end their marriages. A black man with a white wife and two biracial children separated from his wife after he became a Black Muslim. None of his new Muslim friends would have anything to do with his wife. One black woman began to feel uncomfortable about her interracial marriage once she started working for the Legal Defense Fund. It seemed inconsistent "to be worried about racial matters and then on the other hand to be married to a white person."[18]

LeRoi Jones also found it impossible to reconcile his interracial marriage with working in the cause for blacks. Neither whites nor blacks took Jones's new public persona as a black nationalist seriously as long as he had a white wife. As one journalist explained, "After all, LeRoi had been around the Village for years, had run with the white beatniks in the early 1950s, had married a white Jewish girl. So how could he really mean what he was saying? Actually *mean* it . . .?" The fact that he had a white wife "blurred his indictments" of whites, his wife recalled. He was called a white-hating madman, but he was still married to a white woman and had white friends. After Malcolm X was assassinated in 1965, Jones moved to Harlem and founded the Black Arts Repertory Theater, returning home only occasionally to visit his children and, as Cohen recalls, to compare his own situation to that of Jomo Kenyatta's, the Kenyan who had left his white wife in order to lead his people. Jones and Cohen were divorced that same year, and Jones soon changed his name to Amiri Baraka and married a black woman.[19]

Those who did not voluntarily end their relationships with whites were publicly criticized by other blacks for "selling out" and for "acting white." A black woman who married a white man in 1968 remembered that a lot of her friends "exerted a lot of totally negative pressure on me. They felt I had married into the enemy camp, and they saw that as a betrayal of my commitment to blacks." Another young black who dated interracially told a reporter in 1969, "You get a lot of static from the militants in the Afro-American community—you know, the 'Buy Black, think Black, Love Black' guys—and other people. They'll call you 'Tom' or 'white man's flunky' if you date a white girl." Grace McAllester, the black woman who had faced reprimands and worse from whites for marrying a white student she met at Earlham College in 1952, found that in the mid-1960s the backlash came from black students at the high school where she worked. How could she be black if she was married to a white man, they wanted to know.[20]

For the first time, some interracial couples faced more problems from blacks than from whites when they were out together. Two black students who attended an exclusive Ohio prep school recalled their trepidation at taking their white girlfriends to a basketball game at a local black school in the late 1960s. "I was more comfortable going in a white environment with a white date than I would have been going in an all-black or predominantly black environment," one of them explained. Interracial couples were shunned or castigated by blacks. A black man dating a white woman on one college campus found that blacks would speak to him if he was alone, but not if he was with his white girlfriend. One campus leader told his white girlfriend that she should not take it personally if he ignored her when he was around other blacks. Melba Jenkins, a black nurse, could chart the changing political climate in the reactions she faced as half of an interracial couple in Washington, D.C. When she first started dating white men, the hate stares came from whites, but by the early 1970s, it was blacks who stared and whispered more, expressing their disgust that she was "consorting with the enemy." And when St. Clair Drake and Charles Hamilton visited their old high school in 1968, the Black Student Union would not have anything to do with the two black academics because both of them were involved with whites.[21]

It was a particularly difficult time for interracially married political activists, who found their commitment to the black struggle questioned because of the choices they had made in their personal lives. Many black leaders who had been committed to the philosophy of integration had married whites in the days before Black Power. During the civil rights era, there was no inconsistency between political involvement and an interracial marriage, since most activists were fighting for an end to segregation and the integration of blacks into white institutions. In the late 1960s, however, as nationalists fundamentally repoliticized interracial relationships as conservative acts that hindered the fight for black liberation, intermarried blacks faced new questions about their ability to participate in, let alone lead, the racial struggle. As one young black woman noted in 1970, dating a white person signaled one's desire to assimilate into the white race, and no one who assimilated could really participate in the black struggle. It would be schizophrenic, she wrote, "to be talking about black power, black control of our resources and then turn around and go to my white home in the suburbs because I've married this white doctor. I don't see how I could continue to work for black people." At the University of Washington in the late 1960s, students who dated whites were not allowed to play any role in black campus politics. If a student wanted to walk around "with a blond draped on his arm, okay," a student leader told St. Clair Drake. "All we say is don't try to join the black studies association, don't try to be a black leader on this campus, integration is his thing." Those who argued that their personal lives did not reflect on their political commitment were seen as naive. Blacks who chose to date and marry interracially had to understand that their choice meant that they could not be involved in the black freedom struggle, asserted the psychiatrist Robert Tucker. If a person's partner meant more to him than his involvement in black liberation, said Tucker, "he should be prepared to face the scorn of his brothers and sisters." Or as one nationalist magazine put it, one could not separate his "politics from his pussy."[22]

Being involved in an interracial marriage thus became a much greater liability for black leaders, and many were pressured either to end their relationships or to relinquish their leadership positions in the black community. By the late 1960s interracial marriages "were under open attack," remembered James Farmer, a founder of the Congress of Racial Equality, who experienced this pressure firsthand. "Prominent blacks with white wives were dumping their wives and marrying black women with Afro hairdos."[23] Like other integrated civil rights organizations, CORE experienced new tensions during the Black Pride Movement, tensions that were exacerbated by the fact that Farmer's wife of nearly twenty years was white. Farmer was publicly criticized for his marriage by Malcolm X in a 1962 debate and by Harlem nationalist groups, who told him, "We're coming downtown after you next, Farmer, because you got that white wife down there." As CORE moved increasingly toward separatism and support of Black Power, there was no place in the group for a person who had been identified with integration and interracialism. Farmer resigned from CORE in 1966 and was replaced by Floyd McKissick, who quickly moved the group toward a black nationalist orientation.[24] Julius Hobson, a longtime black activist in the Washington, D.C., area, also felt the wrath of black nationalists when he married a white woman in 1969. When one young black activist suggested turning to Hobson for advice, another responded, "That man Hobson's had it. Since he married the white woman, his mind's gone, he's not emancipated." Others snubbed his wife at black political affairs.[25]

Some of these political figures were truly surprised by the depth of the antiwhite feelings of the time. Julius Lester, a folk singer and writer affiliated with SNCC, was dismayed by the ways in which the ideas of Black Power infiltrated the realm of personal relationships. A 1960 graduate of Fisk, in 1962 Lester married a white singer he met at a progressive music camp, and began working with SNCC. Although Lester had strong personal reservations about black nationalism, in 1968 he wrote a book called *Look Out Whitey! Black Power's Gon' Get Your Mama,* which put the modern Black Power program into historical perspective, explaining it as part of the long struggle against white subordination and for cultural autonomy. Lester's popular explanation of Black Power, however, did not call for black separatism, and the book was even dedicated to his white wife.[26]

After the publication of *Look Out Whitey,* Lester was attacked as a hypocrite who was "talking black and sleeping white." People in SNCC let him know in "indirect and subtle ways" that they disapproved of his marriage, and other blacks wondered how he could preach Black Power and still practice integration in his personal life. One reader responded to a story by Lester in *Ebony* with the observation that "interracial marriage

is a form of integration in itself. If interracial marriages are permitted in
the newly formed black nation, how long indeed would it be a black nation?" Another scoffed at the idea that blacks should listen to "a black
man married to a white woman . . . telling us the necessity of separation.
He can't even crawl out of bed with 'it' and [he's] 'gonna' tell us to separate."[27] Lester later wrote that he found it frightening to be identified
personally with what he had written. "Because I can express black anger
does not mean I am angry, and it certainly doesn't mean I hate white
people." He could not understand the hatred of whites that so often went
hand in hand with the black nationalist movement. "If I had not been
married to a white woman, perhaps, I would not have cared (I hope I
would have)," Lester wrote in his 1976 memoir. "But I was and I did not
want her killed by somebody out to get 'Whitey.'"[28]

Lester, however, was out of step with the times. Although he remained
committed to black cultural politics, teaching Afro-American Studies
and writing children's books based on black folktales, his adherence to an
ethic of integration and his interracial marriage made him a target in the
black community of the 1970s. As a young professor at the University of
Massachusetts–Amherst, he discovered that black students shied away
from his classes because he had a white wife.[29] Lester refused to be
cowed, however. Since the 1970s, he has publicly attacked the identity
politics of black nationalism and the black racial hatred he feels it has unleashed. In his 1994 novel, *And All Our Wounds Forgiven,* Lester even suggests that interracial relationships are a necessary step toward racial equality, because they help heal "history's wounds" between blacks and whites.
The "real work" of the civil rights movement might even have been interracial sex, the book suggests.[30] For Lester, interracial sex had important
political benefits.

Not all interracially married black leaders faced such virulent public
attacks for their friendships and marriages with whites. Those who had
proved themselves during the movement were protected from some of
the nationalist rhetoric. Chuck McDew, the SNCC activist who married
a white woman in 1964, was, as he saw it, in a "sort of unique position."
No one could question his commitment to the black struggle, since he
had been repeatedly arrested and beaten and was once held in solitary
confinement in a southern jail for nearly a year. When Malcolm X ques-

tioned his marriage, McDew made it clear that no one, black or white, had the right to criticize his personal choices. "I have paid some heavy dues," he told Malcolm, ". . . and [not] you or nobody else will tell me who I will love." He must have been convincing, since Malcolm ended up sending McDew and his new wife a set of sherry glasses as a wedding present.[31]

Many of those intermarried black leaders who were attacked viewed criticism of their marriages as evidence of black nationalism's limited and misguided political precepts. Julius Hobson, for example, defended his marriage by attacking the exclusive focus that nationalists accorded to issues of race. The real problem facing blacks was economic oppression, Hobson insisted, and he wanted to foster alliances between poor whites and poor blacks rather than organize along racial lines. He was a militant, Hobson asserted, although his was not a "militancy that calls for racial separation."[32] Others criticized the tendency by nationalists to judge people by their personal choices rather than by their political actions. It was misguided to think that being intermarried meant someone was less committed to the black struggle or lacked a sense of racial identity, Julius Lester insisted. "I had one cat tell me that the reason LeRoi Jones was a revolutionary was because he left his white wife. Well, the implication is that one of the primary qualifications to be a black revolutionary is to have a black woman. And I can't relate to that." Having a white wife didn't mean that he was any less black or any less militant, Lester argued. It simply meant that he judged people as individuals. Lester also wondered whether nationalists actually opposed intermarriage because they were insecure in their racial identity. As he wrote in an "interview" with a fictional interracial couple, "If I can be married to a white woman and still maintain my blackness, then it means that they're operating on some pretty wrong assumptions. . . . They would much rather make me leave [my white wife] than see if they could have a close relationship with a white person and still maintain their blackness."[33] James Farmer also argued that there was no inconsistency between interracial relationships and black pride: "If blacks felt black pride in their very bones, then they had nothing to fear from association with others of different ethnicity."[34]

Other blacks found this particular form of identity politics—one that used involvement in interracial relationships as evidence of an individual's political commitment—to be a self-defeating exercise that diverted energy from a more substantive fight against racial inequality. Calvin Hernton, the black literary critic, insisted in his writings that blacks as a group should be concerned with ending white oppression, not with the personal preferences of a minority of people. "Are we fighting to restrict all black people to marrying or being intimate with only black people? Or are we fighting to get some POWER for all black people?" Focusing on these relationships played into the hands of white racists, Hernton insisted, because it reduced "the entire revolutionary struggle to a pseudo issue centered around interracial sex."[35]

Yet throughout the late 1960s and into the 1970s, Black Power advocates pressed their crusade to valorize black women above white, to build a self-sufficient black community separate from whites, and to reinforce strong black families as the center of that community. And despite criticisms from many quarters, the black nationalist critique of interracial marriage resonated with many blacks who were anxious about the possibilities for new types of racial assimilation in a world without segregation. Although it is difficult to assess how many blacks accepted the nationalist repoliticization of interracial marriage, throughout the 1970s, one-fifth of blacks polled opposed interracial relationships, and black rhetoric in letters and magazines was consistently more critical of interracial marriage than it had been even ten years before.[36]

It was not only the evolving meanings of interracial marriage for blacks that galvanized the late-1960s debate about these relationships, but also the emerging new patterns of interracial marriage among blacks. Up until the 1960s, the number of black men and black women involved in interracial relationships had been roughly equal. Indeed, according to the 1960 U.S. Census, there were slightly more black women married to white men than there were black men married to white women. In the 1960s, however, the number of black men who married white women began to soar at the same time that the rate of marriage between black women and white men dropped. In this period the number of black husband–white wife couples increased by 61 percent (from 25,496 to 41,223), while that of white husband–black wife couples decreased by

In the mid-1960s the growth of black nationalism triggered a backlash against interracial marriage in the black
community. Like these demonstrators, many black
women felt that the growing number of black men who
were marrying whites threatened the health and viability
of black families. (©Bettmann/CORBIS.)

9.1 percent (from 25,913 to 23,566). By 1980, 122,000 black men were
married to white women, as compared with only 45,000 black women
married to white men.[37]

Neither structural nor demographic factors explain why the number
of black male–white female couples increased at the same time that the
number of marriages between black women and white men remained

stable or decreased. Black women, especially those in the new black middle class, were not more segregated from whites than black men. Both men and women took advantage of the new opportunities provided by integration. Black women were as likely as black men to attend integrated colleges, to enter white-dominated professions, and to meet potential white partners.[38] If anything, black women should have had higher rates of intermarriage because of a growing gender imbalance in the black community. In the 1960s, the ratio of available black men to black women in the American population began to decline, a result of a shorter life expectancy for men, increasing homicide and incarceration rates, and a higher percentage of female births. In 1950, there were 99 black males for every 100 black females; by 1977, there were only 91. This disparity was even higher for blacks older than fourteen, because more young black men than women either died from violence, drug overdoses, accidents, and disease or were imprisoned. Thus in 1970, for every 100 black women over the age of twenty-five, there were only 84 available black men. This shortage was worst for college-educated black females. In 1970, there were only 88 black male college graduates for every 100 black female graduates; that number decreased to 74 by 1976. In short, as one 1972 *Ebony* article concluded, "a sufficient supply of black males for black females is not available at this time."[39]

This emerging gender imbalance, coupled with a growing sense that intermarriage represented a way to leave the group behind, upset many black women, especially those from the middle class who feared a decreasing pool of potential black husbands. Many black women in the 1960s and 1970s joined male Black Power advocates in criticizing black men who intermarried for deserting the race.

To these critics, the rising visibility of black male–white female couples at a time of renewed black nationalism was evidence of the misguided ways in which black men had been conditioned to think about masculinity and power during years of white racial oppression. Black nationalists, academics, and disgruntled black women insisted that centuries of being punished or lynched for even looking at white women had made having a white woman into a symbol of black male freedom. Michele Wallace, a black feminist and cultural critic, blamed the increase in black male–white female couples in the 1970s on black men's beliefs that free access to white women was a prerequisite to their own freedom and to achieving their manhood. Black men, she argued, had allowed white men to channel their rebellion into the sexual arena; possessing a white woman was the key to liberation, rather than more traditional avenues of achieving power, like seeking control over resources or politics. "A black man can walk down the street with a white woman unmolested. What a victory for the black revolution," Wallace wrote sarcastically.[40] Some nationalists even charged that whites manipulated black men's obsession with white women to keep black men in their place. *Black Male/Female Relationships,* a small black nationalist magazine published between 1979 and 1981, argued that black male–white female relationships were part of a larger racial conspiracy on the part of whites to limit black power by promoting racial disunity. White men used white women as symbolic bait to attract black men and to distract them from more substantive issues. The white man needed the black man to pursue white women "so that he can retain the trap, the mechanism, of keeping you castrated politically, economically, psychologically, sociologically, and culturally."[41]

Most of these relationships were unhealthy, if not depraved, critics charged. Some argued that black men turned to white women not for love, but for revenge. By sleeping with a white woman, the black man could simultaneously assert his own manhood and vent his hatred against white men, the sociologist Calvin Hernton theorized. "Having the white woman, who is the prize of our culture, is a way of triumphing over a society that denies the black man his basic humanity." The black psychologists William Grier and Price Cobbs argued that black men used "sex as a dagger to be symbolically thrust into the white man." Other psychologists argued that black men exploited white women as a means of avenging themselves on the white race. Black men, in other words, associated with white women in order to send white men a message that black men would no longer agree to a subordinate position in American society.[42]

Many black women argued that the rising intermarriage rate was evidence that black men believed white women were inherently superior to black women. Black men had internalized white standards of beauty so thoroughly, black women charged, that they would marry the whitest-looking woman they could find, regardless of her personality, looks, or intelligence. Crystal James, a young fashion sales representative, complained in 1970 that black men often dated white women who were inferior in status to them. The white women could be "dogs," but black men would date them anyway. These men, she contended, would "never go with a black woman in the same category." Black men, a black female lawyer commented, "are looking for a [T]winky and a cup cake; preferably . . . one who is yellow with cream filling and hair that blows in the wind. It doesn't make a difference how smart she is or how far we've come, that's still the case." As another black woman charged in 1970, the rapid increase in black male–white female marriages so soon after the civil rights movement seemed to prove that all those supposed "myths" about black men wanting white women had been true. Although most black women were not this adamant, a 1980 survey of 1,200 black Americans found that 12 percent of the women, as compared with only 4 percent of the men, believed that black men preferred white women to black.[43]

There is no doubt that the cultural stereotyping of white women as "forbidden fruit" who held the key to power and freedom compelled some black men to enter interracial relationships. One of the first black men to marry a white woman in Mississippi explained that he was attracted to his wife in part because of the challenge and thrill associated with having a white woman. For him, "the idea I wasn't supposed to have a white woman" made him want to prove he could have one. These cultural stereotypes led many black men to be curious about interracial relationships. Cautioned all their life to avoid even looking at white women, young black men in freer atmospheres, like that of a college campus, might well want to see what all the fuss had been about. Courtland Milloy, at Louisiana State University in 1968, was admittedly eager to meet white women. "Integration to me meant, in part, what it meant to some white people. It meant race-mixing," Milloy later wrote. He had an image of white women that had come off the cover of glamour magazines, "if not the centerfold of Playboy."[44]

Yet characterizing all interracial relationships between black men and white women as unhealthy manifestations of black men's cultural oppression and misguided attraction to whiteness is unfair. The picture of black men reduced to mad lust by the mere presence of a white woman borders on a modern manifestation of the racist stereotype of the black-beast rapist and obscures the complexity of relationships between black men and white women. Some black men, for example, found that the white women they idealized were quite different in reality. Milloy, for one, seemed surprised to discover that the white women he met at college did not live up to his centerfold expectations. He did not become involved with a white woman while at LSU. Many of those who did experiment with interracial dating on campuses and in other integrated settings, moreover, did not end of up marrying white women. Nearly 90 percent of black male students polled on one Texas campus had dated interracially, for example, but only 56 percent said they would consider marrying interracially. Although black men's sexual and racial curiosity about white women—as well as white women's own interest in black men as their own "forbidden fruit"—brought some interracial couples together, once together they had to move beyond these surface reactions if they hoped to forge a lasting relationship. For one black University of Michigan student, making his interracial marriage work meant that both he and his wife had to overcome their preconceived racial notions. "Once the curiosity and infatuation are over you settle down like any other couple," he explained. But it had taken some "soul-searching" to purge themselves of their racism.[45]

The "forbidden fruit syndrome," while overstated, may have contributed to the gender gap in black intermarriage rates, but just as important was the fact that no similar cultural stereotypes made black women and white men attractive to each other as dating or marriage partners. White men, unlike black men, had not been endowed with a particular sexual mystique, and black women had certainly never been the "forbidden fruit" for white men. In fact, the long history of sexual relationships between black women and white men poisoned rather than impelled modern interracial romances. Under slavery and later under the system of segregation, black women had little recourse against the sexual advances of white men, and many black women were raped, victimized, and sexually abused by white men. Slave narratives abound with stories about the danger black women faced from white men; the historian Darlene Clark Hine has concluded that "the ever-present threat and reality of rape" was one of the important factors that motivated black women to migrate from the South to the North. This exploitation continued after slavery's end, as white men used sexual violence to reassert control over blacks during and after Reconstruction. Until the late 1960s, it was almost impossible for a southern black woman to hold a white man legally responsible for rape. Not all sexual relationships between white men and black women were so abusive and exploitative, but very few of them ended in marriage. Even white men who kept black women as concubines, and treated them well, were rarely willing to marry their black lovers.[46]

This history of sexual abuse and illicit relationships affected many black women's feelings about interracial relationships and left them wary about dating and marrying whites. As the widow of the slain civil rights leader Medgar Evers explained in a 1968 *Ladies' Home Journal* article, her feelings about interracial relationships stemmed from growing up in Mississippi where white men openly preyed on black women, yet black men who even looked at white women might face death. "Sex between whites and Negroes was a one-way street, and the white man was invariably the aggressor." She understood that interracial relationships were dangerous, and that she, as a black woman, had little recourse against a white man's sexual advances other than her own "intelligence and agility." Although she hoped one day to achieve the color blindness her children seemed to practice, her own scars were "deep and deeply rooted in a past where hate was the only commodity in plentiful supply." As late as 1983, a black sociologist argued that black women weren't attracted to white men "because they still have memories of their grandmothers being sexually violated by white men."[47]

Black women were more likely than black men to see interracial dating as potentially exploitative. As one twenty-four-year-old black woman explained in 1968, her skin was still a badge that identified her as a "sexual plaything" to white men. Many were convinced that white men saw black women only as sexual objects, not as suitable spouses. In one study of interracial dating at integrated high schools in the early 1970s, many of the black girls interviewed were suspicious of white suitors, claiming that white boys wanted only sex, not relationships. "Any white boy who asked me out, I'd know what he wants," one black high school student insisted. Although some women refused to allow these historical forces to affect how they saw white men, many had difficulties viewing white men except through the prism of history. A black woman who was dating a white man explained that she sometimes wondered what he saw in her. "Am I the strong, comely wench with the good teeth that the slave master looked for in a black woman back then? Am I the hot Sally that turns him on?"[48]

The gender imbalance in interracial marriage rates also stemmed from a reluctance on the part of white men to date and marry black women. Even those black women who might want to date interracially felt that it was far more difficult for them to do so than it was for white women, in part because black women had few white suitors. White women, they complained, could choose freely among both black and white men, but black women did not have such choices. Black high school and college women complained that male students did not show the same kind of interest in them that black male students showed in white girls. White boys almost never asked out black girls, one high school student said, because it would be a "step down" for him, and friends would want to know if he was "hard-up or something." Dating a white girl could be a status symbol for a black boy, but dating a black girl conferred no status on a white boy. White male college students were far less likely to date outside their race than black men were. One young black woman, a college student on a predominantly white campus, explained in the early 1970s, "Interracial dating makes my jaw tight. . . . White chicks have an advantage over the sisters. Sisters must compete for the black guys; white chicks don't have to. She has her man and whenever she wants to she comes over and raids the black women's territory, something not freely available to black women." This young black woman felt she could not approach white men as easily as a white woman could approach a black man, and she was not alone. Another college student explained that black women on her campus did not have "free access to making it with the white guys."[49]

Given these widely divergent cultural beliefs and legacies, it is not surprising that many young black women not only disapproved of interracial dating far more than black men, but were less likely to date interracially themselves. A 1972 study of black students at four predominantly white college campuses in upstate New York found that nearly one-third of the black women, compared with only 13 percent of the black men, disapproved of interracial dating. Twice as many of the men as the women had dated interracially. On the campus of San Antonio College in Texas, the numbers were even more skewed; 88 percent of the black men had dated interracially, compared with only 28 percent of the black women.[50] Studies of black women professionals conducted in the late 1970s and early 1980s found that many simply refused to date white professionals, even though they knew few black professionals. Although most respondents claimed that they wanted to get married and have children, they saw few possibilities for doing so. "I don't really come in contact with black males and I don't date white males," one woman complained; another explained that she and her friends "don't even look at white men" despite a lack of available black men. Although black men of professional status were "almost extinct," an assistant U.S. attorney in the Civil Rights Division asserted, she refused to date white men because she didn't "want that to be the statement that I'm making in my life."[51] Many women, in fact, seemed to view marrying a white man as a choice of last resort. Some women reported considering becoming single parents, marrying men below their status, sharing husbands, or turning to lesbianism as more positive alternatives to dating whites. Indeed, 67 percent of the black women at a southern university reported in 1988 that they would rather remain single than marry outside of their race.[52]

Black women, especially those in the growing black middle class, thus perceived the trend of black men marrying white women as a serious threat to their own hopes for marriage. In their view, each interracial marriage took one more eligible black man out of a shrinking pool of potential mates for black women. As one young black woman wrote to *Ebony* in 1965, the growing number of black male–white female relationships presented serious problems for single black professional women. "In recent years," she wrote, black women "have begun to be rejected on a grand scale by similarly attractive well-educated Negro men." Black women, no matter how pretty or talented they were, became wallflowers, watching black men pursue white women, she complained. Many similarly frustrated black women expressed their anger at being abandoned by black men. "Black, beautiful, provocative and frustrated sisters" spent long weekends alone watching television while black men sought the company of white women, one woman charged.[53] In the late 1960s and early 1970s, letters from single black women complaining about white women who stole "their" men filled the pages of *Ebony*. One black woman who described herself as attractive and intelligent with a good job wrote to express her anger at white women. "The black woman has been used and misused for so long that apparently non-sister thinks we should accept this. . . . I do not want a white man. I, too, want a black man. The name of the game is 'competition.' Non-sister, you are trespassing." Some black women even founded symbolic "Save Our Men" clubs to protest relationships between white women and black men.[54]

Black men's interracial dating left many black women feeling betrayed, rejected, insecure, or even physically ill. "What's wrong with me?" a college freshman lamented in 1971. "There aren't enough black men to go around and *he's* messing with Charlie's daughter." Black men should be made to realize that interracial dating was both a practical and a symbolic rejection of black women, many women insisted. As one Colorado woman described it, successful black men who chose white wives were responsible for the "mental castration of millions of Black women." Another black woman who had lost two lovers to white women began to buy every book or magazine that might help her understand interracial relationships. She had reached the point where the sight of an interracial couple on the street made her feel sick.[55]

The arguments between black men and black women about rising intermarriage rates were just one manifestation of new gender tensions that were threatening to tear the black community apart, and the gender rift assumed a new public prominence in the wake of black nationalism.[56] Sexism and male chauvinism were crucial aspects of cultural black nationalism, which preached the necessity of black men's reasserting their masculinity and assuming their proper place as heads of black families. Nationalists idealized the strong black man and the submissive black woman. They argued that white racism demasculinized black men and forced black women to be self-reliant and to distrust black men; in fact, black women's independence was seen as a problem rather than a strength for the black community. Women political activists were pressured to resign their positions and let men take over. Angela Davis, who

was one of the few powerful women involved in the Black Power movement, recalled all the myths about black women that black men threw at
her: she was too domineering, she wanted to rob men of their manhood.
By holding a leadership position, male nationalists asserted, she was aid-
ing the white enemy.[57]

Some black men involved in interracial relationships turned to this
nationalist rhetoric to defend their decision to marry white women. Although nationalists condemned intermarriage and castigated blacks who
intermarried for betraying the race, the gender politics of nationalism
provided new ways for black men to justify their involvement in interracial relationships. They turned to white women, some claimed, because
black women were too domineering and demanding. Thus Fred Williamson, a minor black movie star in the 1970s, explained in an *Ebony* interview that he often dated white women because black women were
too aggressive: "Competition is just built into most of them." White
women, however, "didn't have to compete so hard, so they're usually
more able to let their man take complete charge. It so happens that I'm
a take charge man—all the way." Other black men justified their interracial dating on the grounds that black women did not respect or
submit to them like white women did. Black women, the black psychologist Danny Davis contended, were aggressive, coercive, and did not
give black men the same kind of recognition that white women did.
Many black men responded to his comments enthusiastically. "Why does
the black man dig the white woman?" Eddie James from Seattle asked.
"Because she does him good like a woman should. He digs being treated
like a MAN. That's something no black woman will ever do for him." A
black man who had been married to both a black woman and a white
woman complained that his black wife constantly nagged him for lacking ambition. His white wife, however, was undemanding and made him
feel good about himself. In these cases, blaming black women for interracial relationships became a way for men to assert their power over
women.[58]

Black women responded to this pressure in a variety of ways. Some
accepted black men's critique and blamed themselves for driving black
men away. Lisbeth Gant, who represented the voice of black women in a
1970 debate in *Ebony* on the "black man–white woman thing," claimed

that black women would have to abandon their dominant role if they wanted a man. Those who were serious about wanting to be with black men needed "to soften a little," she argued. An Alabama woman criticized black women for walking all over black men. White women respected black men, and it was white women who had "saved our men" from black women's neglect. "Now black women will either learn to appreciate and respect black men or live without them." Black women, another *Ebony* reader claimed, had to be more realistic about black men's economic and social status if they wanted to find partners. Too often, black women judged black men by white standards and were overly particular about the type of black man they would consider marrying.[59]

Many other black women, however, resented the sexism and the chauvinism of black nationalism. One young black woman remembered the fight she and her black boyfriend had after a lecturer on African nationalism told them that women's needs should be subordinate to those of men. "My man and I had the biggest fight because he said that was how I was supposed to act. But I wouldn't fall into it." Other young black women professionals complained that their black boyfriends felt threatened by their career success and their self-assurance. Keeping a man required compromises that not all of these women were willing to make. As one young lawyer explained, she could not imagine keeping her mouth closed "just to make a man feel better." Although 42 percent of black professional women in a 1982 survey agreed that black professional men would not date them because they were not deferential enough, few were willing to change their behavior to attract a man.[60]

For these black women, black men who intermarried proved that they were not secure enough, indeed not manly enough, to handle having a strong female partner. Those who chose to marry white women were not responsible or proud black men. As one black woman explained in 1973, "For black men to show such preference for white women and such disregard for their own women indicates lack of maturity and pride and demeans their manhood." A black New York woman pointedly accused black men of marrying white women as a way to avoid their responsibility to black women and the black community. Intermarried men were "narcotizing themselves behind their white wives as others withdraw from responsibility behind alcohol or drugs," she argued.[61]

Although much of black women's growing opposition to intermarriage in the late 1960s and 1970s stemmed from their personal fears of not being able to find a suitable black husband, their criticism also reflected a deeper gender divide in the black community. In their attacks on interracial marriage, many black women expressed the idea that the key to racial progress was unity. Equality and racial advancement would best be achieved by blacks who built strong black families and worked together in their communities. Individual goals might have to be sacrificed for the good of the race. Many black men, in contrast, argued that racial liberation was contingent upon personal freedom. Only when black people could act like individuals would the race truly be free.

Gender, of course, did not entirely determine an individual's position on the issue of how racial liberation for blacks might best be attained, but there were compelling cultural and historical reasons why black men and women would have different ideas about the measure of racial progress. Black women had long played a role in black communities as the transmitters of cultural values and as the central figures in extended black families. In his study of civil rights organizing in Mississippi, Charles Payne found that a disproportionate number of women were active in the movement, in part because women were so embedded in kin and communal networks that they were often drawn into the movement by other relatives. These black women might well feel a greater sense of responsibility to maintain the future of the community by building strong black families and raising black children.[62] As Alvin Poussaint argued in the late 1970s, "The black woman in some ways sees herself as guardian of the black experience, keeper of the culture and the black family role. She may feel more uncomfortable with the white male as father of her children than the other way around."[63]

Some black women clearly disapproved of interracial marriage because they wanted to keep alive historical traditions and felt a responsibility to pass their cultural knowledge on to black children. A black high school girl who dated both black and white boys in the late 1960s thought she would marry within the race because she had a "good personality and a good intelligence" and wanted to pass these traits to her children. Another black woman, who described herself as "attractive, intelligent and well educated," insisted that she would marry a black man so that their children could benefit from her achievements.[64]

Black women frequently wrote of the need to look beyond individual gratification to do what was best for black people as a whole. Lisbeth Gant argued in the pages of *Ebony* in 1970 that it was a waste of time to discuss how to improve the status of the black race until black men and black women could learn to work together: "The whole black outlook is a fallacy if the reality is that black men are increasingly turning to white women."[65] This position ultimately reflected a belief that black people had to place responsibility to the race and their community over their individual freedom; individuals had to be prepared to sacrifice some of their rights for the greater good. Marrying a white person reflected a lack of commitment to the group, putting selfish needs ahead of those of the race. One black college senior explained in 1970 that "there's really no such thing as an individual when you're speaking of the black race." Once she had thought primarily in terms of her own accomplishments, but now she thought about "what we are going to accomplish for the black race as a whole. To survive, the black community must remain unified." Racial progress, in other words, was incompatible with individualism. Sandra Satterwhite, a graduate of Bennett College, echoed this position. There was no room for interracial relationships in America in the 1970s, she argued. "We need all the black togetherness we can get. In the kind of society in which we are now living, we can't afford to be individuals in that sense."[66]

Some black women could imagine a society where interracial relationships would be irrelevant, but twentieth-century America was not it. In an ideal world, one black woman explained, everyone should have the right to marry whomever they wanted. But practically, the black race would cease to exist without strong black families. Blacks needed to love themselves "so much that we would want to see the blood of our heritage running in and through the veins of our children." Black people, another woman contended, had to "look beyond the individual kinds of gratifications . . . we need to look at what are our responsibilities." Black men and women had a responsibility to work together and nurture black children, she argued.[67] A few critics carried this position to its logical conclusion, arguing that the right to intermarry should be limited by the community for the sake of the greater good. "Until all black people are free, I can't see where any one has the right to deal with whom he pleases at the expense of children and the liberation movement," asserted one black woman in 1970. Another suggested that the very first law that should be passed if blacks ever got their own nation was one banning interracial marriages. As Darielle Watts reminded *Ebony* readers in 1970, "The Jews did not get to where they are today by intermarrying with WASPS."[68]

In these criticisms, black women conceptualized freedom more as the attainment of a group rather than the achievement of a single individual. Yet as many black men saw it, the right to act as autonomous individuals was a measure of their freedom. Having endured a social system where their political, economic, and social lives had been circumscribed and often rigidly controlled by whites, black men often saw individual autonomy and the ability to control their own lives as proof of their masculinity and independence. Thus while black women might define manhood as being loyal to black women, some black men defined manhood as the right to assert their own rights and not to be controlled by anyone, including black women. A poll of black, Chicano, and Anglo students at Texas Tech in the mid-1970s found that black males were the most adamant of all the groups that whom they dated was a personal matter with which society had no right to interfere. Black women, in contrast, were the group most likely to agree that interracial marriage was immoral.[69]

For some black men, having the right to choose their own marriage partners became an important aspect of reclaiming their masculinity. The black psychologist Danny Davis argued in 1970, "The black man needs to have the right to deal socially and sexually with anyone whom he pleases." In Davis's view, the black man had long been repressed and controlled, and now needed to assert his masculinity. "All his life, someone has been telling him what to do, whom he can see, whom he can't see. . . . The white man has done it to him; now I see the black woman wishing to do the same kind of thing." When black women objected to black men's interracial relationships, it suppressed part of their manhood. Julius Lester shared this definition of masculinity, arguing that he wasn't going to listen to criticisms of his interracial relationship. "I'm a man now, and black folks are trying to tell me who I am and what I should do. . . . I don't mind limitations, but there are some things no one has a right to limit me on. One of them is who you love and who you marry."[70]

Charlie Bodi, a black man who married a white woman in the 1970s, understood black women's criticism of his marriage, but refused to accept it. "I know where [black women's criticisms are] coming from because, as African American people, we've had to stay together to move forward, and there's strength and protection in numbers," he explained, but why should black women be able to define who he was, whom he could love, and what he could do? For some intermarried black men, criticisms of their marriage represented a type of "police mentality" that wrongly sought to limit their personal freedom.[71]

Blacks who were not themselves involved in interracial relationships also insisted on the importance of individual freedom, responding both to nationalist rhetoric and to black women's attacks on intermarriage. "We cannot regulate the personal lives of others," one black man argued in 1970. Or as another asked, "Who on God's green earth has the right to tell another human being how to choose his friends and whom to choose?" Some black women also saw calls to limit individual freedom for the sake of the larger good as a form of oppression, particularly in so personal an area as the choice of a mate. Attacking blacks for intermarrying was just another form of slavery, Vanessa Holt insisted in 1984. "The day I let another person tell me who to love, I'll go chop rock in Georgia 'cause I'll be more slave than free." Another woman reminded those black women who complained about black men's interracial dating that the United States had just emerged from a "nightmare" of legislated marrying. Whether or not they liked the idea of black men dating white women, "are my black sisters willing to return to the insanity of law's choosing our dates for us?"[72]

A majority of black Americans in the 1970s would probably have sided with those who stressed the importance of individual rights in the debate about the relative value of racial unity versus freedom of choice. The nationalist attack on interracial relationships reflected an insecurity about how blacks could maintain their racial identity and sense of group re-

sponsibility in a world where integration and assimilation were a possibility. But more blacks supported the right of individuals to marry
whomever they chose than thought the community should castigate
those who married interracially. As the sociologists Charles Willie and
Joan Levy noted in their 1969 study of black college students, on balance,
"the push for individual freedom usually transcends the call for racial solidarity whenever there is conflict between the two." Indeed, although
black disapproval for interracial marriages held steady at around 20 percent throughout the 1970s, the number of blacks who claimed to approve of intermarriage actually increased as the percentage telling poll-
sters they had no opinion declined. In 1972, the first time the Gallup Poll
asked blacks their opinions of intermarriage, 58 percent claimed to approve of such marriages. By 1978, 66 percent approved, and by 1983, 71
percent did.[73] In short, despite the strident opposition of black nationalists, black Americans remained far more tolerant of interracial relationships than whites.

Yet the undercurrent of opposition to intermarriage that had long existed among blacks came to the surface in the late 1960s as black nationalists articulated a forceful critique of interracial marriage. This opposition led some couples to end their relationships and kept other blacks
from dating whites. Although the number of black–white couples increased during the era of black nationalism, given the legalization of interracial marriage, the growing tolerance among whites for the practice,
and increasing integration in schools and workplaces, the rate of black-
white marriage would likely have been greater if not for the intensity of
nationalist opposition. The 20 percent of black Americans who expressed disapproval of interracial relationships in national polls were outspoken in their criticism, and for many more blacks, interracial marriage
was an important symbolic issue that starkly divided those who urged racial solidarity from those who rejected the right of any group, even their
own, to limit their personal choices.

The black nationalist era of the late 1960s and 1970s marked a high
point of vocal black disapproval of interracial relationships. Since the
1970s, most of the radical political organizations of the Black Power
movement have failed, victims of government repression campaigns and
internal divisions. The Nation of Islam remains one of the few active or-

ganizations preaching a Black Power ideology like that of the sixties. Yet recently even Louis Farrakhan, the leader of the Nation of Islam, has softened his traditional stance against interracial marriage, telling the audience at the Million Family March in 2000 that love was stronger than skin color. This departure suggests that some black leaders would like to bring interracially married blacks back into the fold by offering them some form of amnesty.[74] Certainly, many of the cultural values of Black Power remain powerful in modern black America. Legacies of the Black Power era include a positive sense of pride in a black racial identity, recognition of a distinctive African-American culture, and a continued ambivalence about racial assimilation. Yet while some blacks today still view interracial relationships as a sign of racial betrayal, heated condemnation of interracial relationships on strictly nationalist grounds has waned since the heyday of Black Power.

Opposition among black women has abated, but not disappeared. Even though the number of black women married to white men more than doubled between 1960 and 1990 (increasing from 26,000 to 61,000), and the actual number of intermarried black men is relatively small, many black middle-class women still fear that widespread intermarriage between blacks and whites will hurt their own chance of finding a suitable spouse, and many continue to accuse intermarried black men of personally betraying them. For contemporary interracial couples, black women's opposition has a more concrete impact on their lives than the legacies of black nationalism.

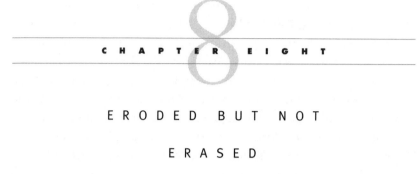

ERODED BUT NOT

ERASED

In 1986 Cherlene McGrady, a black magazine editor, met Doug Fearn, a white audio engineer and pilot. They married a year later, much to the delight of both of their families, who were glad the two had found each other. They had never felt any public hostility or condemnation as an interracial couple, either where they lived in West Chester, Pennsylvania, where they worked, or when they traveled together. People accepted them, McGrady felt, because they were not defensive or apologetic about their relationship. "We know we belong together and act like it!" Their young daughter, she insisted, had "unlimited options and horizons." McGrady had even started a support group to help families raise healthy biracial children with a strong sense of self-esteem.[1]

McGrady and Fearn's story is testimony to the remarkable changes that have taken place since the 1940s. Without riots or revolutions, centuries of barriers to interracial marriage have eroded significantly. Thanks to the legal and cultural shifts of the 1960s and 1970s, interracial couples today face a very different color line than they used to. Interracial marriage has been decriminalized and couples now have some legal protections from egregious job and housing discrimination. Interracial relationships have become far more visible in popular culture, and the most open hostility directed at interracial couples has diminished. As a result, interracial couples today are not forced, as they once were, to become part of the black community. They are as likely to craft lives for themselves among tolerant whites or with other interracial couples, and they are no longer limited to raising their children as black.

Those in this new generation of interracial couples refuse to be put on the defensive about their relationship or to remain invisible. Many aggressively assert their right to be considered normal families, free from the stigma long associated with interracial relationships. Forming their own magazines and support groups to provide for an "interracial community," attacking negative cultural portrayals of interracial marriage, and adamantly raising their children as biracial, modern couples not only are challenging stereotypes about interracial marriage, but are also demanding public recognition as legitimate families. The radical change in racial attitudes and values since the 1960s has made couples more confident and comfortable about and setting the terms for their own lives without compromise.

These changes, however, should not mask the fact of continued discrimination directed at interracial couples. Hostility among whites, while diminished, has by no means disappeared, and many black women remain outspoken critics of intermarriage. Many couples experience some mundane forms of harassment directed at them from both blacks and whites, although they now have more options about how to cope with persecution.

Moreover, at a time when the larger culture is becoming increasingly racially diverse, black-white marriage remains relatively rare. Though the number of black-white marriages has increased dramatically in recent years, from 213,000 in 1990 to 363,000 in 2000, such marriages account for only a small fraction of the approximately fifty-five million marriages in the United States today. The rate of marriages between blacks and whites, moreover, lags behind that of other types of interracial marriage. There are nearly two million marriages between non-Hispanic whites and Hispanics (these marriages are often counted as interracial, although many Hispanics are considered racially white), while there are close to 700,000 Asian-white couples in the United States. Native Americans and Asian Americans are significantly more likely to marry whites than blacks are. Over 50 percent of Native Americans marry outside their racial group, while 25 percent of Asians do. In 1990, by comparison, only

6 percent of married blacks had nonblack (primarily white) spouses. These numbers suggest that marriages between blacks and whites remain more controversial and contested than those between whites and other racial groups.[2]

Even so, the radical nature of the changes that have taken place over the last sixty years cannot be denied. Although the number of black-white couples remains small, the rate of intermarriage has been increasing dramatically. If only first-time marriages are counted, 10.8 percent of all marriages involving a black person in 1990 were interracial. In other words, one out of every ten new marriages involving blacks today is interracial, and the majority of these interracial marriages involve whites.[3] These current trends suggest that the color line separating whites and blacks, once unyielding and inflexible, has become less powerful in recent years.

Since the 1960s the United States has become increasingly racially diverse, and Americans themselves have become more tolerant and accepting of difference. American public culture celebrates multiculturalism and pluralism, and public expressions of racial hostility are no longer tolerated by schools or government officials. Indeed, the belief that race should play no role in government policy has been accepted by many Americans.[4] Although both multiculturalism and the ideology of "color blindness" that have emerged since the civil rights era can be fairly criticized as tokenism or as ideologies that mask continuing racial inequalities, these intellectual and ideological shifts have had an enormous impact on the lives of interracial couples. There is no question that it is easier to be intermarried today than it was thirty or forty years ago.

The years since World War II have been marked by a radical transformation in whites' attitudes toward interracial sex and marriage. In a 1997 Gallup Poll, 61 percent of whites claimed to approve of interracial marriage.[5] In 1987, voters in Mississippi removed the prohibitions on interracial marriage written into the state constitution. Voters in South Carolina and Alabama followed suit in 1998 and 2000, respectively. Although legally meaningless since the 1967 *Loving* decision, these consti-

An Alabama couple in November 2000 prepares to cast their vote to overturn the legally meaningless, but symbolic, ban on interracial marriage written into the Alabama state constitution. The Alabama constitution, like that of South Carolina and Mississippi, continued to criminalize black-white marriages long after the 1967 *Loving* decision invalidated such bans. (AP/Wide World Photos.)

tutional bans were characterized by opponents as archaic symbols of racism that tarnished the image of the South.

Government officials, schools, and the media, furthermore, increasingly characterize opposition to interracial marriage or dating as an outdated and unacceptable form of racism. When at a February 1994 school assembly in the small town of Wedowee, Alabama, principal Hulond Humphries threatened to cancel the school prom if interracial couples planned to attend, it became a national incident. When Revonda Bowen, the junior class president, stood up and asked whom she, a biracial student whose father was white and mother was black, should take to the prom, Humphries told her that her parents had made "a mistake" and he wanted to be sure others didn't do the same. Bowen filed a civil suit against Humphries and the Randolph County School Board on the grounds that his comments caused her "humiliation, embarrassment, and emotional distress." Members of the NAACP and the head of the Southern Christian Leadership Conference attended school board meetings and led the charge against Humphries. And the national media descended on the tiny town, fascinated both by Humphries' outspoken challenge to the increasing social integration in Wedowee and by the racial fault lines his comments exposed.[6] The school board voted to suspend Humphries from his position as principal pending an investigation of his comments, and when the Justice Department sued the school system for racial discrimination, Humphries was reassigned to an administrative position and forbidden to visit any school during school hours. The school district, meanwhile, paid Revonda Bowen $25,000 in an out-of-court settlement.

The Wedowee case illustrates a sea change in the way interracial relationships are discussed in public by whites: public opposition to interracial marriage, instead of being widely accepted, is today characterized as racist. The sole black member of the Wedowee school board thus blamed the incident on the fact that the town had "a lot of hillbillies here who just don't know that mainstream society has gotten beyond this sort of thing." The town mayor argued that the principal's attitude was not representative. Interracial dating was common in Wedowee, he explained. "The red lights don't all quit working when an interracial couple drives through town. This is 1994. We're out in the country, but we get TV. We know what's accepted."[7]

Indeed, the topic of interracial sex and marriage has been largely removed from national political discussions about race since the late 1960s. Contentious racial issues like school busing or affirmative action are not attacked today as steps leading down the path to "race mixing." When Clarence Thomas, a conservative black judge, was nominated to the U.S. Supreme Court in 1991, his marriage to a white woman engendered no comments or criticisms from his conservative supporters, who included former stalwart segregationists like South Carolina's Strom Thurmond. Thomas's marriage was no longer a political issue; his white supporters were far more concerned with his conservative politics.

In fact, voicing opposition to intermarriage has become a liability for white politicians. In 1992 the volunteer coordinator of Pat Buchanan's presidential campaign in New Jersey was removed after he compared mixed marriages to animal cross-breeding. When then candidate George W. Bush gave a speech at fundamentalist Bob Jones University during the 2000 Republican primary, he was widely criticized for not attacking the school's ban on interracial dating. Facing widespread political and media criticism, the university changed its dating policy.[8]

Certainly, approval for black-white relationships among whites is not universal. In Mississippi, South Carolina, and Alabama more than 40 percent of the voters cast ballots to retain their state's symbolic constitutional bans on interracial marriage—evidence, the head of the Mississippi NAACP argued, of "an attitude that still supports segregation."[9] Approval of intermarriage varies significantly by region; whites in the West are most tolerant of the practice, while only one-third of whites in the South say they approve. Nationwide, approval for black-white interracial marriage lags significantly behind that for other forms of integration, such as living in a mixed-race neighborhood or sending one's children to integrated schools.[10] Whites still have a harder time accepting intimate interpersonal relations between blacks and whites than they do accepting more distant social relationships.

Outspoken white supremacist groups such as the Ku Klux Klan and the Aryan Nation, furthermore, continue to be obsessed with interracial sexuality, which they describe as a threat to continued racial purity, to the white race, and to Western civilization. White supremacists, now living in an age of affirmative action and women's liberation, believe that white males have become victims and that white masculinity is in crisis. Through their discourse and their actions, they seek to reassert white male dominance and authority, often by trying to prevent the boundary crossing between blacks and whites that they find so threatening. In the disturbing 1978 novel *The Turner Diaries,* the neo-Nazi William Pierce (using the pen name Andrew Macdonald) tells of a successful race war against the American government, which he portrays as dominated by Jews and "human relations councils" who let ignorant and inferior blacks bully and rule over a terrified white population. Carrying the idea of racial purity to the extreme, the revolutionary "Organization" not only massacres the entire American black and mixed-race population, but also

lynches any whites who are sexually involved with blacks. One particularly graphic scene describes the "Day of the Rope," when whites married to or living with nonwhites are forced to don placards reading "I
defiled my race" and are then hung from trees and lampposts to serve as
public symbols of the new racial order.[11]

Although *The Turner Diaries* is clearly fantasy, members of white supremacist groups regularly target whites and blacks involved in interracial relationships. According to the Klanwatch Project of the Southern
Poverty Law Center, interracial couples are common victims of cross
burnings. In one 1982 case, Klan members in Georgia burst into the
home of a white woman known to date black men. They threw her
across a coffee table and beat her with a leather strap while her teenage
children watched. One of the Klansmen told her that if the family continued to associate with "niggers," the Klan would remove her fifteen-
year-old daughter from the home, for fear her mother's dating habits
would corrupt her.[12]

But these violent acts of hostility are not a fact of life for most interracial couples today; most attest that the growing acceptance of interracial
marriage among whites has markedly improved their quality of life.
Many couples, especially those who have been married for twenty years
or more, report that harassment from whites has markedly decreased. Gail
and Merlyn Hurd, a black man and white woman who married in
Greenwich Village in the early 1960s, did not see, in 1985, the shocked
looks that used to be common when they went out in public. Eloise
Mays, a white woman who married a black man in Michigan in 1962,
describes the shift: "Our relationship isn't the first thing people notice
anymore. I think we are accepted as 'people' a little more quickly. Although inner feelings may not have changed in everyone, it is no longer
acceptable to behave rudely in public and the stares and comments of the
'60's are gone!" Mays notes that whether other whites have truly accepted interracial relationships or not, their behavior toward couples has
changed, as previously accepted forms of overt racial hostility have become less publicly acceptable. As a result, many couples have become
more comfortable going out together in public. A white Boston woman
was excited that by 1980, after fourteen years of marriage, she could

finally walk down the street holding hands with her black husband without fear of unpleasant remarks or hostile stares.[13]

These long-married couples note that the increasing number of interracial couples out on the street has made it easier for them, since they no longer stand out as much as they used to. Marvin Rich, a black New York academic administrator who married a white woman in the late 1950s, remembers being stared at as the only mixed couple whenever they went out in public. By 1980, however, with so many other couples around, they no longer experienced stares. Nathaniel Brown, a black man from Georgia who married a white woman in the early 1970s, also felt that the increased visibility of interracial couples had made life easier for him and his wife. When he first married, his mother gave him a gun in case he ever ran into any trouble, and the couple was in fact stopped once by Georgia state troopers who suspected Brown of abducting his wife. But twenty-five years later, things were completely different. "Now that you see pictures of interracial couples in the newspapers and on television, you can feel free to walk in the malls and out in the street, doing what other people do and enjoying each other," Brown explained. Melissa Moonves, a white woman who married a Haitian man in the early 1980s, echoed Brown's assessment. The strange looks they often received in Miami, Florida, when they were first married were gone. "It's just so common."[14]

Couples who have married more recently are somewhat more circumspect. Recently married couples never experienced the very overt hostility of earlier decades, and for them any racial slight may loom large. The perception of racial intolerance, more than any actual incidents, seems to color the views of couples who have married within the last ten or twenty years Thus the majority of twenty-one Minneapolis-area couples told interviewers in the early 1990s that they had faced few racial incidents, but that they still felt society was somewhat hostile to them. They remembered small instances of racial discrimination—such as slow service at a restaurant or being gawked at in a shopping mall—in vivid detail. Shira-Davida Goldberg-Rathell, a white woman who married her black husband in 1990, remembered two uncomfortable situations in a year of living in Salt Lake City. In each case, it felt like "getting socked in the gut." Another white woman who married a black man in the mid-1990s found it strange that there had only been a "few uncomfortable moments in our almost seven year relationship. People at my job don't bat an eyelash. I guess we keep expecting something to happen."[15] The expectation of potential violence, more than actual incidents, keeps modern couples on their guard.

Indeed, most couples today have suffered few, if any, serious acts of discrimination because of their relationships. In a recent survey of two hundred interracial couples, only 40 percent of the black-white couples reported experiencing any discrimination because of their marriage. The most common problem they encountered, moreover, was unfriendly service in stores and restaurants. Although hurtful, this kind of discrimination is relatively minor. Some couples even see it as humorous when waitresses at restaurants look at them, two people who are obviously together, and ask, "Table for one?" or bring them separate checks after a meal. A St. Louis couple was surprised that they had so few problems. "Most people just mind their own business," they explained. Yvette Weatherly, a black Atlanta woman who met her white husband when she was bused into his nearly all-white high school, felt secure walking around her neighborhood and reported few instances of public discrimination. "Maybe I'm stupid. Maybe I'm naive. Maybe I have a bag over my head. But we haven't had those type of problems."[16]

Not all interracial couples are so lucky, of course. Some regions of the country are less tolerant of interracial couples. In the South, especially outside of the major metropolitan centers, outspoken disapproval by whites remains relatively common. Black men with white women are often made to feel that they have stepped out of line, while their white partners are characterized as depraved and immoral. As recently as the early 1990s, a picture of a teenage interracial couple in a Greensboro, North Carolina, newspaper provoked a storm of protest from whites who complained the picture was "distasteful, demoralizing, suggestive" and promoted race mixing.[17] Not surprisingly, interracial couples who move to the South from elsewhere find it less hospitable than other regions. A black woman married to a white man described how she and her husband were "sneered at" whenever they went out in public in Alabama. Although they had received glares when they lived in the West, it was much worse in the South. The young white wife of a black man echoed these complaints in 1990, claiming that whenever she and her husband went outside the black community in the town in Georgia where they lived, they faced "screams of abuse, stares of hatred and disgust, and rejection at every turn." Interracial couples in the South live less openly than those in other regions, and they report more violent incidents, like being threatened at gunpoint, run off the road, or victimized by vandalism. The violence can be deadly. In South Carolina in 1996, two white men shot and killed a black man riding in a van with his white wife.[18]

Small cities in the Midwest can also be a hostile environment for interracial couples. When Amy and Demeatries Rollison first married in 1997, they settled in Lancaster, Pennsylvania, but people there spit at them and threw things at their car. They relocated to Atlanta, Georgia, which they have found to be more accepting. Shira-Davida Goldberg-Rathell described an oppressive atmosphere for interracial couples in Milwaukee. She and her friends used to describe their efforts to hide their interracial relationships as going "inconnegro." In Sacramento, California, where she now lives, however, people do not seem to think her relationship is an issue. This change was somewhat disconcerting to her, since her time in Milwaukee left her "always ready to explain myself."[19]

Couples seek to minimize problems by avoiding potential trouble spots. Some couples avoid traveling in the South, choose national chains over local restaurants and hotels, and avoid rural roads.[20] Couples routinely relocate from less friendly areas to those they perceive to be more tolerant. Some of the interracial couples in cities like Seattle, San Francisco, Denver, and Minneapolis have moved there from elsewhere, seeking out politically liberal cities with large numbers of other interracial couples. One couple explained that they moved to Seattle from Southern California because they felt much more comfortable in a city where there were more marriages like theirs. In Orange County, people stared at them, but in Seattle, black men with white women were considered normal. Richard Carter, a black man married to a white woman, felt his life improved dramatically when he and his wife decided to move out of Cleveland. "After six years of fighting the stares, subtle slights, and flagrant insults, Janice and I stopped being so confrontational and began rolling with the punches." They moved to Manhattan, leaving behind "a place that tolerated us grudgingly for a city where our abilities and perseverance mean more to other people than our interracial marriage."[21]

Interracial couples today can more easily find areas where they are accepted or tolerated than they could in the first thirty years after World War II. Although many couples in the forties, fifties, and sixties encountered serious housing discrimination and found finding suitable housing a challenge, couples today report far fewer problems in finding a place to live. There are, of course, still instances of real estate agents steering interracial couples to all-black neighborhoods, but many contemporary interracial couples have chosen to live in integrated, racially diverse neighborhoods, and they report few problems in doing so.[22] Only two of the twenty-one couples interviewed for a study in Minneapolis reported having difficulty finding housing. Some lived in predominantly black communities, but they did so out of choice rather than of necessity. One couple chose a "highly interracial neighborhood," because if they had lived in a "predominately white suburban community" their children would not have had enough opportunities to interact with blacks. Other studies have found that interracial couples actively seek out racially integrated neighborhoods because they believe they will feel more comfortable there. These neighborhoods are often multiracial; neighbors might include whites, blacks, Asian Indians, or Latinos.[23]

As overt opposition on the part of whites has become less noticeable, couples have focused more on the often subtle disapproval they feel from blacks, especially black women. Although recent national polls indicate that more blacks than ever before (77 percent) claim to approve of interracial marriage, black opposition has by no means disappeared.[24] Articles in the black media continue to debate whether marrying a white person signals a betrayal of the race or whether black men have a "moral duty" to marry black women.[25] Although criticisms of intermarried blacks have softened somewhat since the heyday of black nationalism, concerns about the danger widespread intermarriage poses to the larger black community remain.

Interracial couples do sometimes feel overt disapproval from blacks. Some couples have encountered criticism in racially segregated cities with large black populations, such as Philadelphia, Chicago, and Washington, D.C., where blacks can express disapproval under the cover of the anonymity a large city provides. When a black stranger beat up the white husband of Jean Elster in their inner-city Detroit neighborhood, he told him, "This is what I think of white men who marry black women!" On college campuses, tensions surrounding the issue of interracial dating remain high. At predominantly white colleges, black students often work through issues of racial identity and assimilation by closing ranks and sticking together. Nya Patrinos, a biracial woman, discovered at her years at the University of Pennsylvania in the early 1990s that "the African-American community at Penn is pretty militant, and they don't want you to hang out with white people." She felt she could not pursue close relationships with whites and remain an active member of the campus black community. A white man married to a black woman since the early 1980s endured a wide variety of negative comments about his marriage from blacks. Followers of the Nation of Islam had tried to separate him from his daughter at the local shopping mall on the grounds that he couldn't really be her father, while black parents in the neighborhood refused to discipline their children who teased his kids for being biracial. The "greatest resistance to our marriage and to our children's biracial identity has come from the black community," this white husband stressed.[26]

The most vocal opposition comes from black women, many of whom continue to be vehement critics of black men's relationships with white women. Black women still disapprove of interracial marriage more than black men and they remain more hesitant to date whites.[27] Their opposition is frequently portrayed in the media. In Spike Lee's 1991 film *Jungle Fever*, a group of black women berate both "white bitches" who steal black men and black men who can't deal with black women. The actresses eventually forgot about the script, Lee claimed. "They were just vomiting that stuff up" from their personal experiences. Black women continue to lament the problem of the "white wife." Bebe Moore Campbell, a black writer, described how she and her friends reacted to the sight of a famous black man out with a blonde at a Hollywood restaurant: "Had Spike Lee ventured in with a camera, he would have had the footage and soundtrack for *Jungle Fever*, Parts II, III, and IV."[28]

With the numbers of interracial couples increasing, some black women openly express dismay about their chances of ever finding a suitable spouse. A migrant to Salt Lake City was shocked and insulted to discover the extent of interracial dating there, which felt to her like a slap in the face of all black women. Living in cities with large numbers of interracial couples can make black women feel "how little value they're assigned in a sexual marketplace where white femininity still has tremendous currency," explains the writer Lisa Jones, and anger and resentment at black men's interracial dating patterns can spill over into overt opposition.[29] Long-married couples find that public disapproval has become less common among whites and more noticeable among black women. A black man who had married his white wife in the mid-1970s characterized the looks he got on the street as "absolutely incredible. It used to be the looks I would get from white men. Now it's looks of hostility from black women." For Joe Hicks, a black resident of Los Angeles married to a white woman since the early 1980s, the most dramatic reaction to his marriage came from black women. "They say, 'Here's another brother with a white woman.'"[30] Couples who have married more recently note the opposition of black women as one of the most significant sources of personal discomfort. A white Boston woman married to a black man calls the looks she gets from black women on public transportation "evil . . . as if I stole their man from them!" while an intermarried white Minneapolis woman feels that "the most negativity towards me personally . . . comes from black women."[31]

Yet despite this sometimes public opposition, the vast majority of blacks today claim to approve of interracial relationships, and blacks are more likely than whites to have dated interracially themselves. In a 1986 poll of one thousand black Americans, 30 percent of the respondents had dated interracially and more than half said someone in their family had gone out with a white person. A 2001 poll found that nearly two-thirds of black men and half of black women responding had dated someone of another race.[32] Although some contemporary observers, like the black sociologist Orlando Patterson, argue that black-white marriage rates remain relatively low today primarily because of opposition from blacks rather than from whites, blacks have consistently approved of interracial marriage more than whites, and they continue to do so today.[33]

Even black women's disapproval of intermarriage may well decrease in the future. Although it is not yet clear whether black women generally have become more open to the idea of interracial dating—deciding, as one black woman remarked in 1983, that she would rather spend time with her white boyfriend than "study the cracks in four walls at home every night"—in the last twenty years interracial marriage rates have begun to equalize somewhat by gender.[34] In 1980 there were only 27,000 black women married to white men, but by 1998 that number had climbed to 120,000. Since 1990, the rate of intermarriage among black women has been climbing faster than that among black men. Today approximately one-third of black-white marriages involve a black woman, a significant increase from 1980 when black women and white men accounted for only one-quarter of all black-white marriages. It seems likely that black women's opposition to interracial relationships will be tempered as more black women marry whites.[35]

Increasing diversity within the black community, furthermore, complicates the issue of interracial marriage. Since the liberalization of immigration laws in the 1960s, approximately two million people have migrated to the United States from the Caribbean.[36] Foreign-born blacks make up nearly 5 percent of the total black population in the United States, and they are significantly more likely to marry whites than their native-born counterparts. Recent black female immigrants (those in the country from five to fifteen years) intermarry twice as often as native-born black women. In 1990, 8.3 percent of native-born married black men and 3.4 percent of native-born married black women were married to nonblacks (primarily whites), while among black immigrants in the United States fifteen years or longer, 15 percent of the men and 10.8 percent of the women were married to nonblacks.[37]

For Caribbean immigrants, both their class status and their position as outsiders in the United States make them more likely to intermarry than native-born blacks. A slightly higher percentage of Caribbean immigrants than native-born blacks are professional workers and well educated, groups that are more likely to intermarry. More important, these immigrants' own distance from America's racist past affects how they see whites and, in turn, how whites see them. The sociologist Mary Waters has found that West Indian immigrants to the United States frequently have better interpersonal relations with whites than American-born blacks, because they don't anticipate personal racism from whites and thus respond to whites as individuals. Although this openness often erodes as the immigrants experience racism in American society, many get along with whites well simply because they did not grow up with the baggage of American race relations. Likewise, black immigrants do not necessarily relate to the American black opposition to interracial marriage. In interviews with West Indian immigrants, Waters found most were open to the idea of interracial marriage. Although they worried that interracial couples might have problems, they did not seem terribly concerned about upholding their own racial or ethnic boundaries through marriage, and some viewed marrying interracially as a way to improve their status and that of their children.[38]

These marriages between whites and Caribbean migrants further highlight America's increasing ethnic and cultural pluralism. Andrea and Winston Christian married in 1984 in California; she is Jewish American, he is Jamaican, and they are raising their two sons as "Jewmaican," while Mharia Ross-Walcott and her Jamaican husband Albert are raising their children as Rastafarians.[39] Cross-cultural exchange, rather than the cultural assimilation of one of the partners, characterizes these couples' relationships.

Interracial couples' lives have been improved not only by the lessening of overt hostility directed toward them, but also by civil rights laws passed since the 1960s that have made it increasingly difficult to discriminate against individuals simply because they are interracially married. Federal fair housing laws, for example, have made it easier for couples to combat common forms of housing discrimination. When a Kentucky owner told a couple that if they moved in, neighbors would come and burn down their house, the couple sued and won, as did an Indiana couple who were evicted because "they were that kind of people." The New York City Commission on Human Rights ordered a Brooklyn landlord to pay a couple $3,500 in compensatory damages when she insisted she had to charge an interracial couple more rent than a white one.[40]

Courts today provide more support to couples who are being harassed in their neighborhood. A South Carolina couple got a restraining order when their landlord began spying on them. When the landlord tried to evict the couple from his apartment building, the couple sued and won.

The couple stayed; the landlord sold the property. In Milford, Connecticut, a judge forced a white couple who was harassing the interracial family next door to move, reversing the usual pattern of hostile racist neighbors forcing an interracial couple out of their neighborhood. Under the Fair Housing Law of 1968, individuals who have burned crosses outside the homes of interracial couples or harass them in other ways have been charged and convicted with violating a couple's right to fair housing.[41]

Employment discrimination laws that emerged from the civil rights era have also afforded blacks and whites who intermarry some protection against harassment or discrimination in the workplace. Title VII of the 1964 Civil Rights Act forbids employers to discriminate on the basis of race. Although Title VII was designed to protect nonwhites, courts have ruled that interracially married whites who are fired for associating with a black person are also victims of discrimination based on race.[42] Susan Partin Moffett, a rental assistant at a large apartment complex in Fort Wayne, Indiana, won a bias suit against her company in 1985 after superiors ignored her complaints that her coworkers called her obscene names, tapped her phone line, and disabled her car because she was dating a black man. Moffett's superiors told her that she would have to get used to "snide remarks from just about anyone and everyone" if she continued to see a black man. The U.S. District Court disagreed, ruling that Moffett had been subject to a "concerted pattern of continuous harassment which pollutes a working environment," harassment that her superiors tolerated. She was awarded nearly $80,000, with the company being ordered to pay another $15,000 in punitive damages. Employees have not always had to take their employers to court to see results. When one white woman warned her boss that she would file a complaint if he didn't stop making disparaging comments about her black husband, her work environment improved. "You can't let people like that get away with it or they'll just keep doing it," she explained.[43]

These legal developments have had perhaps their most significant impact in reducing one of the most painful forms of bigotry an interracial couple could encounter: losing custody of their children from previous same-race marriages. In the 1940s, 1950s, and early 1960s, white women who married black men routinely lost custody of their white children from previous relationships. At the request of hostile ex-husbands or es-

tranged grandparents, courts took children from their white mothers,
ruling that it would harm the children to have black stepfathers or to
grow up in interracial homes. Even after the Supreme Court invalidated
antimiscegenation laws in 1967, courts in southern states continued to
deny interracially married women custody of their white children, although their rulings were often cloaked in racially neutral language.[44] In
1984, however, in the Florida case of *Palmore v. Sidoti,* the U.S. Supreme
Court made even this kind of subterfuge more difficult by ruling that
race could not be a determinative factor in child custody cases. In this
case, a trial court removed Linda Sidoti Palmore's young white daughter
from her custody after she married a black man. The decision was upheld
by the Florida Appeals Court. The U.S. Supreme Court, however, overturned the decision, making clear that courts could no longer rely on
racist thinking or on the argument that a child might be stigmatized by
growing up in an interracial home to justify denying white women custody of their children.[45] *Palmore v. Sidoti* did not make it impossible to remove white children from interracial homes, but it severely limited the
ability of state courts to make custody decisions on the basis of racial
considerations.

   The institution that perhaps best encapsulates this growing acceptance
of interracial marriage over the last thirty years is the United States military. In the 1940s, military authorities desperately tried to control the
sexual lives of black soldiers serving overseas, and interracial couples
were frequently denied permission to marry. Since the 1980s, however,
the military has become perhaps the single most significant source of interracial marriages in the United States. In the 1940s and 1950s, most
military interracial marriages involved American servicemen stationed
abroad who married foreign women of other races. Such marriages still
take place, but the modern military also fosters interracial marriages between black and white enlisted personnel.

   The military has proved a conducive place for interracial relationships
for a variety of reasons. Since the desegregation of the military in 1948, it
has become the most integrated workplace in America. Every branch of
the U.S. military is racially integrated. The army, the most racially diverse
branch of the military, is 26 percent black, 59 percent white, and 8 percent Latino.[46] Although the military is not free of racial discrimination,

and the officer corps is less diverse than the enlisted personnel, its culture fosters cross-racial cooperation; new recruits are stripped of the markers of their individual identity and are treated according to a rigid ranking system that can minimize traditional racial hierarchies. Members of lower rank are expected to obey and respect those of higher rank, no matter their race. Black and white recruits, moreover, train together and live together in close quarters. They are forced to interact and to work together to achieve a common goal. Studies have shown that although casual contact between blacks and whites does little to change racial attitudes or reduce racial tensions, when blacks and whites work together as equals in pursuit of a common objective, as they do in the military, it can promote cross-racial tolerance and friendships. One veteran explains that all sorts of people enter the military, but then "we go in and get these hair cuts and they put us into the same clothes. Then they treat us all like crap. They strip away all of your personality . . . they strip you down to nothing to make you part of a team."[47]

Not only does the military provide an atmosphere that fosters cross-racial contact, but it also takes young Americans away from their hometowns, and sometimes even their country. Being stationed outside the United States can highlight the cultural similarities between Americans of different racial backgrounds. Furthermore, whether stationed abroad or in the United States, recruits are away from their families, so relationships can develop without family interference or pressure. This may be a crucial factor in explaining the frequency of cross-racial relationships among members of the military, since individuals cut off from their family and childhood communities are more likely to intermarry.[48] Cynthia Burton, a white marine, met her husband, Bryan, a black airman, when they were both stationed in Okinawa. They married while still in Okinawa, four months after they met. She told her parents her husband was black only after they had married. Sheree Hunt Gates also met her black husband when they were both in the military and stationed overseas. Both families objected, but the couple married anyway. Fred Holland, a black man sent to Redstone Arsenal Base in Alabama, found that the racially tolerant atmosphere on the base and the distance from community controls made Redstone a "meeting place for many people of different nationalities, cultures and races." He went to a club his first night on the

base and was surprised to see mixed couples on the dance floor. He was
even more surprised when a white army woman from Alaska asked him
to dance. Although Holland initially worried about what others would
think, the newly established social networks on the base were too tenuous to discourage him from dating a white woman. The couple dated
throughout their training, and found military people generally accepting
of their relationship. As Amy Rollison put it, when she met her black
husband-to-be at Fort Benning in Georgia, dating "just came natural" in
the military environment.[49]

The military experience demonstrates the fundamental truth that integration does lead to increased interracial marriage, especially when institutions encourage racial tolerance. Data from the 1990 census suggest
that white men who have served in the military are three times more
likely to marry black women than those who have never served, while
current military service increases white men's odds of marrying a black
woman by eight times. White women who have served in the military
are seven times more likely to marry black men than those who have
never served. Although the numbers are not as dramatic for black men
and women, military service also makes it more likely that they will
marry whites.[50]

Anecdotal evidence also suggests that multiracial families are more
common on military bases than in the general population. Although the
military does not keep records about the racial composition of soldiers'
families, some involved in the military estimate that as many as 15 to 20
percent of all military families are multiracial, whether through interracial marriages or transracial adoptions. A white woman, living on base in
Darmstadt, Germany, in 1992, had "never seen so many interracial couples." Of the forty-three soldiers, medical personnel, and civilian workers
in her husband's unit, only seven were not involved in an interracial relationship and two of those seven were the single parents of biracial children. As she saw it, the fact that they were all overseas and in need of
American company helped minimize racial issues. Some military bases
even have their own support groups for interracial families, like the Eb-
ony/Ivory Support Group, founded by an interracially married marine
sergeant at Fort Ritchie in Maryland. Indeed, many of the interracial
couples living in southern states are associated with the military, and they

have found military bases more tolerant than southern civilian communities. As a black woman married to a white man noted, residents of the military base in Tucson, Arizona, accepted them, but "the further we travel from the base, the more heads we turn."[51] Although the military is today a pioneer in providing a hospitable environment for interracial families, the military experience may well foreshadow the direction the country is heading more generally.

The growing acceptance of interracial couples by communities, workplaces, and the state has slowly begun to filter down to families as well. Family disapproval among whites remains, despite the changes in the political arena and in the broader society, but disapproval is not as universal and in many cases is more transitory than it once was. In one recent poll, 55 percent of whites said they would not object if a close relative married a black person, a dramatic change from the near-universal concern about such marriages in earlier eras. More whites who intermarry are finding that they can retain, or quickly regain, the support of their families. Only nine of the twenty white partners interviewed in a 1988 study reported having serious problems with their parents, and only five had been completely rejected by their families. In another case, one-third of the families of twenty-eight intermarried whites in South Carolina had fully accepted the interracial marriage, and the opposition of families who disapproved diminished over time.[52]

Of course, some parents continue to worry that marrying interracially will adversely affect their children, costing them status, racial privileges, and their class position. One Chicago woman recalled that her father "freaked" when she told him she planned to marry her black boyfriend. He worried that marrying interracially would mean she would have a "hard life." The father of a white South Carolina woman blew up when she told her parents she was marrying a black man. "He was yelling and screaming and told me that I had just thrown my life away." By marrying interracially, these families suggested, their children would never live up to their full promise and would never achieve the kinds of success that they might have been capable of. Thus when Greg Todd told his white parents that he planned to marry a black woman, they were disappointed. Greg was the one who was supposed to make it and do better than others in the family, his father told him, and by marrying a black woman, he threw away that chance. Walt Harrington's parents had a similar reaction when he informed them that he planned to marry his black girlfriend in the early 1980s. As his parents saw it, his marriage mocked their values and the efforts they had made to reach the middle class. Although his girlfriend was from a middle-class background, his parents assumed that their son would lose the social position they had worked so hard to achieve by marrying a black woman. For his parents, Harrington wrote, "race was a stand-in for a whole constellation of class-laden fears."[53]

At their most extreme, such concerns could lead parents to disown their children or to insist that the child hide the marriage from family and friends. When Cynthia Payne told her parents that she planned to marry her black boyfriend in the early 1980s, her father cut her out of his will, she was forced to move out of the family home, and her sisters stopped socializing with her because they didn't want their children playing with any black cousins. Other whites hesitated to tell their parents about their interracial relationships because they knew how hard it would be for their parents to tell their friends and relatives. One white woman who married a black man in the early 1970s was still pretending to be single and childless in 1991. Although her parents knew that she was intermarried, they did not want any of the other relatives to know, and they would allow her and her children to visit their home only after dark, so the neighbors would not see them.[54] Many of these parents came of age in the 1950s and 1960s, when opposition to interracial marriage was the norm, and they are less socialized to an interracial world than their children. Younger whites report much greater tolerance of interracial relationships than their elders, which may well mean that future intermarried whites will encounter less parental opposition.[55]

Indeed, among couples who have married since the mid-1980s, there are far fewer stories of being permanently disowned or estranged from their parents because of their marriage. In part because of the weakening of family ties and the increasing autonomy of young adults since the 1960s, fewer families today express concern that the entire family will be stigmatized because of the act of one child. Initial disapproval, moreover, often gives way to acceptance. In some cases, parents relent when it becomes clear that opposition will not prevent the marriage. Even some

whites who feared they would be disowned by their parents found a father willing to walk them down the aisle. Dawn Skeete, a young Alaskan
woman, secretly dated a black man for years after her father forbade her
to date interracially, but when she announced her intention to wed her
black boyfriend, her father participated in the wedding and welcomed
her black husband into the family. Shira-Davida Goldberg-Rathell saw a
similar change of heart in her mother. Concerned about her own reputation, her mother threw Shira out of the house when she refused to stop
dating her black boyfriend. But by the time she died several years later,
Goldberg-Rathell's mother had become a doting grandmother and
had fully accepted her black son-in-law. It was "such a happy ending,"
Goldberg-Rathell notes.[56]

Some parents had a change of heart when they realized that marrying
interracially did not in fact ruin their child's life. The woman whose father "freaked" when she began dating her black boyfriend came to treat
his black son-in-law like a son. A white father who was violently opposed to his daughter's interracial wedding, refusing to allow her name to
be spoken in his house, gradually grew more accepting as he heard positive things about the relationship and saw how happy his daughter was.
Others relented when it became clear the marriage was going to last or
when children were born. Walt Harrington's parents reconciled themselves to his marriage after several years of estrangement, while many
others told of parents visiting for the first time after a grandchild was
born. In some cases, white parents gradually overcame the stereotypes
they had about black people as they learned about their children's spouse.
One black woman recalled that her husband's mother assumed she
would have nothing in common with her black daughter-in-law. She
was surprised to learn that her son's wife preferred classical music to
gangsta rap.[57] In this case, as in many others, the white in-laws came to
accept the marriage with time.

Black families, despite the lingering undercurrent of hostility to intermarriage in the black community, continue to be more accepting of interracial marriage, both initially and in the long term, than white families. Debates about racial loyalty and solidarity have had a relatively
muted impact on black family reaction. Most blacks today are willing to

accept interracial marriages in their own families. In a 1993 Gallup Poll, 60 percent of blacks questioned said they would favor a relative's marrying someone of another race, while an additional 25 percent volunteered that they would be indifferent about such a marriage. A 1999 *Atlanta Constitution* poll found that 92 percent of blacks would not mind if a member of their own family married a white person.[58]

Of course, family members who consider themselves black nationalists or who see intermarrying as a form of racial betrayal may vehemently disapprove of a potential interracial marriage, to the point of cutting off ties with their intermarried relative. Talitha Johnson's mother threw her out of the house after she began dating a white man, while a black Indiana businessman recalled that when he brought his new white wife to meet his family, his parents accepted her, but a sister who had "been into 'being black' since the seventies" came over and tried to force his wife out of their parents' home. His marriage effectively ended his relationship with his sister. Yet even some of these staunch opponents eventually relented. The sister of Demeatries Rollison initially refused to speak to his white girlfriend when he brought her home, but she eventually accepted his white wife fully into the family.[59]

Nearly every case study of interracial couples has found that the families of the black spouse are less upset by the marriage than the families of the white spouse, and stories of a black child's being disowned because of an interracial marriage are exceptionally rare. Black families seem more willing to judge a relative's white partner on the basis of individual character and the quality of the relationship. When Charles, a black Madison, Wisconsin, man, first brought home his white girlfriend, his sisters and aunts were not at all supportive, treating his decision to date a white woman as a personal insult. But after the two wed in 1993, most of them came to accept her. The family members of Richard Cooper, a Bay Area academic administrator, had mixed feelings when he told them he planned to marry a white woman. Although his mother and sister genuinely liked his white fiancée, they worried that she might not be able to handle the discrimination they were sure she would face, and they wished that Richard had found a black woman instead. But they welcomed the young woman into their homes and planned to attend the wedding.[60] Not every couple is so lucky, but overall, there is little evidence that family disapproval is a greater problem now for blacks than in the first thirty years after World War II.

Yet while few whites or blacks today are permanently estranged from their families because of their marriages, choosing a partner of another race in the face of family opposition remains one of the most emotionally wrenching issues of marrying interracially. As one interracially married white woman wrote in 1995, "Rejection by family members is far more painful than rejection by strangers." She was hurt and disgusted to realize that the members of her family believed many of the stereotypes about interracial couples. Letters, articles, and memoirs written by interracial couples suggest that coping with family disapproval is now probably the most difficult aspect of crossing the color line. An anguished letter by a participant in an interracial relationship suggested the depth of the conflicting emotions generated by family disapproval. "How do we face the decision of choosing between our family and our mate?" the Massachusetts writer asked. "And when we finally choose between the two, how do we go about dealing with the feelings of loss, resentment, anger and so on. What about those of us who avoid decision-making by stringing family and mate along?"[61]

Although the anguish of dealing with family disapproval is similar to that experienced in earlier decades, the emphasis on individual rights and the importance of personal happiness that was a legacy of the 1960s has translated into greater cultural support for couples who choose to go against their parents' wishes. By the 1980s, when couples sought advice from columnists, they were told that should feel free to act without their parents' blessing. In fact, "experts" characterized those couples who hesitated to marry because of their families' opposition as immature and insincere. An *Ebony* advice columnist thus advised a young black woman to demand that her white boyfriend stand up to his disapproving parents. Although it was "an appropriate gesture of respect" for children to take their parents' wishes into consideration, ultimately an individual had to decide for himself whom to marry. "If your friend really loves you and has the maturity to know what he wants and the fortitude to fight for it, he won't let his 'Christian parents' stand in the way" the columnist told her. A nineteen-year-old white woman who was torn between wanting to make her parents happy and wanting to date her black boyfriend was told that her problem was not her parents, but her dependence on their approval. "To live your life as your parents want you to, rather than as you want to, is to live a false life," a marriage counselor advised her.[62]

A growing sense of community among interracial couples has also made coping with discrimination or family disapproval easier in the last fifteen years. Until the late 1980s, there were no ready-made support networks for interracial couples. A handful of couples in major urban areas after World War II formed short-lived associations, while other couples found tolerant spaces in progressive political or religious organizations. But there was almost nowhere a couple could turn for sympathetic advice or for guides on what intermarried life might be like. Maureen Reddy, a white English professor who began dating her black husband in 1976, found almost no positive stories about interracial couples when she began her relationship. Interracial couples, she wrote in her 1994 memoir, "begin not as inheritors of a tradition, but as pioneers. Each of us begins again at the very beginning, with few but negative guides. If we go looking for information, testimony from those who have gone before us, we find mainly cautionary tales of tragedy and loss."[63] Every interracial couple, she felt, had to reinvent the wheel, forging their own path and finding their own ways to deal with societal and family disapproval.

Since the mid-1980s, however, interracial couples have built a type of virtual community for themselves, through magazines, support groups, and websites. These networks, often national in scope, provide interracial couples with information, advice, and support for their relationships; they foster a sense of belonging and shared history. They are manifestations of what might be considered a new militancy among couples to live unrestricted lives; to be seen as typical married couples; and to have their choices and their families recognized as legitimate by the larger society. Couples will no longer accept that wedding cake figurines don't come in black and white, that families that look like them are largely invisible in ads and children's books, or that they are stigmatized as deviant or abnormal for intermarrying.

Several national magazines targeted to interracial couples have been founded since the late 1980s. Yvette Walker-Hollis, a black woman married to a white man, founded *New People,* a magazine designed to show interracial relationships as "a normal part of life," after she underwent a frustrating, and ultimately fruitless, search to find an interracial figurine for her wedding cake. By 1994, *New People* had 2,500 subscribers.[64] *Interrace* was founded in 1989 by Candy Mills, a then twenty-five-year-old interracially married black woman from Schenectady, New York. Living with her white husband and biracial daughter, Mills often read magazines looking for stories of interracial couples, but she found few, and almost none that were written specifically for people who were interracially involved. So with little more than $200, she decided to start a national magazine for interracial couples and their children. The first issue appeared in November 1989, supported by a subscriber base of two hundred; by 1999 *Interrace* had fifteen thousand subscribers and could be found nationwide at bookstores and newsstands.[65]

Interrace targets interracial couples of all racial backgrounds and families who are multiracial, whether through intermarriage or transracial adoption. As Candy Mills describes it, the magazine seeks to "dispel negative stereotypes, 'accentuate the positive'; to offer a wide-open forum for differing views; and to disseminate accurate information to America and the world."[66] Seeking to debunk myths and stereotypes about interracial couples, it has published critiques of psychological and sociological research that portray interracial couples as deviant or maladjusted.

In *Interrace* couples can find advice and share their experiences. Articles provide examples of how to cope with everyday instances of discrimination—using humor to defuse racist remarks, for example. Its popular "Interracial Living Guide" polls readers about the best and worst places for interracial couples to live. *Interrace* advice columnists offer suggestions to young people interested in, but wary about, interracial dating, and caution couples not to panic about their parents' attitudes. "It's their prerogative to disapprove as it is your prerogative to date whomever you like," one such column instructed. "Success Stories" in each issue feature couples who have happy marriages, have overcome family opposition, or who have learned to deal with ongoing disapproval. As one 1994 article chirped, marriages can thrive even under the most adverse conditions: "Yes, you can be happy!"[67]

These magazines also act as a clearinghouse for goods and services aimed specifically at interracial couples. *Interrace* catalogues resources ranging from children's books about multiracial families to support groups around the country. Since 1994 the magazine has even organized an annual Caribbean cruise so readers can meet "other members of the '*Interrace* Family.'" Reinforcing this sense of belonging, the magazine advertises a variety of products aimed at interracial couples, including multicultural books, games, toys, interracial greeting cards, and biracial pride T-shirts. Therapists who specialize in counseling multiracial families advertise there, as do adoption agencies looking for families for children of multiracial heritage.

Although *Interrace* reaches only a minority of black-white couples, it clearly provides some with important positive reinforcements about crossing the color line. Letters from couples have poured into the magazine (as many as ten thousand within its first five years of publication), and many of them express gratitude for the publication. One writer from Albany, Georgia, explained, "My spirit always soars a little bit higher when I find my *Interrace* magazine in the mailbox. Your publication has become a vital source of information and support for me." The magazine "fills a cavernous void for interracial couples," another asserted, while other readers told of the ways in which the magazine had helped them overcome feelings of isolation. *Interrace,* couples attested, could provide a needed sense of community and belonging. A black Brooklyn, New York, woman, who was "speechless" when she discovered *Interrace,* testified that the magazine made her and her white boyfriend feel like they were "part of a special community of our own, 'The *Interrace* Nation.'" This kind of reinforcement and support can fill a need couples were not even aware of. As one interracial couple wrote from Atlanta, before they discovered *Interrace,* "Neither of us had realized how much we need the kind of validity that *Interrace* provides."[68]

The number of clubs and support groups for interracial couples, multiracial people, and their families has also exploded in the last twenty years. Some of these organizations cater to particular interests or subgroups. Steve and Ruth White, both evangelical Christians, founded A Place for Us in Gardena, California, in 1984 after friends and ministers in their church discouraged their 1980 wedding. White friends from Steve's Bible study group told him that marrying a black woman was a "disastrous and unscriptural decision," and his pastor refused to perform the wedding ceremony. Feeling like "a tree whose roots had come loose," the couple decided to form a Christian ministry specifically for interracial couples and their families, a place where couples facing disapproval from family or their churches could receive counseling. Since its founding, A Place for Us has changed from a ministry to a general support group for interracial couples. With at least twenty-eight branches nationwide and a national "Multiracial Hotline," the group provides advice about dealing with parental disapproval and coping with discrimination, and offers interpretations of biblical references to interracial relationships. Shira-Davida Goldberg-Rathell began a support group and website for multi-racial Jewish families after discovering there were few resources available for them. She is adamant that her family is a legitimate Jewish family and believes that it's much easier to be different today because of the growth of support systems.[69]

For those interracial couples seeking support or advice, participating in a club or reading a magazine can reinforce the sense that marrying interracially is not socially aberrant. But joining a club is not the only way for couples to assert their normalcy, and many couples choose not to organize on the basis of their identity as an interracial couple precisely because they see themselves as "normal" or typical, and thus not in need of special groups.[70] Yet whether couples choose to join clubs or not, most share the goal of living as normal families and of being regarded as such by mainstream society. Interracial couples in the forties, fifties, and sixties expressed similar concerns, but since the 1980s couples have become even more assertive about insisting on a legitimate place for themselves within American society.

The reaction many couples have to the depiction of interracial love and marriage in the media illustrates their keen interest in being perceived as normal. Since the mid-1970s, portrayals of interracial couples in films, on television, and in the print media have increased dramatically. While a single touch between black and white singers on a television variety show elicited howls of protest in the 1960s, by 1975 it was possible to feature a married interracial couple on a regular television series. *The Jeffersons,* which premiered in 1975 and ran for ten years, featured Tom and Helen Willis, a white man and black woman, who were the neighbors and friends of George and Helen Jefferson. Although George Jefferson, a black man who had finally struck it rich and "moved on up" to a luxury apartment on New York's East Side, disapproved of their marriage and frequently made bigoted comments about it, the series presented the interracial couple sympathetically. Since then, interracial marriages have taken place on soap operas, with the first black–white soap couple walking down the aisle in 1988 on *General Hospital,* and interracial storylines have become more common on nighttime series. In 1990 the Fox television network developed a short-lived "Brady Bunch" type show about a blended interracial family, and recently storylines involving interracial couples have been featured on *Ally McBeal, ER,* and *The West Wing.* A growing number of films depict interracial relationships, newspapers nationwide print many more articles about interracial couples, and two nationally syndicated comic strips (*Boondocks* and *Jump Start)* feature subplots about interracial marriage.[71] Many interracial couples are highly sensitive about the messages sent by these modern depictions of relationships across racial lines, and they are not shy about expressing their opinions.

Some couples complain that modern portrayals continue to present interracial relationships as extraordinary or abnormal. They wonder why interracial romances in film and on television are often short-lived and seem primarily sexual, why movies starring black men and white women (such as the 1993 film *The Pelican Brief,* starring Julia Roberts and Denzel Washington) often lack any romantic component, or why interracial love depicted in pop culture so often ends in tragedy.[72] Many couples felt special opprobrium for Spike Lee's 1991 film *Jungle Fever,* which focused on an extramarital relationship between a black man and white woman. As Lee described it, the movie was about two people (Flipper and Angie) who are attracted to each other because of sexual mythology, a mythology portrayed as so powerful that both are willing to sacrifice their families and friends for the opportunity to sleep together. Angie's friends and relatives are appalled that she is seeing a black man; her father beats her and throws her out of the house. Flipper throws away a seemingly good marriage and his close relationship with his daughter because of his "Jungle Fever." Their relationship does not survive long.[73]

Many couples complained that *Jungle Fever* made the environment toward them more hostile. Spike Lee had given a "catch-phrase name" to interracial relationships, a black actress engaged to a white man complained: "Now you've got *Jungle Fever.*" Some couples on the street faced new taunts of "Jungle Fever" from passing strangers; others felt that the movie affected the way the world saw them. When Mark Mathabane, a black South African writer, and his white American wife went to see *Jungle Fever,* everyone stared at them as they left the theater. "To our horror, we realized that we had become Flipper and Angie, the maligned interracial couple of the movie."[74]

Jungle Fever, many interracial couples complained, perpetuated stereotypes rather than debunking them. The film upset a Virginia woman because it portrayed interracial relationships "in such a stereotypical and negative light." She worried that people would believe what they saw in the movie, which would only make things harder for her family: "We have enough obstacles to overcome without this negative influence from the media creating new challenges for interracial families." One interracially married white man found the film's allegation that biracial children would be social outcasts particularly disturbing. The movie "didn't give the message that interracial relationships can be based on good reasons."[75] Although some of these couples took the film too literally, missing the fact that some of Lee's depictions are satirical and that Lee included a subplot about a potentially healthy relationship between a white man and a black woman, their criticisms stemmed from a real fear that this kind of complex portrayal could easily be turned against real interracial couples.

Far worse than *Jungle Fever* are the depictions of interracial couples on the daytime television talk shows that have become popular since the 1980s. The *Oprah Winfrey Show,* the *Ricki Lake Show,* and *Geraldo,* among others, have all done shows featuring dysfunctional interracial couples or couples who have faced intense, often violent, opposition from friends and family. As couples have discovered, these shows seek controversy and have little interest in those who have faced few social problems. Candy Mills, the editor of *Interrace,* at first thought she would be educating people by participating in talk shows. She discovered, however, that the shows wanted only negative stories about discrimination and family disapproval. A white man married to a black woman felt as though he and his wife had been asked to participate in a freak show rather than a serious discussion of the issues of being an interracial couple. Producers of the *Geraldo* show were "very disappointed that there was nothing weird about our relationship and that we were accepted by all the people that we socialize with and work for." A white woman married to a black man was rejected for an Oprah Winfrey show about whether people should marry their own kind because she and her husband didn't have enough problems, while the black wife in another interracial couple was told that she was "too reasonable" to appear on the Montel Williams show; they wanted an interracially married black woman who would make derogatory comments about black men. "Talk shows are not interested in seeking out the truth about interracial couples," her husband complained. They "sabotage our normal images by predetermining which voices get heard."[76] Of course, television talk shows rarely seek the truth about any kind of couple or family relationship. They thrive on spectacle and on exploiting weak relationships, no matter what the shows' subject matter. Yet as many interracial couples recognize, a show on dysfunctional interracial relationships may serve to stigmatize all who are intermarried by giving credence to negative stereotypes that still circulate in the wider society.

For interracial couples, the line between the portrayal of interracial marriage on these sensationalist shows and in the "respectable" media often seems blurred, since the print media has also been drawn to tales of controversy and suffering. A typical 1992 article on interracial marriage in the women's magazine *Redbook* began with a dismal description of intermarried life: "Families disown them. Friends shun them. Strangers taunt them." Claudine Edwards, a newly married white woman from Massachusetts, was happy to tell a local reporter that she and her Jamaican husband had been accepted by both of their families, but the reporter was frustrated that all six of the couples she had contacted had only positive things to say. She wouldn't be able to write the article unless she found people with more problems, she told Edwards. Similarly, Dickelle Fonda complained about the "biased and incomplete representation of the reality of lives of interracial couples and families" in a 1991 front-page *New York Times* article, which told of couples who had been spat on in public, rejected by their families, and terrorized by their neighbors. The couple featured most prominently had kept their marriage a secret from the white partner's family for years. "Reading this news story, many of us felt invisible and offended, particularly knowing that several couples whose stories were not as 'juicy' were, in fact, interviewed for the article. Our version of the reality of interracial marriage in the '90s was again ignored in favor of the more sensational stories."[77]

Couples found newspapers and magazines unwilling to tell what they considered the "real story" of the increased social acceptance of interracial marriage, and some blame the media for creating prejudices against them. As *New People* editor Yvette Walker-Hollis saw it, television talk shows and negative media coverage had "set interracial relationships back 20 years" by focusing solely on couples who had problems. Gabe Grosz, the business manager for *Interrace* magazine, urges interracial couples to boycott films and television shows that show interracial marriage in a negative light.[78] For many contemporary couples, such stories are outdated and ultimately harmful.

Contemporary interracial couples' insistence on being viewed as normal, legitimate families on their own terms is also reflected in the decisions couples are making about how to raise their children. In the last twenty years, an increasing number of black-white couples have decided to raise their children as biracial—as part black and part white—rather than telling their children they are black. Well into the 1970s, the majority of children of black-white marriages were raised to consider themselves black, either because their parents accepted the idea that having any black heritage made one black, or because couples knew the outside world would see their children as black. In the last twenty years, however, any consensus among couples that children of interracial marriages should be raised as black has disappeared. This shift is palpable in the way couples talk about raising their children, in the many organizations that exist specifically for multiracial families, and in the political movement begun by some couples to gain government recognition for multiracial identity. Not only are interracial couples increasingly raising their children as biracial, but many are demanding that the larger American society define their children that way as well.

As the number of interracial couples has grown, as they have become less isolated, and as they have found some acceptance outside of the black community, choosing to identify a child as biracial has become easier and, for many, has become a sign that their marriage is one of committed and equal partners. Sharon Howard, a black woman pregnant with her first child in 1994, explained what she and her white husband had decided to teach their baby when it was born: "We're going to teach you both cultures, your black side and your white side, and you're not going to have to choose, if we can help it." Having to choose one identity represented a form of unnecessary compromise to her. A growing number of white parents have also become less willing to raise their children in ways that might deny their white heritage. Deane Nelson, a white woman married to a black man, objected whenever people told her that her child would be considered black. "I was bound and determined that my child would not be raised black, would not be called black, because I'm white and half of her background is white," Nelson explained. Some white parents fear that it is "psychologically damaging" when biracial children are forced to deny their white parentage by choosing a monoracial identity. According to one white Brooklyn mother, her biracial daughter would be better able to handle racism and sexism if she had a strong sense of both parts of her racial identity: "I want her to feel that bi-racial [sic] is an identity unto itself."[79]

Even couples who planned to raise their children as black sometimes found their ideas changed as their children grew up. Maureen Reddy and her black husband decided before their son was born that they would raise him as a black child, teaching him that he was racially black and ethnically African and Irish American. Their six-year-old son, however, upset their plans when he came home one day and told them he wasn't black, he was both black and white. Gradually, Reddy came to believe that by raising their child as black, they were accepting the racist one-drop rule and making their own interracial family invisible. No longer willing to play the part of "martyr" by denying her own racial and ethnic ancestry, Reddy now encourages her children to see themselves as biracial Irish Americans.[80]

The current turn to biracial identity for children of interracial marriage is reflected in an explosion of organizations for multiracial children and their families. With names like the Interracial Family Network, the Interracial Family Alliance, the Biracial Family Network, Parents of Interracial Children, and the Interracial Family Circle, these groups are particularly interested in nurturing biracial children and helping families

Its name taken from the Hebrew word meaning "one who understands," *MAVIN* magazine was founded in 1998 to celebrate the "mixed-race experience." It is one of the many new resources available to multiracial people today. (Reprinted by permission of *MAVIN.*)

meet their children's unique developmental needs. I–Pride, one of the longest running of these groups, was established in 1979 in the San Francisco Bay Area to validate people of multiracial heritage. Besides holding regular meetings and publishing a newsletter, the group also conducts educational workshops on raising healthy multiracial children. The Interracial Club of Buffalo, founded in 1983 by a black husband and white wife team, holds a regular monthly meeting, sponsors picnics and parties, hosts occasional discussions or workshops on issues of particular interest to interracial families, runs a multiracial children's playgroup, and publishes a monthly newsletter. The MAVIN Foundation, created in 2000 by then twenty-year-old multiracial activist Matt Kelley, is a nonprofit group that promotes awareness of the issues facing mixed-race youth. The foundation publishes *MAVIN* magazine (founded by Kelley in 1998) to celebrate the experience of young multiracial people, creates resources on mixed-race children for teachers and child welfare professionals, and runs the MatchMaker Bone Marrow Project to help recruit more multiracial bone marrow donors.[81]

Couples often become involved with these organizations for the sake of their children. Jennifer and Jerome Broadus started attending meetings of the Interracial Family and Social Alliance of Dallas when their three-year-old daughter began to notice that families all around her were either all-white or all-black. "We thought it would be a good idea for her to see other children who looked like her," Jennifer Broadus explained. Clyde Leuchtag, a black man married to a white woman, was reluctant to join the Interracial Family Alliance of Houston when he and his wife were first told about the organization. They weren't having any problems and thought of themselves as independent, not in need of a support group. But they eventually became involved in the hundred-family organization when they decided it was a good idea for their children to play with other biracial kids.[82]

Many of these same families, moreover, are leading a political battle against the invisibility of their children and their families on public records that catalogue race. These records—kept by federal and state government, local schools, and often businesses to help enforce antidiscrimination laws—typically ask individuals to choose between the identities of black, white, Asian, Native American, Hispanic, or "Other." Many interracial couples see the category of "other," the only one in which their children fit, as offensive. Earl and Georgette Dredge of Atlanta, for example, married in 1972 and decided to raise their daughter Ashley to see herself as biracial, teaching her to value both sides of her racial heritage. Careful not to stress one culture more than another, the Dredges resent school forms that force their daughter to choose between the identities of "black," "white," or "other," which they see as degrading. "It's unfair for us to check black or white, when actually she is both, and I don't like to check 'other,'" Georgette Dredge explains.[83]

Experiences such as these have led some parents of biracial children to mount a campaign for a "multiracial" category on school forms and state documents, and in the U.S. Census. Susan Graham, a white woman with two biracial children, founded Project RACE (Reclassify All Children Equally) in 1991 after she realized that there was no appropriate category for her children either on the U.S. Census form or on school forms. "When a child has to pick the race of one of their parents, they are in essence being forced to deny the other parent," Graham claims. Her organization has campaigned in several states to get local and state institutions to establish a multiracial category. By the late 1990s Project RACE had successfully lobbied seven states to add a multiracial category to their public forms. Although the 2000 U.S. Census did not include a multiracial category, for the first time it allowed individuals to check more than one box to indicate their racial heritage. Nearly 785,000 Americans identified themselves as both black and white in the 2000 census, out of a total of 6.8 million Americans who declared themselves multiracial.[84]

Supporters of the movement to recognize multiracial people claim that they are helping to further the fight against racism by making American racial categories more accurate and by asserting the legitimacy of multiracial families. They insist that forcing children of interracial couples into existing racial categories damages their personal self-esteem, and some believe that the rising numbers of multiracial children will undermine the whole concept of race as more and more people are born who do not fit into a single racial category.

Critics, including some parents of biracial children, are more circumspect about the political and psychological implications of embracing the idea of multiracial identity. Opponents of a "multiracial" category point out that being black and having mixed racial heritage has long been more the norm than the exception. By some estimates, more than 70 percent of the current black American population has multiracial heritage. If all of those people checked the "multiracial" box, the political strength of the black community would be seriously depleted. Leaders of the movement for a multiracial category assume that only children born of contemporary interracial couples will check the box, but some critics believe this kind of thinking might contribute to the emergence of a privileged mixed-race class between blacks and whites. Some suggest that the current efforts to get multiracial status legally recognized could produce a triracial society, much like South Africa, where whites remain on top, multiracial people are in the middle, and blacks continue to occupy the lowest rung on the ladder. In a heated letter to *Interrace,* the novelist Danzy Senna, herself a biracial woman who identifies as black, criticized the magazine's advocacy of multiracial identity, which she saw simply as a code word for "not black." It is far more politically radical for people of mixed racial ancestry to boldly define themselves as black, she argued.[85]

The fact that some of those who most actively push for the legal recognition of multiracial status are the white parents of multiracial children only fuels suspicion that the real goal of the multiracialists is to distance their children from the stigma of being considered black. Candy Mills, who had once supported the fight for a multiracial category, was by 1996 criticizing those who wanted such a category. "It's the parents of many multiracial children who have the identity problem, not the children themselves," Mills charged. "Many of these multiracial activists, both black and white, want to minimize the child's African heritage. I think they see a multiracial category as a way to elevate their children."[86]

Others dismiss the idea of biraciality because they believe it underestimates the continued salience of race and racism in American society. Jane Lazarre, a white academic, and her black husband, Douglas, raised their two sons as biracial for many years. As their children grew older, however, and began to experience racism, Lazarre decided "biracial" was problematic, "as if young men with brown skins can ever be considered 'part white' in America." As with any other identity, Lazarre insists, "how one experiences oneself in the everyday outside world must become internal as well, or the mind splits, even sanity may slip, imbalance threatens." To teach her children to consider themselves biracial when the world would categorize them as black would ultimately be destructive to their self-esteem, Lazarre argued. Sometimes the argument over raising children as biracial or as black plays out within a single family, which was the case for a couple in Maryland. The black mother wanted to teach her children that they were black in order to arm them against racial prejudice; their white father wanted to raise them as biracial and fight society's attempts to categorize the children as black.[87]

Interracial couples do not all agree that it is wise or healthy to raise children of black and white parents as biracial, but the vitality of the debate reflects the improved social conditions interracial couples enjoy today. Living in a more tolerant society where they face fewer problems because of their relationships, contemporary couples have more options about how to craft their lives and have become less willing to accept a marginal status within American society. Interracial couples today are challenging the notion that "normal" families include only people who look the same. They are demanding that the society and the state recognize their relationships, relationships that are symbolically erased when children of black-white couples are categorized monoracially.

Among both blacks and whites, the decades since World War II have been marked by increasing acceptance of interracial marriage. Although many blacks remain ambivalent about interracial relationships and whites have not overcome their fears of interracial marriage entirely, the radical nature of the changes that have taken place over the last sixty years cannot be denied. Changing attitudes about race, new legal norms, and cultural shifts toward individual autonomy have affected what is considered publicly acceptable discourse, so that couples no longer face constant criticism, and some positive representations of interracial love can be found in the media and popular culture. These changes have also transformed national politics, ensuring that cries of "no social equality" can no longer be used to stave off civil rights laws. Perhaps most significant, they have improved the quality of life for those who choose to cross the color line in marriage. Once seen as deviant neurotics and forced to be on their guard in public, interracial couples are today far less stigmatized and their marriages appear to be nearly as stable and long-lasting as intraracial ones.[88]

Indeed, interracial relationships today are increasingly being heralded as a sign of the country's success in overcoming racial inequality. Yet the significance of the transformation that has occurred since the 1940s must be kept in perspective. Although the growing numbers of black-white couples demonstrate that the color line in the United States has become considerably more fluid, to take these marriages as proof that racism has disappeared or that race no longer carries much significance in American life oversimplifies the current racial situation. The taboo against interracial marriage has eroded significantly since World War II, but the increased social acceptance of interracial relationships does not necessarily mean that structural and institutional racial inequalities no longer exist.

I S   L O V E   T H E

A N S W E R ?

In March 1977 in Middletown, Connecticut, the short-lived Interracial Clubs of America founded a new magazine that advocated interracial marriage as the solution to America's race problems. *Interracial* was dedicated "to the proposition of developing a totally integrated America through intermarriage." Interracial marriages not only would bring people of different racial and ethnic backgrounds together, but would also produce biracial children who could transcend America's historical racial divide. Individuals who married interracially could achieve what the legal reforms of the civil rights movement had failed to do, *Interracial* asserted. Its motto explained, "Love is the answer, not legislation."[1]

Today politicians, the media, and popular culture commonly describe cross-racial love as a positive good that will help reduce racial animosity. In 1998 the *Washington Post* argued that then-defense secretary William Cohen's marriage to a black woman was "the best advertisement for the kind of dialogue and interpersonal racial progress President Bill Clinton is now pushing, the kind of progress that can't be legislated."[2] Warren Beatty's 1998 political satire, *Bulworth,* preached a similar message about the importance of interracial relationships in overcoming America's racist history. In *Bulworth,* Beatty plays a disillusioned American senator who takes on a role as truth-teller during a reelection campaign. Soon he's wearing hip-hop clothes, rapping his message, and courting a black

woman half his age. Near the end of the film, Bulworth announces to a
crowd of supporters that the only way to end racism is through widespread interracial sex, for "everyone to fuck everyone else." All we need
to achieve racial harmony, the senator raps on national TV, is "a volun-
tary, free-spirited, open-ended program of procreative racial deconstruc-
tion." When asked in an interview about the movie why he had decided
to advocate interracial sex as the solution to the race problem, Beatty replied, "If you're doing a movie about race and you want to offer any kind
of conclusive suggestion, that would be it. It's called love."[3]

Interracial love in these accounts is an, or even *the,* answer to how to
improve American race relations. Proponents of this idea cite a variety of
reasons why love and marriage across the color line have the potential to
undo racial hierarchies. Some focus on the importance of multiracial
children, whose very existence not only will undermine racial categories,
but who also may have a unique ability to serve as racial ambassadors,
shuttling back and forth between each of their racial homes in an effort
to make peace. As one biracial man argued recently, multiracial people
are "uniquely positioned to be sensitive, objective negotiators of intergroup conflict."[4] Others argue that interracial relationships will serve as a
mechanism for the transfer of wealth from whites to nonwhites, that
these relationships will lead a growing number of intermarried whites
and their relatives to redraw their map of "racial self-interest" to include
blacks, or that intermarried whites can best educate other whites about
the damage caused by racism. Interracial marriage will thus produce a set
of whites whose interest in racial justice will be more immediate and
lasting than that of "white liberals who happen to live in the suburbs."
According to the legal scholar Randall Kennedy, "few situations are
more likely to mobilize the racially privileged individual to move against
racial wrongs than witnessing such wrongs inflicted upon one's mother-
in-law, father-in-law, spouse or child." Family ties across racial lines, another legal scholar argues, "will more quickly consume racial animus
than any other social or legal force."[5]

Yet given the still small numbers of black-white marriages, even if
these marriages do serve as a meaningful method of wealth transmission
or lead some whites to become blacks' racial allies, their influence will be
quite limited. With less than four hundred thousand black-white couples

in contemporary America, only a very small minority of blacks will receive any economic benefit from intermarriage. Even if all intermarried whites became crusaders for racial justice, they would still represent only a tiny percentage of whites overall.

Perhaps not surprisingly, then, most assertions that "love is the answer" focus not on actual interracial couples, but on the importance of whites' increased acceptance of interracial relationships more generally. Many social scientists have agreed, as James Weldon Johnston wrote in 1931, that the "sex factor" is rooted in the "core of the heart of the American race problem." Johnston's words serve as an epigraph to several books on the subject of intermarriage, an opening that suggests a crucial relationship between achieving racial equality and dealing with anxieties about interracial sex.[6] Thus the black literary critic Calvin Hernton argued in his classic 1965 work, *Sex and Racism in America,* that the primary reason whites oppose racial integration is "the superstitious imagining of the pornographic nature of interracial sex," while the sociologist Joseph Washington insisted in 1970 that if white Americans could come to terms with their fear of interracial marriage, "the other problems between blacks and white would rapidly fall into their proper perspective and pale into insignificance."[7] Anxiety about racial mixing, in these accounts, lies at the foundation of white racism.

Today similar thinking is manifested in the claim that an individual's attitudes about interracial relationships are the best way to measure whether or not a person is racist. Thus in courtrooms across the country, potential jurors who say they are opposed to interracial marriage are routinely excused by lawyers for black defendants on the grounds that they must be racist. In 2000, a black Connecticut man appealed his conviction for murder on the grounds that the judge did not allow his lawyer to ask prospective jurors their opinions on interracial marriage. Although lawyer Frank Mandanici had been allowed to ask jurors other questions about racial attitudes, he insisted that questions about interracial marriage were an "X-ray of the heart. . . . If you're against interracial marriage, I believe that means you're a racist at heart." The answer to one question about intermarriage was more telling than the answers to "a thousand other bland questions on race," Mandanici asserted.[8] The appeal, though ultimately denied, suggested that attitudes toward intermarriage were a crucial indicator of the state of an individual's racial attitudes.

There is no question that the taboo against interracial marriage has eroded since the 1940s, and that whites' opposition to interracial relationships is not as vehement as it once was. Although whites have not accepted interracial relationships to the same extent that they claim to approve of other forms of integration, the larger pattern is clear: on an individual level, whites have become more willing to accept some blacks as their equals. But what exactly do these changes suggest about the current state of American race relations? Now that white Americans have become more accepting of interracial marriage, will all other racial problems "pale into insignificance," as Joseph Washington predicted in 1970?

Without minimizing the importance of the change in individuals' attitudes, it is crucial to recognize that racism is not simply a reflection of individual hatred. The "love is the answer" discourse implies that whites' willingness to accept blacks as their social equals will automatically lead to meaningful racial equality in the United States. Yet racial inequalities today are primarily structural and institutional, rather than the result of individual racist acts or attitudes. Despite the gains of the civil rights movement and the growth of a sizable black middle class, structural racial inequality remains embedded in American politics and institutions. One of every two black children today lives below the poverty line; four times as many black families as white live in poverty; black unemployment rates are two to three times that of whites. Racial minorities are far more likely than whites to live near toxic waste dumps, to be arrested on drug charges, and to be denied mortgage loans. Blacks are far more likely than Asians or Latinos to live in segregated neighborhoods, no matter what their income level. Blacks live, on average, in neighborhoods that are 60 percent black. The level of segregation in the public schools remains high despite the *Brown* ruling prohibiting segregation in public education. In 1980 nearly one-third of black students attended all-minority schools, and three out of five attended schools that were predominantly black. School segregation today is due more to residential patterns than to laws, but it remains a fact of life for most young blacks and whites.[9]

Although celebrating love as the answer to racial problems seems far less dangerous and divisive than the old demonization of interracial love as a defilement of racial purity, this celebration has in fact become a convenient way to discount the continued significance of institutionalized forms of racism, and it is part of a broader social trend. As the social critic Benjamin DeMott argues in his 1995 book *The Trouble with Friendship*, a new racial orthodoxy in contemporary America suggests that the United States has solved its most serious racial problems. With the passage of laws that guarantee equal rights to black Americans and the end of legally sanctioned segregation, politicians, the media, and popular cultural forms have shifted their attention away from legislative solutions and structural racism to individuals and their racial beliefs and attitudes. Popular representations today suggest that the best way to achieve racial progress is for blacks and whites to work together as individuals; by reaching across the color line and forging personal relationships and friendships, individual blacks and whites can help eradicate the vestiges of racism in America.[10]

As appealing as the discourse celebrating interracial love might be, it ignores the continued salience of race in American society. Focusing on the acts of individual blacks and whites simplifies complex problems and contributes to the removal of racial issues from the public sphere. As the critical legal race theorist Patricia Williams asserts, suggesting intermarriage as the way to end racial inequality in American society is a "romantic solution posing as a political tool."[11] This discourse further reinforces the belief that racism is the work of isolated racists rather than something systemic or structural. The notion that "love is the answer" serves to mask existing inequalities, not to undo remaining racial hierarchies.

Tellingly, this idea has been embraced most emphatically by those on the right who oppose affirmative action programs, believe "identity politics" are balkanizing the nation, and contend that ongoing racial divisions are the artificial creation of a liberal elite. At the core of these writers' arguments is the assertion that rising approval for interracial dating and marriage proves that white racism is no longer a serious problem that limits opportunities for blacks, and thus government-sponsored remedies to benefit blacks are no longer needed. Intermarriage rates are used to discredit pundits and social scientists who insist that high incarceration rates for black males, continuing income inequalities between blacks and whites, and high black poverty rates mean that blacks remain disadvan-

taged in American society. The historian Stephen Thernstrom thus questioned a pessimistic 1998 report on race that called for government initiatives to aid the inner-city poor and to reform the American criminal
justice system by pointing to evidence of better interpersonal relations
between blacks and whites: "If you look at social contact, it is increased
markedly. Interracial dating is up. Interracial marriage, the same. Whatever the fault lines are in our society, the idea that it is the old-fashioned
black and white seems to me fairly simplistic."[12]

Rising intermarriage rates, furthermore, are thought to ensure that
government programs aimed at racial redress are no longer necessary.
Dinesh D'Souza, a political pundit whose book *The End of Racism* argues
that existing racial inequality is due to a deficient black culture, thus
looks forward to the day when the increasing number of multiracial children will make it impossible for the government to sort people into categories for the purpose of enforcing affirmative action policies. Calling
race-entitlement programs "pure political pork" supported by civil rights
activists who have rejected the color-blind principles of predecessors
such as Martin Luther King, Jr., and Frederick Douglass, D'Souza celebrates the growing number of multiracial children who are "literally beyond racial classification." This emerging American "café au lait society"
will soon mean that the government will be unable to count citizens by
race, D'Souza predicts, and thus everything from college admissions to
hiring, government contracts, and voting districts based on race will be
impossible to enforce.[13]

In D'Souza's construction, interracial couples allow for the resurrec-
tion of the old image of America as a melting pot, where people of different cultures and backgrounds will be forged into a new race. That
pot has already worked to reduce the importance of ethnic differences
among whites. Now previously unassimilable groups—Asians, Native
Americans, and even blacks—seem to be "melting" away their differences through intermarriage as well, and they are doing this on their
own, without government intervention. Rising intermarriage rates are
evidence of this increasing social fluidity, a fluidity, the journalist Jim
Sleeper argues, denied by "color-coding bureaucrats, corporate diversity
trainers, foundation-funded ethnocentric advocates, professors of pig-
mentation, and others in our vast national 'race industry.'" The conserva-

tive *National Journal* also criticizes racial liberals for supposedly ignoring the positive racial change demonstrated by the existence of more interracial relationships. In 1998 it attacked the *Los Angeles Times* for burying a story of rising intermarriage rates on page six while the front page was "heavy on stories about racial and ethnic identity."[14] Current racial tensions, in these accounts, are exaggerated by civil rights advocates and the liberal media, which focus on racial strife for their own political gain.

Black Americans, these conservative writers claim, can be seen now as just another ethnic group, rather than as a distinctive racial group. As Stephen and Abigail Thernstrom write in *America in Black and White,*

> One of the sharpest distinctions between the experience of African Americans and of that of the more than 50 million immigrants who came voluntarily to the United States in the nineteenth and twentieth centuries is that blacks were not allowed into the marital melting pot that did so much to blur immigrant group consciousness and foster assimilation. Although Louis Farrakhan and Spike Lee might not approve, that process has at last begun to affect African Americans in significant numbers.[15]

Here rising intermarriage rates become proof that America has overcome its history of racist exclusions, even though the black-white marriage rate lags behind that of other types of interracial marriage. Some more realistic commentators insist that if interracial marriage rates are used as the indicator, blacks are not assimilating as successfully as Asians or Latinos, and they worry that a new American divide might emerge between blacks and nonblacks.[16] Although such predictions are too pessimistic given the changes that have taken place since World War II, they serve as a reminder that old barriers can easily be replaced by newer, perhaps more insidious ones.

The coverage of the Thomas Jefferson–Sally Hemings controversy demonstrates the ways in which focusing on individual interracial relationships can shift focus away from structural racial inequality. When scientists finally established that Thomas Jefferson had indeed fathered at least one child by his slave Sally Hemings, many in the media claimed that the affair affirmed Jefferson's humanity and suggested that he must have been less imbued with the racism of his time than previously

thought. A writer in *USA Today* saw the proof of Jefferson's affair as a
"kind of a relief," because it made Jefferson seem more like a real person
and less like a myth.[17] Others termed the relationship between Hemings
and Jefferson a consensual one, based on love. Orlando Patterson argued
that Jefferson could not possibly have had a long-term sexual relationship
with a black woman and still deny her and her people's humanity. The
longevity of the relationship, Patterson maintains, suggests that Jefferson's
"doubts about his racialist theories may have been far more serious than
he let on in his writings."[18] Yet the fact that Jefferson had a long-standing
sexual relationship with a woman he owned and had mixed-race children that he kept as slaves could as easily be interpreted to mean that
Jefferson was more of a racist and less of a humanitarian than historians claim. The context of the exploitation of institutionalized slavery is
erased in this sentimental story about love.

In a more recent case, when four white New York City police officers
went on trial for the sexual assault on the Haitian immigrant Abner
Louima with a police nightstick, their lawyers denied that they were racist, pointing out that two of the officers, including the one charged with
assaulting Louima, had black girlfriends.[19] That individual police officers
have black girlfriends does not mean that there is not institutionalized
racism within the New York City Police Department or that the officers
in question could not have practiced racism in a vicious act of police
brutality.

The history of black-white marriage since 1940 demonstrates that great
strides have been made in lessening the taboo against interracial relationships. More blacks and whites are marrying each other. Interracial couples, in general, face less hostility from family and friends, and many have
found tolerant communities where they can live and raise their children.
Whites who marry blacks are no longer automatically forced down to
the status of blacks, and couples have more freedom about crafting their
own lives. The stringent color line of the 1940s has softened.

Yet this history also highlights the racial inequalities that remain. Perhaps the most important factor limiting the rate of black-white intermarriage is the kind of structural and institutionalized racism that the

"love is the answer" discourse erases. Income inequality and school and residential segregation not only act as barriers preventing blacks and whites from meeting in situations that might lead to dating, but also continue the racial disadvantages that make blacks less attractive as marital partners. As long as there are real costs associated with being black, whites will think seriously before embarking on an interracial relationship. Marriage between blacks and whites will not become commonplace until race is no longer a marker of privilege or disadvantage.

The old segregationist fear that integration would lead to "race mixing" was well founded. Meaningful integration allows blacks and whites to meet, to transcend the cultural and historical legacies that hinder healthy relationships, and to marry if they so choose. There is no question that interracial love will become more common and even more accepted as racial barriers erode in American society, but it will take more than love to break down those barriers. Old hierarchies must be dismantled for new attitudes about interracial love and marriage to flourish.

Prologue

1. Question from October 17, 1958, in George H. Gallup, *The Gallup Poll: Public Opinion, 1935–1971,* vol. 2, *1949–1958* (New York: Random House, 1972); *Gallup Opinion Index,* November 1972, report no. 89; Maria P. P. Root, *Love's Revolution: Interracial Marriage* (Philadelphia: Temple University Press, 2001), p. 38.

2. David Fowler, *Northern Attitudes towards Interracial Marriage: Legislation and Public Opinion in the Middle Atlantic States of the Old Northwest, 1780–1930* (New York: Garland Publishing, 1987), pp. 339–439; Charles Magnum, *The Legal Status of the Negro* (Chapel Hill: University of North Carolina Press, 1940), pp. 236–273.

3. On endogamy in the 1940s, see Milton L. Barron, "Research on Intermarriage: A Survey of Accomplishments and Prospects," *American Journal of Sociology* 57 (November 1951): 249–255; Ruby Jo Reeves Kennedy, "Single or Triple Melting-Pot? Intermarriage Trend in New Haven, 1870–1940," *American Journal of Sociology* 49 (January 1944): 331–339; William Tuttle, *"Daddy's Gone to War": The Second World War in the Lives of America's Children* (Oxford: Oxford University Press, 1993), pp. 99–100.

4. U.S. Census Bureau, *http://www.census.gov/population/socdemo/race/interrac tab1.txt.;* Jason Fields and Lynne M. Casper, "America's Families and Living Arrangements 2000," *Current Population Reports* (June 2001): 15.

5. Fields and Casper, "America's Families and Living Arrangements, 2000," p. 15; Michael Lind, "The Beige and the Black," *New York Times Magazine,* August 16, 1998, p. 38; *Washington Post,* July 5, 2001, p. A01.

6. For more on this possibility, see Gary Nash, "The Hidden History of Mestizo America," in *Sex, Love, Race: Crossing Boundaries in North American His-*

tory, ed. Martha Hodes (New York: New York University Press, 1999), pp. 10–32.

7. On the colonial regulation of interracial marriage and "fornication," see Peter Bardaglio, "'Shameful Matches': Regulation of Interracial Sex and Marriage" in *Sex, Love, Race,* ed. Hodes, pp. 112–138; Kathleen Brown, *Good Wives, Nasty Wenches, and Anxious Patriarchs* (Chapel Hill: University of North Carolina Press, 1996), pp. 187–222; Paul Finkelman, "Crimes of Love, Misdemeanors of Passion: The Regulation of Race and Sex in the Colonial South," in *The Devil's Lane: Sex and Race in the Early South,* ed. Catherine Clinton and Michele Gillespie (New York: Oxford University Press, 1997), pp. 124–135; A. Leon Higginbotham, Jr., and Barbara Kopytoff, "Racial Purity and Interracial Sex in the Law of Colonial and Antebellum Virginia," *Georgetown Law Journal* 77 (August 1989): 1967–2029.

8. Nancy Cott, *Public Vows: A History of Marriage and the Nation* (Cambridge: Harvard University Press, 2000); Nancy Cott, "Giving Character to Our Whole Civil Polity: Marriage and the Public Order in the Late Nineteenth Century," in *U.S. History as Women's History,* ed. Linda Kerber, Alice Kessler-Harris, and Kathryn Kish Sklar (Chapel Hill: University of North Carolina Press, 1995), pp. 107–121.

9. See David Heer, "Negro-White Marriage in the U.S.," *Journal of Marriage and the Family* 28 (August 1966): 262–273, for a discussion of the ways in which intermarriage could open up avenues of social mobility for blacks. Peggy Pascoe demonstrates that many antimiscegenation cases dealt with the disposition of property. See Pascoe, "Race, Gender, and Intercultural Relations: The Case of Interracial Marriage," *Frontiers* 12 (1991): 5–18.

10. For more on this, see Heather Dalmage, *Tripping on the Color Line: Black-White Multiracial Families in a Racially Divided World* (New Brunswick, N.J.: Rutgers University Press, 2000).

11. The six were Indiana, Georgia, Florida, Nevada, North Dakota, and Utah. Fowler, *Northern Attitudes towards Interracial Marriage,* appendix; Cott, *Public Vows,* p. 42.

12. Martha Hodes, *White Women, Black Men: Illicit Sex in the 19th-Century South* (New Haven: Yale University Press, 1998), chaps. 7 and 8; Glenda Gilmore, *Gender and Jim Crow* (Chapel Hill: University of North Carolina Press, 1996), esp. chap. 4; Nell Painter, "Social Equality, Miscegenation, Labor, and Power" in *The Evolution of Southern Culture,* ed. Numan Bartley (Athens: University of Georgia Press, 1988), pp. 47–67. On the invention

of the term "miscegenation," see Hodes, *White Women, Black Men,* pp. 144–145.

13. On race mixing outside the South, see Leslie Harris, "From Abolitionist Amalgamators to 'Rulers of the Five Points': The Discourse of Interracial Sex and Reform in Antebellum New York City" in *Sex, Love, Race,* ed. Hodes, pp. 191–212; Kevin Mumford, *Interzones: Black/White Sex Districts in Chicago and New York in the Early Twentieth Century* (New York: Columbia University Press, 1997), pp. xi–xix, 37–49.

14. Fredrick Hoffman, *Race Traits and Tendencies of the American Negro* (New York: Macmillan, 1896), reprinted in *Plessy v. Ferguson: A Brief History with Documents,* ed. Brook Thomas (Boston: Bedford Books, 1997), p. 86.

15. Mumford, *Interzones,* pp. 10–11; Mary Berry and John Blassingame, *Long Memory* (New York: Oxford University Press, 1982), pp. 130–132; Cott, *Public Vows,* pp. 163–164.

16. For exemplary studies that focus on the South, see Hodes, *White Women, Black Men;* and Clinton and Gillespie, *The Devil's Lane.* On the legal history of the prohibitions of interracial marriage, see Rachel F. Moran's *Interracial Intimacy: The Regulation of Race and Romance* (Chicago: University of Chicago Press, 2000), and Randall Kennedy's *Interracial Intimacies: Sex, Marriage, Identity, and Adoption* (New York: Pantheon, 2003). Recent notable sociological case studies of couples include Robert P. McNamara, Maria Tempenis, and Beth Walton, *Crossing the Color Line: Interracial Couples in the South* (Westport, Conn.: Praeger, 1999); Paul C. Rosenblatt, Terri A. Karis, and Richard D. Powell, *Multiracial Couples: Black and White Voices* (Thousand Oaks, Calif.: Sage Publications, 1995); and Root, *Love's Revolution.* The historian Paul Spickard's comparative survey *Mixed Blood: Intermarriage and Ethnic Identity in Twentieth-Century America* (Madison: University of Wisconsin Press, 1989) is an exception to the general pattern within the scholarship in that it explores the history of interracial marriage nationwide.

17. F. James Davis, *Who Is Black?* (University Park: Pennsylvania State University Press, 1991); Joel Williamson, *New People: Miscegenation and Mulattoes in the United States* (New York: Free Press, 1980).

18. Cott, *Public Vows,* p. 27; Tomás Almaguer, *Racial Fault Lines: The Historical Origins of White Supremacy in California* (Berkeley: University of California Press, 1994), pp. 57–62; Richard Godbeer, "Eroticizing the Middle Ground: Anglo-Indian Sexual Relations along the Eighteenth-Century Frontier," in *Sex, Love, Race,* ed. Hodes, pp. 91–111.

19. Works that suggest that race relations have improved dramatically since the

1960s include Orlando Patterson, *The Ordeal of Integration* (Washington, D.C.: Civitas Counterpoint, 1997); Stephen and Abigail Thernstrom, *America in Black and White* (New York: Simon and Schuster, 1997). On the continuing importance of race and of structural white privilege, see Andrew Hacker, *Two Nations* (New York: Ballantine Books, 1992); Derrick Bell, *Faces at the Bottom of the Well* (New York: Basic Books, 1992); George Lipsitz, *The Possessive Investment in Whiteness* (Philadelphia: Temple University Press, 1998).

20. This idea is further developed in the Epilogue.

1. The Unintended Consequences of War

1. Hazel Byrne Simpkins, "I Married a Tan Yank," *Tan Magazine,* March 1951, reprinted in *Marriage across the Color Line,* ed. Cloyte M. Larsson (Chicago: Johnson Publishing Co, 1968), pp. 97–106.

2. William Tuttle, *"Daddy's Gone to War": The Second World War in the Lives of America's Children* (Oxford: Oxford University Press, 1993), pp. 91–97.

3. For more on the impact of World War II on the South, see Bruce Shulman, *From Cotton Belt to Sunbelt: Federal Policy, Economic Development, and the Transformation of the South, 1938–1980* (New York: Oxford University Press, 1991); Neil McMillen, ed., *Remaking Dixie: The Impact of World War II on the American South* (Jackson: University Press of Mississippi, 1997).

4. Manning Marable, *Race, Reform and Rebellion,* 2nd ed. (Jackson: University Press of Mississippi, 1991), p. 10; George Lipsitz, *Rainbow at Midnight* (Urbana: University of Illinois Press, 1994), p. 54.

5. Margaret Crawford, "Daily Life on the Home Front," in *World War II and the American Dream,* ed. Donald Albrecht (Washington, D.C.: National Building Museum; and Cambridge: MIT Press, 1995), p. 129; Arnold Hirsch, *Making the Second Ghetto: Race and Housing in Chicago, 1940–1960* (Cambridge: Cambridge University Press, 1983), pp. 4–5.

6. Elaine Tyler May, "Rosie the Riveter Gets Married," in *The War in American Culture,* ed. Lewis Erenberg and Susan Hirsch (Chicago: University of Chicago Press, 1996), p. 128. For more on wartime sexual opportunities, see Allan Bérubé, *Coming Out under Fire* (New York: Plume, 1990); Beth Bailey and David Farber, *The First Strange Place: The Alchemy of Race and Sex in World War II Hawaii* (New York: Free Press, 1992).

7. Sister M. Annella, R.S.M., "Some Aspects of Interracial Marriage in

Washington, D.C., 1940–1947," *Journal of Negro Education* 25 (Fall 1956): 387–389; Sister Annella Lynn, "Interracial Marriages in Washington, D.C.," *Journal of Negro Education* 36 (Fall 1967): 428–433.

8. Pete Daniel, "Going among Strangers: Southern Reactions to World War II," *Journal of American History* 77 (December 1990): 886–911; Arvin D. Smallwood, *The Atlas of African-American History and Politics* (Boston: McGraw-Hill, 1998), pp. 128–129.

9. Crawford, "Daily Life on the Home Front," pp. 111–113; Hirsch, *Making the Second Ghetto,* pp. 40–99; Stephen Grant Meyer, *As Long as They Don't Move Next Door: Segregation and Racial Conflict in American Neighborhoods* (Lanham, Md.: Rowman and Littlefield, 2000), pp. 64–78.

10. Howard Odum, *Race and Rumors of Race* (1943; Baltimore: John Hopkins University Press, 1997), pp. 54–55.

11. George Roeder, "Censoring Disorder: American Visual Imagery of World War II," in *The War in American Culture,* ed. Erenberg and Hirsch, pp. 57–58; Barbara Savage, *Broadcasting Freedom: Radio, War, and the Politics of Race, 1938–1948* (Chapel Hill: University Press of North Carolina, 1999), pp. 124–142.

12. Marilynn S. Johnson, *The Second Gold Rush: Oakland and the East Bay in World War II* (Berkeley: University of California Press, 1993), pp. 64–65; Savage, *Broadcasting Freedom,* pp. 204–206.

13. Odum, *Race and Rumors of Race,* p. 58.

14. Theodore Bilbo to Mississippi Legislature, March 22, 1944, reprinted in *The Development of Segregationist Thought,* ed. I. A. Newby (Homewood, Ill.: Dorsey Press, 1968), pp. 140–144; Stimson diary quoted in Richard Dalfiume, "The 'Forgotten Years' of the Negro Revolution," *Journal of American History* 55 (January 1968): 106; "social equality" quote from James Patterson, *Grand Expectations: The United States, 1945–1974* (Oxford: Oxford University Press, 1996), p. 5.

15. Bailey and Farber, *The First Strange Place,* pp. 95–132; Geoffrey Perret, *There's a War to Be Won* (New York: Random House, 1991), pp. 469–472.

16. Gail Buckley, *American Patriots* (New York: Random House, 2001), p. 183; W. E. B. Du Bois, "The Negro Soldier in Service Abroad during the First World War," *Journal of Negro History* 12 (Summer 1943): 324–334.

17. Graham Smith, *When Jim Crow Met John Bull: Black American Soldiers in World War II Britain* (New York: St. Martin's Press, 1988), p. 200.

18. Ibid., pp. 47, 189.

19. Mary Frances Berry and John Blassingame, *Long Memory* (New York: Ox-

ford University Press, 1982), p. 321; Neil Wynn, *The Afro-American and the Second World War* (London: Paul Elek, 1976), p. 33.

20. Smith, *When Jim Crow Met John Bull,* pp. 57, 79.

21. Ibid., pp. 98–99, 194–196.

22. Ibid., pp. 114, 198.

23. *Ibid.,* p. 223. For accounts of violence, see Smith, *When Jim Crow Met John Bull,* pp. 197–198; "Germany Meets the Negro Soldier," *Ebony,* October 1946, p. 7.

24. Brenda L. Moore, *To Serve My Country, to Serve My Race* (New York: New York University Press, 1996), pp. 80–82, 122–136; Smith, *When Jim Crow Met John Bull,* pp. 191–193. "Companionship" quote is from Moore, p. 80. I found no accounts of interracial marriages involving black women serving abroad and white foreign men.

25. George H. Roeder, Jr., *The Censored War: American Visual Experience during World War II* (New Haven: Yale University Press, 1993), p. 57; Roeder, "Censoring Disorder," p. 56.

26. Elfrieda Berthiaume Shukert and Barbara Smith Scibetta, *War Brides of World War II* (Novato, Calif.: Presidio Press, 1988), p. 20; Jenel Virden, *Good-bye, Piccadilly: British War Brides in America* (Chicago: University of Chicago Press, 1996), pp. 30–38.

27. Virden, *Good-bye, Piccadilly,* p. 34; Shukert and Scibetta, *War Brides of World War II,* pp. 20–23, 131–144.

28. Ibid., p. 30; Shukert and Scibetta, *War Brides of World War II,* pp. 20, 132–133.

29. H. Struve Heusel to Walter White, January 15, 1946; Robert Patterson to Walter White, March 5, 1946; Edward F. Witsell to Dr. M. L. Ogan, April 16, 1946; Captain M. C. Mumma Jr. to M. L. Ogan, April 15, 1946, in *Papers of the NAACP,* Part 9: Discrimination in the U.S. Armed Forces, 1918–1955, Series B, NAACP 1940–1955: Legal File—Soldier Marriages, 1944–1949 (Frederick, Md.: University Publications of America, 1982), microfilm, reel 15. Hereafter referred to as *NAACP Papers,* Soldier Marriages File.

30. Permission to Marry Forms, November 11, 1944, Headquarters, AAF Station, 552, APO 635, U.S. Army; Memo from Colonel Goodall, December 11, 1944, both in *NAACP Papers,* Soldier Marriages File.

31. James D. Givens to Commanding General, Base Air Depot Area, U.S. Strategic Air Forces in Europe, January 8, 1945 (emphasis omitted); Charles Campbell to Commanding General, Base Air Depot Area, U.S. Strategic

Forces in Europe, December 26, 1944, both in *NAACP Papers,* Soldier Marriages File.

32. White to Robert Patterson, December 20, 1945, *NAACP Papers,* Soldier Marriages File.

33. Ollie Stewart, "How War Brides Fare in America," *Negro Digest,* April 1948, p. 26; Shukert and Scibetta, *War Brides of World War II,* p. 150.

34. MP quote in Smith, *When Jim Crow Met John Bull,* p. 164; Memo to Section Commanders from Headquarters, ETO US Army, May 12, 1945; Robert Bradford to NAACP, October 28, 1946, both in *NAACP Papers,* Soldier Marriages File.

35. Sister Annella Lynn, "Communications and Opinion," *American Sociological Review* 18 (October 1953): 57; Hildegard Kaiser to NAACP, December 7, 1946, in *NAACP Papers,* Soldier Marriages File.

36. Shukert and Scibetta, *War Brides of World War II,* pp. 48–49.

37. C. E. Richards to NAACP, October 8, 1946 in *NAACP Papers,* Soldier Marriages File.

38. "Englishwoman in Dixie," *Negro Digest,* June 1948, pp. 29–33; "Till Law Us Do Part," *Newsweek,* January 19, 1948, pp. 25–26.

39. Simpkins, "I Married a Tan Yank," p. 104.

40. Memo to Commanding General European Theater of Operations, APO 887, U.S. Army, December 19, 1944, in *NAACP Papers,* Soldier Marriages File.

41. Marion T. Frederick to National Office of the NAACP, March 16, 1945; Franklin Williams to Marion T. Frederick, March 27, 1946; Franklin Williams to Lawrence Wright, March 27, 1946, in *NAACP Papers,* Soldier Marriages File.

42. Shukert and Scibetta, *War Brides of World War II,* pp. 20, 132–133; in contrast, there were only about ten thousand marriages between American soldiers and French women during World War I. See Evelyn Millis Duvall and Reuben Hill, *When You Marry* (New York: Association Press, 1948), p. 117.

43. Robert L. Carter to Cleophes J. Randall, November 26, 1945, in *NAACP Papers,* Soldier Marriages File.

44. Ernest Porterfield, "Black-American Intermarriage in the United States," *Marriage and Family Review* 5 (Spring 1982): 17–34; M. Belinda Tucker and Claudia Mitchell-Kernan, "New Trends in Black American Interracial Marriage: The Social Structural Context," *Journal of Marriage and the Family* 52 (February 1990): 209–218. On the difficulty of gathering reliable data

on interracial marriage rates, see John H. Burma, "Interethnic Marriage in Los Angeles, 1948–1959," *Social Forces* 42 (December 1963): 156–165; David Heer, "Negro-White Marriage in the United States," *New Society,* August 26, 1965, pp. 7–9; Thomas Monahan, "An Overview of Statistics on Interracial Marriage in the United States, with Data on Its Extent from 1963–1970," *Journal of Marriage and the Family* 38 (May 1976): 223–231.

45. *Baltimore Afro-American,* September 3, 1949, p. 3.

46. Joseph Golden, "Characteristics of the Negro-White Intermarried in Philadelphia," *American Sociological Review* 18 (April 1953): 179; Lynn, "Interracial Marriages in Washington, D.C., 1940–47," p. 64.

47. Quoted in Neil McMillen, "Fighting for What We Didn't Have: How Mississippi's Black Veterans Remember World War II," in *Remaking Dixie,* ed. McMillen, p. 99. See also John Dittmer, *Local People: The Struggle for Civil Rights in Mississippi* (Urbana: University of Illinois Press, 1995), pp. 17–18.

48. Douglas Massey and Nancy Denton, *American Apartheid* (Cambridge: Harvard University Press, 1993), pp. 42–46; Hirsch, *Making the Second Ghetto,* pp. 5–13; Johnson, *The Second Gold Rush,* pp. 222–233.

49. Erenberg and Hirsch, "Introduction," in *The War in American Culture,* ed. Erenberg and Hirsch, pp. 1–2.

50. Robin D. G. Kelley, *Race Rebels: Culture, Politics, and the Black Working Class* (New York: Free Press, 1994), pp. 55–75; Adam Fairclough, *Race and Democracy* (Athens: University of Georgia Press, 1995), pp. 74–134.

51. W. T. Couch, "Publisher's Introduction" in *What the Negro Wants,* ed. Rayford Logan (Chapel Hill: University of North Carolina Press, 1944), p. xv. On the declining legitimacy of scientific racism, see Elazar Barkan, *The Retreat of Scientific Racism* (Cambridge: Cambridge University Press, 1992).

52. Peggy Pascoe, "Miscegenation Law, Court Cases, and Ideologies of 'Race' in Twentieth-Century America," *Journal of American History* 83 (June 1996): 44–69.

53. Alan Brinkley, "The New Political Paradigm: World War II and American Liberalism," in *The War in American Culture,* ed. Erenberg and Hirsch, pp. 313–330; Savage, *Broadcasting Freedom,* pp. 194–245; Walter Jackson, *Gunnar Myrdal and America's Conscience: Social Engineering and Racial Liberalism, 1938–1987* (Chapel Hill: University of North Carolina Press, 1990), pp. 236–241.

54. Theodore Bilbo, *Take Your Choice: Separation or Mongrelization* (Poplarville, Miss.: Dream House Publishing Co., 1947), pp. 55–56.

55. David Cohn, "How the South Feels," *Atlantic Monthly,* January 1944, pp. 47–51.

56. David Southern, *Gunnar Myrdal and Black-White Relations* (Baton Rouge: Louisiana State University Press, 1987), p. 26.

57. Gunnar Myrdal, *An American Dilemma* (New York: Harper and Brothers, 1944), p. 59. On the miscegenation taboo, see pp. 53–64, 573–603.

58. Lewis Erenberg, "Swing Goes to War," in *The War in American Culture,* ed. Erenberg and Hirsch, p. 158.

59. Margaret Halsey, *Color Blind* (New York: Simon and Schuster, 1946), p. 69.

60. Ibid., p. 20.

61. Sterling Brown, "Counting Us In," p. 326; Frederick Patterson, "The Negro Wants Full Participation in the American Democracy," p. 261; Gordon Hancock, "Race Relations in the United States: A Summary," p. 277; Langston Hughes, "My America," p. 306, all in *What the Negro Wants,* ed. Logan.

62. Southern, *Gunnar Myrdal and Black-White Relations,* pp. 82–84; John Egerton, *Speak Now against the Day* (New York: Knopf, 1994), pp. 133–134, 271–275.

63. Couch, "Publisher's Introduction," pp. xxii, xiv; Savage, *Broadcasting Freedom,* pp. 218–222.

64. *South Pacific* has been criticized for its exotification of the "Oriental" other. One can read the film as suggesting that it is progressive for a white man to deign to love the racial other, however, and in any case, the romance ends in tragedy when the white partner is killed in action.

65. Louisa Blackwell and Frances Clay, *Lillian Smith* (New York: Twayne Publishers, 1971); Anne C. Loveland, *Lillian Smith: A Southerner Confronting the South* (Baton Rouge: Louisiana State University Press, 1986).

66. Lillian Smith, *Strange Fruit* (Cornwall, N.Y.: Cornwall Press, 1944), pp. 65, 39.

67. Smith to Frank Taylor, July 26, 1943, reprinted in *How Am I to Be Heard: Letters of Lillian Smith,* ed. Rose Gladney (Chapel Hill: University of North Carolina Press, 1993), p. 72.

68. *Pinky* (Twentieth Century Fox, 1949).

69. For more on the production code, see Chapter 5. Cid Ricketts Sumner, *Quality: A Novel* (1945; New York: Bobbs-Merrill, 1946). For critiques of *Pinky,* see Thomas Cripps, *Making Movies Black* (New York:

Oxford University Press, 1993), p. 235; Daniel Leab, *From Sambo to SUPERSPADE: The Black Experience in Motion Pictures* (Boston: Houghton Mifflin, 1975), pp. 153–156; "Pinky: The Story of Girl Who Passes Will Be Most Debated Film of the Year," *Ebony,* September 1949, pp. 23–25.

70. John Kisch and Edward Mapp, *A Separate Cinema: 50 Years of Black Cast Posters* (New York: Noonday Press, 1992), p. 82.

71. "Ladies, What Would You Do . . . ?" *Life,* October 17, 1949, p. 113.

72. Arnaud d'Usseau and James Gow, *Deep Are the Roots* (New York: Charles Scribner's Sons, 1946), p. 143.

73. Ibid., p. xxi.

74. Ibid., p. 201.

75. For reviews of *Pinky,* see *Time,* October 10, 1949, pp. 96, 98; *New Yorker,* October 1, 1949, pp. 50–51; *New York Times,* September 30, 1949, p. 28; *New York Times,* December 25, 1949, sect. 2, p. 1.

76. On *Deep Are the Roots,* see *The Negro Handbook, 1946–1947,* ed. Florence Murray (New York: Current Books, 1947); Samuel Leiter, ed., *The Encyclopedia of the New York Stage, 1940–1950* (Westport, Conn.: Greenwood Press, 1992), pp. 155–156; *Life,* October 15, 1945, p. 51. On *Strange Fruit,* see Loveland, *Lillian Smith: A Southerner Confronts the South,* pp. 70–71; Mertrice M. James and Dorothy Brown, eds., *Book Review Digest 1944* (New York: H. W. Wilson, 1945), pp. 699–700.

77. The police in Boston objected to the novel's use of the word "fuckin'." The Massachusetts Supreme Court upheld the ban, ruling that *Strange Fruit* was "obscene, indecent, and impure." See Bernard De Voto, "The Decision in the 'Strange Fruit' Case: The Obscenity Statute in Massachusetts," *New England Quarterly* 19 (June 1946): 147–183; Max Lerner, "On Lynching a Book," in *The First Freedom,* ed. Robert Downs (Chicago: American Library Association, 1960), pp. 209–210.

78. Lillian Smith to Frank Taylor, May 2, 1944, reprinted in *How Am I to Be Heard,* ed. Gladney, pp. 84, 83.

79. *Hopesville Statesman* quoted in Loveland, *Lillian Smith: A Southerner Confronts the South,* pp. 70–71.

80. *Stevens v. United States,* 146 F.2d 120 (1944).

81. For legislative history, see dissenting opinion by Justice Shenk, *Perez v. Sharp,* 198 P.2d 17 (1948), p. 38. The case was also known as *Perez v. Lippold.*

82. On the merits of the First Amendment argument, see Ted LeBerthon, "Does the Constitution Uphold Mixed Marriage?" *Negro Digest,* July 1947,

pp. 52–56; David Seidelson, "Miscegenation Statutes and the Supreme Court: A Brief Prediction of What the Court Will Do and Why," *Catholic University of America Law Review* 15 (May 1966): 159; Harvey Appelbaum, "Miscegenation Statutes: A Constitutional and Social Problem," *Georgetown Law Journal* 53 (Fall 1964): 49–91; Pascoe, "Miscegenation Law," pp. 61–67.

83. *Perez v. Sharp*, 198 P.2d 17 (1948), p. 18.

84. Concurring opinion by Justice Carter, *Perez v. Sharp*, 198 P.2d 17 (1948), p. 33.

85. Ibid., p. 22, 24, 25.

86. Ibid., pp. 25.

87. See "A Seventy-Six Year Old Miscegenation. . . . ?" unidentified paper, October 16, 1948, Schomburg Center Clipping File, Intermarriage, vol. 1, Schomburg Center for Research in Black Culture, New York Public Library, New York; Lise Funderburg, *Black, White, Other: Biracial Americans Talk about Race and Identity* (New York: William Morrow, 1994); Seidelson, "Miscegenation Statutes and the Supreme Court," p. 158; "Racial Bill Retained," *New York Times,* May 19, 1951.

88. *Record of Davis Knight v. State of Mississippi*, Circuit Court of First Judicial District of Jones County, no. 37205, December 1948 term, Mississippi Department of Archives and History, Archives and Library Division, Jackson, Miss.; Victoria Bynum, "Misshapen Identity: Memory, Folklore, and the Legend of Rachel Knight," in *Sex, Love, Race: Crossing Boundaries in North American History*, ed. Martha Hodes (New York: New York University Press, 1999), pp. 237–253.

89. "Brief for Appellee to the Supreme Court of Mississippi," *Davis Knight v. State of Mississippi*, no. 37205, p. 13.

90. *Davis Knight v. State of Mississippi*, 42 So.2d 747 (1949); "Davis Knight, white," *Newsweek,* November 28, 1949, p. 16.

91. Bilbo, *Take Your Choice,* preface.

2. The Dangers of "Race Mixing"

1. Philip Klinker with Rogers Smith, *The Unsteady March* (Chicago: University of Chicago Press, 1999), pp. 210–224.

2. Henry Louis Gates, *Colored People* (New York: Vintage Books, 1994), p. 22.

3. Question from October 17, 1958, in George H. Gallup, *The Gallup Poll: Public Opinion, 1935–1971,* vol. 2, *1949–1958* (New York: Random House, 1972).

4. Paul Spickard, *Mixed Blood: Intermarriage and Ethnic Identity in Twentieth-Century America* (Madison: University of Wisconsin Press, 1989), pp. 288–289.

5. James Weldon Johnson, *Along This Way* (New York: Viking Press, 1933), p. 170.

6. Eva Saks, "Representing Miscegenation Law," *Raritan* 7 (Fall 1998): 48.

7. Gunnar Myrdal, *An American Dilemma* (New York: Harper and Brothers, 1944), p. 590.

8. Theodore Bilbo, *Take Your Choice: Separation or Mongrelization* (Poplarville, Miss.: Dream House Publishing Co., 1947), pp. 57–58.

9. Edwin King quoted in Charles Marsh, *God's Long Summer: Stories of Faith and Civil Rights* (Princeton: Princeton University Press, 1997), p. 83.

10. "He Wouldn't Cross the Color Line," *Life,* September 3, 1951, p. 93.

11. For more on white women in interracial couples being taken for prostitutes, see Chapter 4.

12. Ernest May, *Life,* September 24, 1951, p. 13.

13. See Nancy Armstrong, "Why Daughters Die: The Racial Logic of American Sentimentalism," *Yale Journal of Criticism* 7 (Fall 1994): 12.

14. Arlene Skolnick, *Embattled Paradise: The American Family in the Age of Uncertainty* (New York: Basic Books, 1991), p. 65. On family and gender relations in the 1950s, see Elaine Tyler May, *Homeward Bound: American Families in the Cold War Era* (New York: Basic Books, 1988); Jessica Weiss, *To Have and to Hold: Marriage, the Baby Boom, and Social Change* (Chicago: University of Chicago Press, 2000).

15. *Loving v. Virginia,* 388 U.S. Supreme Court (1967), p. 3; question from June 6, 1962, in Gallup, *The Gallup Poll: Public Opinion, 1935–1971,* vol. 3, *1959–1971,* p. 1770. For more on the religious argument against intermarriage, see Myrdal, *American Dilemma,* p. 584; James Cook, *The Segregationists* (New York: Appleton-Century-Crofts, 1962), pp. 215–216; James W. Vander Zanden, "The Ideology of White Supremacy," *Journal of the History of Ideas* 20 (June–September 1959): 385–402; Charles Reagan Wilson, *Baptized in Blood* (Athens: University of Georgia Press, 1980), pp. 100–118; David Harrell, Jr., *White Sects and Black Men in the Recent South* (Nashville: Vanderbilt University Press, 1971).

16. "The Love Story That Rocked the South," *Tan,* October 1960, reprinted as "Mississippi Story" in *Marriage across the Color Line,* ed. Cloyte M. Larsson (Chicago: Johnson Publishing Co., 1965), pp. 114–119.

17. See James A. Adair, "Racial Intermarriage and Christianity" (M.A. thesis, Pittsburgh-Xenia Theological Seminary, 1956), pp. 1–5, 55–60; Helen Schaffer, "Mixed Marriages," *Editorial Research Reports,* May 24, 1961,

p. 383; David Lawrence, "And What about Intermarriage," *U.S. News and World Report,* November 21, 1958, p. 136; Milton Mayer, "The Issue Is Miscegenation," *Progressive,* September 1959, pp. 17–18.

18. George Lipsitz, *The Possessive Investment in Whiteness* (Philadelphia: Temple University Press, 1998), p. 184. On Native Americans and Asians, see Timothy Tyson, *Radio Free Dixie* (Chapel Hill: University of North Carolina Press, 1999), pp. 137–140; Ian Haney López, *White by Law: The Legal Construction of Race* (New York: New York University Press, 1996), pp. 148–153.

19. Quoted in Matt Garcia, "'Memories of El Monte': Intercultural Dance Halls in Post–World War II Greater Los Angeles," in *Generations of Youth,* ed. Joe Austin and Michael Nevin Willard (New York: New York University Press, 1998), p. 164.

20. Matthew Jacobson, *Whiteness of a Different Color* (Cambridge: Harvard University Press, 1998), pp. 8–12.

21. Arnold Hirsch, *Making the Second Ghetto: Race and Housing in Chicago* (Cambridge: Cambridge University Press, 1993), pp. 196–197; Thomas Sugrue, "Crabgrass-Roots Politics: Race, Rights, and the Reaction against Liberalism in the Urban North, 1940–1964," *Journal of American History* 82 (September 1995): 561–562.

22. Robert Roberts, "Trends in Marriages between Negroes and Whites in Chicago," in *Perspectives in Ethnicity,* ed. Regina Holloman and Serghei Arutiunov (The Hague: Mouton Publishers, 1978), pp. 195, 205–206.

23. David Halberstam, *The Fifties* (New York: Fawcett Columbine, 1993), p. 141; Hirsch, *Making the Second Ghetto,* pp. 171–198; Gary Gerstle, "The Working Class Goes to War," in *The War in American Culture,* ed. Lewis Erenberg and Susan Hirsch (Chicago: University of Chicago Press, 1996), p. 118.

24. Stephen Grant Meyer, *As Long as They Don't Move Next Door: Segregation and Racial Conflict in American Neighborhoods* (Lanham, Md.: Rowman and Littlefield, 2000), p. 8; Lorraine Hansberry, *A Raisin in the Sun* (1958; New York: Modern Library, 1995), p. 105.

25. Cheryl I. Harris, "Whiteness as Property," *Harvard Law Review* 196 (June 1993): 1734–36.

26. Ian Haney López, "The Social Construction of Race: Some Observations on Illusion, Fabrication, and Choice," *Harvard Civil Rights–Civil Liberties Law Review* 29 (Winter 1994): 1–62.

27. James Baldwin, *Tell Me How Long the Train's Been Gone* (New York: Dial Press, 1968), p. 61.

28. Charles Smith, "Negro-White Intermarriage—Metropolitan New York: A Qualitative Case Analysis" (Ph.D. diss., Teachers College, Columbia University, 1960), p. 46.

29. Robert K. Merton, "Intermarriage and the Social Structure: Fact and Theory," *Psychology* 4 (August 1941): 369.

30. Skolnick, *Embattled Paradise,* p. 69; Rickie Solinger, *Wake Up Little Susie: Single Pregnancy and Race before Roe v. Wade* (New York: Routledge, 1992), pp. 4–6; Elaine Tyler May, "Explosive Issues: Sex, Women, and the Bomb," in *Recasting America: Culture and Politics in the Age of the Cold War,* ed. Lary May (Chicago: University of Chicago Press, 1989), pp. 155–156.

31. Milton Barron, "Research on Intermarriage: A Survey of Accomplishments and Prospects," *American Journal of Sociology* 57 (November 1951): 249; Henry Yu, "Mixing Bodies and Cultures: The Meaning of America's Fascination with Sex between 'Orientals' and 'Whites,'" in *Sex, Love, Race: Crossing Boundaries in North American History,* ed. Martha Hodes (New York: New York University Press, 1999), pp. 444–463.

32. Everett Parker, "New York City: Negro-White Marriages," *The Christian Century,* November 6, 1945, p. 1383.

33. John D'Emilio and Estelle Freedman, *Intimate Matters* (New York: Harper and Row, 1988), p. 234.

34. George Little, "Analytic Reflections on Mixed Marriage," *Psychoanalytic Review* 29 (January 1942): 22.

35. Robert Seidenberg, M.D., "The Sexual Basis of Social Prejudice," *Psychoanalytic Review* 39 (January 1952): 90–95.

36. May, *Homeward Bound,* pp. 116–117; James Gilbert, *A Cycle of Outrage: America's Reaction to the Juvenile Delinquent in the 1950s* (New York: Oxford University Press, 1986).

37. Eugene Cash, Jr., "A Study of Negro-White Marriages in the Philadelphia Area" (Ph.D. diss., Temple University, 1956), p. 96; Linton Freeman, "Homogamy in Interethnic Mate Selection," *Sociology and Social Research* 39 (July–August 1955): 369–377.

38. Merton, "Intermarriage and the Social Structure," pp. 361–374. See also Kingsley Davis, "Intermarriage in Caste Societies," *American Anthropologist* 43 (July–September 1941): 388–395.

39. Pierre L. Van Den Berghe, "Hypergamy, Hypergeneration, and Miscegenation," *Human Relations* 13 (February 1960): 88–89. For commentary on how widely held the "exchange theory" was, see Thomas Monahan, "The Occupational Class of Couples Entering into Interracial Marriages," *Journal of Comparative Family Studies* 7 (Summer 1976): 175–189; Gary Crester

and Joseph Leon, "Intermarriage in the U.S.: An Overview of Theory and Research," *Marriage and Family Review* 5 (Spring 1982): 3–15.

40. Quoted in Joseph Golden, "Social Control of Negro-White Intermarriage," *Social Forces* 36 (March 1958): 269.

41. Randall Risdon, "A Study of Interracial Marriages Based on Data for Los Angeles County," *Sociology and Social Research* 39 (November–December 1954): 94.

42. "Sociological suicide" is a term used by the black sociologists St. Clair Drake and Horace Cayton to describe the impact of intermarriage on the white partner. See St. Clair Drake and Horace Cayton, *Black Metropolis: A Study of Negro Life in a Northern City,* rev. ed., vol. 1 (1945; New York: Harper Torchbooks, 1962), p. 142.

43. Little, "Analytic Reflections on Mixed Marriages," p. 22.

44. Robin French to Walter White, May 26, 1950, Box A608, Folder: Staff—Walter White General and Personal, 1950 April–May, National Association for the Advancement of Colored People Papers, Group II, Administrative Files (1940–1955), General Office File, Library of Congress, Manuscript Division, Washington, D.C.

45. David Heer, "The Prevalence of Black-White Marriage in the United States, 1960 and 1970," *Journal of Marriage and the Family* 36 (May 1974): 246–258; Paul Glick, "Intermarriage among Ethnic Groups in the United States," *Social Biology* 17 (December 1970): 292–298.

46. *Vetrano v. Gardner,* 290 F. Supp 200 (U.S. District Court N.D. Mississippi, Greenville Division, 1968).

47. *New York Post,* September 7, 1956, Schomburg Center Clipping File, Intermarriage—Laws, 1925–1974, Schomburg Center for Research in Black Culture, New York Public Library, New York; "Davis Knight, white," *Newsweek,* November 28, 1949, p. 16.

48. "The Love Story That Rocked the South," pp. 114–119.

49. Maria P. P. Root, *Love's Revolution: Interracial Marriage* (Philadelphia: Temple University Press, 2001), pp. 22, 60.

50. Anonymous, "My Daughter Married a Negro," *Harper's,* July 1951, pp. 36–40.

51. Interview with Paul and Doris in Albert Gordon, "Negro-Jewish Marriages: Three Interviews," *Judaism* 13 (Spring 1964): 171; Hettie Cohen, *How I Became Hettie Jones* (New York: Penguin Books, 1990), p. 63.

52. Anonymous, "My Daughter Married a Negro," p. 38; mother quoted in "They Live in a Brave Gray World," *New York Daily News,* February 18, 1972, from Schomburg Center Clipping File: Intermarriage, Chronology,

1968–1972; Michelle Ross, "Is Mixed Marriage Jinxed," *Ebony*, August 1953, pp. 36, 38.

53. Interview with Frances and Jackson in Albert Gordon, *Intermarriage: Interfaith, Interracial, Interethnic* (Boston: Beacon Press, 1964), p. 259; Robert S. Bird, "Integration—and a Campus Romance," *U.S. News and World Report*, February 22, 1960, p. 101; SallyAnn Hobson in Lise Funderburg, *Black, White, Other: Biracial Americans Talk about Race and Identity* (New York: William Morrow, 1994), p. 61.

54. Golden, "Social Control of Negro-White Intermarriage," p. 269.

55. Marty Goldsmith, January 6, 1961, part 3, side 2, tape 544a, George Wiley Papers, 1952–1973, State Historical Society of Wisconsin, Madison.

56. Nick and Mary Lynn Kotz, *A Passion for Equality: George A. Wiley and the Movement* (New York: W. W. Norton, 1977), p. 73.

57. Gregory Williams, *Life on the Color Line* (New York: Plume Books, 1995), p. 182.

58. "They Live in a Brave Gray World," February 18, 1972; Lloyd Taylor, "Interracial Romances on Campus," *Crisis*, January 1953, pp. 23–24, 64; "Interracial College Marriages," *Ebony*, July 1954, pp. 89–94; *New York Post*, February 3, 1960, in Schomburg Center Clipping File: Intermarriage: Chronology, 1960–1968; Bird, "Integration—and a Campus Romance," pp. 100–102.

59. "Statement on Policy," *The Earlhamite*, Spring 1952, p. 12, in "McAllester-Cunningham Folder," Earlham College Archives, Lilly Library, Earlham College, Richmond, Ind.; *Chicago Defender*, May 5, 1952, in "McAllester-Cunningham Folder," Earlham College Archives.

60. Walter White to Rufus Allen, Chairman, Board of Trustees, Earlham College, May 28, 1952; Earlham press release on McAllester-Cunningham incident, April 24, 1952; Robert N. Huff, Director of Public Relations, to J. C. Furnas, January 6, 1955, all in "McAllester-Cunningham Folder," Earlham College Archives.

61. Interview with Grace and Robert McAllester by the author, March 1, 1994.

62. Ibid.

63. Press release, April 24, 1952; "A Summary of the Current Interracial Controversy at Earlham," 1952, both in "McAllester-Cunningham Folder," Earlham College Archives.

64. News accounts appeared in *Jet*, *Ebony*, the *Chicago Defender*, the *New York Post*, the *San Francisco Chronicle*, and the *New York Herald Tribune*, among

others. Earlham received letters from the NAACP and the American Friends Service Committee criticizing the college's stand. See Walter White to Rufus Allen, May 28, 1952; Tom Jones to John Willard, May 16, 1952; "Students Sympathize with Two Involved in Mixed Marriage," *Dayton Daily News,* May 5, 1952, all in "McAllester-Cunningham Folder," Earlham College Archives.

65. Interview with Grace and Robert McAllester.

66. See examples in Cash, "A Study of Negro-White Marriages in the Philadelphia Area," p. 53; press release, "Seattle Urban League Reports Wider Acceptance of Interracial Marriages in the Community," April 30, 1967, Schomburg Center Clipping File: Intermarriage.

67. *Associated Negro Press,* December 27, 1950, in Claude A. Barnett Papers, series I: Race Relations, 1923–1965, part 3, Subject Files on Black Americans, 1918–1967 (Frederick, Md.: University Publications of America, 1985), microfilm, reel 78; interview with Paul and Doris, "Negro-Jewish Marriages," pp. 170–171; *New York Post,* February 3, 1960; "The Bursar's Daughter," *Time,* February 15, 1960, pp. 56, 59.

68. Ernest Porterfield, *Black and White Mixed Marriages* (Chicago: Nelson-Hall, 1978), p. 121.

69. Anonymous, "My Daughter Married a Negro," p. 39; Bird, "Integration— and a Campus Romance," pp. 100–102; *New York Post,* February 3, 1960.

70. Interview with Doris in Gordon, *Intermarriage,* p. 286; "Mixed Marriage Nightmare," *New York Amsterdam News,* June 19, 1965, p. 53.

71. For more on this, see Solinger, *Wake Up Little Susie.*

72. Smith, "Negro-White Intermarriage," pp. 126, 128.

73. Cash, "A Study of Negro-White Marriages in the Philadelphia Area," p. 57; Smith, "Negro-White Intermarriage," p. 126.

74. For examples of Jewish families sitting Shiva, see Funderburg, *Black, White, Other,* pp. 123–124; Smith, "Negro-White Intermarriage," p. 129.

75. Anonymous, "My Daughter Married a Negro," p. 59.

76. Scott Minerbrook, *Divided to the Vein* (New York: Harcourt Brace and Co., 1996), p. 35; interview with Grace and Robert McAllester; Drake and Cayton, *Black Metropolis,* vol. 1, p. 144.

77. Smith, "Negro-White Intermarriage," pp. 128, 122–123.

78. Interview with Paul and Doris in Gordon, "Negro-Jewish Marriages," pp. 170–171; Jones, *How I Became Hettie Jones,* pp. 63–64.

79. Hobson in Funderburg, *Black, White, Other,* pp. 60–67 (quote at 64).

80. Minerbrook, *Divided to the Vein,* pp. 35, 14.

81. Interview with Ruth in Gordon, "Negro-Jewish Marriages," p. 184.

82. Lee Chennault, "How I Face the World with My Negro Child," *Ebony,* December 1960, p. 58.

83. Minerbrook, *Divided to the Vein,* p. 6.

84. Interview with Kimani Fowlin in Funderburg, *Black, White, Other,* p. 55. On the difficulty of getting legal abortions in the 1950s, see Solinger, *Wake Up Little Susie,* pp. 37–38.

85. Jones, *How I Became Hettie Jones,* p. 63; Jeanne Campbell, "This Is My Daughter," *Negro Digest,* June 1965, p. 84.

86. Interview with Henry and Violet in Gordon, "Negro-Jewish Marriages," p. 176; Smith, "Negro-White Intermarriage," p. 103.

87. "Pawn in Pigtails," *Newsweek,* November 14, 1949, pp. 28–29.

88. For more on the history of child custody, see Mary Ann Mason, *From Father's Property to Children's Rights: The History of Child Custody in the United States* (New York: Columbia University Press, 1994). For a more extensive discussion of these cases, see Renee Romano, "'Immoral Conduct': White Women, Racial Transgressions, and Custody Disputes" in *"Bad" Mothers: The Politics of Blame in Twentieth-Century America,* ed. Molly Ladd-Taylor and Lauri Umansky (New York: New York University Press, 1997), pp. 230–251. None of these cases involved divorced white fathers who married black women, probably because so few fathers were awarded custody of their children.

89. *Jet,* April 10, 1952, p. 22; *Pittsburgh Courier,* July 11, 1959, p. 9.

90. *Potter v. Potter,* 127 N.W.2d 320 (Michigan, 1964).

91. Charles Claudius Philippe to Poppy Cannon, July 28, 1949, box 11, folder 77, Walter White–Poppy Cannon White Papers, section 2, ser. 1, Beinecke Library, Yale University, New Haven, Conn.

92. "Brief for Defendant-Appellant, Court of Appeals of the State of New York"; "Brief of the New York City Chapter of the National Lawyers Guild as Amicus Curiae," both in National Association for the Advancement of Colored People Papers, Group II, Legal Files (1940–1955), Box B82, Folder: Intermarriage; *People of New York ex rel. Mollie Portnoy v. Ann Strasser,* Court of Appeals, 1951–1952; *People ex rel. Portnoy v. Strasser,* 104 N.E.2d 895 (New York, 1952); *People ex rel. Portnoy v. Strasser,* 195 N.Y.S.2d 905 (New York, 1951).

93. *Murphy v. Murphy,* Appendix to Appellant's Brief, Connecticut Supreme Court Record and Briefs, part 2, June term 1956, pp. 134–135.

94. *Potter v. Potter,* Brief and Appendix for Plaintiff and Appellant, State of

Michigan Supreme Court, Appeal from the Circuit County, Wayne County, October term 1963, p. 11.

95. *Potter v. Potter,* Brief and Appendix for the Appellant, p. 71a; *Potter v. Potter,* 127 N.W.2d 320 (Michigan, 1964).

96. "Are Interracial Homes Bad for Children," *Ebony,* March 1963, p. 135.

97. Brief for Appellant, *Murphy v. Murphy,* Supreme Court of Errors of the State of Connecticut, New Haven County, January term 1956, no. 4529, p. 19.

98. *In re Adoption of a Minor,* 228 F.2d 446 (Washington, D.C., 1955). A higher court eventually reversed this decision.

99. *Commonwealth ex rel. Myers v. Myers,* 360 A.2d 587 (Pennsylvania, 1975).

100. *Potter v. Potter,* Brief and Appendix for Plaintiff and Appellant, pp. 55a, 200a.

3. Ambivalent Acceptance

1. Jay Collins, "*Top Secret* Bombshell! It Will Come as a Shock to Millions of Whites . . . What's Behind those Inter-Racial Marriages," *Top Secret,* June 1960, in Vertical File: Marriage, Moorland-Spingarn Collection, Howard University, Washington, D.C.

2. Gunnar Myrdal, *An American Dilemma* (New York: Harper and Brothers, 1944), p. 56.

3. Beatrice Woodson, *Ebony,* January 1947, p. 4.

4. Henry Louis Gates, *Colored People* (New York: Vintage Books, 1994), pp. 34–35; "Who Wants Intermarriage: Intermarriage Favored but Non-Skilled Females Object," *Pittsburgh Courier,* magazine section, September 6, 1958, p. 1.

5. "Intermarriage Poll Concluded: Do Professional Negroes Have Less Antipathy toward Whites," *Pittsburgh Courier,* September 17, 1958, p. 1; "Who Wants Intermarriage: Most Courier Readers Stand against Interracial Marriage," *Pittsburgh Courier,* September 20, 1958, p. 6.

6. On the politics of respectability, see Stephanie Shaw, *What A Woman Ought to Be and Do* (Chicago: University of Chicago Press, 1996); Evelyn Brooks Higginbotham, *Righteous Discontent* (Cambridge: Harvard University Press, 1993); Kevin Gaines, *Uplifting the Race* (Chapel Hill: University of North Carolina Press, 1996).

7. St. Clair Drake and Horace Cayton, *Black Metropolis: A Study of Negro Life in a Northern City,* rev. ed., vol. 1 (1945; New York: Harper Torchbooks,

316 NOTES TO PAGES 86–90

1962), p. 138; Postcard to Eslanda Robeson, June 19, 1949, in Paul Robeson Papers, Correspondence—Hate Mail, Manuscript Division, Moorland-Spingarn Research Center, Howard University, Washington, D.C.; Carrasco quoted in Lise Funderburg, *Black, White, Other: Biracial Americans Talk about Race and Identity* (New York: William Morrow, 1994), p. 84.

8. Drake and Cayton, *Black Metropolis,* p. 131.

9. Mark Chesler, ed., "How Do You Negroes Feel about Whites: A Collection of Papers by College Students Exploring and Expressing Their Own Racial Attitudes," Center for Research on Utilization of Scientific Knowledge, Ann Arbor, Mich., 1969, pp. 14–15.

10. Henry Haifner, *Ebony,* September 1949, p. 6.

11. The 1960 U.S. Census even found slightly more white male–black female couples than black male–white female couples in the U.S. population (about 26,000 as compared with 25,000).

12. Drake and Cayton, *Black Metropolis,* p. 134; Pamela Allen, *Ebony,* November 1951, p. 10.

13. Violet Coburn to NAACP National Headquarters, February 16, 1950, National Association for the Advancement of Colored People Papers, Group II, Administrative Files (1940–55), Box A610, Folder: Staff—Walter White, Marriage, 1949–51, Library of Congress, Washington, D.C.

14. Anonymous, "Are White Women Stealing Our Men," *Negro Digest,* April 1951, p. 52.

15. Violet Coburn to NAACP National Headquarters, February 16, 1950, in NAACP Papers; Lucy Ridley, *Ebony,* August 1949, p. 10; Nannie Burroughs, "Church Leader Argues against Mixed Marriage," *Ebony,* November 1951, p. 51; John Banks quoted in "Critical Logic Features Interracial Love Advice," *Pittsburgh Courier,* November 27, 1954, p. 2.

16. Lena Horne, "My Life with Lennie," *Ebony,* November 1965, p. 186; Thomasena Allen, *Ebony,* November 1960, p. 18.

17. Julius Kiano, *Ebony,* February 1950, pp. 10–11.

18. Jimmy Bridges, *Ebony,* November 1947, p. 4; H. Finley Trope, *Los Angeles Sentinel,* September 8, 1949, p. 7a; Carl Rowan, "What White People Ask about Negroes," *Ebony,* February 1960, p. 90.

19. A/2C Clarence B. Williams, *Ebony,* March 1954, p. 12; George Schuyler, "Are Negroes More Prejudiced than Whites?" *Negro Digest,* November 1951, pp. 40–43; Schuyler, "Views and Reviews," *Pittsburgh Courier,* October 1, 1949, p. 16; "Who Wants Intermarriage: Majority Would Not Ob-

ject to Children Marrying Whites," *Pittsburgh Courier,* magazine section, September 13, 1958, p. 1.

20. F. V. Seabrook, *Negro Digest,* August 1950, p. 97; "Does Mixed Marriage Hurt Race Relations," *Jet,* July 3, 1952, p. 25; Eva Roberson, *Ebony,* April 1954, pp. 8–9.

21. John Green, *Ebony,* October 1953, p. 6; Miss D. Jones, *Ebony,* July 1953, p. 6, 8. See also Lloyd Forney, *Ebony,* January 1951, p. 8; Julia Watson, *Ebony,* August 1951, p. 6.

22. Sgt. Edward Berry, *Ebony,* August 1954, p. 6; William Kennedy, *Ebony,* August 1947, p. 4.

23. Walter C. Daniel, *Black Journals of the United States* (Westport, Conn.: Greenwood Press, 1982), pp. 159–164, 213–214, 262–264; Ronald Wolseley, *The Black Press, U.S.A.,* 2nd ed. (Ames: Iowa State University Press, 1990), pp. 85–89, 142–147; Cathy Cohen, *The Boundaries of Blackness: AIDS and the Breakdown of Black Politics* (Chicago: University of Chicago Press, 1999), pp. 186–195.

24. In 1968, when the circulation of *Ebony* was about 1,000,000 copies, it was estimated that each issue reached 4,575,000 readers. Walter Goodman, "*Ebony:* Biggest Negro Magazine," *Dissent* 15 (September–October 1968): 403.

25. Quoted in Wolseley, *The Black Press, U.S.A.,* p. 86.

26. Editor's statement, *Ebony,* November 1945, quoted in Paul M. Hirsch, "An Analysis of *Ebony:* The Magazine and Its Readers," *Journalism Quarterly* 45 (Summer 1968): 261.

27. See George and Josephine Schuyler, "Does Interracial Marriage Succeed?" *Negro Digest,* June 1945, pp. 15–17; Dr. Nathanial Calloway, "Mixed Marriage Can Succeed," *Negro Digest,* March 1949, pp. 24–27; Jack Johnson, "Does Interracial Marriage Succeed?" *Negro Digest,* May 1945, pp. 3–5; Mr. and Mrs. William Grant Still, "Does Interracial Marriage Succeed?" *Negro Digest,* April 1945, pp. 50–52; Thryra Edwards Gitlin and Murray Gitlin, "Does Interracial Marriage Succeed?" *Negro Digest,* July 1945, pp. 63–64.

28. "1,000 Witness Interracial Marriage in Chicago," *Jet,* July 17, 1952, p. 27; "Church Wedding for Mixed Couple," *Ebony,* December 1951, pp. 50–52.

29. "Anne Brown Becomes a Norwegian," *Ebony,* September 1948, pp. 26–30; "Famous Negroes Married to Whites," *Ebony,* December 1949, pp. 20–28; "Is Mixed Marriage a New Society Fad," *Ebony,* September 1951, pp. 98–103; Pearl Bailey, "This Time It's Love," *Ebony,* February 1953, pp. 122–128; Cloyte Murdock, "My Daughter Married a White Man–J. Wesley

Dobbs," *Ebony,* January 1954, pp. 86–93; "Do Negro Stars Prefer White Husbands," *Ebony,* May 1954, pp. 41–46; "Why Musicians Choose White Wives," *Jet,* January 8, 1953, pp. 24–29; "Negro Women with White Husbands," *Jet,* February 21, 1952, pp. 24–29; "Are Europe's Men Stealing Our Women," *Jet,* May 7, 1953, pp. 14–17.

30. "Is Mixed Marriage a New Society Fad," pp. 98, 99, 103.

31. "Wanted: Negro Husbands and Wives–Germans Forget Aryan Doctrine, Seek Colored Mates in America," *Ebony,* March 1951, pp. 65–69; "Why German Women Want Negro Husbands," *Jet,* April 3, 1952, p. 20; "I Want to Marry a Negro," *Negro Digest,* August 1948, pp. 12, 14; Oskar Heim, "Why I Want a Negro Wife," *Negro Digest,* July 1954, pp. 64–68.

32. "Negro Women with White Husbands," *Jet,* February 21, 1952, p. 25; "Why More White Men Are Marrying Negro Women," *Jet,* December 3, 1953, p. 19; "Marriages That Criss-Cross the Color Line: Unions of White Men, Negro Women as Numerous, but Less Publicized," *Chicago Defender,* July 29, 1950, p. 13.

33. Hazel Erskine, "The Polls: Interracial Socializing," *Public Opinion Quarterly* 37 (Summer 1973): 286.

34. Pvt. Norman W. Bailey, *Ebony,* August 1954, pp. 6, 8.

35. Dorothy Jones, *Ebony,* January 1947, p. 4; James Connor, *Ebony,* January 1947, p. 51; Herbert C. Barker, *Ebony,* February 1950, p. 10.

36. Audrey Hepburn, *Ebony,* January 1951, p. 8; *Jet,* September 18, 1952, p. 7.

37. Thurgood Marshall, "What the Negro Wants Now," *Ebony,* March 1958, p. 68; "Prominent Negro Leaders Answer Question: Does Interracial Marriage Hinder Integration," *Ebony,* July 1957, pp. 90–91.

38. Quoted in "Gotham Citizens Express Opinions of Mixed Unions," *Pittsburgh Courier,* December 4, 1954, p. 11. See also "Readers Heap Fury on Dr. Peale for 'Advice,'" *Pittsburgh Courier,* November 20, 1954, p. 2; "Critical Logic Features Interracial-Love Advice," November 27, 1954, p. 2. Peale's comments were made in an advice column in *Look* Magazine, November 16, 1954, p. 42.

39. "Jackie Robinson," *New York Post,* February 8, 1960, Schomburg Center Clipping File, Schomburg Center for Research in Black Culture, New York Public Library, New York.

40. Carol Stout to George Wiley, February 9, 1960; Stout to Wiley, February 18, 1960; Stout to Wiley, March 5, 1960, in Box 2, Folder 3 (Personal Correspondence, 1960–1969), George Wiley Papers, State Historical Society of Wisconsin, Madison.

41. Quoted in "The South and the Negro," *Ebony,* April 1957, p. 80.

42. Poppy Cannon, *A Gentle Knight: My Husband Walter White* (New York: Rinehart and Company, 1956), pp. 28–29; White to Cannon, February 9, 1949, Walter White–Poppy Cannon White Papers, Section II, Series I: Box 12, Folder 112, James Weldon Johnson Collection, Beinecke Library, Yale University, New Haven, Conn.

43. White to Cannon, January 11, 1949, Section II, Series I: Box 12, Folder 12, Walter White–Poppy Cannon White Papers.

44. The Round-the-World Town Meeting on the Air was a privately organized tour of representatives from twenty-eight American organizations.

45. Helen Martin to Walter White, May 20, 1949, in Box 4, Folder 131, Walter White–Poppy Cannon White Papers; Madeleine White to Walter White, May 20, 1949, in Box 7, Folder 225, Walter White–Poppy Cannon White Papers.

46. J. Robert Smith, "It's the Truth," *Los Angeles Sentinel,* August 4, 1949, p. B1; *Oklahoma Black Dispatch,* reprinted in "Famous Negroes Married to Whites," *Ebony,* December 1949, p. 22.

47. Madeline White to Walter White, May 20, 1949; "Spaulding Spanks Walter," *Pittsburgh Courier,* September 3, 1949, p. 4.

48. "New York Buzzing With Gossip on NAACP's Walter White," *Charlotte Post,* July 30, 1949, NAACP Papers, Group II, Administrative Files (1940–55), Folder: Staff—Walter White, Marriage, 1949–51; "Walter White and the NAACP," *Norfolk Journal and Guide,* August 6, 1949, p. 8.

49. Booker T. Washington, *Up from Slavery: An Autobiography* (1901; New Brunswick, N.J.: Transaction Publishers, 1997), pp. 176–177.

50. Madeleine White to Walter White, May 20, 1949; *Norfolk Journal and Guide,* August 6, 1949, p. 8; Carl Murphy to Palmer Weber, August 31, 1949, NAACP Papers, Group II, Administrative Files (1940–55), Folder: Staff–Walter White, Leave of Absence, 1949.

51. Palmer Weber to Carl Murphy, September 1, 1949, NAACP Papers, Group II, Administrative Files (1940–55), Box A610, Folder: Staff–Walter White, Leave of Absence, 1949; William Hastie to Carl Murphy, October 3, 1949, NAACP Papers, Box A610, Folder: Staff–Walter White, Marriage, 1949–51.

52. "Meeting of the Board of Directors," June 13, 1949; "Meeting of the Board of Directors," April 10, 1950, both in *Papers of the NAACP,* Part I, 1909–1950, Meetings of the Board of Directors, Records of Annual Conferences, Major Speeches, and Special Reports (Frederick, Md.: University Publications of America, 1982), microfilm, reel 3.

53. Mrs. Charles Ackou, *Pittsburgh Courier,* October 11, 1958, p. 7.

54. "Who Wants Intermarriage: Majority Would Not Object to Children Marrying Whites," p. 1.

55. "Negroes Are Found to Be Uninterested in Mixed Marriage," *New York Times,* May 25, 1964, Schomburg Center Clipping File.

56. Amiri Baraka, *The Autobiography of LeRoi Jones* (New York: Freundlich Books, 1984), p. 149.

57. James McBride, *The Color of Water: A Black Man's Tribute to His White Mother* (New York: Riverhead Books, 1996), p. 195; William Peters, "Are There Boundary Lines in Love," *McCall's,* June 1968, reprinted in *Black Male/White Female: Perspectives on Interracial Marriage and Courtship,* ed. Doris Wilkinson (Cambridge, Mass.: Schenkman, 1975), p. 135.

58. Interview with Paul in Albert Gordon, *Intermarriage: Interfaith, Interracial, Interethnic* (Boston: Beacon Press, 1964), p. 281; Scott Minerbrook, *Divided to the Vein* (New York: Harcourt Brace and Co., 1996), p. 64.

59. Charles Smith, "Negro-White Intermarriage—Metropolitan New York: A Qualitative Case Analysis" (Ph.D. diss., Teachers College, Columbia University, 1960), p. 128.

60. Minerbrook, *Divided to the Vein,* p. 65; Drake and Cayton, *Black Metropolis,* p. 144; Smith, "Negro-White Intermarriage," p. 124.

61. Smith, "Negro-White Intermarriage," p. 123.

62. Interview with Arthur Lambkin in Gordon, *Intermarriage,* p. 237; interview with Paul in ibid., p. 281.

63. Andrew Billingsley, *Climbing Jacob's Ladder: The Enduring Legacy of African-American Families* (New York: Simon and Schuster, 1992); Harriet Pipes McAdoo, ed., *Black Families* (Thousand Oaks, Calif.: Sage, 1997); Niara Sudarkasa, *The Strength of Our Mothers* (Trenton, N.J.: Africa World Press, 1996), pp. 3–11, 123–141; Carol B. Stack, "Sex Roles and Survival Strategies in an Urban Black Community," in *The Black Woman Cross-Culturally,* ed. Filomina Chioma Steady (Cambridge, Mass.: Schenkman, 1981), pp. 349–368.

64. Interview with Yvonne and Chuck Cannon by the author, August 24, 1999; Todd Pavela, "An Exploratory Study of Negro-White Intermarriage in Indiana," *Journal of Marriage and the Family* 26 (May 1964): 210.

65. Interview with SallyAnn Hobson in Funderburg, *Black, White, Other,* p. 66.

66. Sandy Cirillo, "The Lois Jones Story," *Interrace,* June/July 1994, pp. 14, 15, 18; Joseph Golden, "Patterns of Negro-White Intermarriage," *American Sociological Review* 19 (April 1954): 145.

67. Minerbrook, *Divided to the Vein,* pp. 66–67, 71.

68. Interview with Arthur Lambkin in Gordon, *Intermarriage,* pp. 239, 237;

Josephine Schuyler, "An Interracial Marriage," *American Mercury,* March 1946, p. 277.

69. Hazel Byrne Simpkins, "I Married a Tan Yank," *Tan Magazine,* March 1951, reprinted in *Marriage across the Color Line,* ed. Cloyte M. Larsson (Chicago: Johnson Publishing Co, 1968), p. 105; Mrs. C. Jackson, *Ebony,* October 1953, p. 6; McBride, *The Color of Water,* pp. 245, 247.

4. Not Just Commies and Beatniks

1. Lola Aquilera, *Ebony,* October 1953, p. 6.

2. St. Clair Drake and Horace Cayton, *Black Metropolis: A Study of Life in a Northern City,* rev. ed., vol. 1 (1945; New York: Harper Torchbooks, 1962), p. 147.

3. Outline for "Intermarriage: A Study in Black and White" in Box 133, Folder: Research Materials, Intermarriage: A Study in Black and White— Outline for Book, E. Franklin Frazier Papers, Moorland-Spingarn Collection, Howard University, Washington, D.C.; Lee Chennault, "How I Face the World with My Negro Child," *Ebony,* December 1960, p. 54.

4. George Metcalf, *From Little Rock to Boston: The History of School Desegregation* (Westport, Conn.: Greenwood Press, 1983), p. 105.

5. Andrew Billingsley, *Climbing Jacob's Ladder: The Enduring Legacy of African-American Families* (New York: Simon and Schuster, 1992), pp. 178–179. In three major sociological case studies of interracial couples who married in the forties and fifties, only one couple out of fifty-one met in high school or college.

6. *New York Amsterdam News,* June 25, 1949, p. 1; Evelyn Elmar Smith, "Interracial Marriage: A Case Study of Twelve Negro-White Marriages in Washington, D.C." (Ph.D. diss., Howard University, 1965), p. 159; Brett Harvey, *The Fifties: A Women's Oral History* (New York: HarperCollins, 1993), p. 163. See also "Interracial College Marriages," *Ebony,* July 1954, pp. 89–94; Lloyd Taylor, "Interracial Romances on Campus," *Crisis,* January 1953, pp. 23–24, 64.

7. Michelle Ross, "Is Mixed Marriage Jinxed?" *Ebony,* August 1953, pp. 34–42; Smith, "Interracial Marriage," pp. 187, 167.

8. "The Case against Mixed Marriage," *Ebony,* November 1950, p. 56; Smith, "Interracial Marriage," pp. 156–157.

9. Eugene Cash, Jr., "A Study of Negro-White Marriages in the Philadelphia Area" (Ph.D. diss., Temple University, 1956), pp. 55–56; Smith, "Interracial Marriage," pp. 142, 147; decision of Supreme Court of Errors, Waterbury,

Conn., August 5, 1955, in *Dorothy Murphy vs. Edward Murphy,* Connecticut Supreme Court Record and Briefs, Part 2: Mas-W, June Term, 1956, p. 19.

10. "Famous Negroes Married to Whites," *Ebony,* December 1949, p. 24; Martin Luther King, Jr., "Advice for Living," *Ebony,* June 1958, p. 118.

11. Max Lerner, "Only One Race," *New York Post,* November 20, 1952, from Schomburg Center Clipping File: Intermarriage, vol. 1, Schomburg Center for Research in Black Culture, New York Public Library, New York; Lena Horne, "My Life with Lennie," *Ebony,* November 1965, pp. 176–186. See also Pearl Bailey, "This Time It's Love," *Ebony,* February 1953, pp. 122–128; "Why Musicians Choose White Wives," *Jet,* January 8, 1953, pp. 24–29.

12. Chennault, "How I Face the World With My Negro Child," p. 54; Scott Minerbrook, *Divided to the Vein* (New York: Harcourt Brace and Co., 1996), p. 63; William Peters, "Are There Boundary Lines in Love," *McCall's,* June 1968, reprinted in *Black Male/White Female: Perspectives on Interracial Marriage and Courtship,* ed. Doris Wilkinson (Cambridge, Mass.: Schenkman, 1975), p. 134.

13. "He Wouldn't Cross the Line," *Life,* September 3, 1951, pp. 81–94; "Is Mixed Marriage a New Society Fad?" *Ebony,* September 1951, p. 99; Cash, "A Study of Negro-White Marriages in the Philadelphia Area," pp. 46–48.

14. Norman Mailer, "The White Negro," *Dissent* (Summer 1957): 276–293; Wini Breines, "Postwar White Girls' Dark Others," in *The Other Fifties,* ed. Joel Foreman (Urbana: University of Illinois Press, 1997), p. 70.

15. Hettie Cohen, *How I Became Hettie Jones* (New York: Penguin Books, 1990), p. 26; Amiri Baraka, *The Autobiography of LeRoi Jones* (New York: Freundlich Books, 1984), p. 142. See also Joyce Johnson, *Minor Characters* (1983; New York: Anchor Books, 1994), pp. 212–218.

16. Elaine Kaufmann from *Who Wouldn't Walk with Tigers* excerpted in *different beat: writings by women of the beat generation,* ed. Richard Peabody (London: Serpent's Tail, 1997), pp. 108–114; Jones, *How I Became Hettie Jones,* p. 135; Baraka, *Autobiography of LeRoi Jones,* p. 148.

17. Vincent Parks, response to questionnaire designed by the author, August 4, 1994; Smith, "Interracial Marriages," p. 190; interview with Henry and Violet in Albert Gordon, "Negro-Jewish Marriages: Three Interviews," *Judaism* 13 (Spring 1964): 177; James Farmer, *Lay Bare the Heart: An Autobiography of the Civil Rights Movement* (New York: Arbor House, 1985), pp. 168–169.

18. John Egerton, *Speak Now against the Day: The Generation before the Civil Rights Movement in the South* (New York: Alfred A. Knopf, 1994), pp. 167–

174; Fraser Ottanelli, *The Communist Party of the United States: From the Depression to World War II* (New Brunswick, N.J.: Rutgers University Press, 1991), pp. 37–43, 127–128.

19. *Daily Worker*, February 19, 1931, quoted in Mark Naison, *Communists in Harlem during the Depression* (Urbana: University of Illinois Press, 1983), p. 47; Dorothy Ray Healy and Maurice Isserman, *California Red: A Life in the American Communist Party* (Urbana: University of Illinois Press, 1993), p. 125.

20. See Healy and Isserman, *California Red*, pp. 125–129; Don Amter, "Why Didn't I Question?" in *Red Diapers: Growing Up in the Communist Left*, ed. Judy Kaplan and Linn Shapiro (Urbana: University of Illinois Press, 1998), pp. 242–243. Nathan Glazer, *The Social Basis of American Communism* (New York: Harcourt, Brace and World, 1961), pp. 170–179.

21. Drake and Cayton, *Black Metropolis*, p. 138; Glazer, *The Social Basis of American Communism*, pp. 170–172; Naison, *Communists in Harlem during the Depression*, pp. 136–137.

22. Parents of two of the eight biracial children interviewed by Katya Gibel Azoulay met at Communist Party meetings, while at least three of the biracial interviewees in a 1993 study had parents who met or got to know each other through their involvement in Communist Party politics. See Azoulay, *Black, Jewish, and Interracial: It's Not the Color of Your Skin, but the Race of Your Kin, and Other Myths of Identity* (Durham, N.C.: Duke University Press, 1997); Lise Funderburg, *Black, White, Other: Biracial Americans Talk about Race and Identity* (New York: William Morrow, 1994), pp. 28–29, 244–246, 264–266.

23. Susan Moscou, "In My World," in *Red Diapers*, pp. 308–310; author interview with Yvonne and Chuck Cannon, August 24, 1999.

24. Gayle Morrison, *To Move the World: Louis G. Gregory and the Advancement of Racial Unity in America* (Wilmette, Ill.: Bahá'í Publishing Trust, 1982), pp. xvi, 45. See also Robert Stockman, *The Bahá'í Faith in America* (Wilmette, Ill.: Bahá'í Publishing Trust, 1985).

25. Quoted in "When Celebrities Intermarry," in *Marriage across the Color Line*, ed. Cloyte M. Larsson (Chicago: Johnson Publishing Co., 1965), p. 94; "Bahá'í Faith: Only Church in World That Does Not Discriminate," *Ebony*, October 1952, pp. 39–46.

26. Anonymous, "I Want to Marry a Negro," *Negro Digest*, August 1948, pp. 9–14; Sandy Cirillo, "The Lois Jones Story," *Interrace*, June/July 1994, p. 18; Oskar Heim, "Why I Want a Negro Wife," *Negro Digest*, July 1954, pp. 64–68.

27. James McBride, *The Color of Water: A Black Man's Tribute to His White Mother* (New York: Riverhead Books, 1996), p. 107; interview with Ruth in Albert Gordon, *Intermarriage: Interfaith, Interracial, Interethnic* (Boston: Beacon Press, 1964), p. 292.

28. Don Terry, "How Race Is Lived in America: Getting under My Skin," *New York Times Magazine,* July 16, 2000, pp. 32–37+, quote from p. 72; John Blake in Funderburg, *Black, White, Other,* p. 270; Melba Patillo Beals, *Warriors Don't Cry* (New York: Pocket Books, 1994), p. 311.

29. Minerbrook, *Divided to the Vein,* pp. 43–59; Wright in Funderburg, *Black, White, Other,* p. 90.

30. Gregory Williams, *Life on the Color Line* (New York: Plume Books, 1995), p. 187.

31. Author interview with Grace and Robert McAllester, March 1, 1994; interview of Arthur Lambkin in Gordon, *Intermarriage,* p. 239; author interview with Yvonne and Chuck Cannon.

32. James Patterson, *Grand Expectations: The United States, 1945–1974* (Oxford: Oxford University Press, 1996), p. 151; Charles Smith, "Negro-White Intermarriage—Metropolitan New York: A Qualitative Case Analysis" (Ph.D. diss., Teachers College, Columbia University, 1960), p. 54; E. Smith, "Interracial Marriage," p. 73; Werner Cahnman, "The Interracial Jewish Child," *Reconstructionist* 33 (1967): 7–12.

33. Azoulay, *Black, Jewish, and Interracial,* p. 60; Penny Rhodes interviewed in *Of Many Colors,* ed. Peggy Gillespie (Amherst: University of Massachusetts Press, 1997), p. 109.

34. See Matthew Jacobson, *Whiteness of a Different Color* (Cambridge: Harvard University Press, 1998), pp. 187–199; Karen Brodkin Sacks, "How Did Jews Become White Folks?" in *Race,* ed. Steven Gregory and Roger Sanjek (New Brunswick, N.J.: Rutgers University Press, 1994), pp. 79–85.

35. Jones, *How I Became Hettie Jones,* pp. 34, 14.

36. Harvey, *The Fifties: A Women's Oral History,* p. 69.

37. Ibid., p. 77; Jessica Weiss, *To Have and to Hold: Marriage, the Baby Boom, and Social Change* (Chicago: University of Chicago Press, 2000), p. 25.

38. Cirillo, "The Lois Jones Story," p. 18; McBride, *The Color of Water,* p. 43.

39. Jessie Bernard, "Note on Educational Homogamy in Negro-White and White-Negro Marriages, 1960," *Journal of Marriage and the Family* 28 (August 1966): 274–276; John Burma, Gary Crester, and Ted Seacrest, "A Comparison of the Occupational Status of Intramarrying and Intermarrying Couples: A Research Note," *Sociology and Social Research* 54 (July 1970): 508–519; Todd Pavela, "An Exploratory Study of Negro-White In-

termarriage in Indiana," *Journal of Marriage and the Family* 26 (May 1964): 209–211.

40. David Heer, "The Prevalence of Black-White Marriage in the United States, 1960 and 1970," *Journal of Marriage and the Family* 36 (May 1974): 246–258; Paul Glick, "Intermarriage among Ethnic Groups in the United States," *Social Biology* 17 (December 1970): 292–298.

41. Cash, "A Study of Negro-White Marriages in the Philadelphia Area," p. 95; John Burma, "Research Note on the Measurement of Interracial Marriage," *American Journal of Sociology* 57 (May 1952): 589. On national marital patterns, see John Modell, *Into One's Own* (Berkeley: University of California Press, 1989), p. 250; Elaine Tyler May, *Homeward Bound* (New York: Basic Books, 1988), p. 6.

42. Heer, "The Prevalence of Black-White Marriage in the United States, 1960 and 1970," p. 250. In Evelyn Elmar Smith's study of twelve couples in Washington, D.C., 54.7 percent had been married before. Of the seventeen couples Eugene Cash studied, 56 percent had been previously married. Ten of the twenty-four individuals Charles Smith studied were previously married. In addition, Joseph Golden found in his study of fifty Philadelphia couples that one-third of the black grooms and one-fourth of white brides were divorced. E. Smith, "Interracial Marriage"; Cash, "A Study of Negro-White Marriage in the Philadelphia Area"; C. Smith, "Negro-White Intermarriage"; Joseph Golden, "Patterns of Negro-White Marriage," *American Sociological Review* 19 (April 1954): 144–147.

43. E. Smith, "Interracial Marriage," p. 201; Mary Jane Knox, *Ebony,* June 1950, p. 10; Mrs. Glenn, *Ebony,* May 1949, p. 6.

44. Michelle Ross, "Is My Mixed Marriage Jinxed?" *Ebony,* August 1953, p. 53; Jones, *How I Became Hettie Jones,* pp. 36–37, 42; E. Smith, "Interracial Marriage," p. 157; Dorothy Tolonen, "Intermarriage Case History no. 1," *Detroit Tribune,* April 10, 1948, p. 9.

45. Minerbrook, *Divided to the Vein,* pp. 61–62. See also McBride, *The Color of Water,* p. 232; Cirillo, "The Lois Jones Story," p. 18.

46. Hazel Byrne Simpkins, "I Married a Tan Yank," *Tan Magazine,* March 1951, reprinted in *Marriage across the Color Line,* ed. Cloyte M. Larsson (Chicago: Johnson Publishing Co, 1968), p. 105; Mrs. Harry Becker, *Ebony,* May 1954, p. 6.

47. C. Smith, "Negro-White Intermarriage," p. 148.

48. Alex Haley and Malcolm X, *The Autobiography of Malcolm X* (New York: Ballantine Books, 1973), pp. 120–125; Calvin Hernton, *Sex and Racism in America* (1965; New York: Anchor Books, 1988), pp. 63–87; Ernest Por-

terfield, *Black and White Mixed Marriages* (Chicago: Nelson-Hall, 1978), pp. 72–75.

49. *The Negro Handbook* (New York: Macmillan, 1949), pp. 77–78; C. Smith, "Negro-White Intermarriage" p. 147; Shann Nix, "When Love Was a Crime," *San Francisco Chronicle,* September 17, 1992, p. D3.

50. Elaine Neil, "Love across the Color Line," *Tan Magazine,* November 1958, reprinted as "Persecution in New York," in *Marriage across the Color Line,* ed. Larsson, pp. 134–135; "1081 Lines Tapped by Police in 1954," *New York Times,* March 9, 1955, pp. 1, 15.

51. Golden, "Patterns of Negro-White Marriage," p. 147; E. Smith, "Interracial Marriage," pp. 181, 184.

52. Sister M. Annella, R.S.M., "Some Aspects of Interracial Marriage in Washington, D.C., 1940–1947," *Journal of Negro Education* 25 (Fall 1956): 390; "The Case against Mixed Marriages," *Ebony,* November 1950, p. 53; Ross, "Is Mixed Marriage Jinxed?" p. 42.

53. National Urban League Public Relations Department, "Seattle Urban League Reports Wider Acceptances of Interracial Marriages in the Community," press release, April 30, 1967, in Schomburg Center Clipping File.

54. "Where Mixed Couples Live," *Ebony,* May 1955, p. 64. Sister Annella Lynn found two cases in which black-white couples moved to white neighborhoods and whites began to move out. Sister Annella Lynn, "Interracial Marriages in Washington, D.C., 1940–1947" (Ph.D. diss., Catholic University, 1953), p. 70.

55. Interview with Henry and Violet in Gordon, "Negro-Jewish Marriages," p. 179; author interview with Chuck and Yvonne Cannon; author interview with Grace and Robert McAllester.

56. Interview with Doris in Gordon, "Negro-Jewish Marriages," p. 173.

57. Neil, "Love across the Color Line," pp. 122–127.

58. "Where Mixed Couples Live," p. 62; Tolonen, "Intermarriage Case History no. 1," p. 9; McBride, *The Color of Water;* Sallyann Hobson in Funderburg, *Black, White, Other,* p. 67.

59. C. Smith, "Negro-White Intermarriage," p. 58; Henry and Violet in Gordon, "Negro-Jewish Marriages," pp. 175, 180.

60. C. Smith, "Negro-White Intermarriage," p. 153; Bernette Ford in Funderburg, *Black, White, Other,* p. 343.

61. Ross, "Is Mixed Marriage Jinxed," p. 42; Lynn, "Interracial Marriages in Washington, D.C., 1940–1947," p. 70; Golden, "Patterns of Negro-White Intermarriage," p. 14; Pavela, "An Exploratory Study of Negro-White Intermarriage in Indiana," p. 210.

62. Cash, "A Study of Negro-White Marriages in the Philadelphia Area," pp. 96–97.

63. Jonnie Smith, *Ebony*, May 1950, p. 8; McBride, *The Color of Water*, p. 232.

64. "Where Mixed Couples Live," p. 61.

65. Examples include the intermarried black men described in Williams, *Life on the Color Line*, and Minerbrook, *Divided to the Vein*.

66. Interview with Henry and Violet in Gordon, *Intermarriage*, p. 277; author interview with Yvonne and Chuck Cannon; author interview with Grace and Robert McAllester; Moscou, "In My World," in *Red Diapers*, p. 309; Golden, "Patterns of Negro-White Intermarriage," p. 146.

67. Brunetta Wolfman, "Color Fades over Time," in *American Mixed Race*, ed. Naomi Zack (Lanham, Md.: Rowman and Littlefield, 1995), p. 21; Jeanne Campbell, "This Is My Daughter," *Negro Digest*, June 1965, p. 85; Bernette Ford in Funderburg, *Black, White, Other*, p. 247.

68. *Ward v. Ward*, 216 P.2d 755 (Washington, 1950), pp. 755, 756; *Fountaine v. Fountaine*, 133 N.E.2d 532 (Illinois, 1956), p. 534.

69. Ross, "Is Mixed Marriage Jinxed," p. 42; William Peters, "We Dared to Marry," *Redbook*, August 1954, p. 83.

70. David Evans, "My Son Is a Blonde Negro," *Negro Digest*, March 1949, pp. 43–45; Chennault, "How I Face the World With My Negro Child," p. 64.

71. Nix, "When Love Was a Crime," p. D3; Marjorie Shaw, *Ebony*, February 1961, pp. 14–15; interview with Yvonne and Chuck Cannon; St. Claire Drake, "How I Teach My Children about Race," *Negro Digest*, April 1951, reprinted in *Marriage across the Color Line*, ed. Larsson, p. 77.

72. Maria P. P. Root, *Love's Revolution: Interracial Marriage* (Philadelphia: Temple University Press, 2001), pp. 116–117.

73. *Los Angeles Sentinel*, May 4, 1950, p. A2; *New York Post*, May 11, 1959; *New York Post*, May 12, 1959, from Schomburg Center Clipping File, Intermarriage: Chronology, 1949–1960; Neisha Wright in Funderburg, *Black, White, Other*, p. 89; Rose Warder in Funderburg, *Black, White, Other*, p. 30.

74. Peters, "Are There Boundary Lines in Love," p. 130; C. Smith, "Negro-White Intermarriage," pp. 90–92.

75. See Paul C. Rosenblatt, Terri A. Karis, and Richard D. Powell, *Multiracial Couples: Black and White Voices* (Thousand Oaks, Calif.: Sage Publications, 1995), pp. 36–38.

76. "The Case against Mixed Marriage," p. 53; other woman quoted in *Top Secret*, June 1960, from Schomburg Center Clipping File: Intermarriage.

77. A.B.L., *Negro Digest,* December 1948, p. 16; "Negro Women with White Husbands," *Jet,* February 21, 1952, p. 26; William Peters, "We Weren't Supposed to Marry," *Redbook,* September 1960 (continues the story of the couple first interviewed for a 1954 *Redbook* article).

78. Mr. and Mrs. Robert Lee, *Ebony,* January 1951, pp. 8–9; Mrs. Harry Becker, *Ebony,* May 1954, p. 6.

79. "The Case against Mixed Marriages," p. 53; Ross, "Is Mixed Marriage Jinxed," p. 40; C. Smith, "Negro-White Intermarriage," pp. 145, 148; Peters, "We Dared to Marry," p. 84.

80. C. Smith, "Negro-White Intermarriage," p. 147; Neil, "Love across the Color Line," p. 139.

81. "Interracial Couples Setting Pattern for Real Democracy," *Baltimore-Afro-American,* May 15, 1948, sect. 1, p. 13; "Mixed Couples in Three Big Cities Form Clubs to Fight against Social Bans," *Ebony,* January 1951, pp. 52, 55; "Interracial Couples Form Organization for Mutual Benefit," *Pittsburgh Courier,* August 7, 1948, p. 3. See also *Baltimore Afro-American,* July 23, 1949, sect. 2, p. 6; Sister M. Annella, "Some Aspects of Interracial Marriage in Washington, D.C., 1940–1947," p. 386.

82. Interview with Paul in Gordon, "Negro-Jewish Marriages," p. 170; C. Smith, "Negro-White Intermarriage," p. 160; "A World Report on Intermarriage," *Negro Digest,* August 1961, p. 62.

5. Culture Wars and Schoolhouse Doors

1. Richard Kluger, *Simple Justice* (New York: Vintage Books, 1977), pp. 309–310.

2. *Horizons: The Future of Race Relations,* March 23, 1952, American Broadcasting Company, T77:0527, Museum of Radio and Broadcasting, New York.

3. Mary Dudziak, *Cold War, Civil Rights* (Princeton: Princeton University Press, 2000), pp. 79–114.

4. *Brown v. Board of Education of Topeka,* 347 U.S. 483 (1954).

5. Michael Klarman, "How *Brown* Changed Race Relations: The Backlash Thesis," *Journal of American History* 81 (June 1994): 81–118.

6. *Daily News* (Jackson, Miss.), May 18, 1954, reprinted in Waldo E. Martin, Jr., *Brown v. Board of Education: A Brief History with Documents* (Boston: Bedford/St. Martin's, 1998), p. 204.

7. Gunnar Myrdal, *An American Dilemma* (New York: Harper and Brothers, 1944), pp. 587, 606.

8. Speech quoted in Numan Bartley, *The Rise of Massive Resistance* (Baton Rouge: Louisiana State University Press, 1969), p. 121; Adam Fairclough, *Race and Democracy* (Athens: University of Georgia Press, 1995), p. 168; Edwin White, *New York Times,* December 1, 1955, p. 34.

9. Tom Brady, *Black Monday* (Winona, Miss.: Association of Citizens' Councils, 1955), p. 89; John Dittmer, *Local People: The Struggle for Civil Rights in Mississippi* (Urbana: University of Illinois Press, 1995), pp. 60, 61.

10. The Citizens' Councils had an estimated three hundred thousand members in 1956; the Ku Klux Klan had perhaps seventy-five thousand members. James Cook, *The Segregationists* (New York: Appleton-Century-Crofts, 1962), p. 16.

11. *Montgomery Advertiser,* May 12, 1957, quoted in *With All Deliberate Speed,* ed. Don Shoemaker (New York: Harper's Brothers, 1957), p. 23. Segregationist publications that equated integration with intermarriage included *The Citizen,* the journal of the Unified Citizens' Councils of America; the publications of the Ku Klux Klan; *The Virginian,* the official publication of the Virginia League, a group that formed in 1954 with the goal of preventing school desegregation in that state; and *The White Sentinel,* whose masthead read, "Racial Integrity—Not Amalgamation." *The White Sentinel* was the official organ of the National Citizen's Protective Association, a St. Louis group founded by a disciple of Gerald Smith, and it circulated widely in the South.

12. Givhan quoted in James W. Vander Zanden, "The Ideology of White Supremacy," *Journal of the History of Ideas* 20 (June–September 1959): 401; American Nationalist postcards, "What Americans Should Know about the N.A.A.C.P" in Box 5, Folder 19, Daisy Bates Papers, State Historical Society of Wisconsin, Madison.

13. *White Sentinel,* November–December 1959, p. 5. See also *White Sentinel,* March 1957, p. 1; *White Sentinel,* April 1959, p. 3; *White Sentinel,* January 1955, p. 1.

14. Perez quoted in Cook, *The Segregationists,* p. 195; *White Sentinel,* July 1954, p. 1; Shelton quoted in "The Final Question," *fact:,* January–February 1966, p. 12.

15. Herman Talmadge, *You and Segregation* (Birmingham, Ala.: Vulcan Press, 1955), pp. 44–45; Patterson quoted in Cook, *The Segregationists,* p. 65.

16. "Interracial College Marriages," *White Sentinel,* October 1958, pp. 1–2.

17. See "Georgia Aide Attacks Court," *New York Times,* November 3, 1955, p. 27; William Workman, Jr., *The Case for the South* (New York: Devin-Adair Co., 1960), p. 214; *White Sentinel,* September 1963, p. 7.

18. Charlayne Hunter-Gault, *In My Place* (New York: Farrar, Straus, Giroux, 1992), p. 242.

19. "We Fell in Love," *Newsweek,* September 16, 1963, p. 27; "Where Integration Led to Intermarriage," *U.S. News and World Report,* September 16, 1963, p. 10.

20. Medford Evans, "The Five-Point Action Program," *The Citizen,* January 1964, p. 11.

21. Herbert Ravenal Sass, "Mixed Schools and Mixed Blood," *Atlantic Monthly,* November 1956, p. 45; Vander Zanden, "The Ideology of White Supremacy," p. 400; Workman, *The Case for the South,* p. 103.

22. Daisy Bates, *The Long Shadow of Little Rock* (New York: David McKay Company, 1962), p. 89; Melba Patillo Beals, *Warriors Don't Cry* (New York: Pocket Books, 1994), pp. 111, 179–180.

23. "Voices from Central High School," from *New York Times,* October 14, 1957, reprinted in *Eyewitness: The Negro in American History,* ed. William Loren Katz (New York: Pittman Publishing, 1967), pp. 496–499.

24. "What Negroes Want Now: Interview with Walter White," *U.S. News and World Report,* May 28, 1954, p. 54.

25. Hannah Arendt, "Reflections on Little Rock," *Dissent* 6 (Winter 1959): 49; David Spitz, "Politics and the Realm of Being," *Dissent* 6 (Winter 1959): 64. Arendt had been asked to write the piece for the journal *Commentary,* but when they delayed publishing she sent it to *Dissent* instead. For more on the controversy over Arendt's article, see Werner Sollers, "Of Mules and Mares in a Land of Difference; or Quadrupeds All?" *American Quarterly* 42 (June 1990): 167–190.

26. Quoted in David Halberstam, *The Fifties* (New York: Fawcett Columbine, 1993), p. 420.

27. See *Jackson v. Alabama,* 72 So. 2d 14 (1954), and *Naim v. Naim,* 87 S.E. 2d 749 (1955); *Naim v. Naim,* 350 U.S. 891 (1955); *Naim v. Naim,* 90 S.E. 2d 849 (1956).

28. Interview with Philip Elman by Norman Silber, "The Solicitor General's Office, Justice Frankfurter, and Civil Rights Litigation, 1946–1960: An Oral History," *Harvard Law Review* 100 (February 1987): 845–847; Robert Sickels, *Race, Marriage, and the Law* (Albuquerque: University of New Mexico Press, 1972), p. 4.

29. Workman, *The Case for the South,* p. 231. In rural southern communities, schools often played an important role in the social life not just of the students but of the whole town. See Glen Robinson, "Man in No Man's Land" in *With All Deliberate Speed,* ed. Shoemaker, p. 200.

30. Reprinted in Vergil Blossom, *It Has Happened Here* (New York: Harper and Brothers, 1959), pp. 41–43.

31. Blossom, *It Has Happened Here,* p. 200.

32. Luther Williams, *Greensboro Daily News,* August 20, 1954, from Schomburg Center Clipping File, Intermarriage, vol. 1, Schomburg Center for Research in Black Culture, New York Public Library, New York; *White Sentinel,* October 1954, p. 1; *Stell v. Savannah-Chatham County Board of Education,* Civil Action no. 1316, Record on Appeal from the U.S. District Court for the Southern District of Georgia–Savannah Division, reprinted in *The Development of Segregationist Thought,* ed. I. A. Newby (Homewood, Ill.: Dorsey Press, 1968), p. 150.

33. Dorothy Schiff, "Dear Reader," *New York Post,* January 8, 1956, from Schomburg Center Clipping File, Intermarriage: Chronology, 1949–1969; Pauli Murray to the Editor of the *New York Times,* December 7, 1955, in National Association for the Advancement of Colored People Papers, Group II, Legal Files (1940–1955), Box: B82, Folder: Interracial, 1944–1955, Manuscript Division, Library of Congress, Washington, D.C.; J. A. Rogers, "History Shows . . ." *Pittsburgh Courier,* March 7, 1959, p. 13.

34. Brady, *Black Monday,* p. 64; Perez quoted in Cook, *The Segregationists,* pp. 204–205.

35. "The Negro Children in Jail for a Kiss," *London News Chronicle,* December 18, 1958; "Statement by Robert F. Williams to the Press," December 31, 1958, both in Box 2, Folder 7, Papers of the Committee to Combat Racial Injustice, State Historical Society of Wisconsin, Madison. For more on this incident, see Timothy Tyson, *Radio Free Dixie* (Chapel Hill: University of North Carolina Press, 1999), pp. 90–136.

36. Luther Williams, *Greensboro Daily News,* August 20, 1954, from Schomburg Center Clipping File, Intermarriage, vol. 1; Sass, "Mixed Schools and Mixed Blood," pp. 48, 49.

37. R. B. Patterson, "Now Is the *Time,*" *White Sentinel,* September 1954, p. 5; Workman, *The Case for the South,* p. 228; textbook quoted in Andrew Weinberger, "A Reappraisal of the Constitutionality of Miscegenation Statutes," *Journal of Negro Education* 26 (Fall 1957): 445.

38. "PW Interviews Garth Williams," *Publisher's Weekly,* February 23, 1990, p. 202; "Fuss over Integrated Black Bunny," *Life,* June 1, 1959, p. 90; "Racial Fur Flies," *Newsweek,* June 1, 1959, p. 28; "Of Rabbits and Race," *Time,* June 1, 1959, p. 19; "The Rabbit Wedding," *New York Times,* May 24, 1959, sect. 4, p. 2; "Children's Book Stirs Alabama: White Rabbit Weds Black Rabbit," *New York Times,* May 22, 1959, p. 29. Werner Sollers has an ex-

tended discussion of *The Rabbit's Wedding* in *Neither Black nor White yet Both* (New York: Oxford University Press, 1997), pp. 18–23.

39. S. L. Gentry, *Time,* June 22, 1959, p. 2.

40. Jordana Shakoor, *Civil Rights Childhood* (Jackson: University Press of Mississippi, 1999), p. 91; Blossom, *It Has Happened Here,* pp. 15–16.

41. *White Sentinel,* October–November 1960, p. 1; *White Sentinel,* February 1955, p. 1.

42. American Nationalist postcards from Box 5, Folder 13, Daisy Bates Papers.

43. "The Second Battle of Atlanta," *Look Magazine,* April 25, 1961, p. 33; Oliver Allstorm, "The Saddest Story Ever Told," *Apostolic Evangel,* January 1961, pp. 12–13, reprinted in *White Sects and Black Men in the Recent South,* ed. David Harrell, Jr. (Nashville: Vanderbilt University Press, 1971), pp. 64–65.

44. *White Sentinel,* February 1955, p. 1; *The Virginian,* July 1956, p. 3.

45. Halberstam, *The Fifties,* p. 472. See also George Lipsitz, "Land of a Thousand Dances: Youth, Minorities, and the Rise of Rock and Roll," in *Recasting America: Culture and Politics in the Age of the Cold War,* ed. Lary May (Chicago: University of Chicago Press, 1989), pp. 267–284.

46. Reprinted in Martin, *Brown v. Board of Education,* p. 222.

47. Lacy Jeffreys, "Hollywood," *The Virginian,* September 1955, p. 3.

48. James Gilbert, *A Cycle of Outrage: America's Reaction to the Juvenile Delinquent in the 1950s* (New York: Oxford University Press, 1986), pp. 174–176; Garth Jowett, *Film: The Democratic Art* (Boston: Little, Brown and Co., 1976), pp. 404–417; Robert Sklar, *Movie-Made America* (New York: Random House, 1975).

49. *Gelling v. Texas,* 72 S.Ct. 1002 (1952).

50. For more on *Island in the Sun,* see Gail Lumet Buckley, "When a Kiss Is Not Just a Kiss," *New York Times,* March 31, 1991, sect. 1, pp. 1, 20; "Island in the Sun," *Ebony,* July 1957, pp. 33–37; Thomas Cripps, *Making Movies Black* (New York: Oxford University Press, 1993), pp. 253–265; Daniel Leab, *From Sambo to SUPERSPADE: The Black Experience in Motion Pictures* (Boston: Houghton Mifflin, 1975), pp. 209–211.

51. *White Sentinel,* December 1956, p. 9; *White Sentinel,* May 1954, p. 4; *White Sentinel,* April 1958, p. 2.

52. Quoted in Bartley, *The Rise of Massive Resistance,* p. 171; Sass, "Mixed Schools and Mixed Blood," p. 48; Arnold Hirsch, *Making the Second Ghetto: Race and Housing in Chicago, 1940–1960* (Cambridge: Cambridge University Press, 1983), p. 196.

53. Eisenhower quoted in Halberstam, *The Fifties,* p. 421.

54. "What the South Really Fears about Mixed Schools," *U.S. News and World Report,* September 19, 1958, pp. 76–90; "'I Spent Four Years in an Integrated High School': A White Girl's Story of Education and Social Life in a Milwaukee School," *U.S. News and World Report,* November 7, 1958, p. 45.

55. Milton Mayer, "The Issue Is Miscegenation," *The Progressive,* September 1959, p. 8.

56. "Proceedings of the 1958 Valparaiso University Institute on Human Relations," Valparaiso, Indiana, July 25–27, 1958, published by the Lutheran Human Relations Association of America, Miscellaneous Schomburg Collection Titles, Sc Micro R-3643, Schomburg Center; "Symposium on Mixed Marriage: 'Would You Want Your Daughter . . .?'" *U.S. News and World Report,* May 9, 1960, p. 116; "Marriage Phobia Hit by Cleric," *Pittsburgh Courier,* February 20, 1960, p. 11; *Editorial Research Reports,* May 24, 1961, pp. 384–385.

57. *New York Times,* May 18, 1954, reprinted in Martin, *Brown v. Board of Education,* pp. 200–201.

58. Lillian Smith, *Now Is the Time* (New York: Viking Press, 1955), pp. 77, 104–105.

59. Lillian Smith to Charles Johnson, June 10, 1955, reprinted in *How Am I to Be Heard: Letters of Lillian Smith,* ed. Rose Gladney (Chapel Hill: University of North Carolina Press, 1993), p. 170.

60. *New York Times,* March 27, 1956, p. 34.

61. Oscar Handlin, "Where Equality Leads," *Atlantic Monthly,* November 1956, pp. 51–54; Lillian Smith, letter to *New York Times,* October 4, 1957 [not published], reprinted in *How Am I to Be Heard,* ed. Gladney, p. 216; George Schuyler, "Views and Reviews," *Pittsburgh Courier,* December 6, 1958, p. 12.

62. "What the South Really Fears about Mixed Schools," pp. 78, 79.

63. "Dynamite in Dixie: An Illuminating Report on America's Most Explosive Problem," published in the *New York Journal American,* March 1956, from Miscellaneous Schomburg Collection Titles, microfilm R-3643, Schomburg Center.

64. Workman, *The Case for the South,* p. 212.

65. Allan Nevins, "Historian Predicts: Intermarriage of the Races Will Be Inevitable," *U.S. News and World Report,* November 14, 1958, p. 72; L. Geoffrey Feather, "Rankin Was Right," *Esquire,* September 1954, pp. 91+;

Walter W. Stevens, "The Great Myth of the South," *Journal of Human Relations* 10 (Summer 1962): 423; S. April, "Miscegenation Is a Phony Issue," *Negro Digest,* October 1962, pp. 22, 36.

66. "Proceedings of the 1958 Valparaiso University Institute on Human Relations"; Smith, *Now Is the Time,* p. 120.

67. Eleanor Roosevelt, *My Day,* May 5, 1956, reprinted in *Eleanor Roosevelt's My Day: Volume II, 1953–1962,* ed. David Emblidge (New York: Pharos Books, 1991), p. 98.

6. The Rights Revolutions and Interracial Marriage

1. "Tuskegee Mayor Breaks Barriers to Lead Ala. City," *Jet,* December 14, 1972, pp. 20–25; "The Tuskegee Mayor and His Wife: A Very Visible Interracial Couple," *New York Times,* November 9, 1972, p. 54; "Black, White, and Married," TV Lab Special, October 29, 1979, Schomburg Center for Research in Black Studies, New York Public Library, New York City; "Interracial Couples in the South," *Ebony,* June 1978, pp. 65–72; Robert Norrell, *Reaping the Whirlwind: The Civil Rights Movement in Tuskegee* (1985; Chapel Hill: University of North Carolina Press, 1998), pp. 201–216.

2. "Tuskegee Mayor Breaks Barriers to Lead Ala. City," pp. 21–22.

3. St. Clair Drake interview by Robert Martin, July 28, 1969, Civil Rights Documentation Project, Moorland-Spingarn Research Center, Howard University, Washington, D.C.

4. Interview with anonymous white female, CORE Chapter 18, Box 1, Folder 6, KZSU–Project South Papers, Special Collections—University Archives SC066, Stanford University, Stanford, Calif. See also Cynthia Griggs Fleming, *Soon We Will Not Cry: The Liberation of Ruby Doris Smith Robinson* (Lanham, Md.: Rowman & Littlefield Publishers, 1998), pp. 131–134.

5. James W. Hilty, *Robert Kennedy: Brother Protector* (Philadelphia: Temple University Press, 1997), p. 317.

6. Quoted in Doug McAdam, *Freedom Summer* (New York: Oxford University Press, 1988), p. 207; John Lewis with Michael D'Orso, *Walking with the Wind: A Memoir of the Movement* (New York: Simon and Schuster, 1998), p. 265; interview with Chuck McDew by the author, April 17, 1999, New York City.

7. McAdam, *Freedom Summer,* p. 4; Mary Aikin Rothschild, *A Case in Black and White: Northern Volunteers and the Southern Freedom Summers, 1964–1965* (Westport, Conn.: Greenwood Press, 1982), pp. 31–32; John Dittmer,

Local People: The Struggle for Civil Rights in Mississippi (Urbana: University of Illinois Press, 1995), p. 244.

8. Interview with Chuck McDew; Zellner quoted in Belinda Robnett, *How Long? How Long?: African-American Women in the Struggle for Civil Rights* (Oxford: Oxford University Press, 1997), p. 132.

9. Sally Belfrage, *Freedom Summer* (Charlottesville: University Press of Virginia, 1990), p. 13.

10. Donaldson quoted in Fleming, *Soon We Will Not Cry,* p. 134; McDew story in Fleming, *Soon We Will Not Cry,* pp. 132–133; Danny Lyon, *Memories of the Southern Civil Rights Movement* (Chapel Hill: University of North Carolina Press, 1992), p. 33.

11. McAdam, *Freedom Summer,* p. 59; "screw around" quote from Rothschild, *A Case in Black and White,* p. 139.

12. Fleming, *Soon We Will Not Cry,* p. 133.

13. Donaldson quoted in ibid., p. 134; Belfrage, *Freedom Summer,* p. 42.

14. Interview I-9 with male CORE volunteer, Box 1, Folder 9, Project South Papers, pp. 19–21.

15. Chana Kai Lee, *The Life of Fannie Lou Hamer* (Champaign: University of Illinois Press, 1999), p. 76.

16. Candi Law to James Farmer, January 12, 1962; James Farmer to Isaac Reynolds, January 15, 1962; Candi Law to James Farmer, January 20, 1962; Gordon Carey to Walter and Candi Riley, October 10, 1963, all in *Papers of the Congress of Racial Equality, 1941–1967* (Sanford, N.C.: Microfiling Corporation of America, 1979), microfilm, reel 3.

17. Fleming, *Soon We Will Not Cry,* p. 135; Mary King, *Freedom Song* (New York: William Morrow and Co., 1987), p. 464.

18. Alvin F. Poussaint, "The Stresses of the White Female Worker in the Civil Rights Movement in the South," *American Journal of Psychiatry* 123 (October 1966): 404; Hugo Biegel, "Problems and Motives in Interracial Relationships," *Journal of Sex Research* 2 (November 1966): 202.

19. James Wechsler, "Love Story," *New York Post,* September 27, 1962, in Schomburg Center Clipping File: Intermarriage, Chronology, 1960–1968; Clayborne Carson, *In Struggle: SNCC and the Black Awakening of the 1960s* (Cambridge: Harvard University Press, 1981), pp. 72–73; author interview with Chuck McDew; interview with Constancia (Dinky) Romilly by the author, February 3, 2000, New York City; Robnett, *How Long? How Long?* pp. 132–133; "Interracial Wedding Sets Deep South Precedent," *New York Post,* August 14, 1967, in Schomburg Center Clipping File: Intermarriage, Chronology, 1960–1968.

20. "SNCC Wedding Stirs Arkansas Officials," *Student Voice,* November 18, 1963, p. 1; Lewis, *Walking with the Wind,* p. 418; author interview with Chuck McDew.

21. Casey Hayden, "Fields of Blue," in *Deep in Our Hearts: Nine White Women in the Freedom Movement* (Athens: University of Georgia Press, 2000), pp. 351, 345.

22. "Should Churches Back Mixed Marriages?" *U.S. News and World Report,* December 2, 1963, p. 2; Frank Van Vranken to James Farmer, March 28, 1965; Van Vranken to Maria Valdery, March 28, 1965, both in *Papers of the Congress of Racial Equality, Addendum, 1944–1968* (Sanford, N.C.: Microfilming Corporation of America, 1982), reel 2.

23. Byron Curti Martyn, "Racism in the United States: A History of the Anti-Miscegenation Legislation and Litigation" (Ph.D. diss., University of Southern California, 1979); Robert Sickels, *Race, Marriage, and the Law* (Albuquerque: University of New Mexico Press, 1972), pp. 63–64; Allan C. Brownfield, "Will the Supreme Court Uphold Mixed Marriages?" *Negro Digest,* March 1965, pp. 72–73; Roger Hardaway, "Unlawful Love: A History of Arizona's Miscegenation Law," *Journal of Arizona History* 27 (1986): 377–390; *Race Relations Law Reporter* 5 (1960): 136–137.

24. *New York Times,* March 4, 1967, p. 15; *New York Times,* April 2, 1967, p. 57.

25. "One Church's Vote on Mixed Marriages," *U.S. News and World Report,* June 7, 1965, p. 16; *Christian Century,* May 27, 1964, p. 693; *America: National Catholic Weekly Review,* November 16, 1963, p. 619; *Christian Century,* February 10, 1965, p. 164.

26. Ruth Burke, "Handle with Care: How to Protect a Mixed Marriage," *Negro Digest,* May 1964, pp. 26–27.

27. *Louisiana v. Brown,* 108 So.2d 233 (1959), p. 234; Brief for Appellants, *Loving v. Virginia,* Supreme Court no. 395, February 17, 1967.

28. *McLaughlin v. Florida,* 153 So.2d 1 (1963). For a description of the case, see "Race, Sex, and the Supreme Court," *New York Times Magazine,* November 22, 1964, pp. 30, 130–134.

29. *McLaughlin v. Florida,* 153 So.2d 1 (1963), pp. 2–3; *McLaughlin v. Florida,* 85 S.Ct. 283 (1964), pp. 286, 291.

30. "A Mixed Marriage's 25th Anniversary of Legality," *New York Times,* June 12, 1992, p. B9; "When Marriage Was Illegal," *Washington Post,* June 14, 1992, p. C5; "The Couple That Rocked the Courts," *Ebony,* September 1967, pp. 78–86.

31. *Loving v. Virginia,* 388 U.S. S.Ct 1 (1967), p. 12.

32. Harvey Appelbaum, "Miscegenation Statutes: A Constitutional and Social

Problem," *Georgetown Law Journal* 53 (Fall 1964): 91; "Race, Sex, and the Supreme Court," p. 133.

33. *Davis v. Gately,* 269 F.Supp 996 (1967); *U.S. v. Brittain,* 319 F.Supp. 1958 (Alabama, 1970); "Biracial Marriage in Miss.," *New York Post,* August 3, 1970, in Schomburg Center Clipping File: Intermarriage, Chronology, 1968–1972; "Mississippi Allows a Mixed Marriage," *New York Times,* August 3, 1970, pp. 1, 12; Sickels, *Race, Marriage, and the Law,* pp. 112–115.

34. *New York Times,* June 20, 1967, p. 38.

35. Hazel Erskine, "The Polls: Interracial Socializing," *Public Opinion Quarterly* 37 (Summer 1973): 292.

36. Texas poll cited in ibid., p. 284. See also William Brink and Louis Harris, *Black and White: A Study of U.S. Racial Attitudes Today* (New York: Simon and Schuster, 1966); Seymour Martin Lipset and William Schneider, "Racial Equality in America," *New Society,* April 20, 1978, pp. 128–131; George Warheit, Edith Swanson, and John J. Schwam, "A Study of Racial Attitudes in a Southern County: A Confirmation of National Trends," *Phylon* 36 (December 1975): 395–406.

37. Belfrage, *Freedom Summer,* pp. 64, 117, 154–155; Rothschild, *A Case in Black and White,* p. 135; Lyon, *Memories of the Southern Civil Rights Movement,* p. 124. See also James Forman, *The Making of Black Revolutionaries* (1972; Seattle: University of Washington Press, 1997), pp. 188–190.

38. Paul Hemphill, *Leaving Birmingham: Notes of a Native Son* (Tuscaloosa: University of Alabama Press, 1993), p. 288.

39. James G. Clark, *The Jim Clark Story* (Selma: Selma Enterprises, 1966), pp. 29–58. Quote from p. 32. When a group of civil rights workers went to the Greenwood police to swear out an arrest warrant against whites who had beaten them, police threatened one of the white activists with a knife, asking, "Think it's sharp enough to cut your cock off?" Belfrage, *Freedom Summer,* p. 26.

40. Lyon, *Memories of the Southern Civil Rights Movement,* p. 171; Charles W. Eagles, *Outside Agitator: Jon Daniels and the Civil Rights Movement in Alabama* (Chapel Hill: University of North Carolina Press, 1993), pp. 220–228.

41. Clark, *The Jim Clark Story,* p. 30.

42. "Would You Want Your Daughter to Marry One," *Ebony,* August 1965, p. 82.

43. *New York Times,* September 12, 1963, p. 30; "How Whites Feel about Negroes: A Painful American Dilemma," *Newsweek,* October 21, 1963, pp. 48–49; Brink and Harris, *Black and White: A Study of U.S. Racial Attitudes Today,* p. 132.

44. "Would You Want Your Daughter to Marry One," p. 82; Bob Weems, "Interracial Marriage, etc.," *The Citizen,* February 1972, p. 4.

45. "The Final Question," *fact:* 3, no. 1 (January–February 1966): 4; Weems, "Interracial Marriage, etc.," p. 12; *Negro Digest,* April 1965, p. 89.

46. Henry Clark, "Questions for the Questioner," *Community,* July 1964, p. 11.

47. Joseph Washington, *Marriage in Black and White* (Boston: Beacon Press, 1970), pp. 1–2.

48. "Symposium on Mixed Marriage, 'Would You Want Your Daughter . . .?'" *U.S. News and World Report,* May 9, 1960, p. 116; Rev. C. Eugene Askew, "Yes, I Would Want My Daughter to Marry a Negro," *Negro Digest,* July 1965, p. 7.

49. Norman Podhoretz, "My Negro Problem—and Ours," *Commentary,* February 1963, reprinted in *Bridges and Boundaries: African Americans and American Jews,* ed. Jack Salzman (New York: George Braziller, 1992), pp. 113, 116–117.

50. Some critics argue that John's exceptional success, high status, and class position trumped his race, that this portrayal essentially allowed him to transcend his racial identity and turned him into a "white" man. But the point of the film is that, despite his many qualities, his black skin still makes him a controversial choice for a young white woman. See Ann DuCille, "The Unbearable Darkness of Being: 'Fresh' Thoughts on Race, Sex, and the Simpsons," in *Birth of a Nation'hood: Gaze, Script, and Spectacle in the O.J. Simpson Case,* ed. Toni Morrison and Claudia Brodsky Lacour (New York: Pantheon, 1997), pp. 321–322.

51. *Guess Who's Coming to Dinner* (Columbia Pictures, 1967). For more on the racial messages of the film, see Thomas Wartenberg, "But Would You Want Your Daughter to Marry One? The Representations of Race and Racism in *Guess Who's Coming to Dinner,*" *Journal of Social Philosophy* 28 (June 1994): 99–130; Ronald Brunson Scott, "Interracial Relationships in Film: A Critical Analysis of 'Guess Who's Coming to Dinner' and 'Watermelon Man'" (Ph.D. diss., University of Utah, 1984).

52. Charles Wendal Childs, "Black and White Couples: Have Attitudes Changed?" *Redbook,* September 1969, p. 134.

53. "A Marriage of Enlightenment," *Time,* September 29, 1967, p. 28. For other media coverage, see "Weddings: Mr. and Mrs. Smith," *Newsweek,* October 2, 1967, pp. 23–24; Simeon Booker, "A Challenge for the Guy Smiths: Peggy Rusk, Negro Husband Face Their Future with Smile," *Ebony,* December 1967, pp. 146–150.

54. *New York Times,* September 22, 1967, pp. 1, 35; Dean Rusk as told to Richard Rusk, *As I Saw It,* ed. Daniel S. Papp (New York: W. W. Norton, 1990), p. 581.

55. "A Marriage of Enlightenment," p. 30, 28; Ruth Durhan, *Time,* October 6, 1967, p. 13; Carol Lee Gray, *Time,* October 13, 1967, p. 17.

56. "Truman Opposes Biracial Marriage," *New York Times,* September 12, 1963, p. 30; Lady Bird Johnson quoted in "Weddings: Mr. and Mrs. Smith," p. 23.

57. "A Marriage of Enlightenment," p. 29; William Peters, "Are There Boundary Lines in Love?" *McCall's,* June 1968, pp. 65–66, 118–122.

58. Rusk, *As I Saw It,* p. 605; Joe Holley, "Unconventional," *Texas Monthly,* August 1998, p. 22.

59. *Gallup Opinion Index,* November 1968, p. 12; *Gallup Opinion Index,* November 1972, p. 12; *Harris Survey Yearbook of Public Opinion 1971* (New York: Louis Harris and Associates, 1975), pp. 351–352. The 1972 Gallup Poll numbers are slightly inflated because the poll for the first time included blacks, who approved of intermarriage far more than whites.

60. Stanley Kramer, "Guess Who Didn't Dig Dinner?" *New York Times,* May 26, 1968, p. D21.

61. Terry H. Anderson, *The Movement and the Sixties: Protest in America from Greensboro to Wounded Knee* (Oxford: Oxford University Press, 1995), p. 248; Charles Wendal Childs, "Black and White Couples: Have Attitudes Changed?" *Redbook,* September 1969, p. 136; Franklin Yurco, *Ebony,* December 1969, pp. 16–17.

62. Anderson, *The Movement and the Sixties,* p. 89.

63. David Allyn, *Make Love, Not War: The Sexual Revolution, an Unfettered History* (Boston: Little, Brown, 2000), pp. 46, 51; Hans Sebald, "Patterns of Interracial Dating and Sexual Liaison of White and Black College Men," *International Journal of Sociology of the Family* 4 (Spring 1974): 24.

64. "Black and White Dating," *Time,* July 19, 1968, p. 48; Joan Downs, "Black/White Dating," *Life,* May 28, 1971, p. 58.

65. James Patterson, *Grand Expectations: The United States, 1945–1974* (Oxford: Oxford University Press, 1996), pp. 452–453, 565–568.

66. Quoted in Frank Petroni, "Interracial Dating—The Price is High," in *Interracial Marriage: Expectations and Realities,* ed. Irvin Stuart and Lawrence Abt (New York: Grossman Publishers, 1973), p. 127.

67. Smith quoted in Childs, "Black and White Couples," p. 136; Ari Kiev, "The Psychiatric Implications of Interracial Marriage," in *Interracial Mar-*

riage: Expectations and Realities, ed. Stuart and Abt, pp. 163–176; Paul Adams, "Counseling with Interracial Couples and Their Children in the South," in ibid., p. 69.

68. "A Group of College Students Review Their Conceptions," in *Interracial Marriage: Expectations and Realities,* ed. Stuart and Abt, pp. 180, 184; Alice Reid, "A Special Kind of Courage," *Negro Digest,* November 1961, pp. 24–26.

69. Steven Mintz and Susan Kellogg, *Domestic Revolutions: A Social History of American Family Life* (New York: Free Press, 1988), p. 205; John Modell, *Into One's Own* (Berkeley: University of California Press, 1989), pp. 286–287, 322–334.

70. Gordon, *Intermarriage,* p. 58.

71. Interview transcript of subject no.16 in Margaret Taylor Smith, "Mothers: Their Stress and Coping Strategies in Response to 'Non-Traditional Behavior' of Their Children, 1983," dataset, Henry A. Murray Research Center, Radcliffe College, Cambridge, Mass.

72. Interview transcript no. 17 from "Mothers: Their Stress and Coping Strategies."

73. Interview transcript no. 37 from "Mothers: Their Stress and Coping Strategies."

74. For more on the growth of the black middle class, see Bart Landry, *The New Black Middle Class* (Berkeley: University of California Press, 1987), pp. 67–93, 116–132; William Julius Wilson, *The Declining Significance of Race,* 2nd ed. (Chicago: University of Chicago Press, 1980), pp. 129–130; Orlando Patterson, *The Ordeal of Integration* (Washington, D.C.: Civitas Counterpoint, 1997), pp. 20–27.

75. Andrew Billingsley, *Climbing Jacob's Ladder: The Enduring Legacy of African-American Families* (New York: Simon and Schuster, 1992), pp. 178–179; Beth Day, *Sexual Life between Blacks and Whites* (New York: World Publishing, 1972), p. 263.

76. Interview with St. Clair Drake, July 28, 1969.

7. Talking Black and Sleeping White

1. LeRoi Jones, *The Slave* (New York: William Morrow and Co., 1964), p. 72.

2. *The Slave,* Jones admitted, was written to some extent out of his own experience. See C. W. E. Bigsby interview with LeRoi Jones, "The Theatre and the Coming Revolution" (1978), reprinted in *Conversations with Amiri*

Baraka, ed. Charlie Reilly (Jackson: University Press of Mississippi, 1994), p. 133.

3. Amiri Baraka, *The Autobiography of LeRoi Jones* (New York: Freundlich Books, 1984), p. 193. For more on his political transformation, see ibid., pp. 166–168; "A Conversation between Imamu Amiri Baraka and Theodore R. Hudson" in *Conversations with Amiri Baraka,* ed. Reilly, pp. 74–75; Baraka interview with C. W. E. Bigsby in *Conversations with Amiri Baraka,* ed. Reilly, p. 134.

4. "Table 1: Race of Wife by Race of Husband: 1960, 1970, 1980, 1991, and 1992," U.S. Bureau of the Census, http://www.census.gov/population/socdemo/race/interractab1.txt.

5. Katrina Williams, *Ebony,* July 1974, pp. 16–17.

6. William Van DeBurg, *New Day in Babylon* (Chicago: University of Chicago Press, 1992), pp. 43–45; Clayborne Carson, *In Struggle: SNCC and the Black Awakening of the 1960s* (Cambridge: Harvard University Press, 1981), pp. 209–211, 215–228.

7. Stokely Carmichael and Charles Hamilton, *Black Power* (New York: Vintage Books, 1967), p. 54. See also Ruth Turner Perot, "Black Power: A Voice Within," *Oberlin Alumni Magazine,* May 1967, reprinted in *Black Nationalism in America,* ed. John Bracey, Jr., August Meier, and Elliot Rudwick (New York: Bobbs-Merrill Co., 1970), p. 467.

8. Van DeBurg, *A New Day in Babylon,* p. 27.

9. For more on cultural politics, see Robin D. G. Kelley, *Race Rebels: Culture, Politics, and the Black Working Class* (New York: Free Press, 1994); Lisa Jones, "Open Letter to a Brother" in Jones, *Bulletproof Diva* (New York: Doubleday, 1994), pp. 215–216.

10. Charles Hamilton, "How Black Is Black," *Ebony,* August 1969, p. 47.

11. Malcolm X in *Muhammad Speaks,* September 1960, reprinted in *Black Nationalism in America,* ed. Bracey, Meier, and Rudwick, p. 418; Malcolm X interviewed on *Jerry Williams Show,* Boston, WMEX, April 2, 1960, quoted in C. Eric Lincoln, *Black Muslims in America* (1961; Grand Rapids: Wm. B. Eerdmans Publishing, 1994), pp. 84–85.

12. Eldridge Cleaver, *Soul on Ice* (New York: Delta Books, 1968), p. 16.

13. "Home Life of Mai Britt and 'Golden Boy,'" *Ebony,* December 1964, pp. 136–146; J.A.B., *Ebony,* February 1965, p. 20; Charles Johnson, *Ebony,* April 1965, p. 16; Arsola Thompson, *Ebony,* April 1965, p. 16.

14. Victor Denson, *Ebony,* December 1966, p. 13; Vaughn E. Taplin, *Ebony,* July 1967, pp. 12–14.

15. Interview with subject no. 5 from Gwyned Simpson, "Black Women Attorneys, 1982," dataset in Henry A. Murray Research Center, Radcliffe College, Cambridge, Mass.; Richard Zweigenhaft and G. William Domhoff, *Blacks in the White Establishment* (New Haven: Yale University Press, 1991), p. 79; Courtland Milloy, "Black Men and White Women," *Washington Post,* February 23, 1986, p. F4.

16. Stayce Alston, *Ebony,* February 1972, pp. 24–25; Regina Jones, *Ebony,* April 1972, p. 23.

17. "An Individual Student Discusses Her Experience," in *Interracial Marriage: Expectations and Realities,* ed. Irvin Stuart and Lawrence Abt (New York: Grossman Publishers, 1973), pp. 196, 198.

18. Ibid., p. 201; interview with subject no. 10 from Cynthia Epstein, "Black Professional Women, 1969," dataset at Henry A. Murray Research Center, Radcliffe College, Cambridge, Mass.

19. Stephen Schneck, "LeRoi Jones or, Poetics and Policeman or, Trying Heart, Bleeding Heart," *Ramparts,* July 13, 1968, quoted in Theodore Hudson, *From LeRoi Jones to Amiri Baraka: The Literary Works* (Durham, N.C.: Duke University Press, 1973), p. 72; Hettie Cohen, *How I Became Hettie Jones* (New York: Penguin Books, 1990), pp. 217, 223; Baraka, *Autobiography of LeRoi Jones,* pp. 198–201.

20. "Interracial Couples' View of Life as Mixed Marriages Increase," *New York Times,* February 23, 1979, p. A24; Charles Wendal Childs, "Black and White Couples: Have Attitudes Changed?" *Redbook,* September 1969, p. 136. Interview by the author with Grace and Robert McAllester, March 1, 1994.

21. Zweigenhaft and Domhoff, *Blacks in the White Establishment,* p. 90; Leland Bernard Cohen, "Interracial Families Adapt to their Marginality: Between Black and White" (Ph.D. diss., Washington University, 1979), p. 86; Grace Halsell, *Black/White Sex* (New York: William Morrow and Co., 1972), pp. 87–88; St. Clair Drake interview by Robert Martin, Civil Rights Documentation Project, July 28, 1969, Moorland-Spingarn Research Center, Howard University, Washington, D.C.

22. "A Sister Debates a Brother on 'THAT BLACK MAN–WHITE WOMAN THING,'" *Ebony,* August 1970, p. 132; St. Clair Drake interview by Robert Martin; Robert Tucker, *Ebony,* November 1970, p. 26; David Burgest and Joanna Bowers, "Erroneous Assumptions Black Men Make about Black Women," *Black Male/Female Relationships,* Winter 1982, pp. 16–17.

23. James Farmer, *Lay Bare the Heart* (New York: Arbor House, 1985), p. 307.

24. See Malcolm X and James Farmer, "Separation or Integration: A Debate,"

Dialogue Magazine, May 1962, reprinted in *Negro Protest Thought in the Twentieth Century,* ed. Francis Broderick and August Meier (New York: Bobbs-Merrill Co., 1965), pp. 378, 380–381; Farmer, *Lay Bare the Heart,* p. 307.

25. Julius Hobson and Marilyn Robinson, "The Great Conversation with Marilyn Robinson," p. 18 in Box 1, Folder: Conversation with Marilyn Robinson, Julius Hobson Papers, Washingtonia Division, Washington, D.C., Public Library; *Washington Star,* October 23, 1977, p. C4, Julius Hobson Papers; interview with Hobson by William Raspberry, "Hobson Has Goaded Many, Angered Others for Change," *Washington Post,* July 3, 1972, Julius Hobson Papers.

26. Julius Lester, *Look Out Whitey! Black Power's Gon' Get Your Mama* (New York: Dial Press, 1968).

27. Julius Lester, *All Is Well* (New York: William Morrow and Co., 1976), p. 134; Julius Lester, *Lovesong: Becoming a Jew* (New York: Henry Holt and Co., 1988), p. 233; Margarete Henson, *Ebony,* November 1970, p. 19; Nola Aumyers, *Ebony,* November 1970, pp. 18–19.

28. Lester, *Lovesong: Becoming a Jew,* p. 43; Lester, *All Is Well,* p. 134.

29. Lester, *Lovesong,* p. 144. Lester converted to Judaism in the 1980s and has since become a spokesperson on black-Jewish relations.

30. Julius Lester, *And All Our Wounds Forgiven* (New York: Harcourt Brace and Co., 1994), pp. 73, 71.

31. Interview by the author with Chuck McDew, April 17, 1999.

32. *Evening Star* (Washington), January 15, 1971, Box 1, File—Newspaper Articles; Testimonials after Death, Julius Hobson Papers; "Goodbye Mr. Hobson: The Last Interview," *The Washingtonian,* in Box 4, File—Biographical, Julius Hobson Papers.

33. Julius Lester, "White Woman–Black Man (Part II)," *Evergreen Review,* October 1969, pp. 68–70. See also Julius Lester, "Black Man–White Woman (Part I)," *Evergreen Review,* September 1969, p. 78.

34. Farmer, *Lay Bare the Heart,* p. 266.

35. Calvin Hernton, *Coming Together: Black Power, White Hatred, and Sexual Hang-Ups* (New York: Random House, 1971), pp. 26, 27.

36. See *Gallup Opinion Index,* November 1972, Report no. 89, p. 12; *Gallup Opinion Index,* November 1978, Report no. 160, p. 27.

37. Lewis Carter, "Racial Caste Hypogamy: A Sociological Myth," *Phylon* 29 (fourth quarter, 1968): 347–350; Clarence Spigner, "Black-White Interracial Marriages: A Brief Overview of U.S. Census Data, 1980–1987," *Western Journal of Black Studies,* 14 (1990): 214–216; Matthijs Kalmijn, "Trends

in Black/White Intermarriage," *Social Forces* 72 (September 1993): 123. Statistical analysis carried out by Deborah Kitchen suggests that black women's intermarriage rates have fluctuated widely. See Kitchen, "Interracial Marriage in the United States, 1900–1980" (Ph.D. diss., University of Minnesota, 1993).

38. In 1973, 58 percent of all black professionals were women and, by 1982, 58 percent of black undergraduates were women. Bart Landry, *The New Black Middle Class* (Berkeley: University of California Press, 1987), pp. 202–208.

39. Jacquelyne Jackson, "Where Are the Black Men?" *Ebony*, March 1972, p. 99; Patricia Elizabeth White, "Patterns of Marriage among the Black Population: A Preliminary Analysis of the Black Female" (Ph.D. diss., Ohio State University, 1980), pp. 42–58; Robert Staples, *Introduction to Black Sociology* (New York: McGraw-Hill, 1970), pp. 129–133; Leachim Tufani Semaj, "Polygamy Reconsidered: Causes and Consequences of the Declining Sex-Ratio in African-American Society," *Journal of Black Psychology* 9 (August 1982): 29–44.

40. Michele Wallace, *Black Macho and the Myth of the Superwoman* (New York: Dial Press, 1979), p. 49.

41. "How the Black Men's Conference Can Save the Black Man, Woman, and Child," *Black Male/Female Relationships,* Winter 1981, p. 56. See also "Sexual Life between Blacks and Whites," *Black Male/Female Relationships,* June–July 1979, p. 18; "Blues for Snow White," *Black Male/Female Relationships,* Winter 1981, pp. 4–7.

42. Calvin Hernton, *Sex and Racism in America* (1965; New York: Anchor Books, 1988), p. 82; William Grier and Price Cobbs, *Black Rage* (New York: Basic Books, 1968), p. 64; Ernest Spaights and Harold Dixon, "Socio-Psychological Dynamics in Pathological Black-White Romantic Alliances," *Journal of Instructional Psychology* 11 (September 1984): 134–135.

43. James quoted in "Numbers of Black Women Say They Will Not Date White Men," *New York Times,* November 23, 1970, p. 44; interview with subject no. 2 from Simpson, "Black Women Attorneys"; Maxine Swift, *Ebony,* November 1970, p. 22; poll data in Kenneth Clark and Mamie Phillips Clark, "What Do Blacks Think of Themselves," *Ebony,* November 1980, p. 180.

44. Halsell, *Black/White Sex,* p. 178; Milloy, "Black Men and White Women."

45. Philip E. Lampe, "Towards Amalgamation: Interethnic Dating Among Blacks, Mexican-Americans and Anglos," *Ethnic Groups* 3 (June 1981): 102;

Childs, "Black and White Couples: Have Attitudes Changed?" *Redbook,* September 1969, p. 141.

46. Darlene Clark Hine, "Rape and the Inner Lives of Black Women in the Middle West: Preliminary Thoughts on the Culture of Dissemblance," in *Unequal Sisters,* ed. Vicki Ruiz and Ellen Carol DuBois (New York: Routledge, 1990), p. 292. On the sexual exploitation of black women, see Thelma Jennings, "Us Colored Women Had to Go through a Plenty: Sexual Exploitation of African-American Slave Women," *Journal of Women's History* 1 (Winter): 45–74; Catherine Clinton, "Bloody Terrain: Freedwomen, Sexuality and Violence during Reconstruction," *Georgia Historical Quarterly* 76 (1992): 313–332.

47. Mrs. Medgar Evers, "Why Should My Child Marry Yours," *Ladies' Home Journal,* April 1968, reprinted in *Black Male/White Female: Perspectives on Interracial Marriage and Courtship,* ed. Doris Wilkinson (Cambridge, Mass.: Schenkman, 1975), p. 155, 157; Lynn Norment, "What Every Black Man Should Know about Black Women," *Ebony,* August 1983, p. 136.

48. "Black and White Dating," *Time,* July 19, 1968, p. 48; Frank Petroni, "Teen-Age Interracial Dating," *Trans-Action* 8 (September 1971): 54; Patrice Miles and Audrey Edwards, "Black Women and White Men," *Essence,* October 1983, p. 96.

49. Petroni, "Teen-Age Interracial Dating," p. 55; Charles Willie and Joan Levy, "Black Is Lonely," *Psychology Today,* March 1972, pp. 76, 78.

50. Willie and Levy, "Black Is Lonely," p. 76, 52; Lampe, "Towards Amalgamation," p. 102.

51. Interview with subjects nos. 5, 7, and 3, in Simpson, "Black Women Attorneys (1978, 1982)."

52. Semaj, "Polygamy Reconsidered," pp. 38; *Jet,* July 18, 1988, p. 17; interview with subject no. 2 in Simpson, "Black Woman Attorneys"; Robert Staples, "The Myth of Black Sexual Superiority: A Re-Examination," *Black Scholar* 9 (April 1978): 21.

53. Diane C., *Ebony,* December 1965, p. 20; Deborah Pickens, *Ebony,* January 1972, p. 20.

54. Lula Miles, *Ebony,* August 1969, p. 19; Miranda Stevens, *Ebony,* September 1969, p. 22. "Save Our Men" clubs are also mentioned in Frank Petroni's "Interracial Dating—The Price is High," in *Interracial Marriage: Expectations and Realities,* ed. Stuart and Abt, pp. 130–131; Beth Day, *Sexual Life between Blacks and Whites* (New York: World Publishing, 1972), p. 134; Joan Downs, "Black/White Dating," *Life,* May 28, 1971, p. 62.

55. Downs, "Black-White Dating," p. 62; Elizabeth Vaughn, *Ebony*, February 1978, p. 16; Anonymous, *Ebony*, January 1980, p. 16.

56. On the gender tensions, see "Black Women/Black Men: Has Something Gone Wrong," *Ebony*, August 1977, pp. 160–162; Robert Staples, *Black Masculinity: The Black Male's Role in American Society* (1982; San Francisco: Black Scholar Press, 1984), pp. 101–116; Robert Staples, *The Black Woman in America: Sex, Marriage, and the Family* (1973; Chicago: Nelson-Hall Publishers, 1978), pp. 172–182; Cynthia Griggs Fleming, *Soon We Will Not Cry: The Liberation of Ruby Doris Smith Robinson* (Lanham, Md.: Rowman & Littlefield Publishers, 1998), pp. 167–169.

57. Belinda Robnett, *How Long? How Long?: African-American Women in the Struggle for Civil Rights* (Oxford: Oxford University Press, 1997), p. 183.

58. "At Home, Fred's a Nice, Nice Guy," *Ebony*, January 1975, p. 53; "A Sister Debates a Brother on 'THAT BLACK MAN–WHITE WOMAN THING,'" *Ebony*, August 1970, pp. 130–133; Eddie James, *Ebony*, October 1970, pp. 21, 24A; Day, *Sexual Life between Blacks and Whites*, p. 199.

59. "A Sister Debates a Brother on 'THAT BLACK MAN–WHITE WOMAN THING,'" p. 133; Catherine Craig, *Ebony*, December 1969, p. 17; Ms. V. Foster, *Ebony*, March 1981, pp. 19–20.

60. Interview with subjects nos. 4 and 8, in Epstein, "Black Professional Women, 1969"; poll data from Simpson, "Black Female Attorneys," questionnaire, 1982.

61. Laurie Johnson, *Ebony*, November 1973, p. 18; "White Women, Black Man, Black Woman," undated, quoted in Hernton, *Sex and Racism in America*, p. 141.

62. Charles Payne, *I've Got the Light of Freedom* (Berkeley: University of California Press, 1995), pp. 266–283. For discussions of the responsibility black middle-class or elite women felt to the larger community, see Evelyn Brooks Higginbotham, *Righteous Discontent: The Women's Movement in the Black Baptist Church, 1880–1920* (Cambridge: Harvard University Press, 1993); Stephanie J. Shaw, *What a Woman Ought to Be and to Do* (Chicago: University of Chicago Press, 1996).

63. Poussaint in "Interracial Couples' View of Life as Mixed Marriages Increase," *New York Times*, February 23, 1979, p. A24.

64. "Black/White Dating," *Time*, p. 49; "Guess Who's Coming to Dinner Now," *Essence*, April 1987, p. 138.

65. Gant in "A Sister Debates a Brother on 'THAT BLACK MAN–WHITE WOMAN THING,'" p. 130.

66. Downs, "Black-White Dating," p. 63; *New York Times,* November 23, 1970, p. 44.

67. Diane Edwards, *Ebony,* May 1981, pp. 14–15; "Black-White Couples," Episode no. 222, *Woman to Woman* (VT-27), 1983–84, Schlesinger Library, Radcliffe College, Cambridge, Mass.

68. Jacqueline Terry, Babatunde Okelle, and Darielle Watts, *Ebony,* November 1970, p. 20.

69. Emory Davis and Phyllis E. Qualls, "Interracial Dating and Marriage Preferences among Blacks, Chicanos, and Anglos," paper presented at the Southwestern Sociological Association meeting, San Antonio, Texas, 1975, Eric Microfiche: ED 104609, pp. 7, 8.

70. Davis quoted in "A Sister Debates a Brother on 'THAT BLACK MAN–WHITE WOMAN THING,'" p. 130; Julius Lester, "White Woman–Black Man," *Evergreen Review,* October 1969, p. 70.

71. Charles Bodi quoted in Peggy Gillespie and Gigi Kaeser, *Of Many Colors: Portraits of Multiracial Families* (Amherst: University of Massachusetts Press, 1997), p. 18.

72. Johnny Gooden, *Ebony,* March 1970, p. 23; Bukola, *Ebony,* August 1984, pp. 24–25; Vanessa Holt, *Ebony,* August 1948, p. 18; Phyllis Braxton, *Ebony,* November 1970, p. 26.

73. Willie and Levy, "Black Is Lonely," p. 78; *Gallup Opinion Index,* November 1972, Report no. 89, p. 12; *Gallup Opinion Index,* November 1978, Report no. 160, p. 27; *Gallup Opinion Index,* June 1983, Report no. 213, p. 10.

74. *Baltimore Sun,* October 22, 2000, p. 29A; *Denver Rocky Mountain News,* April 14, 1996, p. 59A.

8. Eroded but Not Erased

1. Cherlene McGrady, "The Fearns," *Interrace,* Spring/Summer 1993, p. 29.

2. For the most recent numbers, see Jason Fields and Lynne M. Casper, "America's Families and Living Arrangements, 2000," Current Population Reports, U.S. Census Bureau, http://www.census.gov/prod/2001pubs/ pp. 20–537.pdf; Michael Lind, "The Beige and the Black," *New York Times Magazine,* August 16, 1998, p. 38; *Washington Post,* July 5, 2001, p. A01.

3. Maria P. P. Root, *Love's Revolution: Interracial Marriage* (Philadelphia: Temple University Press, 2001), pp. 187–188.

4. On modern race conditions, see Patricia J. Williams, *Seeing a Color-Blind Future: The Paradox of Race* (New York: Noonday Press, 1998); David

Hollinger, *Post-Ethnic America: Beyond Multiculturalism* (New York: Basic Books, 1995). On the decline of overt racial hostility, see David Sears, "Symbolic Racism," in *Eliminating Racism,* ed. Phyllis Katz and Dalmas Taylor (New York: Plenum Press, 1988), pp. 53–84.

5. 1997 Gallup Poll cited in Root, *Love's Revolution,* p. 38.

6. "Alabama Student Sues Principal Who Nixed Interracial Prom Dating," *Jet,* April 4, 1994, p. 20; "Principal Causes Furor on Mixed-Race Couples," *New York Times,* March 16, 1994, p. A10.

7. "In Prom Dispute, a Town's Race Divisions Emerge," *New York Times,* August 15, 1994, p. A10.

8. Michael Fletcher, "Interracial Marriages Eroding Barriers," *Washington Post,* December 29, 1998, p. A01; *St. Louis Post-Dispatch,* March 4, 2000, p. 3.

9. "Mississippi Repeals Ban on Interracial Marriages," *Jet,* November 23, 1987, p. 18; NPR News, "Morning Edition," April 15, 1999; *USA Today,* November 8, 2000, p. 13A.

10. Root, *Love's Revolution,* p. 39; "Black/White Relations in the U.S.," *Social Audit,* June 10, 1997.

11. Abby L. Ferber, *White Man Falling: Race, Gender, and White Supremacy* (Lanham, Md.: Rowman & Littlefield Publishers, 1998); Andrew MacDonald, *The Turner Diaries,* 2nd ed. (Hisslboro, W.V.: National Vanguard Books, 1980), pp. 160–169.

12. "Confronting America's Hate Crime Crisis," *Klanwatch Intelligence Report,* February 1992, p. 6; *United States of America v. Wood, et al.,* 780 F.2d 955 (11th Cir., 1986).

13. "A New Look at Intermarriage," *New York Times,* February 11, 1985, p. C13; Eloise Mays, response to author questionnaire on interracial marriage, September 17, 1994; *Woman to Woman* (VT-27), Episode no. 212, "Black-White Marriages," Schlesinger Library, Radcliffe College, Cambridge, Mass.

14. "Interracial Marriages: The Problems Haven't Lessened. They've Just Changed," *New York Daily News,* June 17, 1980, in Schomburg Center Clipping File: Interracial Marriage 1989–, Schomburg Center for Research in Black Culture, New York Public Library, New York; "Black-White Marriages Rise, but Couples Still Face Scorn," *New York Times,* December 2, 1991, p. B6; Moonves quoted in "Interracial Marriages Are on the Rise," *Toronto Star,* May 16, 1998, p. L9.

15. Paul C. Rosenblatt, Terri A. Karis, and Richard D. Powell, *Multiracial Couples: Black and White Voices* (Thousand Oaks, Calif.: Sage Publications,

1995), pp. 124–125; telephone interview with Shira-Davida Goldberg-Rathell by the author, October 26, 2001; "Our Daughter, Ourselves," *American Love Stories,* http://www.pbs.org/weblab/lovestories/stories.

16. *Interrace,* October/November 1994, p. 13; Leland Bernard Cohen, "Interracial Families Adapt to Their Marginality: Between Black and White" (Ph.D diss., Washington University, 1979), p. 88; "Marriage in Black and White," *Atlanta Constitution,* July 25, 1988, in Schomburg Center Clipping File: Intermarriage, 1975–1988.

17. Mark and Gail Mathabane, *Love in Black and White: The Triumph of Love over Prejudice and Taboo* (New York: HarperPerennial, 1992), p. 185.

18. *New York Times,* December 2, 1991, p. 1; Glinda Emery, *Ebony,* October 1990, pp. 10–11; Lorraine Challen-Johnson, *Ebony,* October 1990, p. 10; *New York Times,* January 21, 1996, p. 18.

19. Telephone interview with Amy Rollison by the author, October 26, 2001; author interview with Shira-Davida Goldberg-Rathell.

20. For examples, see "The Color of Love," *Washington Post,* August 22, 1994, p. B1; Robert P. McNamara, Maria Tempenis, and Beth Walton, *Crossing the Line: Interracial Couples in the South* (Westport, Conn.: Praeger, 1999), pp. 110–113.

21. Sylvester Monroe, "Love in Black and White: The Last Racial Taboo," *Los Angeles Times Magazine,* December 9, 1990, p. 58; Richard Carter, "Weathering Prejudice," *New York Times Magazine,* August 4, 1991, p. 14. See also Rosenblatt, Karis, and Powell, *Multiracial Couples,* pp. 174–175.

22. McNamara, Tempenis, and Walton, *Crossing the Line,* p. 97.

23. Rosenblatt, Karis, and Powell, *Multiracial Couples,* pp. 141, 205; Cohen, "Interracial Families Adapt to Their Marginality," p. 122; author interview with Shira-Davida Goldberg-Rathell; author interview with Amy Rollison.

24. Root, *Love's Revolution,* p. 38.

25. Lynn Norment, "Black Men, White Women: What's Behind the New Furor," *Ebony,* November 1994, p. 50; Colbert King, "The Fuss over Mixed Marriages," *Washington Post,* September 24, 1999, p. 23; Russell Adams and Ronald Walters, "The Meaning of Mixed Marriages," *Washington Post,* October 5, 1991, p. A17; Edwin Darden, "My Black History Paradox," *Washington Post,* February 24, 1991, p. B5; Charles Mills, "Do Black Men Have a Moral Duty to Marry Black Women," *Journal of Social Philosophy* 25 (June 1994): 131–153.

26. Jean Alicia Elster, "When Violence Hits Home," *Interrace* 7, no. 2 (1996): 27; Nya Patrinos in Lise Funderburg, *Black, White, Other: Biracial Americans*

Talk about Race and Identity (New York: William Morrow, 1994), p. 136; *The Politics of Love in Black and White* (Communique Video, Mountaintop Productions, 1993); "A Father's Experiences," *American Love Stories,* http://www.pbs.org/weblab/lovestories/stories.

27. Pamela Paset and Ronald Taylor, "Black and White Women's Attitudes towards Interracial Marriage," *Psychological Reports* 69 (December 1991, pt. 1): 753–754; Jeanette Davidson and Lawrence Schneider, "Acceptance of Black-White Interracial Marriage," *Journal of Intergroup Relations* 19 (Fall 1992): 47–52; *Jet,* October 2, 1995, p. 22.

28. "Spiking a Fever," *Newsweek,* June 10, 1991, p. 47; Bebe Moore Campbell, "Brothers and Sisters," *New York Time Magazine,* August 23, 1992, pp. 18, 20.

29. Tina Taylor-Carter, *Essence,* July 1983, p. 6; Lisa Jones, "Reckless Igging," *Village Voice,* June 14, 1992, p. 40.

30. Monroe, "Love in Black and White," *Los Angeles Times Magazine,* p. 22; Hicks quoted in "Interracial Marriages Increase," *Chicago Tribune,* September 8, 1998, p. 1.

31. "Nothing Is Just Black and White," *American Love Stories,* http://www.pbs.org/weblab/lovestories/stories/; Rosenblatt, Karis, and Powell, *Multiracial Couples,* p. 150.

32. ABC News/*Washington Post* Poll, January 1986, American Public Opinion Data, microfiche 1 of 53; *Washington Post,* July 5, 2001, p. A01.

33. Orlando Patterson, *The Ordeal of Integration* (Washington, D.C.: Civitas Counterpoint, 1997), p. 196.

34. Quoted in Patrice Miles and Audrey Edwards, "Black Women and White Men," *Essence,* October 1983, p. 95.

35. "Married Couples of Same or Mixed Races and Origins, 1980–1999," U.S. Census Bureau, Statistical Abstract of the United States 2000, Section 1: Population, p. 51; Root, *Love's Revolution,* pp. 187–188.

36. Ransford W. Palmer, *Pilgrims from the Sun: West Indian Migration to America* (New York: Twayne, 1995), pp. 11–20; Mary C. Waters, *Black Identities: West Indian Immigrant Dreams and American Realities* (New York: Russell Sage Foundation, 1999), p. 2.

37. Zhenchao Qian, "Who Intermarries? Education, Nativity, Region, and Interracial Marriages, 1980 and 1990," *Journal of Comparative Family Studies* 30 (Autumn 1999): 579–597.

38. Palmer, *Pilgrims from the Sun,* pp. 35–37; Waters, *Black Identities,* pp. 7, 61–67; Funderburg, *Black, White, Other,* pp. 35, 56.

39. "Close-Up," *Interrace,* May/June 1992, p. 11; Peggy Gillespie and Gigi

Kaeser, *Of Many Colors: Portraits of Multiracial Families* (Amherst: University of Massachusetts Press, 1997), pp. 112–115.

40. *Lamb v. Sallee,* 417 F.Supp. 282 (Kentucky, 1976); *Indiana Civil Rights Commission v. Holman,* 380 N.E.2d 1281 (Indiana, 1978); "Interracial Couple in N.Y. Gets Damage from Landlord," *Jet,* May 4, 1987, p. 29.

41. McNamara, Tempenis, and Walton, *Crossing the Line,* p. 119; *New York Times,* July 19, 2000, p. B6; *United States of America v. Wood, et al.,* 780 F.2d 955 (11th Cir., 1986); *United States of America v. Johns, et al.,* 615 F.2d 672 (1980); *Munger v. United States,* 827 F. Supp. 100 (N.Y. 1992).

42. See *Gresham v. Waffle House,* 586 F. Supp. 1442 (Georgia, 1984); *Whitney v. Greater New York Corporation of Seventh-Day Adventists,* 401 F. Supp. 1363 (New York, 1975).

43. *Moffett v. Glick Co., Inc.,* 621 F.Supp. 244 (District Court, Indiana, 1985), pp. 259, 270; McNamara, Tempenis, and Walton, *Crossing the Line,* p. 118.

44. See Renee Romano, "'Immoral Conduct': White Women, Racial Transgressions, and Custody Disputes" in *"Bad" Mothers: The Politics of Blame in Twentieth-Century America,* ed. Molly Ladd-Taylor and Lauri Umansky (New York: New York University Press, 1997), pp. 230–251.

45. *Palmore v. Sidoti,* 426 So.2d (1981); *Palmore v. Sidoti,* 472 So.2d 843 (1982); *Palmore v. Sidoti,* 104 S.Ct. 1879 (1984).

46. Steven Holmes, "Which Man's Army," *New York Times,* June 7, 2000, p. 1; "Population Representation in the Military Services," Office of the Assistant Secretary of Defense, November 2001.

47. Quoted in McNamara, Tempenis, and Walton, *Crossing the Color Line,* p. 153. For an extended discussion of the military's potential to transform an individual's racial attitudes, see *Crossing the Line,* pp. 132–140.

48. M. Belinda Tucker and Claudia Mitchell-Kernan, "New Trends in Black American Interracial Marriage: The Social Structural Context," *Journal of Marriage and the Family* 52 (February 1990): 214–215.

49. Peter Slavin, "Biracial Couples in the Military," *Interrace,* July/August 1991, p. 12; Sheree Hunt Gates, "Before You Jump the Broom, Consider This . . . ," *Interrace* 6, no. 6, p. 8; Fred Holland, "Black Men/White Women: A Soldier's Story," *Interrace,* March/April 1992, p. 18; author interview with Amy Rollison.

50. *St. Louis Post-Dispatch,* March 26, 1997, p. 7A; Tim B. Heaton and Cardell K. Jacobson, "Intergroup Marriage: An Examination of Opportunity Structures," *Sociological Inquiry* 70 (Winter 2000): 30–41.

51. Carol Landry, "Biracial Unions: An Emerging Social Issue," *Interrace,* November/December 1991, p. 26; Brenda Johnson, *Interrace,* September/Oc-

tober 1992, 4; "Interracial Living Guide," *Interrace,* Fall 1997, p. 10; McNamara, Tempenis, and Walton, *Crossing the Line,* pp. 150–157; *Toronto Star,* May 16, 1998, p. L9.

52. *Washington Post,* July 5, 2001, p. A01; Jerry Bruckner, "Ministry to Blacks and Whites in Interracial Marriages in the San Francisco Bay Area" (Ph.D. diss., San Francisco Theological Seminary, 1988), pp. 154–165; McNamara, Tempenis, and Walton, *Crossing the Line,* p. 85.

53. Quoted in *Interrace,* October/November 1993, p. 24; McNamara, Tempenis, and Walton, *Crossing the Line,* pp. 76, 79; Walt Harrington, *Crossings: A White Man's Journey into Black America* (New York: HarperPerennial, 1992), pp. 20–21.

54. Lois Romano and Janeline Trescott, "Love in Black and White," *Redbook,* February 1992, pp. 88–92+; "Black-White Marriages Rise, but Couples Still Face Scorn," *New York Times,* December 2, 1991, p. B6.

55. *Gallup Poll Monthly,* August 1991, pp. 60–61.

56. Dawn Skeete, "Take Two," *Interrace,* January/February 1993, p. 8; author interview with Shira-Davida Goldberg-Rathell.

57. "What People Are Saying about Interracial Relationships," *Interrace,* September/October 1993, p. 24; Harrington, *Crossings,* p. 21; McNamara, Tempenis, and Walton, *Crossing the Line,* p. 88; "When Your In-Laws Drive You Crazy," *Interrace,* April 1994, p. 8.

58. *The Gallup Poll: Public Opinion 1993* (Wilmington, Del.: Scholarly Resources, 1994), p. 232; "AJC Southern Focus Poll: Attitudes on Race," *Atlanta Constitution,* June 20, 1999, p. 1H.

59. Talitha Johnson, "Brotherly Love," *Interrace,* April/May 1995, p. 26; Kathlyn Gay, *The Rainbow Effect* (New York: Franklin Watts, 1987), p. 74; author interview with Amy Rollison.

60. Root, *Love's Revolution,* pp. 5–6; Monroe, "Love in Black and White," *Los Angeles Times Magazine,* pp. 14–22+. See also McNamara, Tempenis, and Walton, *Crossing the Line,* pp. 87–91.

61. Gates, "Before You Jump the Broom," p. 9; Anonymous, *Interrace,* January/February 1991, p. 27.

62. "The Ebony Advisor," *Ebony,* September 1985, p. 74; "Boy Meets Girl," *Interrace,* January 1990. See also "Ebony Advisor" from August 1982, October 1987, and June 1990.

63. Maureen Reddy, *Crossing the Color Line: Race, Parenting, and Culture* (New Brunswick, N.J.: Rutgers University Press, 1994), p. 10.

64. "Newsletter for Biracial Couples," *San Francisco Chronicle,* August 24, 1994; "Cross Colors," *Los Angeles Times,* March 27, 1994, p. E1.

65. Gabe Grosz telephone interview by the author, March 12, 1994; *Gale Directory of Publications and Broadcast Media,* vol. 1, 132 (Detroit: Gale, 1999), p. 396.

66. *Interrace,* December 1994/January 1995, p. 6.

67. "Tips to Keep in Mind If You Are Interracially Dating," *Interrace,* December 1990, p. 16; Henri Cohen, "Yes You Can Be Happy!" *Interrace,* June/ July 1994, p. 52.

68. Author interview with Gabe Grosz; Robbie Cullen, *Interrace,* November 1990, p. 4; Deborah Struthers, *Interrace,* January/February 1991, p. 27; Erin Barrett, *Interrace,* Vol. 4, no. 1, p. 6; Cyn [and Joe], *Interrace,* December 1993, p. 4.

69. Steve and Ruth Bryant White, *Free Indeed: The Autobiography of an Interracial Couple* (1983; Gardena, Calif.: A Place for Us Ministry, 1989), p. 70; Steve White telephone interview by the author, December 7, 1993; "Messengers of Truth," *Interrace,* December 1993, p. 28; Itabari Injeri, "Faith, Hope, and Racial Disparity," *Los Angeles Times,* August 20, 1989; author interview with Shira-Davida Goldberg-Rathell.

70. See, for example, David Zarembka, response to questionnaire on interracial marriage, June 21, 1994; McNamara, Tempenis, and Walton, *Crossing the Line,* pp. 157–158.

71. "Daytime TV's First Interracial Marriage Set for 'General Hospital,'" *Jet,* February 29, 1988, p. 58; Gail Lumet Buckley, "When a Kiss Is Not Just a Kiss," *New York Times,* March 31, 1991, sect. 2, p. 1; "The Last Taboo? Does Wave of Interracial Movies Signal a Real Change?" *Ebony,* September 1991, pp. 74–78; Mary Murchison-Edwards and Candy Mills, "*Interrace* Goes to the Movies," *Interrace,* December 1990, pp. 38–41; Monroe, "Love in Black and White," *Los Angeles Times Magazine,* pp. 14–22, 58–62.

72. "Does *Pelican Brief* Practice Abstinence for Racial Reasons?" *Gannett News Service,* December 20, 1993; Margo Hammond, "Mixing the Colors of Love," *St. Petersburg Times,* May 13, 2000, p. 1D; "The Last Taboo? Does Wave of Interracial Movies Signal a Real Change?" *Ebony,* September 1991, pp. 74–78.

73. *Jungle Fever* (1991); "Spiking a Fever, *Newsweek,* June 10, 1991, pp. 44–47.

74. Holly Robinson quoted in Harrington, *Crossings,* p. 371; Carter, "Weathering Prejudice," p. 14; Mark Mathabane, "Mixed Couples Break Down Barriers; but Interracial Marriages Still Provoke Strong Opposition," *Newsday* (Nassau and Suffolk Edition), February 24, 1992, p. 35.

75. Lisa Tatum, *Interrace,* September/October 1991, p. 5; Elizabeth Atkins and Tarek Hamada, "'Fever' Too Hot on Negative Side, Say Interracial Cou-

ples," *Gannett News Service, Detroit News,* June 7, 1991. See also "'You Can't Join Their Clubs': Six Mixed Couples Get Together to Talk about Love, Marriage, and Prejudice," *Newsweek,* June 10, 1991, p. 48.

76. Candy Mills, "Editor's Note," *Interrace,* April/May 1995, p. 3; "Step Right Up!" *Interrace,* December 1993, p. 37; "What People Are Saying about Their Interracial Relationships," *Interrace,* September/October 1993, p. 24; Gregory Stephens, *Interrace,* Spring/Summer 1993, p. 2.

77. Romano and Trescott, "Love in Black and White," *Redbook;* Claudine Edwards, *Interrace,* July/August 1992, p. 4; Dickelle Fonda, "Shame, Shame, Shame on You!" *Interrace,* March/April 1992, p. 32.

78. Walker Hollis in "Being Biracial," *Plain Dealer* (Cleveland), April 11, 1993, p. G1; author interview with Gabe Grosz.

79. "The Color of Love," *Washington Post,* August 22, 1994, p. B1; "Not Black, not White, but Biracial," *Atlanta Journal and Constitution,* December 1, 1991, A01; "The Loving Generation," *Newsweek,* February 13, 1995, p. 72; "Our Daughter, Ourselves," *American Love Stories.*

80. Reddy, *Crossing the Color Line,* pp. 40, 72, 99, 101.

81. Gay, *The Rainbow Effect,* pp. 124–129; Mary Murchison-Edwords, "Starting an Interracial Support Group," *Interrace,* July/August 1991, p. 32; Karen West, "One Who Understands," *Washington CEO,* February 2002, p. 58.

82. "Mixed Metaphor," *Dallas Morning News,* March 23, 1993, 1C; Barbara Karkabi, "Love, Marriage, Race, and Kids," *Houston Chronicle,* October 11, 1992, Lifestyle, p. 1.

83. Karkabi, "Love, Marriage, Race, and Kids," p. 1.

84. On the history of the multiracial movement, see Jon Michael Spencer, *The New Colored People* (New York: New York University Press, 1997), pp. 16–26; Lawrence Wright, "One Drop of Blood," *New Yorker,* July 25, 1994, pp. 46–55. Graham quoted in "Between Black and White," *Toronto Star,* July 7, 1994, p. A23; Dowell Myers et al., "Race Contours; USA, California, and Los Angeles in the Census 2000," University of Southern California School of Policy, Planning and Development, http:www.usc.edu/sppd/census2000.

85. Spencer, *The New Colored People,* pp. 57–89; Ellis Cose, *Color Blind* (New York: HarperPerennial, 1998), pp. 1–26; Danzy Senna, *Interrace,* January/February 1994, p. 2.

86. *New York Times,* July 6, 1996, p. 7.

87. Jane Lazarre, *Beyond the Whiteness of Whiteness: Memoir of a White Mother of Black Sons* (Durham, N.C.: Duke University Press, 1996), p. xvii; Romano and Trescott, "Love in Black and White," *Redbook.*

88. There are as yet no national statistics on the divorce rates of interracial couples who married after 1970. A recent study of marriages in South Carolina and Virginia found that the divorce rate among interracial couples was lower than that among white couples. Scholars generally agree that divorce rates for interracial and intraracial couples have become much more similar in the last twenty years. See Lawrence Tenzer, "Are Marriages between Whites More Stable than Marriages between Blacks and Whites?" *Interrace,* May/June 1992, p. 37; *Chicago Tribune,* September 8, 1998, p. 1; Root, *Love's Revolution,* p. 176.

Epilogue

1. *Interracial,* March 1977, p. 17. The complete run of *Interracial,* March 1977–April 1979, is available at the Schomburg Center for Research in Black Culture, New York City.

2. Kevin Merid, "A Candid Couple," *Washington Post,* January 13, 1998, p. B6.

3. *Bulworth* (Twentieth Century Fox, 1998); Judith Miller, "Think Tank: Banishing Racial Strife on the Wings of Love," *New York Times,* May 23, 1998, p. B11.

4. Ellis Cose, *Color Blind* (New York: HarperPerennial, 1998), p. 18. See also *San Francisco Examiner,* February 9, 1992, p. 10.

5. Dr. James Coleman quoted in John T. Becker and Stanli K. Becker, *All Blood Is Red . . . All Shadows Are Dark!* (Cleveland, Ohio: Seven Shadows Press, 1984), p. 127; Randall Kennedy, "How Are We Doing with Loving?: Race, Law, and Intermarriage," *Boston University Law Journal* 77 (October 1997): 819; Jim Chen, "Unloving," *Iowa Law Review* 80 (October 1994): 167.

6. For use of Johnston in epigraphs or introductions, see Grace Halsell, *Black/White Sex* (New York: William Morrow and Co., 1972), p. 13; Calvin Hernton, *Sex and Racism in America* (1965; New York: Anchor Books, 1988); Paul Spickard, *Mixed Blood: Intermarriage and Ethnic Identity in Twentieth-Century America* (Madison: University of Wisconsin Press, 1989), p. 235; Kevin Mumford, *Interzones: Black/White Sex Districts in Chicago and New York in the Early Twentieth Century* (New York: Columbia University Press, 1997), p. xvi; Fernando Henriques, *Children of Conflict* (New York: E. P. Dutton and Co., 1975), p. 78.

7. Hernton, 1988 Introduction to *Sex and Racism in America,* p. xiv; Joseph Washington, *Marriage in Black and White* (Boston: Beacon Press, 1970), p. 1.

8. *Hartford Courant,* June 8, 2000, p. A10; *State of Connecticut v. Sean Smith,* 608 A.2d 63 (Supreme Court of Connecticut, 1993), p. 66; Associated Press State and Local Wire, October 25, 2000.

9. George Lipsitz, *The Possessive Investment in Whiteness* (Philadelphia: Temple University Press, 1998), chap. 1; Douglas S. Massey and Nancy A. Denton, *American Apartheid* (Cambridge: Harvard University Press, 1993), pp. 64–71, 86–88; Gary Orfield, *Public School Desegregation in the United States, 1968–1980* (Washington, D.C.: Joint Center for Political Studies, 1983), pp. 3–7.

10. Benjamin DeMott, *The Trouble with Friendship: Why Americans Can't Think Straight about Race* (New York: Atlantic Monthly Press, 1995).

11. Ibid., p. 27; Patricia Williams quoted in "Think Tank: Banishing Racial Strife on the Wings of Love," *New York Times,* May 23, 1998, B11.

12. Thernstrom quoted in *Hartford Courant,* March 1, 1998, p. A14.

13. Dinesh D'Souza, "The One-Drop-of-Blood Rule," *Forbes,* December 2, 1996, p. 48; Dinesh D'Souza, *The End of Racism* (New York: Free Press, 1995), p. 552.

14. Jim Sleeper, "The Ordeal of Integration: Progress and Resentment in America's Racial Crisis; book reviews," *New Leader,* December 29, 1997, p. 5; Jim Sleeper, *Liberal Racism* (New York: Viking Books, 1997), pp. 67–69, 94, 96–97; William Powers, "Editions and Subtractions," *National Journal,* May 30, 1998, p. 1250.

15. Stephen and Abigail Thernstrom, *America in Black and White* (New York: Simon and Schuster, 1997), p. 526.

16. Nathan Glazer, "Questions about Race and Ethnicity on Census Forms," *New Republic,* October 7, 1996, p. 29; Michael Lind, "The Beige and the Black," *New York Times Magazine,* August 16, 1998, pp. 38–39.

17. Eric S. Lander and Joseph J. Ellis, "Founding Father," *Nature,* November 5, 1998, p. 14; Lorraine Dusky, "We're Jefferson's Legacy in More Ways than One: Men Lied about Sex Then, as Now," *USA Today,* November 4, 1998, p. 27A.

18. J. Tilman Williams, *Los Angeles Times,* November 12, 1998; Orlando Patterson, "Jefferson the Contradiction," *New York Times,* November 2, 1998, p. A27.

19. *New York Times,* March 28, 1999, p. 43.

white women: in colonial America, 4; "racial purity" and, 5, 6, 30, 45, 46–48, 163,
198; World War II and, 14, 15, 17; black
soldiers and, 18, 19–27, *21,* 31–32, 92;
stigma of interracial sex and, 46–47;
taken for prostitutes, 48, 128, 129; liberated sexuality of, 49–50, 193–194; psychologists and, 55; control of daughters,
60, 196–198, 212–213; family pressures
and, 60–63, 71–73, 271; medical establishment and, 66–67, 69; underage girls,
67–69; custody of children and, 77–78,
263–264; beauty standards and, 87, 88,
221–222, 233–234, 260; as "forbidden
fruit," 87, 121, 179, 234–235; relations
with black husbands' families, 105–107;
black jazz musicians and, 115; reasons
for seeking black men, 120–121, 125,
140; as rite of passage for black men,
129, 232–233; employment discrimination and, 130, 131; school desegregation
and, 158–159; high school students,
168, 169; in civil rights movement, 178,
179–184, 193; number of interracial relationships and, 217–218, 230–232; in
U.S. military, 265–266. *See also* rape

Wiley, George, 63, 97
Williams, Gregory, 64
Williams, Patricia, 291
Williams, Tony, 122
Williamson, Fred, 240
Willie, Charles, 246
Wilson, Doris and John, 113
Workman, William, Jr., 160, 171
World War I, 18
World War II, 12–13, 98, 145; end of, 27–
31; social changes in wake of, 42, 44;
American Communist Party and, 117;
nationalization of race question and,
147
Wright, Neisha, 122, 138
Wright, Richard, 33

Young, Adeline, 59
Young Communist League (YCL), 118–
119, 123
youth culture, 164, 165, 209–210

Zanuck, Darryl, 166, 167
Zellner, Dottie, 179